The Terrorism Reader

The Terrorism Reader is an intriguing introduction to a notorious and puzzling inter-national phenomenon. The book draws together material from a variety of experts and makes their opinions on terrorism easily accessible, allowing understanding, conjecture and debate.

The Terrorism Reader explores all the aspects of terrorism from its definition, psychological and sociological effects, legal and ethical issues to counter-terrorism. In a particularly original way, this reader illustrates the growth and variety of terrorism with a series of twelve case-studies from four continents including:

- ETA and Spain
- the Revolutionary Armed Forces of Colombia
- the Shining Path in Peru
- the Liberation Tigers in Sri Lanka
- the IRA and UFF in Northern Ireland
- the Quaddafi Regime in Libya.

David J. Whittaker is recently retired and was formerly Lecturer in International Politics at the University of Teesside. His many books include *United Nations in Action* and *Conflict and Reconciliation in the Contemporary World*.

The Terrorism Reader

Edited by

David J. Whittaker

London and New York

First published 2001
by Routledge
11 New Fetter Lane, London EC4P 4EE

Simultaneously published in the USA and Canada
by Routledge
29 West 35th Street, New York, NY 10001

Routledge is an imprint of the Taylor & Francis Group

© 2001 David J. Whittaker for selection and editorial matter;
individual extracts © the contributors

Typeset in Bell Gothic and Perpetua by
Florence Production Ltd, Stoodleigh, Devon
Printed and bound in Great Britain by
TJ International, Padstow, Cornwall

British Library Cataloguing in Publication Data
A catalogue record for this book is available from the British Library

Library of Congress Cataloging in Publication Data
    The terrorism reader / edited by David J. Whittaker.
        p. cm.
    Includes bibliographical references and index.
    1. Terrorism. I. Whittaker, David J., 1925–
    HV6431 .T493 2001
    303.6'25–dc21   00–051703

ISBN 0–415–22133–1 (hbk)
ISBN 0–415–22134-X (pbk)

Contents

Preface

Vilified by the majority of people, defended by instigators of political action, terrorist outrages claim priority in media coverage. Their incidence has more than doubled in the past twenty years. While most countries have experienced some form of conspiratorial violence, often tragic and indiscriminate, today ten of them bear the brunt of three out of four incidents. Terrorism has become one of the most pressing political problems during the last half-century. Its many-sidedness, inexpensive lethality and unpredictability make prevention and control difficult, costly and undependable. Its manifestations range the gamut of apparent mindlessness to firm faith and rational calculation. Terrorists may be villains, heroes, ruthless criminals, admired trailblazers; some have made the transition from hunted insurgent to state president.

This book offers guidelines for the exploration of a multiple political riddle – its origins, its significant contrasts, the possibility of prevention and control. As a survey, it is not one of those volumes, loaded with theory and full of facts and figures, that crowd library shelves in their hundreds. Rather, it is a 'taster', deliberately designed to introduce students, teachers, researchers and the general public to a topic notoriously complicated to discuss. It is, in fact, a reader, a carefully assembled and edited selection of the views of a number of well-known authorities on political terrorism. Given the diversity of opinion among the contributors, it is hoped that this reader will stimulate plenty of speculation and controversy.

There are three parts to this book. Part One deals with definition, motivation, and the global incidence and typology of terrorism. A list of contemporary terrorist groups will be found there. Part Two illustrates the growth and variety of terrorism with a series of twelve contrasted case-studies from four continents. Part Three looks comprehensively at the topic of counter-terrorism, at its ethical and legal problems, and at the control strategies some governments employ. The book concludes with notes giving, among other things, the origins of the extracts quoted in this reader together with suggestions for further reading and hints as to places where more information may be sought.

This survey of terrorism originated as a gleam in the publishing eyes of Routledge. Its completion would have been impossible without the ready willingness of authors and publishers to have work cited and quoted. Cogency and easy-to-read clarification have been my aims and sometimes extracts have had to be 'filleted'. I apologise for any resulting offence – it was never deliberate.

I am grateful, also, to many people for their unstinted helpfulness and patience. In particular I should like to thank the following: Professor James Connolly, Sindy Goldberg (South Africa House), Walter Kirwan (Secretary-General, Forum for Peace and Reconciliation, Dublin), Simon Partridge, Marianne Whittaker (indefatigable reader of manuscripts), and library staffs in the Universities of Bradford, Durham, Newcastle, St Andrews, and Teesside, and the Sri Lanka High Commission, London. At Routledge I was indebted to Heather McCallum, Victoria Peters, and later to Janice Baiton, Liz O'Donnell and Gillian Oliver. Once more, Jane Thompson has done a splendid job in producing a final manuscript.

For any shortcomings and misinterpretations I alone am responsible.

David J. Whittaker
North Yorkshire

Acknowledgements

The author and publishers wish to thank the following for their permission to reproduce copyright material:

Extracts from *Terrorism in Context* edited by Martha Crenshaw (University Park: The Pennsylvania State University Press, 1995), pp. 7–12, 330–1, 324, 317, 336–7, 339–40, 213, 214, 215–16, 224–5, 226–8, 232–3, 240–1, 243, 246–7, 411–13, 415–17, 418–19, 422, 423, 427–8, 436, 444–5, 441–3, 465, 466–9, 251–3, 254–5, 257, 260–1, 262–3, 265–6, 267–8, 270, 270–8, 285, 280, 301–2, 305, 176–8, 202–5, 156–9, 481–2, 9–10, 21, 22, 23, 24. Copyright by 1995 The Pennsylvania State University. Reproduced by permission of the publisher; 'The Causes of Terrorism' by Martha Crenshaw from *Comparative Politics* reproduced by permission of the publisher and the author; material from www.terrorism.com by permission of the Terrorism Research Center, Virginia, USA; Reich, Walter, ed. *Origins of Terrorism: Psychologies, Ideologies, Theologies, States of Mind* pp. 25–8, 31–2, 33, 35–6, 38, 54–5, 58, 132, 136, 137, 156–7, 163–5, 165–7, 169. © The Johns Hopkins University Press; *The New Terrorism* by Walter Laqueur © 1999 by Walter Laqueur. Used by permission of Oxford University Press, Inc. and by permission of the author; *Inside Terrorism* by Bruce Hoffman 1998 reproduced by permission of Victor Gollancz publishers; *The Legitimization of Violence* by David Apter (1997) by permission of Macmillan Press Ltd; 'Ideology and Practice of Hizballah in Lebanon: Islamization of Leninist Organizational Principles' by A. A. Khalil in *Middle Eastern Studies* by permission of Frank Cass Publishers; *Hib'allah in Lebanon: the Politics of the Western Hostage Crisis* by Magnus Ranstorp (1997) by permission of Macmillan Press Ltd; *Qaddafi and the United States since 1969* by P. Edward Haley © 1984. Reproduced with permission of Greenwood Publishing Group, Inc., Westport, CT, USA; 'British Tamils fund war in Sri Lanka' by Christopher Thomas in *The Times* © The Times Newspapers Limited, 23rd October 1997; *Conflict and Reconciliation in the Contemporary World* by David Whittaker (1999) reproduced by permission of Routledge; *A Rebellious People: Basques, Protests, and Politics* by Cyrus Ernesto Zirakzadeh. Copyright © 1991 by University of Nevada Press. Reproduced with the permission of the University of Nevada Press; *The Establishment of Algeria* by Martin Stone (1997) by permission of C. Hurst & Co. (Publishers) Ltd.; McClintock, Cynthia. 'Why Peasants Rebel: The Case of Peru's Sendero Luminoso'. *World Politics* (1984), pp. 81–2. © Center of International Studies, Princeton University. Reprinted by permission of the Johns Hopkins University Press; NACLA Report on the Americas. Vol. 30:1, pp. 37–8. Copyright 1996 by the North American Congress on Latin America, 475 Riverside Dr., #454, New York, NY 10115–0122; *Colombia: Inside the Labyrinth* by permission of the Latin American Bureau, London; Extracts from *Terrorism in Europe* edited by Y. Alexander and K. A. Myers, Croom Helm (1982) by permission of Routledge Publishers; *United Nations in Action* by David Whittaker, UCL Press (1995) by permission of Routledge Publishers; *Long Walk to Freedom* by Nelson Mandela, Abacus. © 1994 by Nelson Rolihlaha Mandela. By permission of Little, Brown and Company (Inc.) and Little, Brown and Company (UK); Extracts from South Africa's Truth and Reconciliation Commission (TRC) website, www.truth.org.za; Extracts from *The Guardian* 14/12/1999 by Jack Straw MP and John Wadham, by permission of Guardian Newspapers Limited; 'Defence against Terrorism' by Brian M. Jenkins in *Political Science Quarterly*, vol. 101, no.5, 1986, pp. 773–86, by permission of the Academy of Political Science, New York; *Terrorism and International Law* by R. O. Higgins and M. Flory (1997) Routledge, by permission of Routledge Publishers; Extract by M. R. L. Smith in *Terrorism's Laboratory: The Case of Northern Ireland* edited by Alan O'Day (1995) Ashgate, by permission of Ashgate Publishing Limited; Grant Wardlaw, *Political Terrorism: Theory, tactics and counter measures* (1989) Cambridge University Press by permission of Cambridge University Press and the Australian Institute of Criminology: *Countering State-sponsored Terrorism* from the website of the International Policy Institute for Counter-Terrorism, Israel, www.ict.org.il.

Characteristics
of terrorism

PART ONE OF THIS BOOK addresses three issues about terrorism: first, definition; second, motivation; and third, the worldwide occurrence of terrorism.

Chapter 1

Definition of terrorism

THIS CHAPTER ADDRESSES THE QUESTION: what is terrorism and how may it be defined? It presents a selection of straightforward definitions which should help understanding and discussion. This is followed by a brief editorial resumé and by excerpts from two acknowledged authorities in the clarification of issues. The selection defines terrorism as:

- The unlawful use of force or violence against persons or property to intimidate or coerce a government, the civilian population, or any segment thereof, in furtherance of political or social objectives (FBI).
- The calculated use of violence or the threat of violence to inculcate fear, intended to coerce or intimidate governments or societies as to the pursuit of goals that are generally political, religious or ideological (US Department of Defense).
- Premeditated, politically motivated violence perpetuated against noncombatant targets by subnational groups or clandestine agents, usually intended to influence an audience (US State Department).
- The use or threat, for the purpose of advancing a political, religious or ideological cause, of action which involves serious violence against any person or property (United Kingdom Government).
- Contributes the illegitimate use of force to achieve a political objective when innocent people are targeted (Walter Laqueur).
- A strategy of violence designed to promote desired outcomes by instilling fear in the public at large (Walter Reich).
- The use or threatened use of force designed to bring about political change (Brian Jenkins).
- The deliberate, systematic murder, maiming, and menacing of the innocent to inspire fear in order to gain political ends. [. . .] Terrorism [. . .] is intrinsically evil, necessarily evil, and wholly evil (Paul Johnson).

- [International terrorism is] the threat or use of violence for political purposes when (1) such action is intended to influence the attitude and behavior of a target group wider than its immediate victim, and (2) its ramifications transcend national boundaries (Peter Sederberg).[1]

In this list of definitions the common ground is evident but there are differences of emphasis. The first four 'official' definitions reflect institutional positions. The FBI, for instance, stresses coercion and unlawfulness, and offences against property, in furtherance of social as well as political objectives. The US State Department lays stress on premeditation. The potential political motivation of 'subnational groups' is noted. There is no reference to spontaneous violence or to the psychological significance of threatened action. More comprehensively the US Department of Defense gives equal prominence to actual or threatened violence, cites a wider range of objectives, and includes as possible targets not only governments but also whole societies.

The United Kingdom's definition is to be found in a bill laid before Parliament in December 1999. There is controversy that this definition is too wide and that it may lead to the Government restricting or even denying the legitimate rights of a wide range of protest groups.

Reich, a psychiatrist, emphasises the intimidatory strategy which instils widespread fear and a sense of personal vulnerability in the civilian population. Sederberg focuses on the use of deliberate intimidation instancing the effects of this on attitudes and behaviour. Johnson's definition is judgemental, a highly charged voicing of disapproval. Lack of objectivity here throws little light on the nature of terrorism.

DEFINITION WITHIN A CONTEXT

Bald words in a printed definition do not advance understanding very far. Questions spring to mind. By what criteria should terrorists be considered to carry out unlawful or illegitimate acts? How rational are they who advocate and plan the use of force to achieve political objectives? Is the calculated spreading of fear anything other than barbarous and inhumane? How far can intimidation and coercion establish and secure desirable outcomes? Is it possible to appraise terrorist motivation dispassionately and without bias?

Questions such as these are touched upon in Part One of this book and they have received much attention from political scientists. It is generally agreed that it is important to examine the context within which terrorism and terrorists operate, that is to say, the historical, social, economic, ethnic, and even psychological factors which have some influence on thought, behaviour and action. Moreover, these factors change. Two writers, Bruce Hoffman (1998) and Martha Crenshaw (1995), have looked closely at the contexts in which definition becomes more adequate.

WHY IS TERRORISM SO DIFFICULT TO DEFINE?

Hoffman's understanding of terrorism is that it is inherently political and that it is a calculated process. He describes shifts in the meaning of the term and changes, in the way that terrorist organisations regard themselves and in their modes of behaviour, whether it is domestic or international violence. Used pejoratively, the term terrorism is often confused with guerrilla warfare or ordinary criminality. In Hoffman's view intellectual fervour and a degree of altruism may be added to those characteristics which distinguish the terrorist:

What is terrorism? Few words have so insidiously worked their way into our everyday vocabulary. Like 'Internet' – another grossly over-used term that has similarly become an indispensable part of the argot of the late twentieth century – most people have a vague idea or impression of what terrorism is, but lack a more precise, concrete and truly explanatory definition of the word. This imprecision has been abetted partly by the modern media, whose efforts to communicate an often complex and convoluted message in the briefest amount of airtime or print space possible have led to the promiscuous labelling of a range of violent acts as 'terrorism'. Pick up a newspaper or turn on the television and – even within the same broadcast or on the same page – one can find such disparate acts as the bombing of a building, the assassination of a head of state, the massacre of civilians by a military unit, the poisoning of produce on supermarket shelves or the deliberate contamination of over-the-counter medication in a chemist's shop all described as incidents of terrorism. Indeed, virtually any especially abhorrent act of violence that is perceived as directed against society – whether it involves the activities of anti-government dissidents or governments themselves, organized crime syndicates or common criminals, rioting mobs or persons engaged in militant protest, individual psychotics or lone extortionists – is often labelled 'terrorism'.

Terrorism, in the most widely accepted contemporary usage of the term, is fundamentally and inherently political. It is also ineluctably about power: the pursuit of power, the acquisition of power, and the use of power to achieve political change. Terrorism is thus violence – or, equally important, the threat of violence – used and directed in pursuit of, or in service of, a political aim. With this vital point clearly illuminated, one can appreciate the significance of the additional definition of 'terrorist' provided by the *OED*: 'Any one who attempts to further his views by a system of coercive intimidation'. This definition underscores clearly the other fundamental characteristic of terrorism: that it is a planned, calculated, and indeed systematic act.

Given this relatively straightforward elucidation, why, then, is terrorism so difficult to define? The most compelling reason perhaps is because the meaning of the term has changed so frequently over the past two hundred years.[2]

Following the Second World War, in another swing of the pendulum of meaning, 'terrorism' regained the revolutionary connotations with which it is most commonly associated today. At that time, the term was used primarily in reference to the violent revolts then being prosecuted by the various indigenous nationalist/anti-colonialist groups that emerged in Asia, Africa and the Middle East during the late 1940s and 1950s to oppose continued European rule. Countries as diverse as Israel, Kenya, Cyprus and Algeria, for example, owe their independence at least in part to nationalist political movements that employed terrorism against colonial powers. It was also during this period that the 'politically correct' appellation of 'freedom fighters' came into fashion as a result of the political legitimacy that the international community (whose sympathy and support was actively courted by many of these movements) accorded to struggles for national liberation and self-determination. Many newly independent Third World countries and communist bloc states in particular adopted this vernacular, arguing that anyone or any movement that fought against 'colonial' oppression and/or Western domination should not be described as 'terrorists', but were properly deemed to be 'freedom fighters'. This position was perhaps most famously explained by the Palestine Liberation Organization (PLO) chairman, Yassir Arafat, when he addressed the United Nations General Assembly in November 1974. 'The difference between the revolutionary and the terrorist', Arafat stated, 'lies in the reason for which each fights. For whoever stands by a just cause and fights for the freedom and liberation of his land from the invaders, the settlers and the colonialists, cannot possibly be called terrorist.' [. . .]

During the late 1960s and 1970s, terrorism continued to be viewed within a revolutionary context. However, this usage now expanded to include nationalist and ethnic separatist groups outside a colonial or neo-colonial framework as well as radical, entirely ideologically motivated organizations. Disenfranchised or exiled nationalist minorities – such as the PLO, the Québeçois separatist group FLQ (Front de Libération du Québec), the Basque ETA (Euskadi ta Askatasuna, or Freedom for the Basque Homeland) and even a hitherto unknown South Moluccan irredentist group seeking independence from Indonesia – adopted terrorism as a means to draw attention to themselves and their respective causes, in many instances with the specific aim, like their anti-colonial predecessors, of attracting international sympathy and support.

Although the revolutionary cum ethno-nationalist/separatist and ideological exemplars continue to shape our most basic understanding of the term, in recent years 'terrorism' has been used to denote broader, less distinct phenomena. In the early 1980s, for example, terrorism came to be regarded as a calculated means to destabilize the West as part of a vast global conspiracy. [. . .] By the middle of the decade, however, a series of suicide bombings directed mostly against American diplomatic and military targets in the Middle East was focusing attention on the rising threat of state-sponsored terrorism. Consequently, this phenomenon – whereby various renegade foreign governments such as the regimes in Iran, Iraq, Libya and Syria became actively involved in sponsoring or commissioning terrorist acts – replaced communist conspiracy theories as the main context within which terrorism was viewed. Terrorism thus became associated with a type of covert or surrogate warfare whereby weaker states could confront larger, more powerful rivals without the risk of retribution.

Terrorism had shifted its meaning again from an individual phenomenon of subnational violence to one of several elements, or part of a wider pattern, of non-state conflict.[3]

Not surprisingly, as the meaning and usage of the word have changed over time to accommodate the political vernacular and discourse of each successive era, terrorism has proved increasingly elusive in the face of attempts to construct one consistent definition. At one time, the terrorists themselves were far more cooperative in this endeavour than they are today. The early practitioners didn't mince their words or hide behind the semantic camouflage of more anodyne labels such as 'freedom fighter' or 'urban guerrilla'. The nineteenth-century anarchists, for example, unabashedly proclaimed themselves to be terrorists and frankly proclaimed their tactics to be terrorism.

Terrorist organisations almost without exception now regularly select names for themselves that consciously eschew the word 'terrorism' in any of its forms. Instead these groups actively seek to evoke images of:

- freedom and liberation (e.g. the National Liberation Front, the Popular Front for the Liberation of Palestine, Freedom for the Basque Homeland, etc.);
- armies or other military organisational structures (e.g. the National Military Organisation, the Popular Liberation Army, the Fifth Battalion of the Liberation Army, etc.);
- actual self-defence movements (e.g. the Afrikaner Resistance Movement, the Shankhill Defence Association, the Organisation for the Defence of the Free People, the Jewish Defense Organization, etc.);
- righteous vengeance (the Organisation for the Oppressed on Earth, the Justice Commandos of the Armenian Genocide, the Palestinian Revenge Organisation, etc.);
- or else deliberately choose names that are decidedly neutral and therefore bereft of all but the most innocuous suggestions or associations (e.g. the Shining Path, Front Line, al-Dawa ('The Call'), Alfaro Lives Damn It!, Kach ('Thus'), al-Gamat al-Islamiya ('The Islamic Organisation'), the Lantero Youth Movement, etc.

Cast perpetually on the defensive and forced to take up arms to protect themselves and their real or imagined constituents only, terrorists perceive themselves as reluctant warriors driven by desperation – and lacking any viable alternative – to violence against a repressive state, a predatory rival ethnic or nationalist group, or an unresponsive international order. This perceived characteristic of self-denial also distinguishes the terrorist from other types of political extremists as well as from persons similarly involved in illegal, violent avocations. A communist or a revolutionary, for example, would like to readily accept and admit that he is in fact a communist or a revolutionary. Indeed, many would doubtless take particular pride in claiming either of those appellations for themselves. Similarly, even a person engaged in illegal, wholly disreputable or entirely selfish violent activities, such as robbing banks or carrying out contract killings, would probably admit to being a bank robber or a murderer for hire. The terrorist, by contrast, will *never* acknowledge that he is a terrorist and moreover will go to great lengths to evade and obscure any such inference or connection.

On one point, at least, everyone agrees: terrorism is a pejorative term. It is a word with intrinsically negative connotations that is generally applied to one's enemies and opponents, or to those with whom one disagrees and would otherwise prefer to ignore. 'What is called terrorism,' Brian Jenkins has written, 'thus seems to depend on one's point of view. Use of the term implies a moral judgement; and if one party can successfully attach the label *terrorist* to its opponent, then it has indirectly persuaded others to adopt its moral viewpoint.' Hence the decision to call someone or label some organisation 'terrorist' becomes almost unavoidably subjective, depending largely on whether one sympathises with or opposes the person/group/cause concerned. If one identifies with the victim of the violence, for example, then the act is terrorism. If, however, one identifies with the perpetrator, the violent act is regarded in a more sympathetic, if not positive (or, at the worst, an ambivalent) light; and it is not terrorism.[4]

Terrorists, as we have seen, deliberately cloak themselves in the terminology of military jargon. They consciously portray themselves as bona fide (freedom) fighters, if not soldiers, who – though they wear no identifying uniform or insignia – are entitled to treatment as prisoners of war (POWs) if captured and therefore should not be prosecuted as common criminals in ordinary courts of law. Terrorists further argue that, because of their numerical inferiority, far more limited firepower and paucity of resources compared with an established nation-state's massive defence and national security apparatus, they have no choice but to operate clandestinely, emerging from the shadows to carry out dramatic (in other words, bloody and destructive) acts of hit-and-run violence in order to attract attention to, and ensure publicity for, themselves and their cause. The bomb-in-the-rubbish-bin, in their view, is merely a circumstantially imposed 'poor man's air force': the only means with which the terrorist can challenge – and get the attention of – the more powerful state.

International terrorism disdains any concept of delimited areas of combat or demarcated battlefields, much less respect of neutral territory. Accordingly, terrorists have repeatedly taken their often parochial struggles to other, sometimes geographically distant, third party countries and there deliberately enmeshed persons completely unconnected with the terrorists' cause or grievances in violent incidents designed to generate attention and publicity.[5]

Terrorism is often confused or equated with, or treated as synonymous with, guerrilla warfare. This is not entirely surprising, since guerrillas often employ the same tactics (assassination, kidnapping, bombings of public gathering-places, hostage-taking, etc.) for the same purposes (to intimidate or coerce, thereby affecting behaviour through the arousal of fear) as terrorists. In addition, both terrorists and guerrillas wear neither uniform nor identifying insignia and thus are often indistinguishable from non-combatants. However, despite the inclination to lump both terrorists and guerrillas into the same catch-all category of 'irregulars', there are nonetheless fundamental differences between the two. 'Guerrilla', for example, in its most widely accepted usage, is taken to refer to a numerically larger group of armed individuals, who operate as a military unit, attack enemy military forces, and seize and hold territory (even if only ephemerally during daylight hours), while also exercising some form of sovereignty or control over a defined geographical area and its population. Terrorists, however, do not function in the open as armed units, generally do not attempt to seize or hold territory, deliberately avoid engaging enemy military forces in combat and rarely exercise any direct control or sovereignty either over territory or population.

It is also useful to distinguish terrorists from ordinary criminals. Like terrorists, criminals use violence as a means to attaining a specific end. However, while the violent act itself may be similar – kidnapping, shooting, arson, for example – the purpose or motivation clearly is not. Whether the criminal employs violence as a means to obtain money, to acquire material goods, or to kill or injure a specific victim for pay, he is acting primarily for selfish, personal motivations (usually material gain). Moreover, unlike terrorism, the ordinary criminal's violent act is not designed or intended to have consequences or create psychological repercussions beyond the act itself [. . .] the fundamental aim of the terrorist's violence is ultimately to change 'the system' – about which the ordinary criminal, of course, couldn't care less.

Finally, the point should be emphasized that, unlike the ordinary criminal or the lunatic assassin, the terrorist is not pursuing purely egocentric goals – he is not driven by the wish to line his own pocket or satisfy some personal need or grievance. The terrorist is fundamentally an *altruist*: he believes that he is serving a 'good' cause designed to achieve a greater good for a wider constituency – whether real or imagined – which the terrorist and his organization purport to represent. The criminal, by comparison, serves no cause at all, just his own personal aggrandizement and material satiation. Indeed, a 'terrorist without a cause (at least in his own mind)', Konrad Kellen has argued, 'is not a terrorist'. Yet the possession or identification of a cause is not a sufficient criterion for labelling someone a terrorist. In this key respect, the difference between terrorists and political extremists is clear. Many persons, of course, harbour all sorts of radical and extreme beliefs and opinions, and many of them belong to radical or even illegal or proscribed political organizations. However, if they do not use violence in the pursuance of their beliefs, they cannot be considered terrorists. The terrorist is fundamentally a *violent intellectual*, prepared to use and indeed committed to using force in the attainment of his goals.

By distinguishing terrorists from other types of criminals and terrorism from other forms of crime, we come to appreciate that terrorism is

- ineluctably political in aims and motives;
- violent – or, equally important, threatens violence;
- designed to have far-reaching psychological repercussions beyond the immediate victim or target;
- conducted by an organization with an identifiable chain of command or conspiratorial cell structure (whose members wear no uniform or identifying insignia); and
- perpetrated by a subnational group or non-state entity.

We may therefore now attempt to define terrorism as the deliberate creation and exploitation of fear through violence or the threat of violence in the pursuit of political change. All terrorist acts involve violence or the threat of violence. Terrorism is specifically designed to have far-reaching psychological effects beyond the immediate victim or object of the terrorist attack. It is meant to instil fear within, and thereby intimidate, a wider 'target audience' that might include a rival ethnic or religious group, an entire country, a national government or political party, or public opinion in general. Terrorism is designed to create power where there is none or to consolidate power where there is very little. Through the publicity generated by their violence, terrorists seek to obtain the leverage, influence and power they otherwise lack to effect political change on either a local or an international scale.[6]

THE PROBLEM OF OBJECTIVITY IN DEFINITION

Crenshaw, in regard to understanding what terrorism is and is not, writes of the search for objectivity in addressing the concept and the contexts in which it takes place. For her, terrorism is highly symbolic and perceptual: it is difficult to be neutral in the task of definition. Labelling activity as terrorist may relate to policies for dealing with it together with moral judgement. Where the context within which a terrorist group operates is that of an organised military force, namely an 'army' or resort to 'warfare', then Crenshaw like Hoffman acknowledges the difficulty of deciding what terrorism really is and how its forceful myths, images and messages may be countered:

The context for terrorism does not consist entirely of objective historical factors. Equally important to understanding terrorism is its symbolic, or perceptual, context, based on what could be termed subjective conditions. These factors are contingent upon our understanding of terrorism as a political issue – the self-presentation of those who use terrorism and the construction governments and publics place on it.

[. . .] There are few neutral terms in politics, because political language affects the perceptions of protagonists and audiences, and such effect acquires a greater urgency in the drama of terrorism. Similarly, the meanings of terms change to fit a changing context. Concepts follow politics.

The task of definition, which necessarily involves transforming 'terrorism' into a useful analytical term rather than a polemical tool, must be considered in light of the relation between language and politics. One of the goals of analysis is to establish a referential context for terrorism and to explicate the grounds on which the concept is contested. Critics of the term may charge that these grounds are ideological rather than intellectual and that terrorism has been appropriated by conservative thinkers who wish to condemn the proponents of revolutionary change. This criticism is not surprising, since concepts are part of the belief systems of political actors and they are given meaning through political use. [. . .]

Scholars who deal with the subject of terrorism try constantly to resolve this contradiction between the need to develop a bounded concept on which theoretical explanation can be built and the desire to avoid the appearance of taking sides in the political conflict that motivates the activity or the label of terrorism. They are aware that political sympathies affect interpretations of actions as legitimate or illegitimate and that the term 'terrorist' is often meant to imply 'illegitimate'.

[Terrorism] is not a neutral descriptive term. Even scholarly definitions of terrorism are subjective because they must take into account ordinary language uses of the term, which contain value judgments. Because of this we are led to ask who calls what terrorism, why, and when. Since 'terrorism' is a political label, it is an organizing concept that both describes the phenomenon as its exists and offers a moral judgment. A label is a useful shorthand, combining descriptive, evocative, and symbolic elements, but its meanings are inherently flexible and ambiguous. They may even be contradictory.

When people choose to call the actions of others 'terrorist' or to label others as 'terrorists', this choice often has a prescriptive police relevance as well as a moral connotation. As a way of framing consciousness, the choice of terminology has a particular relevance to assessing the legitimacy of political authority. Political language affects the perceptions of audiences and their expectations about how the problem thus evoked will be treated. That is, by defining and identifying a problem, labels may also indicate a preferred solution. It is well to remember, however, that the users of political language are not entirely free to shape it; once concepts are constructed and endowed with meaning, they take on a certain autonomy, especially when they are adopted by the news media, disseminated to the public, and integrated into a general context of norms and values.

That terms like terrorism should be contested is a normal part of the political process. Political language evolves through challenges. Critics of policies that labels serve to legitimize are quick to question the usefulness and appropriateness of the labels. Politics involves competition to define terms, as actors attempt to impose their own interpretations of history. In contemporary politics, calling adversaries 'terrorists' is a way of depicting them as fanatic and irrational so as to foreclose the possibility of compromise, draw attention to the real or imagined threat to security, and promote solidarity among the threatened. Using the term terrorism can imply not only that an adversary employs a particular strategy or style of violence but also that the 'true nature' of the opponent is thereby revealed. By defining the PLO [Palestine Liberation Organization] as a terrorist organization, for example, Israeli policy makers precluded recognition or negotiations. Furthermore, the government was bound by its own label; dealing with the PLO appeared as a major concession. This example also reminds us of the international dimensions of political labeling. The United States and Israel tend to share common conceptions of terrorism, but when talking to the PLO became a matter of American political interest, these conceptions diverged. In 1988 the United States accepted the PLO's formal renunciation of 'terrorism' (although the two sides did not agree on a precise definition), but to Israel the group remained a 'terrorist organization'.

Thus, conceptions of terrorism affect the ways in which governments define their interests, and interests also determine reliance on labels or their abandonment when politically convenient. The label can, however, blind governments to the distinction between violent and nonviolent dissent. It can also influence the selection of targets for state repression. For example, because the Argentine military conceived of terrorism as the symptom of a disease to be eradicated, the whole of society was seen as contaminated, and thus society itself became the target of terrorism from above. The government determined not only to destroy organized opposition but to cleanse society of the tendencies that had motivated resistance. In Italy, the term 'terrorism' was not used until midway through the Red Brigade's campaign of violence, although their activities remained essentially the same. In Northern Ireland, the official criminalization of the IRA was part of an effort to deny special status; such criminalization led to prison hunger strikes. West Germany pursued a similar policy. Labeling minorities as terrorist may intensify communal conflict, as it has in India. Labeling revolutionary movements terrorist risks minimizing their importance. The Peruvian government may have delayed responding to Sendero Luminoso, because it was initially dismissed as a mere 'terrorist organisation', implying the absence of popular support or military power. Possibly reintegration of 'repentant' terrorists was easier in Italy because left-wing militants were considered misguided youth, not professional revolutionaries.[7]

Oppositions who use terrorism also attempt to provide frames of reference and comparisons that place them in a morally advantageous light (for example, appealing to the analogy of resistance to fascism in the 1930s and 1940s). Both sides try to situate terrorism in a broader conceptual context. What is curious is that oppositions also seem to wish to appropriate the metaphor of warfare to describe terrorism, although for reasons that appear incompatible with those we are ascribing to governments.

An underground organization using terrorism probably defines terrorism as warfare in order to acquire political recognition and status, which in turn can confer legitimacy, which is exactly what governments resist. To be engaged in warfare is a justification for terrorism as well as a claim to powerful status. The smaller and the more extreme the group becomes, it seems, the more likely it is to call itself an 'army' (such as the Red Army Faction, the Japanese Red Army, or the Red Brigades); but one would not want to overlook the Irish Republican Army, which uses the term to remind us of its heritage. Most underground groups borrow the symbols and trappings of military discipline and procedure. Yet acts of terrorism do not typically resemble acts of warfare. 'Hard' or well-defended targets of military or defensive value to the enemy are rarely the targets of terrorism; to the contrary, terrorists seem to prefer noncombatants. When military units engage in actions that we might refer to as terrorism, they are called 'unconventional' or 'special' operations. A military self-conception can even be self-defeating. According to Richard Gillespie, when the Montoneros of Argentina began describing themselves as an armed force, they were compelled to recognize that they were inferior to government security forces. As a terrorist organization without military pretensions, they seemed powerful.

Nevertheless, in criticizing this metaphor for its political implications, we recognize that it forces us to ask what terrorism is. Where should terrorism be situated in the continuum between peace and war? What analogies and historical comparisons are relevant? What does terrorism tell us about the changing nature of military force in the contemporary world? Should it be seen in the context of warfare in some cases, protest in others? Is it a sign that modern warfare is steadily becoming less 'conventional', that is, politicized?

Defining terrorism becomes particularly troublesome when it occurs against a background of extensive violence. We cannot assume that terrorism is discontinuous with collective political violence. Even the best scholarly intentions may not suffice to distinguish terrorism from protest, guerrilla warfare, urban guerrilla warfare, subversion, criminal violence, paramilitarism, communal violence, or banditry. For example, which elements in the broad spectrum of violence in Ireland since the eighteenth century should rightly be called terrorism? Which revolutionary or counterrevolutionary practices during the eight years of the Algerian war consti-tuted terrorism? In Argentina, terrorism developed as oppositional violence but became an even more important part of the government response. The prolifera-tion of sometimes confusing terms (paramilitarism, urban guerrilla warfare, militarism, national liberation, armed struggle, or gang warfare) is indicative of the dilemma of distinguishing terrorism in particular from political violence in general. Since the word has a readily available negative meaning and distinctions seem inconsistent, it is easy to attribute terrorism to one's enemies and anything else to one's friends. The problem of definition is thus exacerbated when actors do not use terrorism exclusively but combine it with other modes of political action, which is frequently the case.

One reason for the power of terrorism as a political label, and hence for its controversialism, is not only its usefulness but its symbolic appeal. Terrorism has acquired a political value that can outlast short-term strategic failures. It persists despite negative outcomes. Terrorism projects images, communicates messages, and creates myths that transcend historical circumstances and motivate future gener-ations. These myths may of course be deceptive or contradictory. [. . .] It may be true of much terrorism (especially the more discriminating forms) that audiences react with both admiration for its daring and revulsion at its cruelty. It is easy for terrorism to become the cutting edge of a movement and to define an ideology. Undeniably it possesses an aura of perversely tragic glamor.[8]

Chapter 2

Motivation for terrorism

THIS CHAPTER ADDRESSES the question: why do some men and women resort to terrorism?

Once terrorism has been defined, with the importance of context acknowledged, it is useful to examine situational variables and causative factors as a background to motivation.

Martha Crenshaw (1981) explores settings in which political violence is likely to occur. Her standpoint, which may not be acceptable universally, is that terrorism is an expression of logical choice and political strategy. Terrorists appraising the parameters of a situation display a collective rationality. Crenshaw's argument, first of all, isolates a number of preconditions which set the stage for terrorism and then, as permissive factors, stimulate and direct motivation, providing opportunities for violent action. Concrete grievances, a lack of opportunity for political participation, above all, disaffection among an élite, are all considered reasons for terrorism.

Finally, a 'precipitating event' may trigger violence, seen then as the only feasible option:

To develop a framework for the analysis of likely settings for terrorism, we must establish conceptual distinctions among different types of factors. First, a significant difference exists between *preconditions*, factors that set the stage for terrorism over the long run, and *precipitants*, specific events that immediately precede the occurrence of terrorism. Second, a further classification divides preconditions into enabling or permissive factors, which provide opportunities for terrorism to happen, and situations that directly inspire and motivate terrorist campaigns.

First, modernization produces an interrelated set of factors that is a significant permissive cause of terrorism, as increased complexity on all levels of society and economy creates opportunities and vulnerabilities. Sophisticated networks of trans-portation and communication offer mobility and the means of publicity for terrorists.

Urbanization is part of the modern trend towards aggregation and complexity, which increases the number and accessibility of targets and methods. The popular concept of terrorism as 'urban guerrilla warfare' grew out of the Latin American experience of the late 1960s. Yet, as Hobsbawn has pointed out, cities became the arena for terrorism after the urban renewal projects of the late nineteenth century, such as the boulevards constructed by Baron Haussmann in Paris, made them unsuit-able for a strategy based on riots and the defense of barricades. In preventing popular insurrections, governments have exposed themselves to terrorism. P. N. Grabosky has recently argued that cities are a significant cause of terrorism in that they provide an opportunity (a multitude of targets, mobility, communications, anonymity, and audiences) and a recruiting ground among the politicized and volatile inhabitants.

Social 'facilitation' [. . .] is also an important permissive factor. This concept refers to social habits and historical traditions that sanction the use of violence against the government, making it morally and politically justifiable, and even dictating an appropriate form, such as demonstrations, coups, or terrorism. Social myths, traditions, and habits permit the development of terrorism as an established political custom. An excellent example of such a tradition is the case of Ireland, where the tradition of physical force dates from the eighteenth century, and the legend of Michael Collins in 1919–21 still inspires and partially excuses the much less discriminate and less effective terrorism of the contemporary Provisional IRA [Irish Republican Army] in Northern Ireland.

The most salient political factor in the category of permissive causes is a govern-ment's inability or unwillingness to prevent terrorism. The absence of adequate prevention by police and intelligence services permits the spread of conspiracy. However, since terrorist organizations are small and clandestine, the majority of states can be placed in the permissive category. Inefficiency or leniency can be found in a broad range of all but the most brutally efficient dictatorships [. . .] as well as modern liberal democratic states whose desire to protect civil liberties constrains security measures.

Turning now to a consideration of the direct causes of terrorism, we focus on background conditions that positively encourage resistance to the state. These insti-gating circumstances go beyond merely creating an environment in which terrorism is possible; they provide motivation and direction for the terrorist movement. We are dealing here with reasons rather than opportunities.

The first condition that can be considered a direct cause of terrorism is the existence of concrete grievances among an identifiable subgroup of a larger popu-lation, such as an ethnic minority discriminated against by the majority. A social movement develops in order to redress these grievances and to gain either equal rights or a separate state; terrorism is then the resort of an extremist faction of this broader movement. In practice, terrorism has frequently arisen in such situa-tions: in modern states, separatist nationalism among Basques, Bretons, and Québeçois has motivated terrorism. In the colonial era, nationalist movements commonly turned to terrorism.

This is not to say, however, that the existence of a dissatisfied minority or majority is a necessary or a sufficient cause of terrorism. Not all those who are discriminated against turn to terrorism, nor does terrorism always reflect objective social or economic deprivation. In West Germany, Japan, and Italy, for example, terrorism has been the chosen method of the privileged, not the downtrodden. Some theoretical studies have suggested that the essential ingredient that must be added to real deprivation is the perception on the part of the deprived that this condition is not what they deserve or expect, in short, that discrimination is unjust.

The second condition that creates motivations for terrorism is the lack of opportunity for political participation. Regimes that deny access to power and persecute dissenters create dissatisfaction. In this case, grievances are primarily political, without social or economic overtones. Discrimination is not directed against any ethnic, religious, or racial subgroup of the population. The terrorist organization is not necessarily part of a broader social movement; indeed, the population may be largely apathetic. In situations where paths to the legal expression of opposition are blocked, but where the regime's repression is inefficient, revolutionary terrorism is doubly likely, as permissive and direct causes coincide.

Context is especially significant as a direct cause of terrorism when it affects an élite, not the mass population. Terrorism is essentially the result of élite disaffection; it represents the strategy of a minority, who may act on behalf of a wider popular constituency who have not been consulted about, and do not necessarily approve of, the terrorists' aims or methods. [. . .] Many terrorists today are young, well-educated, and middle class in background. Such students or young professionals, with prior political experience, are disillusioned with the prospects of changing society and see little chance of access to the system despite their privileged status. Much terrorism has grown out of student unrest; this was the case in nineteenth-century Russia as well as post-World War II West Germany, Italy, the United States, Japan, and Uruguay.

Perhaps terrorism is most likely to occur precisely where mass passivity and élite dissatisfaction coincide. Discontent is not generalized or severe enough to provoke the majority of the populace to action against the regime, yet a small minority, without access to the bases of power that would permit overthrow of the government through *coup d'état* or subversion, seeks radical change. Terrorism may thus be a sign of a stable society rather than a symptom of fragility and impending collapse. Terrorism is the resort of an élite when conditions are not revolutionary.

The last category of situational factors involves the concept of a precipitating event that immediately precedes outbreaks of terrorism. Although it is generally thought that precipitants are the most unpredictable of causes, there does seem to be a common pattern of government actions that act as catalysts for terrorism. Government use of unexpected and unusual force in response to protest or reform attempts often compels terrorist retaliation. The development of such an action–reaction syndrome then establishes the structure of the conflict between the regime and its challengers. There are numerous historical examples of a campaign of terrorism precipitated by a government's reliance on excessive force to quell protest or squash dissent. [. . .] The British government's execution of the heroes of the Easter Rising set the stage for Michael Collins and the IRA. The Protestant violence that met the Catholic civil rights movement in Northern Ireland in 1969 pushed the Provisional IRA to retaliate. In West Germany, the death of Beno Ohnesorg at the hands of the police in a demonstration against the Shah of Iran in 1968 contributed to the emergence of the RAF [Red Army Faction].

This analysis of the background conditions for terrorism indicates that we must look at the terrorist organization's perception and interpretation of the situation. Terrorists view the context as permissive, making terrorism a viable option. In a material sense, the means are placed at their disposal by the environment. Circumstances also provide the terrorists with compelling reasons for seeking political change. Finally, an event occurs that snaps the terrorists' patience with the regime. Government action is now seen as intolerably unjust, and terrorism becomes not only a possible decision but a morally acceptable one. The regime has forfeited its status as the standard of legitimacy. For the terrorist, the end may now excuse the means.[1]

TYPES OF TERRORIST MOTIVATION: RATIONAL, PSYCHOLOGICAL AND CULTURAL

There have been many studies of the motivation presumed to underlie terrorist acts. Most studies assume that political violence follows a calculated rationale to which a collective subscribes at least for a time. Not all commentators would go as far as Crenshaw to term a line of action with its priorities, its planning, and its execution as a logical process. Those attempting to analyse terrorist thinking as a prelude to decisive action have had to consider factors which inspire both a group as a whole and the individual within it. An example of such analysis is to be found in an essay from the US Army's Command and General Staff College printed by the Terrorism Research Center in the United States. There is a concise and clear outline of goal-centred terrorism with a recognition that the common objectives of 'old-school' terrorism have given way to modern variegated motives, targeting and techniques. Consequently, counter-terrorism by way of prediction and combat has become very much more difficult. The essay goes on to deal with motivation classified into three categories – rational, psychological, and cultural – stating that terrorist action may be shaped by combinations of these:

Terrorism may be motivated by political, religious, or ideological objectives. In a sense, terrorist goals are always political, as extremists driven by religious or ideological beliefs usually seek political power to compel society to conform to their views. The objectives of terrorism distinguish it from other violent acts aimed at personal gain, such as criminal violence. However, the definition permits including violence by organized crime when it seeks to influence government policy. Some drug cartels and other international criminal organizations engage in political action when their activities influence governmental functioning. The essence of terrorism is the intent to induce fear in someone other than its victims to make a government or other audience change its political behavior.

Terrorism is common practice in insurgencies, but insurgents are not necessarily terrorists if they comply with the rules of war and do not engage in those forms of violence identified as terrorist acts. While the legal distinction is clear, it rarely inhibits terrorists who convince themselves that their actions are justified by a higher law. Their single-minded dedication to a goal, however poorly it may be articulated, renders legal sanctions relatively ineffective. In contrast, war is subject to rules of international law. Terrorists recognize no rules. No person, place, or object of value is immune from terrorist attack. There are no innocents.

This situation did not always prevail. Throughout history, extremists have practiced terrorism to generate fear and compel a change in behavior. Frequently, terrorism was incidental to other forms of violence, such as war or insurgency. Before the nineteenth century, terrorists usually granted certain categories of people immunity from attack. Like other warriors, terrorists recognized innocents – people not involved in conflict. Terrorists usually excluded women, children, and the elderly from target lists. For example, in late nineteenth-century Russia, radicals planning the assassination of Tsar Alexander II aborted several planned attacks because they risked harming innocent people. Old-school terrorism was direct; it intended to produce a political effect through the injury or death of the victim.

The development of bureaucratic states led to a profound change in terrorism. Modern governments have a continuity that older, personalistic governments did not. Terrorists found that the death of a single individual, even a monarch, did not necessarily produce the policy changes they sought. Terrorists reacted by turning to an indirect method of attack. By the early twentieth century, terrorists began to attack people previously considered innocents to generate political pressure. These indirect attacks create a public atmosphere of anxiety and undermine confidence in government. Their unpredictability and apparent randomness make it virtually impossible for governments to protect all potential victims. The public demands protection that the state cannot give. Frustrated and fearful, the people then demand that the government make concessions to stop the attacks.

Modern terrorism offers its practitioners many advantages. First, by not recognizing innocents, terrorists have an infinite number of targets. They select their target and determine when, where, and how to attack. The range of choices gives terrorists a high probability of success with minimum risk. If the attack goes wrong or fails to produce the intended results, the terrorists can deny responsibility.

Ironically, as democratic governments become more common it may be easier for terrorists to operate. The terrorist bombings of the New York City World Trade Center and the Oklahoma City Federal Building prove how easy it is for terrorists to operate in a free and democratic society. Authoritarian governments whose populace may have a better reason to revolt may also be less constrained by requirements for due process and impartial justice when combatting terrorists.

As commanders and staffs address terrorism, they must consider several relevant characteristics. First is that anyone can be a victim. (Some terrorists may still operate under cultural restraints, such as a desire to avoid harming women, but the planner cannot count on that. Essentially, there are no innocents.) Second, attacks that may appear to be senseless and random are not. To the perpetrators, their attacks make perfect sense. Acts such as bombing public places of assembly and shooting into crowded restaurants heighten public anxiety. This is the terror-ists' immediate objective. Third, the terrorist needs to publicize his attack. If no one knows about it, it will not produce fear. The need for publicity often drives target selection; the greater the symbolic value of the target, the more publicity the attack brings to the terrorists and the more fear it generates. Finally, a leader planning for combatting terrorism must understand that he cannot protect every possible target all the time. He must also understand that terrorists will likely shift from more protected targets to less protected ones. This is the key to defensive measures.

The terrorists

Terrorists are inspired by many different motives. Students of terrorism classify them into three categories: rational, psychological, and cultural. A terrorist may be shaped by combinations of these.

Rational motivation

The rational terrorist thinks through his goals and options, making a cost–benefit analysis. He seeks to determine whether there are less costly and more effective ways to achieve his objective than terrorism. To assess the risk, he weighs the target's defensive capabilities against his own capabilities to attack. He measures his group's capabilities to sustain the effort. The essential question is whether terrorism will work for the desired purpose, given societal conditions at the time. The terrorist's rational analysis is similar to that of a military commander or a busi-ness entrepreneur considering available courses of action.

Groups considering terrorism as an option ask a crucial question: can terrorism induce enough anxiety to attain its goals without causing a backlash that will destroy the cause and perhaps the terrorists themselves? To misjudge the answer is to risk disaster. Recent history offers examples of several groups that had apparently good prospects for success which paid the price of misjudging reaction to terrorism. In the early 1970s, the Tupamaros in Uruguay and the ERP (People's Revolutionary Army) and Montoneros in Argentina misjudged a hostile popular reaction to terrorism. They pushed the societies beyond their threshold of tolerance and were destroyed as a result.

Psychological motivation

Psychological motivation for terrorism derives from the terrorist's personal dissat-isfaction with his life and accomplishments. He finds his *raison d'être* in dedicated terrorist action. Although no clear psychopathy is found among terrorists, there is a nearly universal element in them that can be described as the 'true believer'. Terrorists do not even consider that they may be wrong and that others' views may have some merit. Terrorists tend to project their own antisocial motivations onto others, creating a polarized 'we versus they' outlook. They attribute only evil motives to anyone outside their own group. This enables the terrorists to dehumanize their victims and removes any sense of ambiguity from their minds. The resulting clarity of purpose appeals to those who crave violence to relieve their constant anger. The other common characteristic of the psychologically motivated terrorist is the pronounced need to belong to a group. With some terrorists, group acceptance is a stronger motivator than the stated political objectives of the organization. Such individuals define their social status by group acceptance.

Terrorist groups with strong internal motivations find it necessary to justify the group's existence continuously. A terrorist group must terrorize. As a minimum, it must commit violent acts to maintain group self-esteem and legitimacy. Thus, terrorists sometimes carry out attacks that are objectively nonproductive or even counterproductive to their announced goal.

Another result of psychological motivation is the intensity of group dynamics among terrorists. They tend to demand unanimity and be intolerant of dissent. With the enemy clearly identified and unequivocally evil, pressure to escalate the frequency and intensity of operations is ever present. The need to belong to the group discourages resignations, and the fear of compromise disallows their acceptance. Compromise is rejected, and terrorist groups lean towards maximalist positions. Having placed themselves beyond the pale, forever unacceptable to ordinary society, they cannot accept compromise. They consider negotiation dishonorable, if not treasonous. This may explain why terrorist groups are prone to fracturing and why the splinters are frequently more violent than their parent group.

The psychodynamics also make the announced group goal nearly impossible to achieve. A group that achieves its stated purpose is no longer needed; thus, success threatens the psychological well-being of its members. When a terrorist group approaches its stated goal, it is inclined to redefine it. The group may reject the achievement as false or inadequate or the result of the duplicity of 'them'. Nicaragua's Recontras, The Basque ETA (Euskadi Ta Askatasuna, 'Basque Fatherland and Liberty'), and many Palestinian radical groups apparently suffer from fear of success. One effective psychological defense against success is to define goals so broadly that they are impossible to achieve. Even if the world proclaims the success of a political movement, the terrorists can deny it and fight on.

Cultural motivation

Cultures shape values and motivate people to actions that seem unreasonable to foreign observers. Americans are reluctant to appreciate the intense effect of culture on behavior. We accept the myth that rational behavior guides all human actions. Even though irrational behavior occurs in our own tradition, we seek to explain it by other means. We reject as unbelievable such things as vendettas, martyrdom, and self-destructive group behavior when we observe them in others. We view with disbelief such things as the dissolution of a viable state for the sake of ethnic purity when the resulting ministates are economically anemic.

The treatment of life in general and individual life in particular is a cultural characteristic that has a tremendous impact on terrorism. In societies in which people identify themselves in terms of group membership (family, clan, tribe), there may be a willingness to self-sacrifice seldom seen elsewhere. [. . .] At times, terrorists seem to be eager to give their lives for their organization and cause. The lives of 'others', being wholly evil in the terrorists' value system, can be destroyed with little or no remorse.

Other factors include the manner in which aggression is channelled and the concepts of social organization. For example, the ambient level of violence is shaped by the political structure and its provisions for power transfer. Some political systems have no effective nonviolent means for the succession to power. A culture may have a high tolerance for nonpolitical violence, such as banditry or ethnic 'turf' battles, and remain relatively free of political violence. The United States, for example, is one of the most violent societies in the world. Yet, political violence remains an aberration. By contrast, France and Germany, with low tolerance for violent crime, have a history of political violence.

A major cultural determinate of terrorism is the perception of 'outsiders' and anticipation of a threat to ethnic group survival. Fear of cultural extermination leads to violence which, to someone who does not experience it, seems irrational. All human beings are sensitive to threats to the values by which they identify themselves. These include language, religion, group membership, and homeland or native territory. The possibility of losing any of these can trigger defensive, even xenophobic, reactions.

Religion may be the most volatile of cultural identifiers because it encompasses values deeply held. A threat to one's religion puts not only the present at risk but also one's cultural past and the future. Many religions, including Christianity and Islam, are so confident they are right that they have used force to obtain converts. Terrorism in the name of religion can be especially violent. Like all terrorists, those who are religiously motivated view their acts with moral certainty and even divine sanctions. What would otherwise be extraordinary acts of desperation become a religious duty in the mind of the religiously motivated terrorist. This helps explain the high level of commitment and willingness to risk death among religious extremist groups.[2]

TERRORIST BEHAVIOUR

Psychodynamic theories of terrorist motivation and behaviour have been outlined recently by Jerrold M. Post (1998), a psychiatrist and political scientist working in Washington DC. Under the rubric, 'Terrorist psycho-logic: terrorist behaviour as a product of psychological forces', Post argues that individuals are drawn to terrorism by means of a special 'logic' which is used to justify their violence. Frequently, terrorist rhetoric strikes us as absolutist; terrorist personalities reveal aggressiveness, a degree of flawed self-concept, a tendency to blame and scapegoat others, and a proneness to failure. Post, having suggested these traits, warns against their generalisation. Individuals feeling 'significant' for the first time readily succumb to leader dominance and group pressure. In conclusion, Post sees a terrorist group's 'success' in achieving a cause as a threat to the goal of survival:

[. . .] *Political terrorists are driven to commit acts of violence as a consequence of psychological forces*, and [. . .] their special psycho-logic is constructed to rationalize *acts they are psychologically compelled to commit*. Thus the principal argument of this essay is that *individuals are drawn to the path of terrorism in order to commit acts of violence*, and their special logic, which is grounded in their psychology and reflected in their rhetoric, becomes the justification for their violent acts.

Considering the diversity of causes to which terrorists are committed, the uniformity of their rhetoric is striking. Polarizing and absolutist, it is a rhetoric of 'us versus them'. It is a rhetoric without nuance, without shades of grey. 'They', the establishment, are the source of all evil, in vivid contrast to 'us', the freedom fighters, consumed by righteous rage. And if 'they' are the source of our problems, it follows ineluctably, in the special psycho-logic of the terrorist, that 'they' must be destroyed. It is the only just and moral thing to do. Once the basic premises are accepted, the logical reasoning is flawless. Shall we then conclude, because their reasoning is so logical, that terrorists are psychologically well balanced and that terrorist campaigns are the product of a rationally derived strategic choice?

If we dismiss the notion of a terror network with a central staff providing propaganda guidance, what accounts for the uniformity of the terrorists' polarizing absolutist rhetoric? The author's own comparative research on the psychology of terrorists does not reveal major psychopathology, and is in substantial agreement with the finding of Crenshaw that 'the outstanding common characteristic of terrorists is their normality'. Her studies of the National Liberation Front (FLN) in Algeria in the 1950s found the members to be basically normal. Nor did Heskin find members of the Irish Republican Army (IRA) to be emotionally disturbed. In a review of the social psychology of terrorist groups, McCauley and Segal conclude that 'the best documented generalization is negative; terrorists do not show any striking psychopathology'.

Nor does a comparative study reveal a particular psychological type, a particular personality constellation, a uniform terrorist mind. But although diverse personalities are attracted to the path of terrorism, an examination of memoirs, court records, and rare interviews suggests that people with particular personality traits and tendencies are drawn disproportionately to terrorist careers.

What are these traits, these personality characteristics? Several authors have characterized terrorists as action-oriented, aggressive people who are stimulus-hungry and seek excitement. Particularly striking is the reliance placed on the psychological mechanisms of 'externalization' and 'splitting', psychological mechanisms found in individuals with narcissistic and borderline personality disturbances. It is not my intent to suggest that all terrorists suffer from borderline or narcissistic personality disorders or that the psychological mechanisms of externalization and splitting are used by every terrorist. It is my distinct impression, however, that these mechanisms are found with extremely high frequency in the population of terrorists, and contribute significantly to the uniformity of terrorists' rhetorical style and their special psycho-logic.

In this regard, it is particularly important to understand the mechanism of 'splitting'. This is believed to be characteristic of people whose personality development is shaped by a particular type of psychological damage during childhood which produces what clinicians have characterized as narcissistic wounds. This leads to the development of what Kohut has termed 'the injured self'.

Individuals with a damaged self-concept have never fully integrated the good and bad parts of the self. These aspects of the self are 'split' into the 'me' and the 'not me'. An individual with this personality constellation idealizes his grandiose self and *splits out* and *projects* onto others all the hated and devalued weakness within. Individuals who place high reliance on the mechanisms of splitting and externalization look outward for the source of difficulties. They need an outside enemy to blame. This is a dominant mechanism of the destructive charismatic, such as Hitler, who projects the devalued part of himself onto the interpersonal environment and then attacks and scapegoats the enemy without. Unable to face his own inadequacies, the individual with this personality style needs a target to blame and attack for his own inner weakness and inadequacies. Such people find the polarizing absolutist rhetoric of terrorism extremely attractive. The statement, 'It's not us – it's them; they are the cause of our problems', provides a psychologically satisfying explanation for what has gone wrong in their lives.

In summary, most terrorists do not demonstrate serious psychopathology. Although there is no single personality type, it appears that people who are aggressive and action-oriented, and who place greater-than-normal reliance on the psychological mechanisms of externalization and splitting, are disproportionately represented among terrorists. Data indicate that many terrorists have not been successful in their personal, educational, and vocational lives.[3]

Although not all the people who find their way into a terrorist group share the characteristics just described, to the degree that many in the group do, the group takes on a particular coloration. For many, belonging to the terrorist group may be the first time they truly belonged, the first time they felt truly significant, the first time they felt that what they did counted. As Bion has persuasively demonstrated, when individuals function in a group setting, their individual judgment and behavior are strongly influenced by the powerful forces of group dynamics. This is true of psychologically healthy people, including successful business executives and educators. Bion's constructs are particularly useful in understanding the group dynamics of terrorist behavior.

In every group, according to Bion, there are two opposing forces – what Bion calls 'the *work group* and 'the *basic assumption group*'. The work group is that aspect of the group that acts in a goal-directed manner to accomplish its stated purposes. But as anyone who has ever worked on a committee or task force will ruefully testify, the occasions when a group proceeds to work in a fully cooperative manner to accomplish its goals in a conflict-free manner are rare indeed. Rather, groups, in their functioning, often sabotage their stated goals. They act, to use Bion's words, as if they are operating under 'basic assumptions', in what Bion calls the basic assumption group. He has identified three such psychological symptoms: the '*fight-flight*' group, the '*dependency*' group, and the '*pairing*' group:

1.   The *fight-flight* group defines itself in relation to the outside world, which both threatens and justifies its existence. It acts as if the only way it can preserve itself is by fighting against or fleeing from the perceived enemy.

2.   The *dependency* group turns to an omnipotent leader for direction. Members who fall into this state subordinate their own independent judgement to that of the leader and act as if they do not have minds of their own.
3.   The *pairing* group acts as if the group will bring forth a messiah who will rescue them and create a better world.

If these states characterize the healthiest of groups, it should hardly be surprising that, when the group contains a disproportionate number of members who have fragmented psychosocial identities as well as a strong need to strike out against the cause of their failure, there should be an especially strong tendency to fall into these psychological postures, with extremely powerful group forces emerging. In my judgment, the terrorist group is the apotheosis of the 'basic assumption' group, and regularly manifests all three 'basic assumption' states.[4]

Given the intensity of the need to belong, the strength of the affiliative needs, and, for many members, the as-yet incomplete sense of individual identity, terrorists have a tendency to submerge their own identities into the group, so that a kind of 'group mind' emerges. The group cohesion that emerges is magnified by the external danger, which tends to reduce internal divisiveness in unity against the outside enemy. 'The group was born under the pressure of pursuit' according to members of the Red Army Faction, and group solidarity was 'compelled exclusively by the illegal situation, fashioned into a common destiny'. Another Red Army Faction member went so far as to consider this pressure 'the sole link holding the group together'.

Doubts concerning the legitimacy of the goals and actions of the group are intolerable to such a group. The person who questions a group decision risks the wrath of the group and possible expulsion.[5]

In attempting to clarify whether acts of political violence are chosen as a wilful strategy or are products of psychological forces, it is of central importance to evaluate the goal of the act of violence. The rationalist school, as explicated by Crenshaw in the previous chapter, would aver that in an unequal political struggle, acts of political terrorism become an equalizer. These acts of political violence call forceful attention to the group's legitimate grievances and are designed to have an impact on a much wider audience than the immediate target of the violence. (Schmid has observed that it is very important to differentiate between the target of the violence and the target of influence; what distinguishes terrorism from other forms of political violence is the differentiation of the target of violence, that is, the innocent victim or noncombatant, from the target of influence, that is, the broader public or élite decision makers.) But implicit in this line of reasoning is an assumption that the political violence is instrumental, a tactic to achieve the group's political goals, to help it achieve its cause.

The position argued in this essay – that political violence is driven by psychological forces – follows a different line of reasoning. It does not view political violence as instrumental, but as the end itself. *The cause is not the cause.* The cause, as codified in the group's ideology, according to this line of reasoning, becomes the rationale for acts the terrorists are driven to commit. Indeed, the central argument of this position is that *individuals become terrorists in order to join terrorist groups and commit acts of terrorism.*

That is surely an extreme statement, but since we are discussing political extremism, perhaps that excess can be forgiven.

Consider a youth seeking an external target to attack. Before joining the group, he was alone, not particularly successful. Now he is engaged in a life-and-death struggle with the establishment, his picture on the 'most wanted' posters. He sees his leaders as internationally prominent media personalities. Within certain circles, he is lionized as a hero. He travels first class, and his family is provided for should his acts of heroism lead to his death as a martyr to the cause. Heady stuff that; surely this is the good life, a role and position not easily relinquished.

Now if authenticity is defined as 'revolutionary heroism', then this definition has important implications for the outcomes of debates and personal rivalries within the group. A leader who advocates prudence and moderation is likely to lose his position quickly to a bolder person committed to the continuation of the struggle. Indeed, on the basis of his observations of underground resistance groups during World War II, Zawodny has concluded that the primary determinant of underground group decision making is not the external reality but the psychological climate within the group. He has described the unbearable tension that builds when a resistance group is compelled to go underground. For these action-oriented people, forced inaction is extremely successful. What, after all, are freedom fighters if they do not fight? *A terrorist group needs to commit acts of terrorism in order to justify its existence*. The wise leader, sensing the building tension, will plan an action so that the group's members can reaffirm their identity and discharge their aggressive energy. Better to have the group attack the outside enemy, no matter how high the risk, than turn on itself – and him.

For any group or organization, the highest priority is survival. This is especially true for the terrorist group. *To succeed in achieving its espoused cause would threaten the goal of survival*. This fact suggests a position of cybernetic balance for the group. It must be successful enough in its terrorist acts and rhetoric of legitimation to attract members and perpetuate itself, but it must not be so successful that it will succeed itself out of business.[6]

Post's rather deterministic line of argument ends with a grim declaration. 'Terrorists whose only sense of significance comes from being terrorists cannot be forced to give up terrorism, for to do so would be to lose their very reason for being.'[7]

Chapter 3

Terrorism's worldwide occurrence

THIS CHAPTER ADDRESSES the question: what form does terrorism take and where is it mostly to be found? First, excerpts from a recent overview of terrorism since 1945 are presented. A number of the groups referred to there are described in detail in the twelve case-studies in Part Two of this book. Second, the excerpts are followed by a note on terrorist organisation. In the third place, there is an outline typology of terrorism which, despite its being a rather bare framework, may offer scope for discussion and comparison. Finally, there is a list of the main contemporary terrorist groups with a note about state-sponsored terrorism.

OVERVIEW OF TERRORISM SINCE 1945

Walter Laqueur (1999), an authoritative and prolific writer on terrorism, has surveyed terrorist activity after the Second World War in broad detail. The following text contains excerpts from Laqueur:

With the end of the Second World War, the terrorist action shifted from Europe to the Middle East and Asia. There was no neo-Nazi or neo-fascist terrorism in the years after 1945, as many had feared; with the defeat of the Axis powers, the fanatical enthusiasm had vanished. In Eastern Europe and the Balkans, including those areas in which terrorism had been endemic, the presence of the Red Army and, later on, the heavy hand of the local secret police were sufficient to act as a deterrent.

But in the colonies and other dependencies in North Africa and the Middle East, violent campaigns were launched by nationalist groups striving for independence. Terrorist acts had, of course, taken place before in the East, for example, prime ministers had been assassinated in Iraq and Egypt. But with the weakening of the colonial powers, violence gained a new, powerful momentum.

Terrorism in Palestine, spearheaded by Irgun, had first appeared on the eve of the Second World War, but then Irgun called an armistice and some of its members joined the British forces. However, even before the war ended, the group renewed its attacks against the mandated power. A smaller, even more radical offshoot, the Stern Gang (Fighters for the Freedom of Israel), had attacked ceaselessly, and their leader was hunted down and shot by the British police in Tel Aviv in 1942. The politics of the Stern Gang were more than a little confused; in the early phase of the war they had looked for cooperation from the Italians and even the Germans, and later on they were attracted to Soviet communism. Their anti-imperialist manifestos often read as if they had been composed in Moscow. But their left-wing motivation was not deeply rooted. Both Irgun and the Stern Gang dissolved after the state of Israel came into being. [. . .] The leader of Irgun, Menachem Begin, and one of the leaders of the Stern Gang, Yitzhak Shamir, in later years became prime ministers of Israel. These are just two examples of the many cases of guerrilla or terrorist leaders having a second, political career after their fighting days were over.

The Algerian war for independence began in 1954 in the mountainous regions of the country, was carried to the cities, and lasted for seven years. The terrorist part of the campaign was not too successful – the French smashed the rebel FLN cadres in the capital and the campaign did not go well in the countryside. But the rebels had the great advantage of having sanctuaries in the neighbouring countries. Twenty thousand of their fighters were assembled outside the reach of the French, who gradually lost the stomach for making the effort needed to keep the renitent country under its control.

As in Israel, the terrorist campaigns were followed by decades of peace, but eventually radical elements again asserted themselves. This led to the second Algerian war in the 1990s and, in Israel, the murder of Prime Minister Rabin in 1995.

Generally speaking, Middle Eastern politics remained violent, marked by the assassination of a great many leaders – among them King Abdullah of Jordan in 1951 and Anwar Sadat of Egypt in 1981 – and a variety of Syrian, Lebanese, and Iranian government ministers. After the emergence of radical Muslim elements, terrorism became even more rampant. Political assassinations, needless to say, occurred in many other parts of Asia and Africa. The murder of Gandhi in 1948, and in later years of Indira Gandhi and Rajiv, her son who succeeded her as prime minister, are particularly striking examples. But it was above all in the Muslim countries of North Africa and the Middle East that systematic and sustained terrorism prevailed in the 1950s, even before anti-Israeli terrorism became a major and well-publicized feature of world politics in the 1960s.

Latin American terrorism

In Latin America, there was a recurrence of terrorism in the late 1960s that was not nationalist–separatist in character but drew its inspiration from the extreme left. The Tupamaros of Uruguay were the prototype of this new terrorism. They emerged in a country that for years had been the most progressive in Latin America, and even in the 1960s was among the more liberal. The Tupamaros, who stood for radical political and social change, attracted some of the best and most idealistic from the younger generation, and they engaged in bank robberies and kidnappings but not in indiscriminate murder. Initially their activities were quite successful, proving that a civilian government could be easily disrupted. The Tupamaros attracted a great deal of attention in the world media, but in the final analysis the only result of their operations was the destruction of freedom in a country that almost alone in Latin America had an unbroken democratic tradition, however imperfect. The campaign of the Tupamaros caused the rise of a military dictatorship and destroyed the democratic system, and, at the same time, brought about the destruction of their own movement. By the 1970s, the remaining Tupamaros were in exile bemoaning the evil doings of an oppressive regime they themselves had helped to bring to power.

Terrorism in Argentina began a few years after the outbreak in Uruguay. It was on a far more massive scale, and both the terrorist operations and the backlash were more indiscriminate and bloody. In contrast to their Uruguayan comrades, Argentinian terrorists consisted of two groups: the Montoneros (basically Peronist in orientation and social composition) and the smaller but better-equipped and organised ERP (more doctrinally left-wing in character, consisting mainly of students). The Montoneros, who had the whole Peronist left wing as a base of recruitment, began their campaign with the killing of ex-President Aramburu in May 1970. Initially, a considerable number of foreigners (or locals representing foreign economic interests) were among the victims, but gradually the terrorism turned against the army, the police, politicians, and moderate union leaders. There were also a great many unintended victims who died because they happened to be where bombs exploded.

Argentina is perhaps the only recorded example of urban guerrilla activity – that is, where terrorists came close to establishing liberated zones in urban areas. But the terrorists over-reached precisely because they engaged in large-scale operations that made it easier for the army to combat them. Once the army received a free hand to retaliate, no mercy was shown. Four thousand members of the Montoneros and the ERP were detained, thousands more were arrested, and many were tortured or disappeared without a trace, including many innocent people. Thus, a terrible price was paid for the ill-conceived terrorist campaign. True, within a decade military dictatorship in Argentina, as in Uruguay, gave way to a civilian government that gradually became more democratic, but the experience of these countries did show that even weak and ineffective governments were capable of defending themselves when terrorists had no hope of gaining the support of significant sections of the population.

Left-wing terrorism in Germany and Italy

A new wave of terrorism of left-wing inspiration appeared in Europe in the late 1960s, partly in the wake of the student revolt of 1968. The German 'Red Army' (the Baader Meinhof group) was active for about seven years, and it was succeeded by the movements 'June 2nd' and the 'Red Cells'. According to Red Army ideology, this group was the vanguard of the exploited and oppressed Third World, terrorism being the only feasible strategy of weak revolutionary movements. But the Third World they invoked was a figment of their imagination, and if it had existed, it would not have wanted any part of these three dozen young men and women who called themselves an 'army', and who lived in a world of infantile dreams.

Over the years the Red Army attacked several banks, burned a department store or two, and killed a number of bankers, industrialists, and judges. But none of the victims was very prominent, nor could they have been regarded as major enemies, of either Baader Meinhof, of the revolutionary movement, or of the Third World. Their names seem to have been picked out of a telephone directory.

Initially, the Red Army had hundreds of supporters, some of whom were willing to give active help. But gradually they lost sympathy, as it became obvious that the terrorists were living in a fantasy world and that their ill-conceived actions had no political impact whatsoever, except perhaps to tarnish the image of the left.

If Baader Meinhof had originally been deeply if unrealistically motivated by ideology, the second and third generation of German left-wing terrorists did not tend towards reflection. They engaged in terrorism because their predecessors had done so. If they had a specific political orientation, they were unwilling or unable to express it. A few terrorist acts took place during the 1980s and early 1990s, but by and large these groups had become irrelevant, and even the media, which originally had devoted inordinate attention to their activities, lost interest.

Italian left-wing terrorism was conducted on a considerably wider scale; it was spearheaded by the Brigate Rosse, which came into being in 1970. The inspiration in Italy came less from the New Left, which had never been very strong in that country, and more from radical groups within the Communist Youth League and, to some extent, from the student groups of the left wing of the Christian Democrats, which had undergone a rapid process of radicalization. As the Red Brigades saw it, Italy was not a democratic country but a bourgeois dictatorship; the language of arms was the only language understood by the ruling class. The Communist Party, these young radicals believed, was a reformist party that had lost its belief in revolution and radical fervour. The movement was also helped by a general feeling of discontent with the lack of progress on the domestic front; the social structures had been frozen since the end of the war, and one party had been in power throughout the period. As in Germany, the membership was predominantly middle class. [. . .]

The Red Brigades engaged in some 14,000 terrorist attacks within their first ten years. While some parts of Italy were relatively free of terrorism, Rome and the industrial regions of the north were strongly affected. The legal system was almost paralysed, since jurors were afraid to fulfill their duty; not all judges were prepared to be heroes, and the police were by and large unprepared to deal with this unprecedented challenge. Nevertheless, the Red Brigades alienated many of their erstwhile well-wishers as the result of their attacks on journalists and union officials, and above all their murder of Aldo Moro, who had been the most leftist of all the Christian Democrat prime ministers. Far from bringing about a weakening of the state apparatus, the abduction and murder of Aldo Moro caused a closing of ranks of all the democratic parties, including, for once, the Communists.

Gradually, the Italian police and the courts began showing greater sophistication in dealing with the terrorists. By 1982, some 1,400 leftist terrorists were in prison and more than a few of them, the so-called *pentiti*, had recanted. This led to splits in the ranks of the terrorists who had not been arrested. By 1984, only one member of the high command of the Brigades had not been apprehended, and the movement had ceased to exist.

America and Japan

The upsurge in terrorism of the 1960s was not limited to Europe. It manifested itself in various ways in the United States and Japan. In America, it appeared on the radical fringe of the New Left in groups like the Weathermen. In a largely unconnected development, terrorism found adherents among black militants, above all the Black Panthers. The motives that induced young blacks to join the terrorist scene were quite different from those that made middle-class white students join the Weathermen. The students knew nothing about the problems of the ghetto and about unemployment. They were motivated by a crisis of identity, suburban boredom, and the desire for excitement and action. For them, more often than not terrorism was the cure for personal problems. All this was immersed in intellectual confusion that espoused the idea that almost anything was permitted and denounced the absence of values. But the things the white radicals were saying about the wickedness of American culture were *a fortiori* true of the radicals themselves.

Contemporary Japanese terrorism, which was limited principally to the Japanese Red Army, reflected native traditions as well as Western influences. Many of the ideological disputations of Japanese terrorists were imported from the West, but they also invoked the spirit of the samurai. Japanese terrorists hijacked a Japanese aircraft, committed murders, including several of their own comrades, and perpetrated a few acts of sabotage, most notably of a Shell refinery in Singapore and of the French embassy in the Hague. They were also instrumental in the massacre at Lod Airport in Israel, and they collaborated with Carlos, the famous multinational terrorist, as well as the Palestinians, and ultimately found asylum in Lebanon. This being the whole extent of their terrorist activities, the Japanese Red Army was much less dangerous than the Japanese sectarian terrorists of the 1990s, who had a true base inside Japan, which the Red Army never had.[1]

The Palestinians

Palestinian terrorism grew out of the Palestinian resistance movement against Israel. There had been attacks against Israeli settlements since the state came into being, mainly small raids across the border, but it was only after the war of 1967 and the occupation of the West Bank that a major terrorist campaign began.

Eventually the PLO, which was both a political organization and something akin to a guerrilla movement, also opted for terrorism through Black September

and other ad hoc groups. The Palestinians engaged in a variety of horrific operations, such as the killing of Israeli athletes at the Munich Olympic Games in 1972
and the blowing up of several jumbo jets at Dawson Field in Jordan in September
1970. But these major operations usually backfired: for example, the Dawson Field
incident threatened the existence of Jordan, whereupon Black September was
suppressed by the Jordanian army. The Israelis retaliated with counterterror inside
Israel and abroad, and the hijacking of planes, which at one time had been a main
strategy, was given up.

Palestinian terrorism [. . .] although not a success per se, had a great advantage over most other terrorist movements – namely, the support extended by many
Arab countries, which created considerable political difficulty for Israel. Eventually
this pressure exerted by the Arab states through the major powers, combined with
the Intifada (which was mass rather than individual violence), brought about concessions from Israel. Israel was also hurt by the enormous publicity given even to very
minor terrorist events in Israel as compared with the much more destructive
terrorism in Sri Lanka and Algeria, for example. The reason was obvious: the media
were concentrated in Jerusalem rather than Sri Lanka or Algeria.

Terrorism old and new: IRA and ETA

A new age of terrorism is dawning, but the old terrorism is far from dead, even
though it has declined markedly in Europe. An example is provided by the situation in Northern Ireland. [. . .] Terrorism in Ireland developed in 1968–69
following Catholic and Protestant demonstrations and has not ceased since. The
last phase of the Troubles in Northern Ireland began in 1969. The early years of
the Troubles (1972–76) were by far the bloodiest. Thereafter the annual number
of victims declined to about a third of what it had been in the early years.

But the IRA could have conducted many more widescale and frequent attacks,
given the financial support they received and the arms supply at their disposal.
What kept their activities down to relatively low levels? The IRA leadership seems
to have realized early on that their campaign against the British would be long, and
that if it became too formidable a danger, especially on the British mainland, they
would not only turn public opinion against themselves but also invite much sharper
and more effective counterblows. Nor could they hope to substantially strengthen
their position in their own community; in parliamentary elections they hardly ever
scored more than 15 per cent of the vote.

Their strategy from the late 1970s on seems to have been to wear out the
British, perhaps to await a time when Britain would be in so weak a position that
it would have to make concessions it had been reluctant to consider in the past.
The aims of the Republicans were, after all, limited in scope compared with those
of Palestinian groups such as Hamas. They wanted not the total destruction of their
enemy but merely a united Ireland.

Hence the political negotiations that began in 1993. [. . .] After many setbacks,
these talks led to agreement in 1998.

Whether the peace will last cannot be predicted with certainty. But as of this
writing in 1999, terrorism in Ireland has come to an end after long negotiations

and the intervention of the American president, Bill Clinton, and the British prime minister, Tony Blair.

The parallels between the IRA and the Basque ETA are striking in many respects: both are motivated by enormous enthusiasm, even though the groups constitute only a minority within their own community. Basque opposition against what is perceived as oppression by the Madrid centralists goes back to the nineteenth century and possibly even further.

The ETA has achieved considerable political concessions, but this success has not been remotely sufficient to satisfy the nationalists. The aim of the extremists remains an independent Basque state.

The high tide of ETA terrorism came in 1978–80, certainly as far as the number of victims is concerned.

ETA's prospects seem dim. [. . .] Nevertheless, ETA still has the support of a fanatical minority in their own region. Eventually, a political solution might be found; this will undoubtedly lead to a split, as in the case of the IRA, since the ultranationalists cannot possibly achieve all they want.

In the Basque region, as in Northern Ireland, a culture of violence has developed over the years that tends to perpetuate itself. It is, in all probability, a generational question. As one generation of professional terrorists ages and by necessity opts out of the armed struggle, a new one may or may not emerge. Or it may appear after an interruption of a few decades, as has happened in Irish history time and again.[2]

TERRORIST ORGANISATION

Earlier chapters have shown that for the most part terrorist activity is the work of organised groups, some simple, perhaps of a fleeting nature, others more complex and long-lasting. The Terrorist Research Center in the United States published, in December 1998, a note about the main points of terrorist organisation:

Organizational details are situation-specific. There are, however, a few general organizational principles. Because terrorists must operate in a hostile environment, security is their primary concern. Security is best served by a cellular structure in which members do not know and cannot identify more than a few of their colleagues in the event of capture or defection. Defection is rare in most groups; defectors or even dissenters are frequently killed or maimed. Yet, terrorists are not immune to human weaknesses. Unless they are united by a charismatic leader, terrorists are affected by group dynamics that produce both problems and opportunities for security forces. Opportunities arise because internal dissension causes security leaks; problems arise because operational patterns may change as different factions prevail.

Terrorist groups that are not supported by a government usually create a support structure of sympathizers and people who have been coerced into helping them. The support structure may comprise active and passive members. It furnishes the active terrorists with logistic support, intelligence, dissemination of propaganda, recruiting, and money.

Terrorist recruitment and training are, predictably, security-sensitive. Among groups that are not ethnic-based, the usual sources of recruits are high school and college students who show commitment to the cause. Ethnically based terrorist groups recruit new members personally known to them, people whose backgrounds are known and who often have family ties to the organization. Intelligence penetration of organizations recruited in this way is extremely difficult.

Terrorist training varies considerably. Those with military experience or who have received prolonged training at sophisticated facilities are the equals of most state security forces. At the other end of the spectrum are 'throw away' operatives who get little more than inspirational talks before being activated. Typical training includes instruction in the use of small arms and explosives along with intelligence collection and indoctrination in the group's cause.

Contemporary terrorist actions include the traditional assassinations, bombings, arson, hostage-taking, hijacking, kidnapping, seizure and occupation of a building, attacks on a facility, sabotage, and perpetration of hoaxes. Newer categories of operations include ecological terrorism and the still largely potential 'high-tech' terrorism using nuclear, biological, and chemical (NBC) weapons and materials. Target selection considerations are equally diverse but include the target's value in terms of its contribution to group goals, its accessibility given group capabilities, and the purpose of the attack, such as to gain attention, collect resources, eliminate a threat, or demonstrate a capability. All these factors are reflected in the group's organization and training.[3]

AN OUTLINE TYPOLOGY

Richard Schultz (1978) developed a typology of political terrorism which provides a useful outline framework that is summarised below and illustrated in an accompanying figure. There are three generalised categories of political action by internal or external agents:

1. Revolutionary terrorism – the threat or use of political violence aimed at effecting complete revolutionary change.
2. Sub-revolutionary terrorism – the threat or use of political violence aimed at effecting various changes in a particular political system (but not to abolish it).
3. Establishment terrorism – the threat or use of political violence by an established political system against internal or external opposition.

There are seven possible variables:

1. Causes – any one or more of observable economic, political, social, psychological factors (long-term or short-term) underlying a decision to use violence.
2. Environment – (internal) urban/rural movements within the nation state; (external) global, other nation states.
3. Goals – objectives as long-range plans or as short-term tactics.

Table 1 Typology of political terrorism

Selected variables	Causes	Environment	Goals	Strategy	Means	Organisation	Participation
General categories							
Revolutionary terrorism	Economic, Political, Social, Psychological factors	Internal (urban or rural revolutionary groups)	Long Range/Strategic Objectives	Primary or secondary role in the overall strategy	Various capabilities and techniques employed	Nature – degrees of organisational structures	Participant profiles
		External (autonomous non-state revolutionary actors)	Short Term/Tactical Objectives				Leadership style/attitude
Sub-revolutionary terrorism	Economic, Political, Social, Psychological factors	Internal (urban-rural non-revolutionary groups)	Long Range/Strategic Objectives	Primary or secondary role in the overall strategy	Various capabilities and techniques employed	Nature – degrees of organisational structures	Participant profiles
		External (non-revolutionary, autonomous, non-state actors)	Short Term/Tactical Objectives				Leadership style/attitude
Establishment terrorism	Economic, Political, Social, Psychological factors	Internal (repression of urban or rural opposition)	Long Range/Strategic Objectives	Primary or secondary role in the overall strategy	Various capabilities and techniques employed	Nature – degrees of organisational structures	Participant profiles
		External (aimed at other nation-states or non-state actors)	Short Term/Tactical Objectives				Leadership style/attitude

4.   Strategy – overall plan with necessary policies, actions, and instruments.
5.   Means – capabilities and techniques varying in destructive effort, cost, practicality and frequency of use, propaganda.
6.   Organisation – structure, leadership, delegation, specific responsibilities, training, recruitment, logistic support, intelligence, funding.
7.   Participation – committed activists, full-time and part-time members, passive sympathisers.[4]

The Schultz typology is presented as Table 1.

CONTEMPORARY TERRORIST GROUPS

It is not easy to compile a list of terrorist groups which are active today. The tally worldwide is never a static one. There are high-profile organisations with dynamic leaders and enterprising and consistent strategies. Many of these have been 'in business' for many years and the counter-terrorist institutions know them well. There are small organisations with shifts in management, numbers, motives, and political action. Their goals and intentions may be difficult to discern. This list (derived from the International Policy Institute for Counter-terrorism, Herzliya, Israel, and published in December 1999) is far from comprehensive but it does show contemporary terrorism as both diverse and far-flung. The list gives the organisational names and national affiliation or locales.

Organisation	National affiliation (or locale)
Abu Nidal Organization (ANO)	Lebanon
Abu Sayyaf Group (ASG)	Philippines
Al-Gama'a al-Islamiyya (The Islamic Group, IG)	Egypt
Al-Qa'ida (the Base)	Afghanistan
Armed Islamic Group (GIA)	Algeria
Aum Shiryinko	Japan
Basque Fatherland and Liberty (ETA)	Spain
Chukaku-Ha (Nucleus or Middle Core Faction)	Japan
Democratic Front for the Liberation of Palestine (DFLP)	Palestine
Fatah – Revolutionary Council (Abu Nidal Organization)	Lebanon
Hamas (Islamic Resistance Movement)	Palestine
Harakat ul-Ansar (HUA)	Pakistan
Hizballah (Party of God)	Lebanon
Irish Republican Army (IRA)	Northern Ireland
Jamaat ul-Fuqra	Pakistan
Japanese Red Army (JRA)	Japan
Jihad Group (Islamic Jihad)	Egypt

Kach and Kahane Chai	Israel
Kurdistan Worker's Party (PKK)	Turkey
Lautaro Youth Movement (MJL)	Chile
Liberation Tigers of Tamil Eelam (LTTE)	Sri Lanka
Loyalist Volunteer Force (LVF)	Northern Ireland
Manuel Rodriquez Patriotic Front (FPMR)	Chile
Moranzanist Patriotic Front (FPM)	Honduras
Mujahedin-e Khalq Organization (MEK or MKO)	Iran
National Liberation Army (ELN) Colombia	Colombia
Nestor Paz Zamora Commission (CNPZ)	Bolivia
New People's Army (NPA)	Philippines
Palestine Liberation Front (PLF)	Iraq
Palestinian Islamic Jihad (PIJ)	Palestine
Party of Democratic Kampuchea (Khmer Rouge)	Cambodia
Popular Front for the Liberation of Palestine (PFLP)	Palestine
Popular Front for the Liberation of Palestine – General Command	Palestine
Popular Struggle Front (PSF)	Syria
Quibla and People Against Gangsterism and Drugs (PAGAD)	South Africa
Real IRA (RIRA)	Northern Ireland
Red Army Faction (RAF)	Germany
Red Brigades (BR)	Italy
Revolutionary Armed Forces of Colombia (FARC)	Colombia
Revolutionary Organization 17 November	Greece
Revolutionary People's Liberation Party/Front (DHCP/F)	Turkey
Revolutionary People's Struggle (ELA)	Greece
Sendero Luminoso (Shining Path, SL)	Peru[5]
Tupac Amaru Revolutionary Movement (MRTA)	Peru[6]

STATE-SPONSORED TERRORISM

This note is also from the same Israeli institute and is published in December 1999:

For many years, terrorism was perceived as a contest between two sides: on the one hand, a group of people or an organization, and on the other, a sovereign state. However, during the course of the second half of the twentieth century, various countries began to use terrorist organizations to promote state interests in the international domain. In some cases, states have established 'puppet' terrorist organizations, whose purpose is to act on behalf of the sponsoring state, to further the interests of the state, and to represent its positions in domestic or regional fronts. In other cases, states sponsor existing organizations, on the basis of mutual interests.

The patron state provides its beneficiary terrorist organization with political support, financial assistance, and the sponsorship necessary to maintain and expand its struggle. The patron uses the beneficiary to perpetrate acts of terrorism as a means of spreading the former's ideology throughout the world, or in some cases, the patron ultimately expects the beneficiary to gain control of the state in which it resides or impart its ideology to broad sections of the general public.

State-sponsored terrorism can achieve strategic ends where the use of conventional armed forces is not practical or effective. The high costs of modern warfare, and concern about nonconventional escalation, as well as the danger of defeat and the unwillingness to appear as the aggressor, have turned terrorism into an efficient, convenient, and generally discrete weapon for attaining state interests in the international realm.

These states are generally acknowledged to be sponsors of international terrorist activity: Iran, Iraq, Lebanon, Libya, Sudan, and Syria.

PART TWO

Twelve terrorism case-studies

EACH OF THE FOLLOWING case-studies is titled under the name of the host country. There is a final chapter by way of conclusion.

Chapter 4

Lebanon

HIZBULLAH (also known as Hizb'allah or Hizballah), the Party of God, is one of the most significant terrorist organisations operating today. It was formed in June 1982 in Lebanon as the militant wing of a religious group, the Shi'a (also known as Shi'ite, Shi'i, Shi'ia or Shiite), to provide an activist front in a protest against social and political marginalisation and deprivation. The Hizbullah goal, expressed cogently and forcefully, was the ousting of foreign influences and the creation of an independent, Islamic Lebanon. Muslim clergy, secular politicians, and firebrand journalists all voiced strident opposition to the United States and to Israel in particular. They soon gathered support from the fundamentalist regime in Iran. More extreme elements within Hizbullah have lost no time in moving beyond propaganda, intimidation and coercion to the use of violent, terrorist tactics such as assassination, the harassing of Israeli settlements, the hijacking of aircraft, and suicide car bombing. There are now many splinter groups. Hizbullah, as an instrument of revolutionary terrorism, has inevitably acquired a high media profile. Less well studied in the West, beyond condemnation of its violence and inhumanity, are the complexities of its origins and development.

THE REACTIVE NATURE OF HIZBULLAH VIOLENCE

In numerous respects Hizbullah is an idiosyncratic movement. Elizabeth Picard (1997) argues that the origins of Hizbullah are best understood within the historical context of political mobilisation and violence and within the Lebanese community. Thus, she regards their violence, first, as largely reactive, taking the forms of extra-institutional protest, revolutionary insurrection, and terrorist acts, and second, as a dynamic for dealing internally with Lebanese dissension and externally with Western interference. Hizbullah's violence is seen to raise four main questions: the distinction between terrorism and liberation struggles, the relation between terrorism and foreign sponsors; the effects of terrorism on Lebanese society, the ideological linkage between terrorism and Islam.

In the Middle East, indeed throughout the entire Arab–Muslim region stretching eastward from Morocco to the Gulf and from Caucasia down to Sudan, few countries offer a better example of political violence than Lebanon. Not even Algeria which has suffered a large number of deaths in recent years. The only exception, it could be argued, is Iran. But the political violence in Iran, under Islamic rule since 1979, is quite specifically state-sponsored violence; whereas in Lebanon the example of the Shi'i community lends itself better to a theoretical model of political violence. The Lebanese case seems to correspond even more precisely to such a model than a country such as Libya, with its role not only in the internal conflicts of neighboring countries but in international terrorism as well. It seems to correspond to a model of political violence more precisely than Egypt or Syria, too.[1] [. . .]

Attempts to address political violence in the geo-politically important region of the Middle East have tended to approach the question from either a political economy perspective (though not strictly class-based) or a cultural perspective.[2] [. . .]

Irrespective of theoretical approach (political economy or culturalist), cultural origin, political beliefs, or personal distance to the Lebanese Shi'a, there is the unanimously held view that the violence committed within the Shi'ia community itself, or outside the community, is mainly a reactive form of violence. The birth and acceleration of this violence can be explained by demographic, sociological, economic, legal and constitutional, as well as strategic and military, variables. Three phenomena in particular are especially significant. First, the Lebanese Shi'ia, as a group, was transformed in the space of forty years from an under-developed and submissive group to a community capable of rapid economic mobility and social mobilization. Second, because the Lebanese communitarian system is governed by a set of rigid rules, there was no continuity in the Shi'i transition from social mobilization to political mobilization. Consequently, the Shi'a saw their identity reinforced, their borders established, and their mobilization as a 'community' strengthened. Third, by using to their own advantage the failure of a new consensus within the Shi'i community and the impossibility of expanded political participation, outside forces – not only armed but 'arming' – intervened and propelled the discourse and practices of the Shi'ah [sic] towards conflict and violence.[3] [. . .]

At the outset of the 1970s, the Shi'a showed all the signs of readiness for social mobilization. Their contact with other, more prosperous segments of Lebanese society made their unfavorable situation, and their lack of social mobility, all the more painfully obvious. Indeed, it did not result in a process of assimilation, but on the contrary, one of rejection.[4] [. . .]

One of the paradoxes of Lebanon's civil violence during the 1970s and 1980s was that the discourse of all the Lebanese groups squarely laid the blame for internal dissension on foreign elements: either the *ajnab* – the West, and particularly Israel – or the *gharib*, those who do not share Lebanese bloodlines. Not only was the notion of *gharib* instrumental at de-emphasizing the internal cleavages in Lebanese society, but it also stirred up local passions against non-Lebanese and protracted the life of an indecisive political system that was mainly threatened by its own internal divisions. The belief in a foreign 'plot' (American, Syrian, Saudi, etc.) thus allowed the Lebanese to forge some semblance of a 'national' consensus. Seeking to avoid mutual accusations and self-criticism, they preferred to deny the existence of an internal dimension to the violence in their country. But in doing so, they are rendered incapable of understanding the real causes and the function of this violence – which of course meant that they could not heal its causes.

What must be underscored is not so much the phenomenon of foreign inter-ference itself, but rather the juncture between international conflict and internal violence. After 1975, it became difficult to distinguish, concretely and analytically, self-defensive violence, deliberate political violence, and violence resulting from international conflict. External and internal violence became interactive.[5] [. . .]

Besides the defensive and competitive community violence, a third form of violence, qualified as 'terrorism', emerged during the revolutionary phase of the struggle. Bomb attacks aimed chiefly at spreading terror (such as the 1983 attacks against American and French army barracks of the Multinational Force in Beirut), hostage-taking (more than twenty Westerners were held in Lebanon between 1984 and 1990), and suicide missions were carried out (Israeli headquarters in Tyre were destroyed by an automobile packed with explosives in 1983). This form of violence, spectacular though marginal, raises four main questions.

First, at what point does one cross the line between 'struggle for liberation' and 'terrorism'? These acts of terrorism were acknowledged and interpreted by Shi'i militants, ideologues and tacticians as acts of war against an occupying power, Israel, and its allies, both local (the Christian militia in Lebanon) and international (the Western powers). The Shi'a, who constituted the majority of the population in South Lebanon, were the principal victims of the Israeli–Palestinian war after 1970 and the Israeli occupation after 1978. They were thus the first to adhere to the armed struggle against foreign enemies. Neither the Lebanese government nor the international community contested in principle their struggle for liberation. The issue was rather the use of violence against foreign civilians as part of the conflict, which raises the casuistical question of legitimacy as well as the existence of unequal forces between local militia groups and an over-armed state.

Second, putting terrorism in an international perspective, the relation between terrorist groups and the foreign states that sponsor must be examined. Both the study of the Fu'ad Ali Saleh's 'Shi'i' terrorist network in France and the process of liberation of the last hostages in 1991 following the end of the Gulf War show that most of these groups are financed by those states, including Iran and Syria, which opted in favour of a terrorist strategy in the second half of the 1980s. When, at the outset of the 1990s, they abandoned this strategy due to a changed interna-tional situation, they quickly and with almost total success imposed a return to international legality.

Third, the instrumental use of terrorist groups by foreign states raises the ques-tion of the relation between the Shi'i social movement and such groups. Here, the problem is not so much the organizational aspect of this relationship. On the one hand, the testimony of liberated hostages and the biographical information on certain of the authors of anti-Israeli attacks in South Lebanon indicate a definite social, even

psychological, alienation on the part of extremist militants, as well as their doctrinaire rigidity. They show the characteristics that can be found among similar groups
in Europe (Red Brigades, *Action Directe*), whose implacable logic led to their self-
destruction. But on the other hand, the hagiographic literature, and the number
and strength of popular demonstrations commemorating the memory of the
martyrs, indicate that the action of terrorists, even if criticized by those in the Shi'i
population who are victimized by reprisals, was in line with a majority political
vision, all the more so that this action fit [sic] into a culture of violence. In this
sense, 'terrorism' does not involve an inversion of the social movement but rather
the extreme accomplishment of its aims.

Finally, we must question the relationship between terrorism and Islam. This
link has been denounced by rightists in the West for whom the confrontation with
Islam, and above all with Shi'i Islam as embodied by the Islamic Republic of Iran,
has replaced the struggle against Communism. Shi'i publications such as *al-Ahd* and
al-Badil, and the sermons and writings of religious authorities, show the contradiction between, on the one hand, a doctrine committed to the respect for life (by
condemning suicide, for example) and the realization of earthly happiness and, on
the other hand, the casuistry invented in the context of *jihad* in order to justify
terrorist actions, including martyrdom. [6] [. . .]

HIZBULLAH'S RELIGIO-POLITICAL IDEOLOGY

Hizbullah ideology, welding fundamentalist religious belief and political observance,
usually leftist, has been surveyed by A. A. Khalil (1991). In common with Picard,
Khalil sees Hizbullah's emergence as the product of Lebanese tensions and conflict
which converge with external policy orientations, especially those of Iran. Hizbullah
goes beyond the Quaran (Koran), it is stated, to emulate Leninist thinking, discipline
and organisation. For Khalil the mosque becomes a rallying point for alienated
Shiites who move towards campaigning as a jihad. Inevitably, and radiating beyond
Lebanon, Hizbullah's assertiveness is viewed in the West as uncompromising
'terrorism', relying on sacrifice and suicide missions and martyrs. In many parts of
the Arab world, though, the terrorists of Hizbullah are venerated as leaders of the
'faithful'.

The study of Islam and Islamic political movements has become a popular enterprise in the West. The religion and the world of Islam are still exotic and are hence
a sensational topic. What made the study of Islam suddenly fashionable in the West
is not an intellectual trend, but is rather a result of the belief that Islam is intrinsically responsible for the surge of 'international terrorism'. Western studies of
Islam, however, are shrouded in generalities and reductionism. The rise of Islamic
consciousness cannot be understood without specific references to the concrete
conditions in every geographic area witnessing the emergence of Islamic fundamentalist movements. Islam does not mean the same thing to the people of Islamic
countries; the practice and interpretation of the religion differ from one country
to another. Consequently, the underlying causes behind the rise of the various

fundamentalist movements are not standard or universally uniform. The subject should be approached with much more specificity.

Lebanon is one of those countries that is witnessing an intense resurgence of Islamic identification. It is the country which – in the eyes of the West at least – has made the study of Islam and 'international terrorism' indistinguishable. Yet, the causes behind the rise of Islam as an ideology are complex and not necessarily religious in nature.

Two words can sum up the deep social conflict in Lebanon. They are *al-Ghabn* (prejudice) and *al-Khawf* (fear). *Al-Ghabn* is used by Muslims to express their sense of injustice, and *al-Khawf* is used by Christians to express their fear of Arab–Muslim hegemony. While Muslims call for the redistribution of national wealth and political power, the Christians consider the privileges that they have enjoyed since the founding of the Lebanese republic in 1920 as 'guarantees' (*damanat*), as factors contributing to their psychological and political security. In other words, the National Pact, which set the official arithmetical formula for the distribution of political power on a sectarian basis, is a constant that is not subject to change according to Christians; while it is an invalid doctrine that time and reality had long transcended, in the eyes of Muslims.

This paradoxical view of the foundation of the Lebanese political system accounts for the deep tensions in society. Any diminution in Christian powers adds to the powers of the Muslims, and vice versa. Moreover, who is to say how to distribute power within the Muslim community? Relations within the Muslim faith are far from harmonious. It is almost impossible to come up with a formula that pleases all the sects at once.

Hizballah is the product of the tensions and conflicts within the Shiite community. The underlying causes for its emergence are deeply rooted in indigenous Lebanese conditions and in the aftermath of the Israeli invasion of Lebanon in 1982. Thus, it is inaccurate to maintain that Hizballah is an Iranian creation. It is also inaccurate to maintain that the idea of Hizballah 'was the brainchild' of Muhammad Husayn Fadlallah [a religio-political leader and writer]. Rather, it emerged as a result of the convergence of Lebanese Shiite interests with Iranian foreign policy orientations.[7] [. . .]

The word *hizb* in Arabic does not have the same connotation that the word party has in English. According to the classical origins of the root of the word, *hizb* means a community, sect, or a group of followers. However, Hizballah ideology emphasizes the Quranic origins of its political terminology. Almost all of the political terms that the Party uses in its political literature are derived from the Quran.[8] [. . .]

Hizballah is not an Islamic stipulation. It is an Islamic adaptation to the era of Leninist revolutionary organizations. The model of Leninist party organization was convenient to all those groups in the Arab world who favoured one-party rule and who are based on absolute self-righteousness and intolerance. Nasserism, Ba'thism, and some Islamic fundamentalist groups benefit from the undemocratic party structure of the Leninist organization which undermines the ability of the party members to bring about change and restructuring. Thus, any change has to emanate from above in a manner that suits the interests of the leadership in a given situation. Ironically, the Party of God, which professes a strong enmity to communism,

emulates the Leninist model of party organization and borrows some of its political terms with some necessary modifications.[9] [. . .]

In Leninist theory, the factory should be the major venue of political agitation
and mobilization. In the ideology of Hizballah the mosque occupies the central
stage. The mosques are transformed into arenas of political, cultural and Jihad
actions, in addition to being places of worship of course, in which the decision-
making process is based. The mosques are also places that provide their occupants
with relative safety and security in countries where there is no freedom of expression and association.[10] [. . .]

In Hizballah's ideology, injustice is caused by people; it is the result of what
some people do to others. Like Leninist thought, Hizballah believes that justice and
equality can be achieved through human efforts, through a revolutionary process.
Hizballah represents a revolutionary version of Shiite Islam.[11] [. . .]

Like the Leninist global outlook, Hizballah's ideology splits the world into two
camps, the exploited and the exploiters. According to its vision, Lenin's 'international imperialism' becomes 'international arrogance', in reference to the USA. But
some Hizballah ideologists deny the existence of a similarity between the ideology
of the Party and Leninist ideas, and maintain that Islamic revolutionary thinking is
far more comprehensive than Marxian analysis which is confined to the realm of
economic exploitation while Hizballah ideology is more encompassing as it takes
into consideration all aspects of human life.

It is ironic that a Shiite fundamentalist party should borrow ideas and organizational principles from the Leninist tradition. But this is not surprising when viewed
within the context of the Lebanese situation where Hizballah emerged. In many
ways, the rise of Islamic fundamentalist groups in Lebanon is the by-product of the
failure and perceived bankruptcy of the Lebanese and Palestinian left. Slogans of
change and revolution were monopolized by the left at a time when religious movements in Lebanon were generally conservative. The Shiites were until the late
seventies drawn into leftist political organizations because they were alienated from
the political system in the country.[12] [. . .]

THE PERVASIVE SENSE OF MISSION

The concept of Jihad has been misunderstood in the West [Khalil believes], it has
also been misused by contemporary Islamic organizations. Under the name of Jihad,
hostages were taken, battles have been fought, and suicide missions have been
ordered. [. . .] The revolutionary ideology of Hizballah broadened the definition of
Jihad to include all facets of party activity.[13] [. . .]

The Islamic (religious) dimension of the concept of Jihad as practised by
Hizballah should not be exaggerated. The Jihad of Hizballah should be equated with
the concept of *an-Nidal* (struggle) as used by leftist parties in Lebanon. While
Leninist parties attribute working-class motivations to their actions, Hizballah attrib-
utes Islamic motivations to its activity. The word also adds 'revolutionary credibility'
to the practice of the Party because the word has been associated with spectacular bombing attacks against the enemies of fundamentalist groups. But Hizballah

broadens the definition of the word to legitimize and 'Islamize' all of its alleged activities, from suicide bombing to kidnapping.

The notion of martyrdom in Shiism is often presented as an explanation for the military activity of Hizballah. While it is true that the promise of heavenly reward motivates some of the suicide fighters of Hizballah, suicide operations have been initiated by Palestinian groups in Lebanon long before Hizballah came into being. Thus, the 'martyrdom' of Hizballah is an 'Islamized' version of the Palestinian notion of al-Fida' (sacrifice). It should be remembered in this respect that Hizballah was not the only party in Lebanon to send fighters on suicide missions against Israeli targets. The Syrian Social National Party, the Lebanese Communist Party, the Arab Socialist Ba'th Party, the Progressive Socialist Party, and the various Palestinian organizations, have all launched suicide attacks against Israeli targets in South Lebanon.

Moreover, all Parties in Lebanon, from right-wing parties to ultra-leftist communist parties, use the word shuhada' (martyrs) to depict all those members who died in the course of the civil war. The religious significance of the term is often exaggerated. Of course, it could also be argued that certain religious trends and terms have permeated most political parties in Lebanon, including those who ostensibly espouse secular ideologies.

Hizballah benefits from the international attention focused on its activities. Even the depiction of its attacks as terrorist does not necessarily affect negatively the image of Hizballah in the eyes of its supporters and in the eyes of the Shiite community in Lebanon. The excessive focus on Hizballah by the USA and Israel adds to its reputation of effectiveness and combativeness. Moreover, the criterion by which the USA and Israel judge whether an act is 'terrorist' or not is not shared by people in the Arab world, particularly among Lebanese and Palestinians. A Hizballah leader, Shaykh Ibrahim al-Amin, did not even reject the 'terrorist' label of his party. He believes that the Quran 'ordered' them to engage in the fight against the USA and Israel. To support his argument, al-Amin cites a verse from the Quran which states: 'Muster against them [the believers] all the men and cavalry at your disposal, so that you may terrorize the enemies of Allah and the faithful.'[4]
[. . .]

Khalil equates the concept of Jihad (mission) with that of a struggle to earn 'revolutionary credibility'. Primarily, most followers of Islam would regard a jihad as a directly sanctified mission: this confers an obligation, partly religious and partly political (political in its broadest sense), to campaign on behalf of principles and to combat disbelief and heresy. Hizbullah's violence, seen in these terms, is proactive as well as reactive. That Hizbullah as a movement is something other than a mere political party is a point which Martin Kramer (1998) considers:

Hizballah's official spokesman maintains that the movement is 'not a regimented party, in the common sense', for the idea of an exclusive 'party' is foreign to Islam. Hizballah is a 'mission' and a 'way of life'. Another Hizballah leader has insisted that Hizballah 'is not an organization', for its members carry no cards and bear no specific responsibilities. It is a 'nation' of all who believe in the struggle against injustice and all who are loyal to Iran's Imam Khomeini. Still another Hizballah leader maintains that 'we are not a party in the traditional sense of the term. Every Muslim is automatically a member of Hizballah, thus it is impossible to list our membership'. And in the mind of Iran's chargé d'affaires in Beirut, Hizballah is not 'restricted to a specified organizational framework [. . .] There are two parties, Hizballah or God's party, and the Devil's party'.[15]

The cause of warding off those who would thwart Hizballah's mission has been embraced by Islamic Jihad. Islamic Jihad claimed credit for the spectacular bombing attacks that helped to drive US and Israeli forces out of Lebanon. Islamic Jihad has done much to purge Lebanon of foreign influence by waging a campaign of kidnapping against foreign nationals. It is difficult to say much that is authoritative about Islamic Jihad or to do more than speculate about the precise relationship between Hizballah and Islamic Jihad. Leading figures in Hizballah, as well as Hizballah's spokesman, disavow all knowledge of the persons behind Islamic Jihad. Western intelligence sources regard Islamic Jihad as a group of clandestine cells run by several of Hizballah's military commanders, in most instances in collaboration with Iran. But conventional thinking on this matter has changed more than once. Those communications issued by Islamic Jihad that are deemed to be authentic are too brief to open a window on this closed universe of belief and action.

But Islamic Jihad need not interpret itself to the world, for this is done on its behalf and with great effectiveness by the leaders of Hizballah. Whatever the relationship of accountability between Islamic Jihad and Hizballah, their ideological compatibility finds daily expression in the public statements of Hizballah leaders.[16]

Two categories of action have posed unique challenges to these leaders, precisely because they employ methods that on their face seem to violate some principle of Islamic law – the very law that Hizballah has championed as a solution to all of Lebanon's ills. These are the suicidal bomb attacks and the kidnappings of foreigners. The arguments within Hizballah over both these extraordinary means provide much insight into how morality, law, and necessity may be distorted and remade under the relentless pressures of great collective distress.[17]

THE TAKING OF HOSTAGES

The act of hostage-taking, a common manifestation of political terrorism, has been something that Hizbullah has frequently resorted to. In the glare of media publicity, hostages have been taken where the players in the scenario are besieged or they are known to have been forcibly detained in a secret location. Generally, this is followed by a credible threat to kill, injure, or continue detention of a victim. The terrorists' threat faces a third party with the anguished choice of either meeting the hostage-takers' demands or submitting to blackmail. Hizbullah's relentless employment of hostage-taking and the management of hostage-crisis by Western powers is examined in detail by Magnus Ranstorp (1997) who believes that Hizbullah's motives are complex and easily misunderstood. The complicity of Iran is evident despite it being subject to volatile political developments in Teheran. The response of Western governments to Hizbullah's abduction of their nationals is considered by Ranstorp to demonstrate firmly held no-concessions positions in public while in private there may be a resort to secret negotiation.

In a ten-year period, between 1982 and 1992, a number of enigmatic and obscure organisations, seemingly loosely or indirectly affiliated with the Hizb'allah organisation in Lebanon, not only launched spectacular and deadly suicide operations against the Western presence but also engaged in political acts of hostage-taking of Western civilians. While the shadowy Hizb'allah movement has denied any active involvement in these acts of terrorism, though applauding these operations in concert with Iran, its self-proclaimed main enemies of the United States, Great Britain, and France, collectively sustained casualties of over 300 individuals killed by the organisation while it has held over forty-five citizens in captivity for various lengths of time over a ten-year period. While the chaos and insanity of the fifteen-year protracted civil war in Lebanon contributed to the difficulty in extracting the Western hostages from among a multitude of confessional militias, it also led to the association and image of Hizb'allah in the West as a crazy and fanatic religious group, bent on martyrdom through suicide-operations and engaged in the random abduction of foreigners, under the assumed strict control and direction of Iran's clerical establishment.

Although the West crossed paths in Lebanon with the radical and militant aspects of the Shi'a community and the Islamic Republic of Iran through Hizb'allah's abductions of foreign citizens, the highly complex nature of the internecine conflict involving an array of confessional warring factions, with foreign patrons, prevented a clearly defined understanding of the Hizb'allah's motives and organisation from emerging. In the murky underworld of Lebanon's civil war, where conduct was regulated by regional, national, sectarian and family interest, the nature of the shadowy groups, acting under the umbrella of Hizb'allah, further compounded the complexity of the hostage-crisis and the involvement of Iran. The ambiguous nature of the organisation itself and its affiliation with Iran led to an array of misperceptions by Western governments and outside observers in their attempts to both understand and confront the prolonged hostage-crisis in Lebanon, at times with disastrous consequences.[18] [. . .]

Analysis of the hostage-crisis in Lebanon yields that Hizb'allah was indisputably responsible for the aforementioned abductions of Westerners despite attempts to shield its complicity through the employment of cover-names. Its organisational framework was not only sophisticated and assimilated according to Iranian clerical designs but also integrated with several key Iranian institutions which provided it with necessary weaponry and training to successfully confront self-proclaimed Islamic enemies and invaluable financial support for it to generate as well as sustain massive support and recruitment among the Shi'a community at the expense of other confessional groups.[19] [. . .]

The responses by the American, French and British governments to the abduction of its citizens in Lebanon have underlined the inherent difficulty in striking a balance between their moral obligation towards providing safety and protection for their citizens abroad without having to sacrifice national interests in the conduct of foreign policy. While all three states have pursued a firmly held and coordinated public position of no-negotiations with terrorists and no-concessions to their demands in the Lebanese hostage-crisis, the reality of actual conduct behind this façade has revealed not only the conduct of secret negotiations, either directly with the Hizb'allah, Iran, and Syria or indirectly through third party intermediaries, over the release of hostages, at times resulting in complex and murky deals, but also that the hostage-issue was intimately influenced by the conduct of foreign policies by these Western states in the Middle East. Although the two Western states and the United States have shared similar types of problems and challenges in efforts to manage and secure the extraction of its citizens from captivity in Lebanon, each individual state has pursued its own overt and covert policies to accomplish this task. Apart from their almost equal standing in Hizb'allah's Western demonology, largely due to their colonial past and present involvement in the Middle East, the divergence of approach to the hostage-crisis reflected not only the individual experiences of these Western states in confronting terrorism within their own borders, but also the nature and status of their relationships with both Iran and Syria as well as their policies in the Middle East, driven by different sets of political motivations as well as economic considerations. The differences from state to state in the frequency, time periods, and number of its citizens abducted by the Hizb'allah, coupled with the specific nature of demands, also contributed to the way in which the Western governments have crafted individual or concerted strategies to the problem of obtaining the release of their citizens from captivity.[20] [. . .]

The responses by the United States and the two West European states to the hostage-crisis in Lebanon have been governed by a uniform policy of refusal to negotiate or make concessions to terrorists under any guise. This policy of no-negotiations and no-concessions to terrorists has been embodied in a series of unilateral or joint declarations of principles which reflects not only the previous experience of liberal democracies in countering terrorism at home, based on the principled position that hostage-taking constitutes an unforgivable act that must not be rewarded through concessions and that a readiness to negotiate as well as a willingness to concede to demands only encourages further terrorist acts, but also that state support for terrorism in any form constitutes unacceptable international behaviour subject to punishment. While principles of US no-concessions policy have been unilaterally proclaimed by policymakers on countless occasions in response to new hostage-takings of American citizens, as outlined by public policy statements and documents, the European states have adopted not only unilateral policies in alignment with the uniform principle of no-concessions but also a concerted European approach to the hostage-problem, as evident by their solemn promise to make 'no concessions under duress to terrorists or their sponsors' at the 1986 European Community (EC) summit in London. The inconsistency between the declaratory policy of not negotiating or conceding to any demands and the actual conduct by Western governments in dealing with the hostage-crisis in Lebanon can be attributed to the often incompatible nature of firmly held counter-terrorism principles as an integral component of foreign policy in the Middle East towards Iran and Syria, who exercise any [sic] degree of control over the Hizb'allah. Despite the fact that both Iran and Syria have concealed the exact nature of their close relationship with the Hizb'allah, the recognition of Iran and Syria as intermediaries for Western governments in dealing with the Hizb'allah posed problems in upholding a non-flexible no-concessions policy as these states benefited indirectly from concessions made to influence the movement despite their own complicity in some of the movement's terrorist acts.[21] [. . .]

THE TERRORISTS' CONTINUING DIALECTIC

Hizbullah in the minds of Western political leaders remains part-enigma by virtue of its complex origins and its labyrinthian development. It is not easy to face down such a vigorous and violent movement. In January 1995 the Clinton Administration forbade its nationals to have any transactions which might imperil the Middle East peace process. World pressure has been increased recently against states suspected of sponsoring international terrorism and on all sides stern trading sanctions have been levied. Nevertheless, Iran and Syria have not relented and Hizbullah remains one of the world's most deadly terrorist organisations. There is no straightforward answer to the double-question: what does Hizbullah gain by its terrorist activities and when are these likely to cease? There is no doubt that Hizbullah's 'culture of violence' will endure so long as the movement yearns at all costs strategically to promote a pan-Islamic cause and tactically to reinforce its own revolutionary identity as defender of the Shi'ite community. Moreover, Hizbullah willingly acts as a 'conduit' for Iran's own revolutionary message to the Islamic masses. Ranstorp (1997) believes that Hizbullah is unlikely to abandon its missionary zeal, directing its militancy and violence towards the goal of eradicating Israel and its Western associates.

For the Hizb'allah movement itself, the hostage-taking activity has served many important functions which reinforced the movement's ideological and political *raison d'être*, assisted in the expansion of its influence within the Lebanese Shi'ite community as well as defined and forged the movement's ties to Iran's clerical establishment. [. . .] In a wider sense, Hizb'allah's hostage-taking activity also served to enhance its revolutionary credence and image as the true defender of the Lebanese Shi'a community against the enemies of Islam, especially as it played an instrumental role in expelling foreign forces out of Lebanon and through its tireless armed campaign against Israel. In this revolutionary struggle, the Hizb'allah was very successful in achieving not only its practical goals but also in accomplishing a psychological atmosphere of fear in the West of the actual threat and capability of the movement which served to enhance the status of the movement within Lebanon and beyond as a major nemesis of Western governments.

While Hizb'allah activity served to consolidate Iran's material assistance to the movement, its rapid transformation from a rag-tag militia into a tightly organised movement with an impressive military and extensive social services programme for the Shi'a community meant that the Hizb'allah positioned itself as a true political, ideological, and economic defender of the Shi'a community, filling the vacuum in place of the scant protection and assistance provided by the Lebanese government and other militias [. . .] While Hizb'allah's terrorism stereotyped the image of Lebanon's Shi'ites as religious fanatics bent on martyrdom in the Western world, the profound role and service of the Hizb'allah movement, fighting and buying its

way into the hearts and minds of the Shi'ite community, far outweighed the consequences of any non-Islamic moral constraints imposed by Western public opinion.
Apart from the fact that Hizb'allah veiled its justifications of violent activity solely
to Muslim believers and according to Islamic law, the movement also provided the
dispossessed Shi'ite community within a lawless civil war environment with a divine
Islamic purpose and mission, which transformed from revolutionary struggle to a
political vehicle aimed at addressing Shi'ite grievances and enhancing its wider
agenda in Lebanon.[22]

Ranstorp sees the Hizbullah terrorists as a well-organised movement able to reinforce its ideological and political *raison d'être* through a strong sense of mission
and a succession of violent strikes, regarded by the West as atrocities. A different
view is that of Martin Kramer (1998), convinced that in some respects Hizbullah
lacks agreement, certainly over the question of hostage-taking apart from other
aspects of violence:

Hizballah is divided over the question of hostage taking. That is perhaps inevitable,
for Hizballah began as a coalition and it remains one. The movement is devoted to
one purpose: the eventual establishment of an Islamic state in Lebanon. But its
leaders continue to debate among themselves the morality and legality of the means
to that elusive end. The extraordinary means employed by some within the coalition have prompted an extraordinary debate. It is unusual because in Shi'ite Islam,
only the cleric can morally disengage the common believer from his acts. In that
limited sense, bombers, hijackers, and hostage takers are morally dependent on
Hizballah and Iran, and the verdicts of their learned scholars are hardly academic.
Yet their interpretations of Islam's dictates often differ in important and even fundamental ways. The evidence for their debate in interviews and speeches only hints
at what must be an intense internal disputation over the future course of the 'nation'
of Hizballah.

   As a coalition, Hizballah is liable at any time to split. Yet Lebanon's tribulations seem only to strengthen it. Hizballah has seen its enemies retreat time and
again, reinforcing its view that Lebanon's crisis will be resolved through Hizballah's
ultimate triumph. But Syria proposes a very different resolution to that crisis, one
in which Hizballah has no place. The movement cannot confront Syria in conventional ways and expect victory. Hizballah is also unlikely to succeed in its bid to
rid South Lebanon of all Israeli political and military influence if it resorts only to
conventional methods. The debate over extraordinary means will not soon end.[23]

POSTSCRIPT

Kramer (1998), writing about Hizbullah, 'the Party of God', and their lack of
consensus about some of their activities (e.g. hostage-taking, hijacking, kidnapping,
car-bombing), concludes that lack of agreement does not vitiate their enthusiasm
and dedication:

It is certain that there is disagreement within Hizballah over how Lebanon's Islamic revolution should be hastened and whether this is an opportune moment to articulate a full plan. There are also differences on this score between certain leading figures in Hizballah and the movement's Iranian guides, who themselves are divided over how best to transform Lebanon. But for Hizballah's rank and file, these debates are of no great importance. The young men and women of Hizballah are fired by the pure image of a future Lebanon that will regain stability through Islamic law and justice and embark on a redeeming struggle against those who would banish Islam from this Earth.[24]

Chapter 5

Libya

FOR THIRTY YEARS, certainly in the Western world, Libyans and their leader, Colonel Quaddafi (also known as Qaddafi, Khadafi) have been regarded as the pre-eminent exponents of state terrorism. Why, though, should any state and state leader deliberately adopt terrorist policies? To understand how this can come about and how the rest of the world responds to it, a number of issues deserve scrutiny. First, an outline of the geographical context. Second, how is the persona of Quaddafi best described? Third, since Libya is a revolutionary state, what ideals and policies energise political action and lead to violence? Fourth, what are the initiatives and the scale of state-sponsored violence as it has been directed at other countries? Fifth, what has been the shape of international response to sponsored terrorism? Why is it that Libya's relations with the United States, in particular, have deteriorated so markedly since the early 1980s? Finally, is it possible to see an end to the terrorism, which, at the end of the 1990s, has been much reduced in scale?

LIBYAN TERRORISM: AN OVERVIEW

A useful introduction to the Libyan scenario, before we give it a more detailed examination, is the overview of Walter Laqueur (1999):

In the 1970s and 1980s, Libya was one of the foremost sponsors of international terrorism. Its involvement was almost as pervasive as that of Iran, a much larger and more populous country. Libya's sponsorship of terrorism predates that of Iran, dating back almost to the coup in 1969 that brought Colonel Khadafi [Quaddafi] to power. Khadafi's ambition was to spearhead an Arab–Islamic revolution in which he saw himself not only as the chief ideologist (by virtue of his little 'Green Book') but also as chief strategist. Libya's income from the sale of oil provided the where-withal to finance a variety of terrorist activities, but in subsequent years it became apparent that the country was too small and backward to sustain any major polit-ical and military initiatives. Furthermore, Khadafi's erratic behaviour (to put the best possible gloss on it), his inordinate ambitions, and his rapidly changing alignments antagonized virtually everyone in the Arab world and isolated him from all but his most needy clients. Doubts were expressed concerning his mental state, not only in the West but also in the Arab and Third World capitals. Was he a madman in the clinical sense, or just highly emotional, unbalanced, and un-predictable? Khadafi even became an embarrassment to those closest to him in outlook.

Though Libya experienced strong economic growth in the early years of the Khadafi regime because of massive oil exports, its growth stalled after 1985 and eventually declined by 1995. Nevertheless, the Libyan regime was still able to spend considerable sums sponsoring terrorist activities abroad and on the construction of factories to produce poison gas and other chemical weapons. Support was given primarily to Arab terrorist groups, but also to a variety of Central and West African groups, and eventually to terrorists from Ireland to the Philippines. Among the recipients of Libyan help were the German RAF as well as the so-called Black September. According to unconfirmed reports, about eight thousand foreign terror-ists, most of them Arabs, were trained each year in Libyan camps in the 1980s, and those select Palestinian groups favoured by Khadafi received an annual subsidy of $100 million. Among the most famous terrorists on the Libyan payroll was Carlos the Jackal, who had been enlisted by the Popular Front for the Liberation of Palestine.

However, the list of recipients of Libyan money changed quickly, sometimes overnight. While relations with Fatah and Arafat had been close at one time, they deteriorated later, and the PLO (and many thousands of Palestinian guest workers) were expelled from Libya as Khadafi shifted his support to the most extreme Palestinian factions, such as the one headed by Abu Nidal. Even Carlos, who had been of so much use to the Libyans, was ultimately refused entry to Libya.

Libyan-sponsored terrorism manifested itself in a variety of other activities, including attacks against Libyan political émigrés. In 1984, some twenty-five such attacks were counted in Europe and the Middle East, and the assassinations continued in later years, albeit on a reduced scale. In one famous instance, Khadafi personally gave orders to his agents in London to open fire on the British police in front of the Libyan legation, an action that annoyed even the Soviets. Khadafi, they felt, was giving international terrorism a bad name. Attacks were carried out by Libyan agents against American and European targets but also against moderate Arab countries. To give a few examples, mines were laid in the Red Sea near the entrance to the Suez Canal after plots to kill President Mubarak of Egypt failed. The bombing of the Berlin nightclub La Belle Discothèque in April 1986 killed three American soldiers, wounded eighty, and claimed some two hundred German civilian victims. Six years later a German court established that while the attack had been carried out by a Palestinian, two officials of the Libyan legation in East Berlin had provided the explosives and logistic support and cover, and that East German espionage services had also been indirectly involved. In Africa, Libyan agents tried to destabilize and overthrow the then moderate government of Sudan, as well as those of the Central African countries of Chad, the Central African Republic, and Zaire.

By 1985, Khadafi's prestige was high among the terrorists, even though they were aware that the Libyan dictator tended to promise more than he delivered. But he certainly seemed more willing to accept the risks of provoking major powers than any other country. The more extreme the group, the more likely it was to find help and, if need be, a refuge in Tripoli. At the same time Khadafi's active and seemingly successful opposition to Islamic fundamentalism made some of Libya's unfriendly neighbours hesitate to take drastic action against Khadafi. Those who did not admire him seemed to fear him, at least in the Arab world. Khadafi's successes made him lose whatever remnants of a sense of reality he still possessed. He overstepped the limits of what was internationally acceptable, and invited a reaction that led to a drastic decline in his standing and a reduction of Libyan-sponsored terrorist operations.

Following Libyan terrorist attacks in Vienna and Rome airports, the Belle Discothèque bombing in West Berlin, and an attempt to bring down a TWA plane over Greece, the United States launched an air strike called El Dorado Canyon in April 1986 against selected targets in Libya. El Dorado Canyon was a one-time strike, not all targets were hit, and the damage caused was not very great. Nevertheless, to the surprise of most of America's European allies, the attack had an immediate effect. The Libyans showed much greater caution afterward, whereas earlier they had boasted of not being afraid to tackle a superpower.

America's European allies assumed that the American attack would have the opposite effect. France and Spain banned the F-111 aircraft engaged in the operation from flying over their territory. However, their fears were misplaced. During 1986–9, there was a decline in terrorist operations all over the Arab world, not just on the part of Libya. The fear that once America lost patience and felt that its vital interests were involved it might react violently and indiscriminately on a massive scale had been planted. While this might not have frightened small extremist groups, it certainly frightened their sponsors.

It was clear that the effect of a limited operation such as El Dorado Canyon would wear off, and after a number of years the bombing of Pan Am flight 103 over Lockerbie, Scotland, and the French airliner UTA flight 722 over Chad took place. (Khadafi apparently wanted to humiliate the French for having ousted the Libyan armed units from Chad, which Tripoli thought part of its sphere of influence.) In both cases, no one claimed credit for the operations, and traces of Libyan involvement were well hidden. Indeed, it seems likely that in the case of the Lockerbie disaster Iran and Syria might also have been involved. However, only Libyan involvement could eventually be proven with reasonable certainty. The matter was taken to the United Nations, where the Security Council unanimously adopted resolution 731, according to which the Libyan government was requested to hand over two of their agents who had been indicted in the United States and in Britain for their part in the Lockerbie disaster. The Security Council resolution also stipulated that Libya accept responsibility for the downing of the French airliner, disclose all evidence, and pay appropriate compensation. The Libyans refused to do so and brought upon themselves a series of sanctions, including an aviation embargo, limitations on the Libyan diplomatic presence in foreign capitals, drastic reductions in oil sales, and other measures that did considerable harm to the Libyan economy and to Libya's international standing. It was a humiliation for Khadafi, and for once he had no response.

The Libyan refusal to comply had no immediate dramatic consequences inasmuch as Khadafi remained in power. But it soon appeared that he had underrated the long-term consequences of being branded an outcast. While the Tripoli government continued to harass exiles from Libya (there were reports of the abduction of a human rights activist in Cairo and a murder in London), these occurred on a much smaller scale than before. Tripoli continued to give some help and shelter to the most extreme Arab terrorist groups, particularly those unwilling to contemplate peace with Israel under any conditions, but reduced its support of non-Arab terrorism. Libyan propaganda was almost as violent as before, but there was one considerable difference: hardly anyone in the outside world paid it any attention. Prior to 1985, Khadafi seemed to have almost gained the stature of a world leader. By the 1990s he was virtually ignored, not just by the outside world but even by his fellow Arabs. He had started his career with far-flung schemes to promote Arab unity, and terrorism had been one of the main means to that end. By the 1990s he had reached the conclusion that Libyan expansion to the south, towards Africa, was more promising and certainly less risky. The Khadafi saga demonstrates what should have been clear from the beginning: that an unscrupulous and relatively unimportant government could buy influence by investing heavily in international terrorism, but once it became more than a mere irritant, a backlash was inevitable and its power would wane.[1]

LIBYA'S GEOGRAPHICAL CONTEXT

Libya has a Mediterranean coastline of 1,200 miles with a fertile coastal strip giving way to the desert, the Sahara, which stretches eastwards to Egypt and the Sudan, southwards to parts of Niger, Chad and the Sudan and then to Algeria and Tunisia in the west. Its sheer size is impressive (two and a half times Texas, seven times the United Kingdom), its strategic importance is momentous as a natural trading route between Africa and Europe. It is not a crowded land with just over five million people, mainly Sunni Muslim Arabs, settled there since the seventh century a.d. What is significant for this case-study, however, are the ways in which certain aspects of Old Libya have been transformed by its people into a New Libya, a process regarded perhaps superficially and not too objectively by outside observers.

A revolution that is geographical as well as political is outlined historically by Henri Pierre Habib (1975), a Canadian scholar:

When Libya was granted its independence by the United Nations on December 24, 1951, it was described as one of the poorest and most backward nations of the world. The population at the time was not more than 1.5 million, was over 90 per cent illiterate, and had no political experience or knowhow. There were no universities, and only a limited number of high schools which had been established seven years before independence. All this had been the result of centuries of Turkish domination and Western imperialism. Every effort was made to keep the Arab inhabitants in a servile position rendering them unable to make any progress for themselves or their nation. The climax of this oppression came during the Italian administration (1911–43) when the Libyans were not only oppressed by the authorities, but were also subjected to the loss and deprivation of their most fertile land which went to colonists brought in from Italy. The British and French who replaced the Italians in 1943 attempted to entrench themselves in the country by various divisive ways, ultimately to fail through a combination of political events and circumstances beyond the control of any one nation.

Despite the attempts made by a number of powers to keep Libya divided and weak after 1951 by establishing a federal system in a homogeneous state, the Libyans amended their own constitution in 1963, established a unitary state and removed a major obstacle to the unity of the nation. This obstacle was an administrative or structural impediment to the fuller evolution of independence which the Libyans sacrificed so much to achieve. More important than this administrative change, there were two major events which were to change fundamentally and drastically the Libyan make-up, and challenge the post-independence Libyan generation. The first event came in 1959 when highly marketable oil of superior quality was discovered in large commercial quantities. The impact of this oil discovery was to change within a decade the whole economic potential of the nation. This was the first challenge of the post-independence period. It meant that for the first time Libya was in a position, without outside help, to remove and eradicate poverty, raise the standard of education, and give itself the first real opportunity to face the challenges of the twentieth century. It was essentially the first step taken towards a still larger and more vital change that was to come and transform Libya into a modern state.

This larger and more significant change constitutes the second major event which was to revolutionize Libya and give it a new and dynamic face. This was the Revolution of September 1, 1969. It was a political, social and economic revolution permeating all facets of Libyan life. It was to rid Libya of the remaining vestiges of colonialism and endow it with a truer and fuller independence than nominally achieved in 1951. It would also allow the country to pursue its authentic Arab–Islamic vocation and perform its special role on the African continent. For Libya belongs to the Arab, Islamic and African world.

The new Libya has established relations with the African continent to an extent never seen before. It has also created closer rapport with Islamic nations and peoples all over the globe. And it is anxious to consolidate these policies particularly with the peoples of Africa and the Islamic world.

Since 1969 Libya has become a challenge to its own people in attempting to modernize itself and to create a viable nation with its own values and traditions independent of alien influences and pressures. It is providing its people with the benefits of their own natural resources, transforming the raw wealth of the country into services in agriculture, education, housing, health and welfare. Rarely has a nation done so much for itself in such a short time.[2]

QUADDAFI: THE ARCH-TERRORIST PERSONA

Muammar al-Quaddafi was born in a desert tent, twenty miles south of the seashore town of Sirte in the spring of 1942. The family were illiterate herders of camels and goats, Bedouin Arabs, who passed on to their son stirring stories of tribal heroes and memories of harsh Italian rule ever since the annexation of Libya in 1911. Primary and secondary schooling followed and Quaddafi struck all his teachers as gifted, serious, rather taciturn, and a most devout Muslim.

Libyan independence in December 1951 led to a flow of books, magazines and newspapers from the wider world, above all from Egypt. Young students now listened eagerly to the radio and to the impassioned rhetoric of the Egyptian leader, Gamal Abdul Nasser. The following year, Nasser's 'army officer's club' overthrew a weak sovereign in Cairo and, reasserting Arab nationalism, unity and pride, replaced King Farouk with a republic. Many Libyan students, dubbed 'irresponsible hotheads' by their teachers (Quaddafi was expelled for his outspokenness) saw their own ineffectual and corrupt monarchy as needing the potent medicine Egypt had distilled. Quaddafi's zest for change (Muammar means 'he who builds up') is summarised by Blundy and Lycett (1987):

He had soaked up the Arab revolutionary ideas which poured out of Egypt under Nasser and, although he seemed to have no clear ideology of his own, he had produced a potent cocktail of revolution and Islamic fundamentalism. He was disciplined and immensely hard-working, and he had tapped into the reservoirs of underground discontent that existed in Libya under King Idris. He was poised to plan the revolution and he decided that the most fertile ground lay in the Libyan armed forces.[3]

As an officer cadet in Benghazi, Quaddafi's charisma was strong enough to persuade others, interested in sedition, to join his 'Free Officers Movement'. In 1966 the future leader was given permission to attend a four-month training course in Britain. That experience disappointed him as he sensed all around social and moral decay and racial prejudice. His return to Libya put into fast gear the planning for an overthrow of the weak government of King Idris who was overly dependent upon imperialist oil companies. The revolutionary coup, when it finally happened in September 1969, was a remarkably bloodless one. (There is still debate over how far Washington and London knew in advance of the revolutionary intent. They may well have felt that the oil and strategic interests of external powers would be more secure in the hands of a strong and popular Libyan regime.) Quaddafi as head of state promoted himself from captain to colonel as Blundy and Lycett recall:

He quickly developed a political style, based on the rhetoric of Nasser, but with disquieting echoes of Benito Mussolini. His watchwords were liberty, socialism and unity, and always, incessantly, 'the people'.

In one not particularly long speech in Sebha on 22 September 1969 he used the word 'people' seventy-seven times:

> The armed forces are an integral and inseparable part of this people, and when they proclaimed the principles of liberty, socialism and unity they proclaimed nothing new. It is the people which believes in liberty, socialism and unity and inspired them to the armed forces, its vanguard, which imposed them on the enemies of the people with the force of arms, thus, the people is the teacher, the inspirer and the pioneer.

As there were no elections, unions, free newspapers or even opinion polls, what 'the people' thought was entirely dependent on what Quaddafi decided they would think.[4]

With Quaddafi safely established as head of state, his ministers competently and confidently settled down to negotiations with the great international oil concerns as a prelude to their wholesale nationalisation in 1971 of all the Western oil companies operating in Libya. The economy was now clearly in the ascendant as Blundy and Lycett note:

Quaddafi had every reason to feel pleased with himself. He had taken on the Western imperialists and won a resounding victory. Foreign troops had left Libyan soil and the most powerful corporations in the world, the oil companies, had been forced to play his game. The Libyan national coffers, already packed with oil revenues, were overflowing.

The money paid by the West was to be used, in part at least, to undermine it.[5]

LIBYA'S REVOLUTIONARY IDEALS AND POLICIES

Master of the Libyan revolution, Quaddafi is generally presented in the media of Europe and the United States as a political prima donna, devious, untrustworthy and prone to using violence capriciously. All too often, the foreign policies of someone the *New York Times* described as a 'warring, whirling dervish' are stated as degenerating into terrorism at its worst. Less frequently is Quaddafi described as a studious reader, a careful listener, a pragmatist who with an ideological 'think tank' converts dreams into feasible programmes of reform.

The pronouncements of Libya's September Revolution may appear to lack logic, clarity and brevity, none the less, they have been powerful stimulants to Libyan action, at home and abroad. A brief outline, only, must suffice for this case-study. Habib (1975) has this to say about the cardinal precepts of the revolutionaries:

The basic ideals of the September Revolution can best be described in the triple slogan of: Freedom, Socialism and Unity. It is by turning to the three slogans that the Arab would rediscover his dignity and his place in history.[6]

Freedom is a human need that goes back into history. Freedom is one of the basic objectives and ideals of the Revolution. The Revolution believes in the freedom of the nation and its citizens, in the freedom of the individual, in the freedom of the Arab in Libya in political, economic and social matters. The individual is to liberate himself from past centuries of oppression, emancipate himself from humiliation, injustice, ignorance and serfdom. He is to liberate himself from the domination of poverty and backwardness, from the nightmare of injustice, and from oppression. This is the freedom needed to emancipate the Arab from his intolerable position. Freedom is the natural right of each individual.[7]

But political freedom which was achieved on September 1, 1969, was not enough in itself. It was a means to achieve social freedom and a social revolution, that is to say, a revolution in agriculture, industry, legislation, laws, justice, etc. 'To fulfil social freedom,' says Quaddafi, 'one must proclaim socialism in its Arab and Islamic context.'

Socialism as understood in the ideals of the September Revolution lies in the collective participation in production and work, and in the distribution of production with justice and equality. It is not to distribute poverty among people, but it is to give an equal share of prosperity to all. Above all, socialism in the Libyan–Arab context must be understood as the socialism of Islam which stems from the heritage of the Arab–Muslim peoples, their beliefs, and the events in their great history. It is a unique experience – it does not advocate class struggle but insists on harmonizing class differences.[8]

When Unity was raised as the third ideal of the Revolution, the leaders of the Revolution were not addressing themselves to national unity, which was taken for granted. They were addressing themselves to the larger question of Arab unity. Total unity of the Arabs is the ideal objective sought by the September Revolution.[9]

Most importantly, these socialist principles, the so-called Will of the People, represent the gospel of the *Jamahiriyah* in which the old entity of state is replaced by the concept of the people's 'command' or 'congress'. These principles are held to be unparalleled elsewhere as Habib relates:

The political ideals of the September Revolution included a comprehensive political, social and economic system to be linked through the basic Islamic heritage of Libya as a fundamental point of reference. Libyans rejected the capitalist and communist systems in both domestic and international matters. They believed that Capitalism has failed because it elevated man without considering the collectivity, while the Communists failed because they emphasized the collectivity and forgot man. The Libyans came out with the Third Theory in order to correct what they believed were the shortcomings of both Communism and Capitalism. They called it the Third Theory not because it was the third in order of importance but because there already existed two other theories.[10]

This collection of principles, gathered together in 1975 as a Green Book and elaborated as the Third Theory, is seen by Quaddafi himself as 'a humanitarian theory, not an aggressive theory [...] it serves humanity, unlike Capitalism, Communism and Zionism'. Yet on numerous occasions, in Quaddafi's own rhetoric and that put about by his disciples, there is less stress on universalism and more on watchful guardianship. The Third Theory, part catechism and part manual for good governance, is to be protected and defended resolutely against, by implication, a host of unbelievers and adversaries. There are frequently rallying cries for urging unity for 'battles yet to be fought'. Moreover, 'if war has to be fought it should be fought on enemy territory', and above all 'there must be no lost battles'. These remarks, with Israel or imperial Anglo-American interests in mind, do raise questions as to Libya's preparedness to use violence for political ends. Libya's 'sacred duty towards all revolutions' is understood as firing enthusiasm for aiding national liberation movements in Angola, Northern Ireland, the Philippines, Latin America, and South Africa — places where sectarian protest has become terroristic. Consequently, Libya has earned a reputation as a political troublemaker on a global scale. Revolutionary zeal is considered by most outside observers as leaping beyond the boundaries of the state, exporting intolerance, virulence, aggression. Readiness to use lethal violence, the bullet and the bomb is thought to be both deliberate in its targeting and on occasion indiscriminate.

STATE-SANCTIONED VIOLENCE

An account of Libya's resort to terrorism is introduced with reference to the sense in which Libyan revolutionaries use the term 'violence'. One of their publications (1983) has a two-part discussion of the term, although the meaning is not clear at times. First, they ask, what do Libyan revolutionaries understand by 'violence'? Is it not justifiable as a tool against those who would destroy a hard-won revolution?

According to our concept of violence, it does not constitute a doctrinal issue, it is no more than a stage which circumstances impose at a moment in which the complications of these circumstances become very critical.

We do not think that violence is important and inevitable as Marxism claims. In our opinion, the conflict may be settled without violence — in the Marxist sense. But this does not mean that violence is not necessary as a sole means and way of reacting against anti-revolutionary violence.

We think that, in the dialectics of revolutionary struggle, there are stages with which it is wrong to deal without violence.

Yet, reactionary forces will have to face another discovery which is more horrible for them than the previous one: they will find out that revolutionaries are determined to answer violence with violence.

[...] If violence will be practiced in the future, it will be total and all-inclusive; it will be exercised by peoples (societies) incited by revolutionary committees; it will be an organized violence, popular and overwhelming; it will be conducted by the people and for the people.[11]

A second question is: do revolutionary committees practice [sic] violence? The practice is justified only when it consolidates revolutionary advance and that is the responsibility, it is inferred, of revolutionary leaders. This point, however, is expressed somewhat quixotically when the leaders:

[. . .] lead the masses throughout the stages of revolution and this implies leading them also in the practice of violence so that this practice be psychologically and culturally fruitful, effective and human.[12]

The last statement in this part of the rhetoric may suggest to some observers that violence will very likely be action-beyond-words aiming to bring tangible achievements and possibly taking the action on to the 'enemy's' ground as the chosen arena.

Quaddafi and his associates never secured effective political roles on the international stage; humiliated, they turned to instruments of violence. The Libyans went on to back insurgents in Uganda, Morocco and the Philippines and to support them with money and military hardware after 1972. There seemed every chance that such initiatives would establish Libya as an exporter of violence, and usher in a wave of state-sponsored terrorism. Haley considers the inevitable question: at what point does the support given to foreign revolutionaries by an internationally recognised government become criminal? This is the argument of P. Edward Haley (1984):

Qaddafi failed to extend his influence and win agreement with his ideas in 1973 in the two critical areas of oil and the Arab–Israeli conflict. Sadat, Faisal, and Assad shut him out of the October War, and he was unable to stop Egypt and Syria from entering direct negotiations with Israel. In regard to oil diplomacy, it was the Gulf producers that called the tune both as to the imposition of the embargo and its termination, which plainly was in preparation as the year ended. As humiliating as it must have been for him to be forced aside and ignored in this way on the main issues, Qaddafi none the less possessed other weapons that could be used in other policy arenas. He had toyed with them from the beginning of his regime; now he turned to them in earnest. The policy arenas lay for the most part in Africa, Asia, Europe, and even the United States, places far from the cockpit of the Eastern Mediterranean and the Gulf. The weapons on which Qaddafi began increasingly to rely were those of terror, subversion, and intervention. It was not simply that Qaddafi had been denied a more conventional role. His passionate hatred of Israel and the West and his strong convictions about Islam, not to mention his exalted conception of his own role in the scheme of things, would undoubtedly have pushed him into opposition sooner or later. Rebuffed in a humiliating way, he turned all the more wholeheartedly to the dark sides of power and politics and clung to his ambitions and expectations.[13]

Although it is a violation of international law to intervene in the domestic affairs of another country, governments regularly support armed rebellions in other states.

This support certainly falls within accepted international diplomatic and military practice, and Qaddafi's backing of revolutionaries in Morocco and the Philippines accords with it. But Qaddafi did not stop with this kind of aid. He went on to give money, arms, and sanctuary to terrorists who committed random acts of horror. The activists in every cause will claim to represent the 'will of the people', and in the absence of a supervised plebiscite the validity of their competing claims is difficult to assess. The appropriate standard, in my view, is whether or not the assistance is used directly in support of the revolutionary cause on behalf of which it was given in the first place. The critical responsibility of the donor is to ensure that the recipients of his aid are not swept away by the fanaticism and moral relevatism that permeate desperate life-and-death struggles in every part of the world. If they are, the donor must stop the aid or become an international outlaw. It is difficult to make simple judgments because of the unavoidable dependence of most revolutionaries on outside help. What is difficult to judge in the abstract becomes far easier to discern when one examines specific concrete cases. As one considers example after example of the uses made by revolutionaries of outside government assistance, it becomes clear that the use is sometimes so tenuously connected with the original revolutionary cause as to be merely criminal. When the donor government declines to halt its aid and in fact even increases it in face of the obvious criminality and irrelevance of the violence it has helped unleash, then the government has become no less an outlaw than the terrorists it has nourished.[14]

Beginning in the early 1970s Qaddafi began to support terrorist and revolutionary groups and to initiate terrorist violence without regard for prudence or proportion. There was, of course, a consistent pattern to the acts. They were anti-Western and anti-Israeli, and they were designed to weaken the democracies of Western Europe and North America, to reduce their international influence, and to destabilize the countries bordering the Mediterranean. No acts of terror were launched or sponsored by Qaddafi in Eastern Europe or the Soviet Union. For a year or two before the October 1973 War Qaddafi criticized the Soviet Union for allowing Jews to emigrate to Israel. Once he decided to seek massive Soviet military aid even this feeble criticism stopped, and Qaddafi began to align Libyan foreign policy with that of the Soviet Union. This was particularly noticeable on matters of great importance to the Soviet Union, such as Soviet intervention in Ethiopia or, later, the invasion of Afghanistan.[15]

Qaddafi continued his support for terrorism, and within two years vastly increased his involvement. According to the former Libyan minister of planning, Omar el-Meheishi, Qaddafi had set aside $580 million for terrorism and paramilitary activities in 1976. At this point, of course, Qaddafi had passed beyond supporting terrorism – although he continued to do this – to the subversion, destabilization, and overthrow of foreign governments.

The motives for Qaddafi's extensive support for and practice of terrorism are clear. He wished to strike at Israel, the West, and enemies of his regime, domestic and foreign. Moreover Qaddafi's public, rhetorical diplomacy is not the most important problem he poses for the United States and its allies in the Middle East and Western Europe. Terrorism sponsored or initiated by Libya is one part of the problem. The other part is foreign intervention – the systematic training in Libya of thousands of guerrillas to be used to destabilize or overthrow neighboring governments.[16]

Haley quotes the observations of John W. Amos II (1980) that Libya went out to enlist the operational help of a range of terrorist groups:

Qaddafi's strategy of attacking Western positions in the Middle East, Israel, and all Arab states perceived to be pro-Western, logically led to a theory of targeting Western countries in their 'own backyard', meaning attacking them in their own territories. Tactically, this required the creation of an ability to hit targets located in Western countries as well as elsewhere. For this Libya did not possess a sufficiently extensive and sophisticated intelligence organization (at least at the outset) to carry out clandestine foreign operations. This lack, plus Libya's oil wealth, led to the obvious conclusion: utilize existing terrorist groups; coordinate, finance, and supply them. [. . .] The selection of these groups, while seemingly random, was actually very carefully done to further the goals of the larger Libyan strategy. [. . .] By 1976, the list of groups armed and trained [by Libya] had grown to encompass FROLINAT, Philippine Muslims, Thailand Muslims, Eritrean groups, and a variety of African organizations. [. . .] The arms supplied were usually Soviet, and Libyan embassies served as supply and communications centres. Tripoli itself became the meeting place of almost every terrorist or insurgent group in the Middle East, Africa, and Asia.[17]

Laqueur's overview of the Libyan scenario, quoted earlier, outlined the scope and intensity of terrorist incidents generally ascribed to Libyans. Precisely pinning blame on a Libyan has, however, frequently proved difficult, largely because Quaddafi moved into terrorism by means of his own 'hit-men' (whose identities were carefully shrouded) and also by entering the multi-representative terrorist network. Haley comments on this strategy of Quaddafi:

[. . .] He opened his land and his treasury to existing terrorist organizations. In May 1972 the PFLP played host in Tripoli to a terrorist summit attended by representatives of Black September, Fatah, the IRA, Baader-Meinhof, the Iranian National Front, and the Turkish People's Liberation Army. This meeting was followed by others, such as the conferences in Baghdad (sponsored by the Soviet Union) and Trieste in 1974, with Libyan and Algerian officials in November 1976, at Larnaca in July 1977, and in South Yemen in 1978. These meetings are important because they facilitate joint planning and the sharing of organizational, intelligence, material, and intelligence resources. This in turn extends the reach of any single group – using Portuguese terrorists to attack an Israeli official, for example – and makes the attacks harder to anticipate.[18]

In general terms, Haley adds, 'the terrorist network, of which Libya was and is an integral part, significantly increased instability in the Middle East including Iran and the Arabian Peninsula and arguably in Western Europe as well'.

Terrorism sanctioned apparently by an irresponsible (and irrepressible) Libyan government was to flourish for a whole decade between 1978 and 1988. The world watched, with growing distaste and alarm, Quaddafi's adventurism abroad ending as it generally did in a welter of violence. In 1978 Tripoli dispatched commandos and tanks into neighbouring Chad to aid a National Liberation Front and to 'take out' any members of the legitimate government they came across. Twelve months later there was a symbolic, ultimately futile, expedition to back the maverick Ugandan dictator, Idi Amin. Quaddafi then turned towards civil strife in Algeria and Tunisia and in the guise of mediator used guerrilla bands to intimidate all sides in the conflict. Libyan embassies in Vienna, Prague, Bonn, Athens and Berne were converted into 'people's bureaux'. Western governments, confronted with fortified revolutionary cells in their own domain, anxiously wondered where the next terror outrage might strike as aircraft were hijacked, buildings were bombed, and 'death squads' hunted their victims in London and the United States. What were the implications of Quaddafi's mission-statement that Libyans must ensure 'the physical elimination of the enemies of the revolution abroad'?

During all this time Libya remained steadfast in support of the Palestinian liberation movement (though not of Arafat himself) and its hatred of Israel and of their United States backer went undiminished. Haley reports a declaration of Quaddafi aimed at Washington:

It is your attitude that drives the fedayeen to die and to kill the Israelis in Palestine. Your giving of arms to Israel! Your unwillingness to understand the Palestinians, your refusal to help them! You Westerners are the ones who make war the only possible solution.[19]

Inevitably, as the intensity of Libya's state-sponsored terrorism grew, governments came together to treat Libya as a pariah state with whom they could not continue to exercise civilised relations. In Haley's view, it was now clear that Quaddafi was 'running out of room' as he acknowledged a consensus refuting his policies:

Libya's increasingly aggressive and militant international actions in 1980 produced an astonishing series of foreign policy setbacks for the North African country. No less than thirteen nations in Africa and the Middle East as well as the United States either broke diplomatic relations with Libya or expelled Libyan diplomatic personnel. In addition there were tensions or a serious deterioration of relations between Libyan and eight other governments, from Uganda to France. During the months from July 1980 to January 1981 Libyan diplomats were expelled from four West African countries: Gabon in July, Ghana in November, and Niger and Nigeria in January. Much more serious were the tensions between Libya and Gambia, Senegal, the Central African Republic, Iraq, and Saudi Arabia.[20]

INTERNATIONAL COUNTER-TERRORISM

Libya's reputation as a nest of hornets did not always elicit a uniform response from outside. Blundy and Lycett in 1987 inferred that politico-strategic objectives were not consistently spearheading the counter-actions of the United States and of Britain. There were commercial factors to take account of although, of course, these would not override response to violent attack:

Western leaders are [still] inclined to see a kind of schizophrenia in Qaddafi's foreign policy. Qaddafi the diplomat carries out energetic and often successful initiatives, dealing with such issues as trade and oil competently and sometimes brilliantly. Then there is the Qaddafi who funds terrorists and revolutionaries. Qaddafi himself sees no contradiction, although he is often puzzled by the reaction of Western governments who criticize his policies, condemn him as a lunatic, but are still prepared to do business with him. He believes that conventional diplomacy and revolutionary politics can operate in a complementary, not a contradictory, way and be means to the same ends: Arab unity, a Palestinian state, and the overthrow of imperialist or monarchist governments. He believes that if other rulers do not take the revolutionary path then they should be overthrown. He has no doubt that the United States acts in a similar way in its efforts to destabilize such regimes as Castro's in Cuba and the Sandinistas in Nicaragua.[21]

US policy towards Libya, perhaps a little less than its policy over nuclear arms limitation, is a battleground of conflicting views between different agencies and between departments of the same agency. The CIA, for example, contained at least two schools of thought, according to a Middle East analyst with special responsibility for Libya, who worked for it. The mainstream CIA analysts on the Libya desk saw all the information about Libyan terror but, like the members of the British Foreign Office, they were not impressed. They did not deny that Qaddafi funded, assisted and often instigated terror. They simply thought that among the players in Middle East terror he was not as significant as their masters in the White House believed. Their strong recommendation in dozens of memoranda was that the best policy towards Qaddafi was to ignore him unless he seriously increased his involvement in terrorism. They noted that Qaddafi had been cautious about hitting US targets and had only on rare occasions exported terrorism to the mainland United States. Their analysis of the majority of raw intelligence material about the movement of personnel and materials was that it really did not amount to much.

The clandestine services of the CIA, which are concerned more with covert operations than analysis, thought differently. They argued, in this war of memoranda, that the best way of dealing with Qaddafi was to confront him. They believed that from the raw intelligence a real threat to the US could be pieced together. Their counsel held sway with the President when he decided to launch the raid against Libya, and the clandestine services urged that action should be taken after the raid to topple Qaddafi.[22]

At last, in April 1986 the United States launched a punitive air-strike against Tripoli and other targets. Laqueur, as we have seen, believes that this operation had a lasting deterrent effect. On the other hand, a good deal of European and Arab opinion was outraged to judge from public demonstrations and opinion polls in Britain, Spain, Greece, Germany, and Egypt. The strike was judged in some quarters as an over-hasty, badly thought-out response by the Reagan administration determined to show 'America strong'. Richard Falk (1986), an international law professor at Princeton, discerns a strange relationship between terrorism and counter-terrorism:

There is an odd convergence of motives between the terrorist who seeks to paralyze the adversary society and the counter-terrorist who seeks to mobilize that society in support of unilateralism and retaliatory violence. To break these linkages is crucial.

One observation stands out. If we seek to deprive terrorist activity of its impact, and therefore weaken the incentives to practice it, then we must put its exploits in proper context, and provide reassurances about safety and security. No counter-terrorist politics can succeed unless they include an appreciation of why terrorist preoccupations have gripped the body politic to such an extent.[23]

Another opinion from the United States is that of Bruce Hoffman (1998) who considers that state-sponsorship of terrorism has not been forestalled by certain counter-terrorism measures:

Today, state sponsorship of terrorism continues unabated. In 1996, for example, the US State Department designated seven countries as terrorism sponsors: Cuba, Iran, Iraq, Libya, North Korea, Sudan and Syria. With the exception of Sudan, which was added in 1993, each of these countries has remained on the list of terrorism's patron states for more than a decade. The reason, as noted above, is that neither economic sanctions nor military reprisals have proven completely successful in effecting positive changes to these countries' policies on terrorism. Even seasoned US government counterterrorist analysts are somewhat dismissive of their effects. A recent high-level discussion paper circulated within the American intelligence community noted that

In theory, the threat or imposition of embargoes and sanctions would appear to be a powerful leveraging tool in the conduct of foreign relations between countries. In practice, no state sponsor of international terrorism against which the US has enacted an embargo or sanctions has renounced it[s] role of sponsorship or denounced terrorism as a tool of its foreign policy. Nor has any state once placed on the state sponsors list ever been removed.

Military reprisals against state sponsors of terrorism have arguably proved no more effective; worse still, in some respects they have been counterproductive.

For example, the aforementioned 1986 US air strike against Libya is frequently cited as proof of the effectiveness of military retaliation; yet, rather than having deterred the Qaddafi regime from engaging in state-sponsored terrorism, it appears that it may have had precisely the opposite effect. In the first place, so far from stopping Libyan-backed terrorism, the US air strike goaded the Libyan dictator to undertake even more serious and heinous acts of terrorism against the United States and its citizens. Indeed, after a brief lull, Libya not only resumed but actually increased its international terrorist activities.[24]

POSTSCRIPT

Terrorist incidents of Libyan origin are seldom reported in the contemporary press. From time to time there is discussion as to the best way to bring to justice those suspected of responsibility for the Lockerbie disaster. Libyan terrorism is an 'irritant' to be guarded against watchfully in the hope that one day it will disappear.

Already in 1990 there was eased tension between Libya and other countries. The *Financial Times* commented that Quaddafi's new-found international respectability was a reward for his decision to return to more conventional foreign and economic policies. Quaddafi was reported as admitting that Libya had founded some terrorist groups but that when their aims and role had been discovered as leading to more harm than benefit then support had been withdrawn. It was in 1991 that Libya had found, in its isolation, an opportunity to resume diplomatic normality. Oil revenues were rising by 40 per cent as a consequence of the Gulf War crisis and a world fuel shortage and the time seemed right to renew international trade contacts and investment. The terrorists donned new clothes and entered the marketplace.

For the next two years, Libya's new pacific countenance was not widely thought credible and tough sanctions were implemented by United Nations member states. Quaddafi now seemed more mercurial than ever, strongly condemning his brothers-in-violence among Islamic fundamentalists as 'mad dogs' and 'terrorists'. At the same time, in 1994, as he approved of President Clinton as 'a good man and a man of peace' he uttered a sombre warning that Washington should never interfere in Tripoli's affairs. Libya was capable of being a 'safety-valve' for peace in North Africa yet capable also of removing the safety-valve and blowing up the whole of North Africa along with itself and its enemies. In 1995 Libya applied to join the United Nations Security Council, declaring an interest in international work for peace. While Council members were considering the request of this penitent state, the applicant withdrew, observing tartly that the Security Council was a tool of United States imperialism.

The position of Libya in 1999 was, indeed, that of a state slowly regaining its respectability despite the unpredictable manoeuvrings of Quaddafi, 'Leader of the Revolution'. United Nations' sanctions were lifted in April 1999. The Lockerbie issue was eventually settled when two suspected Libyan terrorists were indicted and extradited with Libyan permission to be tried under Scottish law in the Netherlands in a court located on soil temporarily designated part of Scotland. In February

2001 three judges found one of the Libyans guilty and gaoled him for life. His co-defendant was acquitted and returned to Tripoli to be welcomed by Quaddafi once more voicing vituperation against Western powers.

Most people now live in towns with motorways, ring roads, and a car for every seven Libyans. Erstwhile terrorists own restaurants for tourists, sell clothes and television sets, study diligently in universities. Women ex-freedom fighters now have full sex equality in the army and in civilian life. Libya now has to fight drug addiction rather than foreign interference. The revolutionary slogan, thirty years old and a mantra for terrorism, was 'No future without unity'. A new gloss was put on this in September 1999 as Quaddafi, the former and foremost arch-terrorist, addressed twenty African presidents at a summit in Tripoli:

Now that [Libya's] liberation stage has ended, the world wants to know Muammar Gadafy as the leader of peace and development in Africa and other countries.[25]

Chapter 6

Sri Lanka

SRI LANKA IS A STATE lacerated by two bitter conflicts. One is that of the state versus the People's Liberation Front (JVP or Janatha Vimukthi Peramuna, the name of its founder), a Sinhalese extreme nationalist organisation anxious to bring down the moderate Colombo government. The other is that of the Tamil Tigers, whose demand is for an altogether separate state. JVP has largely been contained by vigorous counter-terrorism; the Tamil Tigers continue to rage unabated and it is with them that this case-study is mainly concerned.

As the smoke cleared away from another bomb explosion in downtown Colombo, Sri Lanka's capital, in March 1998, an excited radio commentator was heard to declare, 'There are another seventy million terrorists out there'. This is perhaps the chief difference between Sri Lanka's Tamil Tigers and those we have already studied in other case-studies, namely, that this group claims the adherence and financial backing of an international web of supporters. They recruit additional disciples and well-wishers and radiate propaganda through sophisticated publicity channels such as an Internet site, radio and television. The so-called Tamil Tigers (the Liberation Tigers of Tamil Elam (LTTE)) represent a terrorist faction whose activities have been a growing source of concern to thirty states over four continents. Nor is there any sign that the conflict which is devastating society in Sri Lanka shows any prospect of reconciliation. Most worrying of all is that few commentators can find an explanation for the Tigers' suicidal and indiscriminate violence.

THE EARLY POLITICAL HISTORY

The Tamils themselves, using their Internet site, Tamilnation, are at pains to present a factual account of the history of their present homeland, Sri Lanka, or, in their language, Eelam, in a 'brief overview':

The island known to Tamils as Eelam (and known under British rule as Ceylon and under Sinhala rule as Sri Lanka) is about 25,000 square miles in extent, situated about twenty miles from the southern extremity of the Indian sub-continent.

About one-fifth of the island's population of 17 million are Tamils and somewhat less than three-quarters are Sinhalese. The Tamils reside largely in the north and the east and on the plantations in the central hills, whilst the Sinhalese reside in the south, west and in the centre as well. The area of the Tamil homeland in the north-east is around 7,500 square miles. A large number of Tamils are Hindus, some are Christians and the overwhelming majority of the Sinhala people are Buddhists.

The Tamils are an ancient people. Their history had its beginnings in the rich alluvial plains near the southern extremity of peninsular India which then included the land mass known as the island of Sri Lanka today. [. . .] The Sinhala people trace their origins in the island to the arrival of Prince Vijaya from India, around 500 BC. The early political history of the people of Eelam, in the centuries before the advent of the European powers, is largely a chronicle of the rise and fall of individual kingdoms. When the Portuguese landed on the island in 1505 there was not one but three kingdoms viz. the Tamil Jaffna Kingdom, the Sinhala Kotte Kingdom and the Sinhala Kandyan Kingdom. The Jaffna Kingdom was captured by the Portuguese when the king of Jaffna was defeated in 1619. The Portuguese ruled the Jaffna Kingdom from 1619 to 1658. The Dutch who captured the Jaffna Kingdom from the Portuguese ruled till 1795 and the British till 1948. Even when the island was ruled by the Portuguese and the Dutch, the Tamil homeland in the North and the East was administered as an entity separate from the rest of the country. In 1833, the British amalgamated the north and east with the rest of the island for administrative convenience.[1]

SRI LANKA'S CONFLICT: A GENERAL OVERVIEW

Walter Laqueur (1999) has compiled a factual and objective overview of Sri Lanka's conflict with the Tamil Tigers. It ends on a note of conjecture: what really is the explanation of the Tamil Tigers and their fanaticism?

Sri Lanka, an island just south of India formerly known as Ceylon, became independent of British rule in 1948. Its politics have been turbulent almost ever since. The Sinhalese majority faces a Tamil minority of less than 20 per cent (about 3 million people), who are concentrated in the north of the country. However the Tamils, some of whom were originally brought to the island from India as labourers, have the backing of a much larger Tamil population in South India, concentrated in the state of Tamil Nadu. The policy of the Sinhalese majority ruling the country has been less than enlightened towards the minority; this manifested itself in an illiberal language policy (Sinhalese only), the refusal to give all Tamils in Sri Lanka citizenship, and the attempt to repatriate some of them to India, even though they had been born in Sri Lanka. Sri Lankan politics, furthermore, has had a strong radical element; this was one of the very few countries in the world in which the

Communist and Trotskyite parties had been strong simultaneously. At the same time, there was equal militancy on the right wing; when the then prime minister Bandaranaike was assassinated in 1959, the murderers were two Sinhalese monks for whom Bandaranaike was insufficiently nationalist.

The Tamil majority felt itself threatened once the British left, and various militant organizations developed in the 1950s and 1960s. Originally the inspiration was revolutionary, and the writings of Castro and Guevara, of General Giap and Regis Debray, which reached them by way of India, had a powerful impact. But gradually the Marxist element faded, and what remained was militant separatism pure and simple. The tension was fuelled by economic stagnation and a high unemployment rate, especially among the young. For an enterprising young Tamil, there seemed to be little to do but become a terrorist. But this explanation is not entirely satisfactory, as unemployment was equally high in Sinhalese and Muslim parts of the island. The fact that religious inspiration was not decisive among the Tamil should be stressed, because religion has often been thought to be the decisive factor in suicide bombing. The Tamil Tigers had the highest rate of suicide missions in the world, with many hundreds of victims over the years. Their motives were not to be found in their religion or ideology but, like Colombia, in their cultural and social traditions – in brief, in their history.

Conflicts between Tamil and Sinhalese continued throughout the 1960s. At the same time, various Tamil groups were fighting each other in a struggle for leadership. The Tigers fighting for Eelam, a homeland, developed out of a revolutionary student's association in Britain, and in 1976 the LTTE (Liberation Tigers of Tamil Eelam) was founded. It became one of the most effective guerrilla/terrorist groups in the world within a year. Its ideological guru was a Marxist-Leninist turned extreme nationalist named Balasingham, but the undisputed political military leader was Prabhakaran. From the very beginning, he was less influenced by Marxism–Leninism than by various Hindu thinkers. One of these was Vivekananda, who taught him to concentrate on training and indoctrinating the very young; another was Gandhi (short of nonviolence but with an emphasis on sexual abstinence); and above all, Subhas Chandra Bose, a chameleon-like man who served as a left-wing Congress leader and strongly supported the Japanese and Nazis during World War II.

What is commonly referred to as the 'Insurgency' began even earlier, in 1973, but during its first phase fighting was on a relatively minor scale. Growing Tamil militancy produced a Sinhalese backlash in 1981, resulting in riots and the murder of imprisoned Tamil leaders, which in turn led to a far bloodier Tamil campaign. This came to a halt only in July 1987, when Indian army units landed on the island in a peacekeeping effort. But the Indians faced Sinhalese resentment in addition to constant attack by the Tamil, who rejected the peace accord that had been worked out by Rajiv Gandhi, then Indian prime minister, and the Sri Lankan president. The Indians had little stomach for guerrilla fighting, and though some twelve thousand Tamils were killed, much of the Jaffna peninsula destroyed, and the Tamil Tigers forced to retreat to the jungle, the Indians decided to withdraw their troops from the island once they realised that peace between the two communities could not be achieved. Ever since then, civil war has continued on the island, with ambushes in the countryside as well as terrorist attacks in the towns, and while the

Tigers have not achieved a significant victory, the Sri Lankan army has been unable to stamp out the insurrection.

The Tamil Tiger leadership committed two major political blunders: one, when they assassinated Rajiv Gandhi in 1991, and, two, when they rejected a generous autonomy offer by the Sri Lankan government in 1995. Despite the rebels' count-less acts of indiscriminate violence, often against innocent civilians, the Tamil Tigers somehow preserved the reputation of an underdog, and thus attracted a certain amount of sympathy from the outside world. But much goodwill in India was lost following the assassination, and whatever sympathy was left disappeared when the Tigers showed extreme intransigence. It took six years for an Indian official inquiry committee to disentangle the circumstances of the assassination (its report was published only in December 1997); it appeared that not only had Tamil Nadu officials been involved, but that at an earlier stage in the insurgency the Tigers had been helped by the Indian secret services. The appeal of the Tamil Tigers was from then on restricted to the Tamil diaspora in foreign countries and their contri-butions, whether voluntary or forced, dwindled.

The Tamil Tigers, in their long fight against the ethnic majority, have shown inventiveness and extraordinary persistence. Mention has been made of the indoc-trination of young Tigers in a spirit of national fanaticism, spiritualism, sexual ascesis, and a cult of suicide. The last usually involved cyanide, and is said to give the Tigers extra confidence in that they have an alternative to capture and impris-onment. They have been waging a guerrilla war based on the Chinese and Cuban pattern, and for a number of years they virtually ruled the Jaffna peninsula as a little state of their own, just as Mao had run Yenan. They had modern high-tech weapons, such as Soviet-made SA 7 ground-to-air missiles obtained from Cambodia, and dozens of tons of RDX, a powerful explosive, obtained from the Ukraine. They operated their own small navy, which plied between Sri Lanka and the Indian main-land, as well as Myanmar (Burma) and Thailand. They operated in large units of several thousand fighters, some of whom received their military training in Tamil Nadu and others in Lebanon [. . .] and for years they maintained a military base in Myanmar. Like the IRA, they ran corporations and businesses, and have smuggled arms, drugs, and other commodities.

Despite the relative weakness of the Sinhalese army, and for all the Tigers' proficiency in guerrilla warfare, they have been unsuccessful in fighting in the open. They lost their main base in the Jaffna peninsula as the result of a government offensive in December 1995, and had to abandon their last urban base in Kilinochi in September 1996. In the latter operation alone, about a thousand Tamil Tigers were killed or taken prisoner. But as so often before, they still had enough strength to inflict major blows on the government. In July 1996, four thousand Tamil Tigers attacked and seized a government military base northeast of Colombo. All 1,200 military personnel at the base were killed, and it was the most severe military defeat the government suffered since the beginning of the war. In addition, there were frequent bomb attacks. In January 1996, almost a hundred civilians were killed and 1,400 injured in the Colombo banking district. On another occasion four Tiger frogmen blew up two gunboats at the naval base of Trinkomalee. On the other hand, a naval blockade imposed by India severely hampered Tamil Tiger arms supplies, which mainly came from across the sea. The small Tiger navy, consisting partly of speedboats, interferes with ships of other nations fairly regularly, committing acts of piracy against China, Malaya, and Indonesia, and this had not added to their popularity.

Tamil propaganda has been far more astute than government propaganda, and the Tigers have established a foreign service of their own with representations in thirty-eight countries, issuing daily news bulletins and running their own illegal radio station in Sri Lanka. Use is widely made of the Internet and video clips, which are distributed to leading media in foreign countries. Yet, with all this, the insurgency in Sri Lanka remains one of the most underreported in the world media.

The main bases of Tiger operations, such as the Jaffna peninsula, have been virtually destroyed; most of the peninsula's inhabitants have emigrated abroad. The war effort of the LTTE is mainly paid for by expatriate Tamil communities in Canada, the United States, Australia, South Africa, and several European countries. Some of the money has come in voluntarily, but the LTTE has also enlisted enforcers, extracting contributions from those reluctant to pay. This in turn has led to the arrest of the more aggressive collectors, and in some countries the Tamil Tigers have been banned altogether. The small Tamil community (some 25,000) in Switzerland allegedly contributed $8 million a year, a sizeable sum considering that most of them recently were very poor asylum seekers. In 1996, the Tiger leadership in Switzerland was arrested and charged with extortion.

In the shadowy world of drug smuggling there is little hard evidence of official LTTE participation, but there is some circumstantial evidence that individual Tamils have played a considerable role in smuggling heroin from Asia to Europe. The Tiger leadership has certainly tolerated it and in all probability benefited from it, but has not advertised its active involvement. The Colombo government, however, has claimed that drug smuggling constitutes the single most important item in the war treasury of the LTTE, and ships that smuggle arms and other commodities are also used to carry drugs.

In the guerrilla and terrorist war against the government, at least ten thousand Tamil Tigers have been killed. There has been enormous material damage to the north of Sri Lanka and the creation of many refugees. Nevertheless, the Tigers claim that despite these losses and many major setbacks they will continue to fight until they have a fully independent state of their own. The most they are willing to concede is a loose economic union with the majority patterned on that of the European Community.

What makes them fight with such tenacity and fanaticism? Religious and ethnic differences do exist but are not crucial; the Sinhalese hail from northern India, the Tamil from the south. The Tamil originally had the Hindu caste system; the Sinhalese are predominantly Buddhist. The Tamil claim that they cannot possibly live with the Sinhalese in the framework of one state; they always had a state (a kingdom) of their own, and it was against their wishes that they were fused into one country under British rule. This state of affairs is obviously true for a great many nationalities and tribes all over the world, and it would be impossible to reconstitute all of these kingdoms, duchies, and principalities. The Tamil militants are not, however, impressed by considerations of this kind. Their leadership, originally Marxist–Leninist, has transformed itself into an intense nationalist group, preaching a fanaticism and a ruthlessness that in Europe could be found only in the fascist movements of the 1930s.

The extraordinary ruthlessness of the campaign waged by the Tamil Tigers has shown itself in the indiscriminate killing of Sinhalese and Muslim peasants in addition to the political murders committed against rivals within the Tamil camp. The Tigers were originally only one of several militant groups among the Tamil community, and their rise to power left a bloody trail of assassinations in their wake, including, for instance, the elected mayor of Jaffna, who was killed by the young Prabhakaran, who in later years became the undisputed commander of the Tigers. In 1998, yet another elected mayor of Jaffna, a Tamil woman, was killed by terrorists. By this time it was no longer clear whether the assassins were Tiger surrogates or a smaller group competing with them. Such internecine warfare has weakened the cause of the Tigers and other militant separatists.

The virulence of Tamil terrorism and its proclivity to suicide cannot be blamed on social and political circumstances. While it is true that their treatment by the Sinhalese majority has often been unjust, only a feverish imagination can refer to it as 'genocide'. Learning from bitter experience and its own mistakes, the Colombo government has made far-reaching concessions to the Tamils over the years, and Tamils have been represented in prominent positions in the government. (The Sri Lankan foreign minister, at the time of writing, is a Tamil by origin.) It is true that the rate of suicide in Sri Lanka is among the highest in Asia, and indeed in the world, and has been steadily rising, but this seems not to be true with regard to Tamil Nadu in India. Poor economic conditions (some 40 per cent of the population live in absolute poverty) are largely the result, not the cause, of the civil war. The combination of a relatively well-educated young generation and youth unemployment can make for political radicalism and possibly even terrorism, but not necessarily for suicide. Hate is not directed against a foreign occupant or members of a religion distasteful to the Tamils, and the difference in language alone cannot explain the deep division, especially since the central government has made Tamil its second official language. Rather, there is a veritable 'cult of the martyrs' among the Tamil. One day of the year is celebrated as Martyrs' Day, but this is recent; it is not part of Tamil history or Hindu religion. It seems more Christian or Muslim than Tamil.

It is certain that the Tigers would not have lasted so long and been able to inflict so many losses on their enemy if it were not for their fanaticism. Assistance from Tamil Nadu and the Tamil diaspora, from Norway to Botswana, has also played an important role. But this, again, does not fully explain the riddle, because while there is Tamil solidarity in Tamil Nadu, there is no intense fanaticism equal to that found in Sri Lanka, nor has there been a movement for separatism in Tamil Nadu. Therefore, in the final analysis, there is no satisfactory explanation for the Tamil Tigers and their fanaticism.[2]

THE TAMIL TIGERS' CASE

The Tamils say (in an Internet overview which the Sri Lankan government would regard as unwarranted propaganda) that 'belligerent Sinhala chauvinism' has attempted to force the Tamil minority to merge with the majority to form one nation, claiming that the country has been united for 2,500 years. The Sinhala approach is vigorously contested by Tamils as grossly unfair and undemocratic:

With the departure of the British in 1948, the re-emergence of a separate Tamil national identity was reinforced by the actions of a Sinhala majority which regarded the island of Sri Lanka as the exclusive home of Sinhala Buddhism and the Tamil people as 'outsiders' who were to be subjugated and assimilated within the confines of a unitary Sinhala Buddhist state.

Majority rule within the confines of a unitary state and the constraints of a Third World economy served to perpetuate the oppressive rule of a permanent Sinhala majority. It was a permanent Sinhala majority, which sought to consolidate its hegemony over the Tamils of Eelam, through a series of legislative and administrative acts, ranging from disenfranchisement, state sponsored colonisation of the Tamil homeland, and discriminatory language and employment policies.

Consequently, in the light of such widespread discrimination, the Tamils hold that armed resistance to this 'oppression' is lawful.

When the Tamil people sought to resist these oppressive legislative and administrative acts by resort to Parliamentary agitation and non-violent protests, they were attacked physically, some of them burnt alive, and their homes destroyed and looted. The genocidal attacks in 1956, 1958, 1961 are illustrative of these Sinhala attempts to terrorise and intimidate the Tamil people into submission at a time when Tamil protest was confined to entirely non-violent forms of agitation. Again, successive Sinhala-dominated Sri Lankan governments dishonoured agreements solemnly entered into with Tamil parliamentary parties.

In 1972, a new Constitution was proclaimed by the Sinhala majority who constituted themselves a Constituent Assembly, changed the name of the island from Ceylon to the Sinhala, Sri Lanka, and proclaimed Buddhism as the state religion and removed even the meagre safeguards against discrimination contained in the earlier Constitution. The plea of the Tamil parliamentary parties for a federal constitution was rejected and the leader of the Tamil parliamentary group resigned his seat in Parliament and sought a mandate from the Tamil people for a separate state. It was a mandate which was later overwhelmingly endorsed by the Tamil people at the General Election in July 1977. The response of the Sinhala people to this parliamentary struggle was yet another genocidal attack on Tamils to intimidate them into submission.

The lawful armed resistance of the Tamil people led by the Liberation Tigers of Tamil Eelam arose in response to decades of an ever widening and deepening oppression under alien Sinhala rule. The armed resistance of the Tamil people was met with wide ranging retaliatory attacks on increasingly large sections of the Tamil people with intent, to compel them to accept Sinhala rule. In the late 1970s large numbers of Tamil youths were detained without trial and tortured under emergency regulations and later under the Prevention of Terrorism Act which has been described by the International Commission of Jurists as a 'blot on the statute book of any civilised country'. Torture was almost a universal practice for the Sri Lankan authorities.

During the past several years the Sinhala-dominated Sri Lankan government has continued with its efforts to conquer the Tamil homeland and rule the Tamil people. The record shows that in this attempt, Sri Lanka's armed forces and para-military units have committed increasingly widespread violations of humanitarian law.

In the East whole villages of Tamils have been attacked by the Army and by the so-called Home Guards. In the North aerial bombardment and artillery shelling of Tamil civilian population centres by the Sri Lankan armed forces has been under-taken on a systematic basis.

The attacks on the Tamil homeland were coupled with the declared opposi-tion of successive Sri Lankan Governments (including that of President Kumaratunga) to the merger of the North and East of the island into a single admin-istrative and political unit and the recognition of the Tamil homeland.

THE TAMIL DIASPORA: A TRANS-STATE NATION

It is claimed by the Tamils that seventy million of their kinsfolk live dispersed in many lands. What they describe as their 'growing togetherness' is publicised in the Tamil website in these terms:

Given the armed struggle for Tamil Eelam in the island of Sri Lanka, and the hundred and fifty thousand Tamil asylum seekers and refugees in many countries in the world, including Great Britain, USA, Australia, New Zealand, Canada, Netherlands, Germany, France, Italy, Switzerland, Norway, Denmark, Sweden, and Finland it may be tempting to conclude that the dispersal of the Tamils is of recent origin. But that would be wrong.

It is true that the genocidal attack on the Tamil people in 1983 in the island of Sri Lanka and the heightened conflict led to the large numbers of Tamil asylum seekers in the 1980s and 1990s. In the 1980s, for instance, during the period of the Cold War and Germany's relatively liberal asylum policies, many Tamils entered Europe via Germany.

However, as far back as the 1950s, the enactment of the Sinhala Only act in 1956 in Ceylon (as the island of Sri Lanka was then known), the genocidal attacks on the Tamil people in 1958, as well as discriminatory employment policies in the state sector led many Tamil professionals, including doctors and engineers, to seek employment in Great Britain, USA, Australia and New Zealand. Later, in 1972, discrimination in respect to University admissions in Sri Lanka saw a second wave of Tamil professionals leaving the island, to secure not only a future for themselves but also to provide an adequate education for their children.

Today, the Tamil diaspora is a growing togetherness of more than 70 million people living in many lands and across distant seas, many thousands as refugees and asylum seekers. It is a togetherness rooted in an ancient heritage, a rich language and literature, and a vibrant culture. But it is a togetherness which is not simply a function of the past. It is a growing togetherness consolidated by struggle and suffering and given purpose and direction by the aspirations of a people for the future – a future where they and their children and their children's children may live in equality and freedom in an emerging post-modern world.[3]

The term 'diaspora' is commonly understood to refer to the forced exile of the Jews from the Roman Empire and to their scattering throughout the lands of the Gentiles in the first two centuries of the Christian era. In the case of the Tamils the dispersion is mainly a voluntary one. In modern parlance it might best be described as a 'supporters club' which actively disseminates the case for Tamil self-determination within Sri Lanka and which has a cardinal role in accumulating funds (one estimate is that of $1 million a month) to support the case. How far the scattered Tamils represent 70 million 'terrorists' and to what extent their financial resourcing fills the coffers of a terrorist treasury are matters for debate. The Sri Lankan Government's view from Colombo is couched in very plain terms, for instance, in the newspaper *Asiaweek* (26 July 1996) under the heading – 'Tiger International – a Secret Global Network Keeps Sri Lanka's Tamil Guerrilla Organization Up and Killing':

The increasingly bloody tempo of the war has thrown into sharper focus than ever the international dimension of the LTTE. A complex, shadowy network developed over more than a decade, it mirrors the sophistication of the quasi-governmental structure built by the Tigers in Sri Lanka itself. Drawing on the loyalties and resources of members of a global Tamil diaspora, the network – call it LTTE International Inc. – links commercial companies and small businesses, informal banking channels, a fleet of ships, political offices, aid and human rights organizations, arms dealers and foreign mercenaries.

The transnational and often secretive presence of the LTTE and its front organizations is increasingly unsettling governments in Asia and the West. Goaded by Colombo, countries including Switzerland, Canada, Australia, Malaysia, Thailand and the Philippines have expressed concern in recent months over LTTE activities – and in some cases moved against them.

Broadly, say analysts, LTTE International functions on three distinct levels: publicity and propaganda, arms procurement, and fundraising. While the networks overlap to some extent, operationally they remain separate. The war for international hearts and minds is conducted at a level of sophistication far more advanced than anything Colombo has reached. Diplomatic missions and news organizations receive daily faxes detailing – albeit selectively – battlefield reports transmitted by satellite phone links. The LTTE puts out slick videos projecting in gut-churning detail the results of government air strikes (while editing out LTTE military units the planes are trying to target). And it uses the Internet both as a propaganda tool and as a means to appeal for funds.[4]

In the opinion of the Sri Lankan and a number of other governments there is clear evidence that **LTTE** derives much of its considerable funds from crime-related activities in many countries. A Canadian research unit in 1995 made a detailed investigation of the matter (Mackenzie Briefing Notes, 1995) and has reported in these terms:

The intimate relationship between terrorism and criminality is not new. Criminal endeavours have often provided cash for political struggles, or have been used as a weapon to attack a social order. Secret societies and underground terrorist networks, initially founded to achieve political or social objectives, are easily redirected towards purely criminal activities. They can easily transpose their organizational structures, methods of operation and ruthlessness towards new objectives.

The demand for resources to maintain such a protracted conflict has never been met in LTTE controlled areas. From the earliest days of their struggle in the 1980s, the organization recognized that it would have to go abroad. Squeezing the local Tamil economy would never meet the LTTE's needs.

The Liberation Tigers of Tamil Eelam and related Tamil insurgents are engaged in organized criminal activities. These began in Sri Lanka and have spread to Western Europe, North America and Australia – wherever Tamil refugees have landed. While crime in a newly arrived migrant community is not unknown, normally the victims of the criminals are members of their own community. In this case, the experiences of Tamil refugees began with extortion, by paying for exit visas to leave insurgent-controlled areas. Many have paid for the insurgents to bring them to a new country, only to have the extortion resume – at an even more costly level.[5]

Britain, particularly, in Sri Lankan eyes, is a gathering ground for Tamil expatriates who are surely standing four-square behind the **LTTE**. In October 1997, *The Times* carried this report about terrorist financing:

The Tamil Tigers, who have been waging a civil war against the Sri Lankan Government for the past 14 years, can keep going indefinitely, funded by the biggest international financial empire ever built by a terrorist organisation. Most of their money comes from Europe, the US and Canada. London is the propaganda headquarters, feeding information – much of it more credible than Colombo's accounts of battlefield developments – to Tamil organisations, embassies and newspapers worldwide. The failure of the international community to stem the Tigers' activities demonstrates the ineffectiveness of the global fight against terrorism.

Britain has all but admitted it is powerless to curb the Tigers, who raise, according to Sri Lankan estimates, £250,000 a month from Tamils living in Britain. The worldwide income is believed to be about £1.25 million a month, some of which goes to humanitarian causes, but most of which funds a sophisticated war machine.

More than 450,000 Sri Lankan Tamils live abroad, many of them victims of ethnic riots, especially those in 1983. They are thus inclined to support armed rebellion. There are 50,000 Tamils in Britain, most of them relatively prosperous, and many Tamils actively support the cause.[6]

THE POWER OF THE MAKING OF MYTHS

This case-study of the Tamils and the following one of Northern Ireland both touch on the apparent significance of myth to terrorists. The process of making myths assume a realistic shape in order to lend credibility and force to LTTE rhetoric has been closely examined by Kapferer (1997). One Tamil myth suggests that there must be played out 'an age-old conflict: that the present situation is merely the reproduction of annual events established in pre-colonial contexts'. There is, by inference, a tradition of violent struggle which may be necessary to attain definable ends. Kapferer believes this to be a distorted premise; the current conflict, he argues, is entirely the result of recent colonial and post-colonial circumstances. Another Tamil myth, soon accepted by them as credible, was to present the state as thoroughly decadent, corrupt, an impersonal bureaucracy threatening the freedom of an individual and even that of a local village community. The myth reinforces the notion of opposable threat and of legitimate active response. Self-respect and rightful autonomy had long been eroded by the alienating policies of a government and of an intolerant majority; only struggle – the process of revolution – could restore basic human rights. Building myths was, as one might expect, a deliberate strategy to inspire the revolutionary cadres, to fortify their resolve, and to consolidate their strength in numbers. For Kapferer there is an inevitable linkage of cause and effect where myths help to heighten identity, and violence, ultimately terroristic, affirms identity where any confrontation contains an ethnic element:

Thus, Tamil guerrilla attacks in the interests of ethnic autonomy sparked violent anti-Tamil rioting much of which received the support of agents of the state. [. . .] The violence of the riots created a deepening of ethnic division which gave the myths of ethnic identity greater relevance. Moreover, the riots generated the expansion of Tamil resistance.[7]

Violence, then, may move towards the objective of annihilation, Kapferer points out, towards the point when terror ousts terror, in a contra-terrorist campaign to 'rub out' suspect supporter groups. The picture is a familiar one: what happened in Sri Lanka has been seen in South America and the Middle East:

Thus, in government action, evidence of individual JVP [Janatha Vimukthi Peranmuna] activists in a village area occasionally became a pretext for action against the village as a whole. Government forces engaged in mass killings: 'guilt' via category-membership and the grim evidence is now being revealed in public enquiries. The bureaucratic/technical order of the state is not just the means or the instrument of state violence, it becomes itself generative of an expanding situation of violence.[8]

Another point characteristic of the Sri Lankan conflict is, for Kapferer, its 'religiosity'. Tamils are chiefly Hindu, observing the distinctions of the caste system; the Sinhala majority are Buddhist in the main. In regard to the Buddhist faith and its followers, Kapferer detects a marked distortion of value and a paradox that is grim in its implications:

Moreover, in the current context of intra-ethnic and inter-ethnic violence officers of the state make intense appeals to the key Buddhist value of non-violence. Further, there is, in the current situation, an implication that the state as constituted in reference to the Buddha ideal of non-violence is the supreme agent of Buddhist morality, a morality which is even present in the exercise by the state of extreme violence. It is a violence in the interest of the order of a Buddhist state.[9]

ETHNIC WAR AND ITS TALLY

Manoj Joshi (1996) has traced the terrorist tactics of the Tigers since 1975:

The 'honor' of carrying out the movement's first political assassination belonged to a young 17-year-old Tamil called Vellupilai Prabhakaran, who managed to shoot the Tamil mayor of Jaffna, Alfred Duriappah, in July 1975. The following year, Pirabhakaran had another 'first', a successful bank raid that netted him over half a million rupees. He then founded the Tamil New Tigers, which became the Liberation Tigers of Tamil Eelam (LTTE). In September 1978, another first was credited to the outfit, a time-bomb blast in an Air Ceylon passenger jet.

A key impetus to Tamil militancy was provided by the anti-Tamil riots of July 1983 and the massacre of a number of militant leaders. [. . .] This led to a stream of refugees fleeing to India across the narrow neck of water dividing the two countries. Most, if not all of these refugees went to the Indian State of Tamil Nadu just twenty-eight kilometers across the Palk Strait. India therefore has been an important reference point for the groups for cultural as well as logistical reasons.[10]

Kapferer (1997) has made a detailed study of state-and-insurrectionary violence in Sri Lanka. He is chiefly concerned with the Sinhalese JVP (the People's Liberation Front) but most of the points he makes and the conclusions drawn are also directly relevant to Tamil terrorism and are well worth reproducing here. Kapferer's argument isolates a number of significant factors leading to conflict: the contrasts between affluence and poverty, above all, in towns, the unconvincing assurances of Colombo government, the messianic and symbolistic postures and resolution of a liberating force (like the LTTE and the JVP), the part played by motives of vengeance, the prevalence of rumour and confusion. There were too many 'contradictions' in Sri Lankan society to lead to anything other than disruptive protest, aggression, and terror:

The ethnic war exacerbated contradictions at the heart of the Sri Lanka state and in the political and social worlds of the Sinhala population. The JVP revolt of 1989–90, and its furious suppression by government forces, was a violent expression of the forces, emergent in such contradiction and the engagement of violence as the key weapon of resolution. The JVP drew on the energies of increased class suffering, especially among the rural and urban poor intensified by the economic strains of the war. The timing of the revolt coincided with the apparent emptiness of the Sinhala nationalist rhetoric of the government (evidenced in the Sri Lanka–India Accord which occasioned serious mass rioting). The state appeared weak, too, in its confrontation with the Tigers whose fighting capacity had reached legendary proportions among the Sinhalese population. In the representations among numerous Sinhalese, the Tigers are depicted as messianic in their commitment and, for many, present an aura of invulnerability. Prior to the JVP uprising rumour had circulated in Colombo that the Tigers were planning a surprise attack on the city and this had led to a small panic among the city's populace, some fleeing towards the countryside. There was wide belief that the ranks in the armed forces were highly sympathetic to the JVP and this undoubtedly encouraged the JVP leadership to embark on its final terror drive, in August 1989, to take over the government. It is generally understood that a JVP mistake (the enormity of which was almost unbelievable at the time and even more so in retrospect) in its discourse of violence at this time was responsible for its failure. The JVP leadership announced that it would attack the families of the armed forces if they did not disobey government directives to move against the JVP. This remarkable error is regarded as being instrumental in the turning of the tide against JVP fortunes and impelling a period of massive human destruction. This destruction often expressly took the form of 'righteous' vengeance.[11]

The conflict in Sri Lanka is much more complex than A versus B – it was a 'total situation of violence' in Kapferer's words:

The distinct dynamics of JVP and government violence expanded the dimensions of the violent context to create for a while a total situation of violence. [. . .] As much as a struggle for controlling power, the violence was a vital element for constituting a social world in which a particular kind of dominating power was possible. Thus the Sinhalese population as a whole was increasingly drawn into the conflict and consumed in its fury.[12]

Moreover, in a very rough and quixotic way, the terrorists assumed the role of moral arbiters:

People executed by the JVP were not only identified as government stooges, or as behaving in defiance of JVP authority, they were also presented as offending local moralities. The JVP executioners often presented themselves as exerting customary or rightful justice, as asserting the justice that the agents of the government had ignored or themselves had abused. People killed by the JVP included rapists, seducers, thieves, etc. The killing occasionally followed the course of long-standing village disputes and exhibited the passions of local enmities and the desire for revenge.

Broadly, the violent discourse of the JVP engaged the dynamic of the war-machine. It expanded through social relations and to some extent became driven by the violence already integral within them. Thus, its energy of destruction joined with the enmities already present and often of a long-standing nature in local areas. The JVP violence became part of pre-existing structures of vengeance and a vehicle for the settling of old scores. The government's need to destroy the JVP and to attack it at base progressively involved government forces in similar processes of local vengeance which expanded the destruction as a whole.[13]

The Sri Lankan tally of terrorism is enormous among a relatively small population. Estimates of the number of terrorists vary but are likely to be in the region of 6,000 fully armed and desperate fighters. They include women guerrillas, the 'freedom birds', and perhaps half of the Tigers are still in their teens. They have their own highly organised intelligence service. An élite brigade, the Black Tigers, operates a battlefield strategy known as 'Unceasing Wave' targeting key members of the government and the armed forces, public buildings and important parts of the economic infrastructure such as power stations, fuel depots, commuter trains and stations. Terrorist strikes will be launched carefully before the security forces are called or when most people are asleep. The terrorist arsenal and methods are substantial and lead to horrendous damage and casualties. People are gunned down in the streets, bombs are detonated in vehicles, trains, ferry boats. Mortars and heavy artillery are launched at public buildings. Muslim and Buddhist clergy and worshippers have been slaughtered. No village community can feel itself safe. Something causing much disquiet in Colombo is the extent of terrorist linkage between their 'front-line' operations in Sri Lanka and a supply and communications base in peninsular India. Manoj Joshi has a note about this:

Safe houses and communications centres were purchased in Tamil Nadu and Karnataka. The LTTE used local contacts for the purchases, but insulated their organization from them. Likewise the LTTE used small workshops and industrial facilities in Tamil Nadu to manufacture uniforms and even items like rifle-fired grenades. Communications were of great importance, and the LTTE had a sophisticated network using high frequency and very high frequency wireless sets, international direct dialling, all with security provisions. This network linked Indian safe houses with each other and with Jaffna and provided real-time control of shipping and smuggling operations.[14]

Sri Lanka's terrorism has known no bounds since 1983. The loss of life that terrorists have caused since 1972 is reckoned to be some 58,000 civilians and military personnel, two-thirds of whom died in the years 1984–97. Seventeen prominent political leaders met their deaths. In the course of violent dissension within the LTTE's own ranks, thirty-two Tamil leaders have been killed.

FANATICISM AND SUICIDE

Laqueur (1999) acknowledges the searing fundamentalism of aggression–hate–fanaticism in members of a group such as the Tamil Tigers but warns that their 'political' beliefs and attitudes should not be simplistically defined. The old definitions of 'revolutionary' or 'reactionary' or 'left wing' or 'right wing' are inappropriate or inadequate in helping us understand terrorist motives and the degree of emotional involvement. As for the Tamils' fanaticism, Laqueur suggests that suicide by Tamils, while appearing horrific and pathologically extreme to others, may have for the individual activists and for their collaborators a positive value where martyrdom is a rational terminal decision demonstrating a worthy and invincible cause. (This seems to be the case with the Hizbullah in Lebanon.)

Being absolutely convinced of the rightness of his cause, the fanatic needs an enemy, and he is bound to have enemies since the majority will seldom agree with him. Hate plays a central role in his personality structure; paraphrasing Descartes, he can rightly say *Odio, ergo sum* – I hate, therefore I exist. The substance of his belief system may vary greatly according to history, culture, or the influence of charismatic leaders. But the burning passion is primary; ideological content is secondary.

Where does the fanaticism, the passion, originate? To what extent are biological factors involved, and to what degree social and cultural factors? Is there a biochemical trip wire that is set off by a childhood trauma? These issues have been widely but inconclusively discussed for many years. But it is not helpful to define radicals of this and similar persuasion as right wing or left wing, as is often done. The usual defining characteristics such as 'reactionary' and 'revolutionary' get mixed up in these mindsets. Some fanatics are simply nihilists, even though they will seldom admit it.

To argue that the Algerian terrorists, the Palestinian groups, or the Tamil Tigers are 'left' or 'right' means affixing a label that simply does not fit. Taken from early nineteenth-century Europe, these terms have little meaning in other times and parts of the world. The Third World groups to which we refer have subscribed to different ideological tenets at different periods, and it is as wrong to take Leninist slogans seriously as it is to subscribe to fascist rhetoric. The foundation of their movements is extreme nationalist orientation, frequently including religious motives in recent times. Such a religious-nationalist-populist movement can to Western eyes appear to be left wing one moment and right the next, as history has shown time and again. Why should one even try to classify terrorist groups using categories that are no longer relevant?

To begin to understand the mind-set of this new breed of terrorist, his cruelty and hate, the shedding of all moral restraints, the great rage about everything and nothing in particular, the joy generated by killing and destruction, one has to go, initially at least, over familiar ground: fanaticism and paranoia.[15]

The indoctrination of the positive value of suicide has been especially intense in Sri Lanka where almost all the candidates among the Tamil Tigers are in their teens. Carrying cyanide on their persons is considered to be an expression of their commitment to their cause: 'We are married to our cyanide; it makes us clear-headed and purposeful'. This commitment to self-destruction is combined with training in the commission of acts of the greatest cruelty.[16]

COUNTER-TERRORISM

Understandably the Sri Lankan authorities, like most governments, have sought to contain and then eliminate anti-state terrorism by means of a mixture of political and diplomatic moves allied to the employment of force. Manoj Joshi (1996) has examined particularly the course of Colombo's attempt at enlisting a mediator, in this case, India. There was an element of force to be used in the approach:

In an important interregnum, between July 1987 and March 1990, the Indian Army, constituted as an Indian peace-keeping force, fought the LTTE in a bid to compel it to accept the Indo–Sri Lanka Peace Accord that had been signed by Indian Prime Minister Rajiv Gandhi and Sri Lankan President J. R. Jayawardene in June 1987.

Beginning as a two-brigade force to enforce the Indo–Sri Lanka Peace Accord, the Indian Peace Keeping Force (IPKF) confronted the LTTE in an aborted two-and-a-half year campaign which left twelve thousand dead and over five thousand wounded. In this period the LTTE showed themselves to be adaptive as well as innovative as guerrillas and terrorists. They first took on the IPKF from their urban redoubt of Jaffna and then, when forced out, from the jungle stronghold of north-central Sri Lanka.

The principal reason for Indian intervention in the affairs of Sri Lanka was to prevent the aggressive assertion of a Tamil identity in Sri Lanka from having a reflex influence in Tamil Nadu. Following Mrs Gandhi's assassination at the hands of her Sikh bodyguards in October 1984, India shifted gears in Sri Lanka. It first attempted to play honest broker between the Tamils and the Sinhala-dominated government of Sri Lanka. After two futile years, at the behest of both sides, it inserted itself as a party, as well as a guarantor, of an Accord signed with the Sri Lankan government on July 29, 1987.

However, in reality, the LTTE was relentlessly opposed to the deal and began a systematic campaign to sabotage the accord. This led to a confrontation with the IPKF, who launched an assault on the town of Jaffna. The Indian Army built up a four-division force that kept Jaffna free from major hostilities for eighteen months and bottled up the LTTE in the Wanni jungles of north-central Sri Lanka.

The 1987–1989 period was the most dangerous for the LTTE, but it adapted well to jungle fighting after being forced out of Jaffna. In some ways the organization actually became stronger and gained greater depth and experience. It was able to exploit the three-way relationship between itself, the Sri Lankan government, and the government of India.

By late 1988, badly bruised by the IPKF actions, the LTTE realized the imperative of getting the Indians out of Sri Lanka. The elections, unrepresentative to the interim northeastern state, boded ill for them in the long run. Neither their attacks nor the casualties they could inflict could compel the IPKF to pull out. The only way the Indians would go out was the way they came in, at the request of the government in Colombo.

The beginning of the end had arrived, as the new foreign minister of India, Inder Kumar Gujral, gratuitously declared in early 1990 that Indian troops would 'never again' be sent to Sri Lanka. India now was left with no leverage to insist on even a token implementation of the Indo–Sri Lanka Accord.[17]

Wider perspectives engaged the Sri Lankan government in January 1998 when the United Nations completed the draft of an International Convention for the Suppression of Terrorist Bombings and opened it in New York for signature. As chairman of the Ad-Hoc Committee working on the draft, Sri Lanka had played an important role in moving discussion into print, declaring frequently and vigorously that only concerted international action could combat terrorism especially where, as in Sri Lanka, a terrorist group could call on backers and funding elsewhere. Effective action against terrorism had been frustrated, in Colombo's view, by too much sterile philosophical debate about the nature of terrorism. The Convention with its legislative and practical proposals had to be adopted and implemented without delay.

POSTSCRIPT

A concluding question is: what future is there for any resort to force among the Tamils of Sri Lanka? In May 1997 there appeared in a newspaper, The *Indian Express,* a number of points certain to exercise minds in contemporary Sri Lanka. The heading reads: Tamed Tigers Add to Tamil Trauma:

Just as the war can never end as long [as] the LTTE remains a force, Tamil aspirations for equality and political autonomy will certainly remain an unfulfilled dream if there were to be no LTTE.

[. . .] Tamil political parties are desperate that a solution must be found and finalised before the Sri Lankan army brings the LTTE to its knees. Third party assistance is urgently required more to push a political deal for the Tamils through the maze of Sinhalese politics but this must happen before the Tigers are eventually crushed by the Sri Lankan army, because sadly, the LTTE is the only lever that the Tamils have now.[18]

Taming the Tigers has certainly been an enormously traumatic experience for Sri Lankans. The civil war, flaring most obviously in 1983, has brought seventeen years of misery and despair. There are today slight signs of moves towards settlement, provided LTTE and Colombo can agree on what must be a compromise for a minority even though that minority disputes the term. A real sticking-point in most negotiations is the Sri Lankan government's fear that giving autonomy to six or eight mainly Tamil regions might shift a possible and acceptable federal solution towards an unacceptable full independence for the Tamils. Many Tamils among the 70 million believe that sometime, somehow their claims for equality of representation and opportunity must be met and there can be few of them who believe that a continuation of terrorism in Sri Lanka will do anything other than decimate the community. There seems no alternative to Colombo's pressing ahead with strategies that build on concessions already offered together with a disarmament programme that may have to be monitored by an outside agency.

Chapter 7

Northern Ireland

NORTHERN IRELAND HAS BEEN called many things – the Land of Wide Sunsets, the Land of Dreams. For most of the present century, though, the romantic appellations have given way to tragic ones – the Land of Long Memories, the Land of Myth, the Land of Terror. Romantic associations of gentle fantasy and humorous irrationality have been displaced by the grim realities of unreconciled conflict and widespread violence. It seems likely that long memories of discrimination, confrontation, and struggle reinforced by quasi-religious myths of victimisation and sacrifice have done much to shape attitudes and behaviour in a community divided by intolerance, suspicion and resort to arms, and that memory and myth play a role in decelerating the momentum of a peace agreement signed in April 1998. Northern Ireland's terrorism is in a state of suspense. This case-study considers three things – the significance of shared memories, the significance of myth, and the controversy over disarmament, that is, 'arms decommissioning'. What will not be found in this case-study, however, is any simplistic deduction of cause-and-effect. First, some historical introduction is needed.

IRELAND'S TROUBLES: HISTORICAL ANTECEDENTS

There is an outline of Ireland's conflict scenario and of the difficulties of settlement and reconciliation in Whittaker (1999):

'The trouble with the Irish is the English' is a traditional Irish refrain shared more often by Catholics in the southern Republic of Ireland than in Northern Ireland. The English connection through history has brought them harsh oppression, tumult and tragedy, high-handedness from absentee landowners, detached and apathetic government from Westminster. Seven hundred years ago Anglo-Norman overlords forced the barbarous Irish tribes beyond the confines of their defended 'Pale'. Four hundred years ago Tudor monarchs exported rapacious nobility to Ireland once more to grab land. Three hundred years ago Northern Ireland was a battleground for the followers of William of Orange to establish Protestant dominance over Catholics, loyal to James II in England and very likely disloyal enough to favour Louis XIV of France. Two hundred years ago the English were intent on penalising the Irish for being influenced by the seductive egalitarian ideas of revolutionary France. Throwing off the yoke of a Hanoverian king and his Protestantism in the name of equality and liberty would invite remorseless retribution. There was a brighter moment in 1800 when the English Liberal Prime Minister, William Pitt, put on the statute book an Act of Unity uniting England, Scotland and Ireland, and granting 100 House of Commons seats to Irishmen – Protestant Irishmen. Catholics had to await any degree of emancipation for another twenty-nine years. Where now was the reputed British belief in democracy and liberalisation? Was the concept of 'British' a euphemism for the hypocritical and untrustworthy English? Victorian times did nothing to satisfy resentments in Dublin and the association between London and their dependency in Northern Ireland grew stronger. In 1886, W. E. Gladstone, the veteran Liberal at Westminster, campaigned eloquently and passionately for Home Rule to placate the troubled Irish.

Hostile Tories and the suspicious Unionists of Northern Ireland would have nothing to do with this proposed breaking of imperial bonds. Home Rule would turn out to be Rome Rule. Buoyed by the message to them from Winston Churchill's father, Lord Randolph Churchill, that 'Ulster will fight, Ulster will be right', they made preparations for manning defences against Catholics in north and south.

The First World War brought trouble in Ireland to breaking point. By 1915, among Catholics there was fury at the injustice and anomalies in English and Protestant ascendancy. Rifles were smuggled in from Europe, and German sympathies for Irish dissolution were evident. In the United States powerful Irish lobbies in New York and Boston voiced loud concern and this was amplified in the influential Hearst press. In Dublin, with its underground links to Belfast, Irishmen planned to cut moorings from London and to expel the English. There was an angry alliance of idealists within the Sinn Féin nationalist movement seeking a Celtic Revival and of armed men mustering determined forces. English excesses in the past, English prevarication against Ireland's contemporary demands, and the prospects of English curbs on future progress were not so much dreams as motivating forces pushing the Irish towards complete independence.

Against gathering clouds of conflict, part-religious, part-political, there were firm constitutional gains for Ireland. In 1920, the Government of Ireland Act conferred self-government on Dublin. Two years later the Irish Free State was born in Dublin, made up of twenty-six Irish counties. At the same time, Ulster was given six counties and a frontier drawn up between the two Irelands. Constitutionally this may have suited the English. For the Irish there were the beginnings of conflict here, with the south rejecting partition, hoping for eventual unification of the entire island, and with Ulster absolutely determined never to permit unification. For many hardened Protestants it was the 'no Popery' of their forebears again. A conflict of intention and will was inevitable. It was to be a conflict with deep historical roots.[1]

ULSTER'S CONTEMPORARY DIVIDE

The Whittaker outline continues looking at the battle for rights among rival elements, the political and religious affiliations of the contending groups, and the socio-economic contrasts at the heart of conflict:

The civil conflict in Northern Ireland reveals three components – a battle for civic rights, that is, socio-economic rights, a nationalistic North–South contest and a politico-military struggle mainly between extremists on the political flanks. These elements are interdependent, relating political controversies to the gulf between an oligarchy and a disadvantaged minority. There is a polarisation of religious affiliation in this conflict, which has made consensus difficult to achieve. There are strident voices in Ulster and vigorous, often bloody, action. Most conflicts have political leaders, their profiles highlighted by the media, their personalities often demonised. In Northern Ireland there is no Mandela to bring discordant elements together in another rainbow nation.

In Ulster the divide reveals most Protestants supporting Unionist or Loyalist parties – the Ulster Unionist, the Official Unionist, the Democratic Unionist. At the time of the April Agreement of 1998 David Trimble was the Unionist spokesman. (Dr Ian Paisley, a maverick to the hilt, headed his own creation, the Democratic Unionists.) These people play the 'Orange Card' of attachment to Great Britain. Two-thirds of their men belong to the fraternal, uncompromising Orange Order. Nine out of ten members of Ulster's own security force, the Royal Ulster Constabulary (RUC) are Protestant. Overall, Unionists feel themselves hemmed in politically and geographically. Catholics, in the main, are loyal either to Sinn Féin, whose President is Gerry Adams, or to the Socialist and Democratic Labour Party (SDLP) where John Hume has been active for twenty-five years. There is a small Alliance Party. Some idea of the proportionate representation of these parties may be roughly estimated from the voting patterns in the 1993 local council elections, which gained Unionist parties almost 50 per cent of the votes, the SDLP 25 per cent, Sinn Féin 15 per cent, the Alliance Party 6 per cent and other groups 8 per cent. [. . .] Many Catholics, terming themselves Nationalists or Republicans, are wedded to the ideal of a united Ireland, and they see the Unionists as Disunionists and the Loyalists as Disloyalists. Threaded through the political stance of the Catholic protest are symbols of sacrifice, of martyrdom, of a 'colonial freedom' movement against imperial subjection.

Northern Ireland's other divide is its socio-economic diversity. Social contrasts are now less marked than they were when industry and commerce were booming and affluence and poverty co-existed uncomfortably. Protestant and Catholic now share unemployment (Europe's worst) and reliance upon welfare [. . .] the test of progress and the possibility of reconciliation for ordinary people in Northern Ireland will be the provision of fairer shares and fairer chances. Gerry Adams, in August 1997, put this squarely to a Sinn Féin meeting in Belfast: 'A settlement where the poor remain poor and the dispossessed remain dispossessed would not be a real change of lives. A cobbled-together political settlement and an end to killings are not enough.' [. . .].[2]

THIRTY YEARS OF STRIFE

The upheaval of society in Northern Ireland remains the theme of Whittaker (1999) where Nationalist and Protestant contestants have suffered grievous losses together with the general population. It is seen that there are many factors bringing about violence among sectarian adversaries and their military and paramilitary wings. Successive Whitehall governments never moved far away from supporting the Protestant Unionists and savagely condemning the 'terrorism' of the Catholic nationalists, principally that of their IRA. It was not until the 1980s that secretive exploration of the prospects for peace were steadfastly pursued between London, Belfast and Dublin. The peace agreement of April 1999 was to bring all sides together in a general cease-fire and round of negotiations. The ultimate fashioning of a definitive end to terrorism is still debatable and in the balance:

Contemporary Ulster has to look back over three decades of bloodshed. Mainly since 1969 Northern Ireland has been convulsed by sectarian violence as rival groups have taken arms against each other and against the British army which has been endeavouring to maintain the peace. In that time the casualties and damage have been horrendous, with 3,500 civilians dead, 30,000 injured and a loss to property totalling many millions of pounds. In a province with only 1.6 million people this is a toll that touches nearly everybody in some fashion. Northern Ireland's police force, the Royal Ulster Constabulary (RUC) has had 300 officers killed and over 9,000 wounded. Mainland Britain has tried to staunch the flow of dissolution, at times deploying 20,000 soldiers together with 8,000 armed police, all at a cost of £3 billion a year. Thirty years of carnage have prompted emotional responses in the rest of Britain, which span everything from outrage to scapegoating and, at times, feelings of utter inability to do anything in terms of pacification and conflict solution.

Armed confrontation has brought groups termed 'paramilitaries' face to face. The Nationalist (Catholic) vanguard is led by the Irish Republican Army (IRA) and three other splinter groups. Unionist (Protestant) forces, calling themselves Loyalists, are the Ulster Defence Association (UDA) and again three splinter groups. Altogether, there is an impressive armoury of thousands of rifles, home-made machine-guns and grenade throwers, anti-tank weapons, and a great deal of Semtex and other explosives.

The IRA has acquired notoriety as an agent of destruction. Founded in 1919 as a commando unit against British rule in Ireland, the organisation split three years later with the proclamation of the Irish Free State. The majority of these 'Freedom Fighters' rejected the new state, the minority accepted it with regret. With detachments of British soldiers Whitehall now had to fend off an armed band of insurrectionists who were to be outlawed in 1931 and again in 1935. During the Second World War there were even those in IRA brigades who regarded themselves akin to the French Resistance movement, fighting an army of occupation in the same way. Otherwise, the conflict in Ireland was low-key.

It was in the 1960s that the mood of many Irishmen changed. They became interested in United States protest movements, particularly those connected with the Civil Rights Movement and the Vietnam War. The thrust of their demands had to do with a better deal for Catholics in regard to local government reform and improved housing. As their agitation brought little response both from the Protestant majorities on local councils and from Whitehall, a largely peaceful demonstration by the working class turned sourly into a popular uprising. In Belfast and Londonderry (Derry) barricades went up and angry words gave way to priming of weapons and the making of petrol bombs. By 1969 there were running battles in the streets, a curfew had been imposed and arrests were widespread. The IRA was now on a war footing, though somewhat split between an extreme element, the Provisional IRA (Provos) forming assassination and punishment squads to deal with Loyalist opponents, and a more moderate Official IRA, prepared, so they said, to substitute talk for bullets.

The 1970s brought wavering fortunes for all sides. There was little prospect of any negotiation in a situation now aflame with destruction and death. British use of internment after the rounding up of suspected 'terrorists' merely served as a recruiting office for the IRA. Closing down the Belfast parliament at Stormont in 1972 and the imposition of Direct Rule from London of course angered Nationalists, who saw themselves condemned to live in a British fiefdom, and it also distressed those Unionists who championed the right to substantial self-determination within the orbit of a protective Great Britain. Direct Rule was reimposed in 1974. Violence soared and atrocities were committed by all sides. The English press, reporting outrage after outrage, soon voiced the questions: how can Britain deal with street guerrillas who appear to know what they are against but have little notion of what they are for? How far is it possible to dethrone the martyr-image? Apart from the confrontations with rifle and bomb there was the more political tactic of detainees who resorted to a hunger strike. How was Britain to deal with that?

The Northern Ireland conflict was beginning to enter a different phase as the 1980s brought bombing and murder to places in the Republic of Ireland and to the British mainland. Although the IRA and the Loyalist paramilitaries vilified each other and there was much wringing of hands in British government circles, there now began a series of covert probing by all sides as to the tentative possibilities of settling the conflict. Quite clearly, contestants, the protesters and the security forces, had underestimated the determination of others to keep the action going, and had over-estimated the extent to which they could wear them down. The only rational way out of this was to initiate a peace process. Sinn Féin made clear that they distanced themselves from the violent tactics of the IRA.

Inching forwards, through enquiry and discussion, towards a prospect of peace received frequent hammer blows when town centres were blasted by high explosives and gunmen wreaked havoc. Attempts to bring about an unconditional ceasefire succeeded finally in 1994, only to be aborted two years later when London's prestigious business centre at Canary Wharf and the heart of Manchester suffered immense bomb damage. The British government now made the bottom line of its negotiating position quite clear: no talk without unequivocal repudiation of all violence. Only then would Sinn Féin be allowed a place at the table. Terrorism would never win anything. In South Africa and in the Middle East the ANC and the PLO had been permitted to engage in resolution discussion only when they had agreed to relinquish strategies of violence. As a first step to Northern Ireland's demilitarisation all weapons must be 'decommissioned'. A special commission to devise ways of doing this was to be set up under the chairmanship of Senator George Mitchell from the United States. These moves did not find favour with Sinn Féin. Their simple retort was: remove the circumstances which lead men to resort to arms and the arms will then be laid down. In 1997 there seemed to be an impasse. Decommissioning must be implemented before peace talks began; no decommissioning would be started before peace talks were under way. In autumn 1997 good sense prevailed with the IRA militarists agreeing with their political allies in Sinn Féin that the issue of decommissioning and an end to violence should not block the beginnings of real conflict settlement. 'Speedy demilitarisation of the entire [Northern Ireland] situation' was their demand.

Efforts to design a peace process acceptable to all participants at last brought diminished violence and in April 1998 a peace agreement. There were times in 1997 and 1998 when the very real concessions made by the Nationalists were in danger of being derailed by Unionist disaffection and by the resentful opportunism of their extremists. Would a peace agreement be a sell-out? Would that be surrender? No conflict of interests should be resolved through selling short the basic rights of a majority.[3]

SHARED MEMORIES AS ENERGISERS

Paul Arthur (Apter, 1997) argues that many in Northern Ireland 'use' memories of the past as agents of reinforcement, inspiration and consolidation, and as preludes to purposive action (which may not always be violent). Arthur begins by quoting the description of Denis Donaghue, a fellow-Ulsterman, that memory is 'agglutinative' – memories of the past are kept alive, the refreshed memories justify the events that occur:

> History is only one way of being significant. Memory gives the unofficial sense of history, effects an order not sequential but agglutinative. That is why we never ask our memories to line up rationally or sequentially, like soldiers on parade: they obey our orders, but not always or in the form we prescribe.

The uses of history as memory, not only to keep the past alive but sustain a sense of loss, deprivation, marginalization, not to speak of the affronts, discrimination, prejudice, and the like has sustained the tensed boundaries of the Irish working-class community extremely well and not only in places like Derry or West Belfast. Everywhere in the Six Counties there is evidence of the past. Handed out generationally, the stories of the fall, victimization, colonialization, pariahization, etc., are almost as deeply relevant as were myths of the eternal return among the Jews. Such memory was important not only within Northern Ireland but the Republic and the diaspora as well. For it fed the clienteles. To be sure, to keep alive, and use memory to intensify yearning, fresh events are required. And where the IRA was not the perpetrator, the various Protestant paramilitary organizations obliged.

Between both sides, and of course under the watchful eyes of the British army, there were political events galore.[4]

For Arthur three things stand firm particularly in Ulster memories – the sense of shared 'victimhood', the feeling and fact of dispossession, the concept of striving for emancipation. He finds agreement with Apter in understanding compulsions towards a continuous resistance campaign which becomes, in a black sense, a 'treasured' memory. Opponents are demonised, traditionally so:

The point of departure for contemporary emancipatory movements 'is not equality but *victimhood*. This is what distinguishes them from "old" social movements which fought for equality or greater participation. [. . .]'
    The IRA fits into this model in that they are [a] protest movement which is

> confrontational and violence-prone and relatively uninterested in rectifying this or that economic, social, or political ill, or providing greater political access to those deprived by reason of religion, gender, ethnicity, race, language, class, role, or other affiliations. Such affiliations are interesting only as provocations requiring the violation of standing jurisdictions.

    Viewed from below – and Ireland is essentially a bottom-up society with a demotic culture – in place of civilization and progress people read conquest and dispossession and a loss of patrimony and a historic sense of grievance. Theirs was not

> a world of choice from which some have been excluded but a universe of meaning in which insight is inspired by victimhood and confrontation [where] inversionary discourse is a means of altering prevailing boundaries and jurisdictions on the ground and in the mind. If they reject ordinary claims and demands and remain aloof from negotiation and the bargaining that accompanies democracy the intent is to create moral and symbolic capital in opposition to economic capital.[5]

[There is] a profound sense of piety, a deep sense of history and of grievance, and an essential sense of the contemporaneousness of the past. It is a narrative of dispossession overlaid by a fundamental religiosity secularized by a doctrine of manifest destiny. It is what has sustained Irish nationalism through centuries of failure.[6]

A shared memory of something denied, something lost, something to be fought for, stood proudly in Irish minds as their small independent state was established in the south in 1916. The Republican mission then and now goes further than passive 'remembering' – the past must be made to live and 'live forward', a strategy which Arthur sees the Sinn Féin leader, Gerry Adams, holding to fervently:

The Irish Free State was born with its national ideal unfulfilled, an embittered and armed minority within its boundaries, a humiliating economic reliance on its traditional enemy, the United Kingdom, and an economy which supported too many unproductive people. And yet it endured. Its very endurance was an affront to those who believed that the 1916 rising had been betrayed. They believed that the new political establishment indulged in what the Japanese call *mokusatsu*, that is killing with silence.

The mission of contemporary republicanism is no less than to restore that 'memory', to rediscover Ireland's soul. And that entails tackling all those vested interests who have recreated modern Ireland. It means moving beyond the status of double marginality – the loss of patrimony in the past and the removal of 'voice' in the present. It is a historic task in the heroic mold and it means returning to first principles. It works on the assumption of splendid failure within a characteristic Irish time-frame which

> inclines Irishmen to a repetitive view of history and that such a view inclines them – perhaps in defensive wariness and from fear of failure – to prize the moral as against the actual, and the bearing of witness as against success. The *locus classicus* of this cast of mind is the Proclamation of the Republic on Easter Monday 1916.[7]

In this century the 1916 Rising is the crucial event which explains all others. The President of Sinn Féin, Gerry Adams, has no doubts as to its significance and relevance to today's struggles:

> Oglaigh na hEireann (the IRA) today takes its historical and organizational origins from the forces which engaged in the Easter Rising of 1916, though one can trace its ancestry much further back if one wishes. But the circumstances which shaped the support for the IRA are above all the experience of the barricade days from 1969–72. These days are of continuing importance not just in terms of the IRA but because they saw the development of tremendous communal solidarity, more than a memory of which remains today.

'Memory' again and that umbilical link between 1916 and the barricade days of the 1970s!

The problem with 1916 is that the 'philosophers and political thinkers of the 1916 Rising did not survive it, and this set the stage for counter-revolution. What we have done is that we have taken a step towards reversing the effects of the counter-revolution'. There is an obvious tactical advantage in taking such a step. It removes republicanism from its conspiratorial ethos onto centre-stage as a mass movement built on communal solidarity. It combines the heroic failure of 1916 with the self-reliance and mutual solidarity created in the mobilization spaces of West Belfast, Free Derry and elsewhere. It has a wider *political* meaning:

> We are not engaged in any new departure. We are committed absolutely to the objective of Irish independence. [. . .] In the past the republican

movement was a separatist movement with radical tendencies. In its current embodiment the radical tendency is for the first time in control.

1916 was a significant historical punctuation mark, an exercise in calculated martyrdom whereby the blood of the fallen would irrigate the barren soil and create the climate for a new generation to continue with the struggle. It was another step along the road to national liberation begun by Wolfe Tone in 1798 and continued by the Fenians in the nineteenth century. It was part of a *narrative* – 'the universal desire to make sense of history by retelling the story to ourselves'. Narrative can serve to release new, and hitherto concealed possibilities, of understanding one's history [. . .] the contemporary act of rereading (i.e. retelling) tradition can actually disclose uncompleted narratives which opens up new possibilities of understanding. That was what the 1916 Rising was about. [. . .][8]

Thus, for Northern Ireland's Catholics, the 'four glorious years', 1918–21, strike a note of justified martyrdom, going much further than nostalgia. What the British Government of the day in London condemned as the irresponsible terrorism of gun-battles and fire-raising was for the fighters of Dublin and for their allies further north the arming of a rightful nationalism. When protracted violence re-erupted in Northern Ireland in 1969 the Catholic community was to some extent taken by surprise at first, until past memories bore down upon present reality and in Arthur's words led to a 'circularity' of violence when each side mobilised to defend what it regarded as its civil rights:

[. . .] republicanism was unprepared partially because it had been engaged in its own internal debate. It lacked the resources to defend its community but, paradoxically, that meant a stronger sense of communal solidarity because often it was the ordinary citizen rather than a revolutionary élite which organized the barricades to defend the areas of Catholic west Belfast against an onslaught launched by protestant mobs with RUC complicity. It was in this milieu that the new generation began to assert themselves.

They started with several assets, the most crucial being that 'the whole process was so *natural* as to be beyond comment'. Attitudes were more important than weapons, and that was to be the key to republican strategy: 'Nothing had to be imported, nothing fashioned by ideologues, nothing sold to the people, nothing secretly arranged because of events. All that was needed was to exploit the existing reality'. That reality was based on a memory of past oppressions and the nature of an intimidatory culture with the emphasis on territoriality and the need for vigilance. Settler vigilance, whether in the form of loyalist mobs or locally recruited militias (official and unofficial), 'taught the natives that power and self-assertion were the property of those who could successfully inflict violence'. The result was a circularity of violence whereby 'vigilance of power perpetually generates the symptoms of rebellion it purportedly guards against; while rebellion on the principle of collective responsibility validates the anxieties of the dominant'.

[. . .] sections of Protestant Ulster perceived the civil rights campaign as a challenge to their very existence and entered into a form of public banding because they believed that state power could not monopolize coercive relationships. In that situation 'the whole system is one of threatened violence in which the state is a feeble pivot between its ostensible supporters [. . .] and the natives'.[9]

For the beleaguered Catholics in Northern Ireland there was the predicament that their violent politics of resistance and of sacrifice needed to find a more logical basis for conflict resolution, as Arthur points out:

They [the Republicans] were able to present politics as a narrative of oppression. They found no difficulty in revealing the state's hegemony in incidents like the introduction of internment in August 1971 when only republicans were lifted. They demonstrated their capability to resist compromise when the Northern Ireland government and parliament were prorogued in March 1972. Rather than accept that as a 'victory' they followed the predictable pattern of emancipatory move-ments 'to move from immediate ends to ultimate values and to define their objects in terms of the widest moral imperative'. But by standing outside the normal frame-work of politics 'using doctrine, ideology and theory to challenge the *doxa*' they confront the problem that adherents 'of violence as a political technique need to show that violent acts can have political consequences. They must demonstrate that some kind of exchange relation holds – or can be created – between the worlds of violence and politics'. Equally governments 'need to tread a delicate line between showing that violence is powerless to acquire any kind of political exchange value and formulating the political responses which demonstrate their commitment to its repression'. Irish republicans relied on two components: repression and the eleva-tion of the symbolic side of political life.

It might be argued that Irish political violence of the past twenty years has moved from the extra-institutional protest of the civil rights movement through a politics of oppression to a politics of sacrifice in search of a logical project.[10]

Could it be that memory as an imprint of history and as an impelling force for defen-siveness loses any logical thrust when confronted by the ambiguities of myth? This is a question which has caught the attention of a number of writers on terrorism and something to which we now turn.

MYTHS AS REINFORCERS

Two aspects of the concept of myth seem significant here. First, the conventional understanding of a fictitious story or legend embodying ancient beliefs and inter-pretations. Second, and taking it further, what is known as a *mythopoeia*, the making of myths. We see in some of the other case-studies, those of the Hizbullah, the Montoneros of Argentina, the Tamils of Sri Lanka, the German Baader-Meinhof Group, that myths, perhaps refashioned, can be incorporated quite deliberately into a political repertoire. This is perhaps what Eric Hobsbawm (1995) had in mind when he referred to 'the invention of tradition'. For Kearney (1997) what he terms 'foundational' myths disclose the original sense of the word 'tradition'.

Foundational myths disclose the original meaning of tradition – *tradere* – carrying the past into the present and the present into the past. So myths of tradition may be said to defy the normal logic of *either/or* by conflating not only opposite time-scales but also such opposed orders as living and dead, divine and human, redeemed and damned. Here we are confronted with another logic – that of imagination and dream – where laws of contradiction and causality no longer operate.[11]

Elsewhere, Charles Townshend (in Crenshaw, 1995), writing about political violence in Northern Ireland (especially the terrorism of paramilitaries), sees the myth proving useful there in many ways. Primarily, it is used to mobilise both the revolutionary cadres and the mass of the people. Second, it assists the creation of social solidarity. Third, it may help heal the wounded heroes of a cause in the event of failure:

Mobilization for revolution has two elements that often prove to be as distinct in practice as they can be made in theory. The first is the organization of the revolutionaries; the second the mobilization of the people. Historically, the first has been more common than the second. Irish history contains plenty of examples of this discrepancy. Indeed, a mass rising of the kind expected by most nineteenth-century revolutionaries never happened, even in 1798. None the less, 1798, like 1789 and Year II in France, became a potent myth that mobilized successive generations of revolutionaries. The Anglo–Irish war of 1918–21 fell well short of the ideal type, but through the brilliance of republican publicity, it generated a myth that was at least as potent. These are myths, I would suggest, in the strictly Sorelian sense that they simplify the world sufficiently to make action possible. A nationalist contemplating any actual 'people' would be driven rapidly to loss of faith, if not suicidal despair. Simplification or idealization is the essence of the notion of the *Volksgeist* and the essential condition for nationalist activity. The myth of the nation provides the reason for action; the myth of popular mobilization underwrites the feasibility of action.

   Anarchist terrorists had posited an alternative mechanism of revolutionary violence, propaganda by deed. [. . .] Propaganda would arouse the people, who would ultimately triumph by sheer weight of numbers.

   In Ireland, however, a quite novel mechanism for interlocking revolutionaries and people was emerging at this time – pragmatically rather than theoretically. Michael Collins's repudiation of traditional IRB insurrectionism in favour of guerrilla methods arose naturally out of Irish conditions. The IRA established the viability of the numerical formula first laid down in print by T. E. Lawrence and later the staple of counterinsurgency manuals: 'Rebellions can be made by two per cent active in a striking force and 98 per cent passively sympathetic'. The IRA did not dispense altogether with the old myth of the people. But the new relation provided a more sophisticated basis for the republican claim that they stood for the Irish popular will.[12]

[. . .] The 'four glorious years' of 1918–21 stand out as the climax of the nationalist myth of the 'risen people', a myth whose power has fueled republican intransigence ever since. Defeat in the civil war was accommodated by a cerebral sleight of hand that one penetrating historian has called the 'triumph of failure'. [. . .] But it remains impossible to grasp the nature of the present armed resistance without recognizing the imprint that history lays on it.[13]

[. . .] Even 'total devastation' has proved transient, noiselessly repaired by the deep and steady force of republican sentiment, historically armored against the shock of failure.[14]

Reliance on myth has played some part in influencing the attitudes and actions of Northern Ireland's Protestant Unionists according to Townshend, who instances the mythical association of eighteenth-century Protestant victories when the Orangemen routed the Catholicism of James II, a feat of arms commemorated today (in an oddly derivative style) by asserting a provocative right to march through Catholic housing estates in Londonderry and Belfast. There is also the mythical claim that Ulster's Unionists represent a nation when the single-issue of legitimate hegemony is trumpeted, a call which, in Townshend's view, is now less strident and less dependent on myth:

The loyalist incorporation of history has been, if anything, more vivid and concrete than that of the nationalists. For contemporary Protestants the symbolic weight of the Ulster Covenant and the Ulster Volunteer Force of 1912 is vast and seems to have been transmitted effectively through superficially different organizations like the 'B' Special Constabulary and the Ulster Defence Regiment.[15]

The unionist mobilization into violence at many points prefigured that of the nationalists. It would be hard to say which of the two is likely to prove the more irreducible. Currently, the prestige of loyalist paramilitary organizations (Ulster Defence Association, Ulster Freedom Fighters, Ulster Volunteer Force) is not high, but the Protestant community has its own myths of popular mobilization, which parallel those of the nationalists.

Yet despite pervasive and novel uncertainty about the proper mode of action in the present crisis, there is little sign that fundamental unionist attitudes have become less monolithic in their simplicity. The general notion of a Protestant 'way of life' retains wide currency, and though the visual symbol of King Billy on his white horse may be less in evidence, the old slogans – We will not have Home Rule; No surrender; Not an inch; and, more disreputably, No popery – remain powerfully expressive definitions of the ground on which loyalists are prepared to fight, or at least to threaten to fight by organizing in military fashion. The best observer study of Protestant activism accepted the view that modern paramilitary groups can be seen as products of traditional Northern Ireland society, not subverters of the old order but extreme versions of it. Those who formed and joined them were used to uniforms, punitive discipline, parades, and a system in which one gave and received orders. But they were unfamiliar with democratic organizations and unused to making their own decisions.

There have been a number of attempts to demonstrate that the components of Protestant identity meet the criteria of nationality and that Ulster unionists are thus a nation. None of these demonstrations has been wholly successful, though since in practice the ultimate proof of nationhood is the capacity to vindicate it by force of arms, there is a degree of circularity in all such analysis. Plainly, Ulster Protestants have come close to such self-assertion on several occasions over the last century but have never taken this collective responsibility. At present the principal barrier is lack of confidence in any specific outcome; exponents of United Kingdom integration (the original antidevolution position of 1886), Northern Ireland devolution à la Stormont (with or without power sharing), and Ulster independence vie for support. It is possible that in the future terrorist violence will be used in a bid for control by one of these persuasions, but so far Protestant paramilitarism has been limited to the traditional single-issue politics of communal ascendancy.[16]

While the myth of 'victimisation' is perhaps shared among activists on all sides, it must be among Catholics that it arouses most resonance. 'When it comes to myth,' Kearney has said, 'the past is never past.' Above all, for Townshend, the hunger strikes demonstrated this. He quotes Apter (1997) about the making of myths as political symbols and goes on to present the imprisoned terrorists under the rubric of 'the egoism of victimisation'. In certain eyes, in Belfast and Whitehall, gunmen were audaciously pressing for status as political prisoners. Surely, though, these terrorists were deservedly locked away as common criminals? Arthur (1997) makes the point that starvation to death was a not an unknown form of sacrifice in Ireland and in its modern version it conferred a sacrificial ideology upon a revolutionary one. The prisoners had gone to the Long Kesh gaol not to win but to die:

Apter (1997) may well have had the hunger strikes in mind when he wrote that endowing 'confrontational events with political symbolism is itself a strategy which changes the political process from accountability and consensus to a politics of spectacle, theatre, violence, drama . . .'. Here was a confrontational event imbued with political symbolism which challenged the *doxa* in a highly theatrical manner. While the republican campaign had been launched against the prevailing accountability and consensus no one single incident or event invested as much spectacle as did the hunger strikes. They raise fundamental questions about the place of the IRA in a typology of violence-prone movements; about the extent to which it is an archetype of emancipatory movements; about whether we can 'read' the strikes as a version of the authenticity paradigm which challenges the impersonality of man-made mass deaths and, as such, as an inversion of the death-world; and finally, once again, whether contemporary republicanism has a logical project.

If any one episode explains the resilience of republicanism it is the hunger strikes of 1980–1. The background is simple: since the introduction of internment in 1971 a battle has been waged between the prisoners and the authorities over the question of political status inside the prisons. Republicans considered they were not criminals. Adams (1986) [. . .] insists that the importance of political prisoner status 'has nothing to do with any contempt for the "ordinary criminals" who are so often the victims of social inequality and injustice. From Thomas Ashe to Bobby Sands the concern has always been to assert the political nature of the struggle in which the IRA has been engaged'. Generally the Catholic community shared Adams's belief that the profile of the prisoners was not that of a criminal class. The emotional reaction by the Cardinal (O'Fiach) after a visit to protesting republican prisoners in 1978 was a precursor of things to come: 'they prefer to face death rather than submit to be classed as criminals [. . .] anyone with the least knowledge of Irish history knows how deeply rooted this attitude is in our country's past'.

By putting it in this historical perspective the Cardinal was drawing attention to the fact that before 1980 no less than twelve republicans had starved to death for their beliefs in this century. It was a practice which flourished in pre-Christian times in Ireland [. . .] Sean MacBride, former IRA Chief of Staff and Nobel Peace Prize winner in 1974, argued that 'it was not some isolated political happening of our time but a deep symptom of a historically recurring persecution: "a fall-out resulting from the cruel interference by Britain in the affairs of the Irish nation" '.

More importantly the prisons' campaign made the distinction between a *sacrificial* ideology and the *revolutionary* ideology of the military campaign.[17]

Kearney also takes up sacrificial ideology as demonstrated by the hunger-strikers:

The most dramatic instance of the myth of sacrificial martyrdom in recent times has been the hunger-strike campaigns of republican prisoners in Northern Ireland, culminating in the death of Bobby Sands. The hunger-strikers in the H-Block at Long Kesh were driven by politics but inspired by myth. The distinction is, I believe, important. If asked why they were doing what they were doing, the prisoners would invariably reply – to defeat the British. But if asked why they saw the self-infliction of suffering and hunger to the point of death as a way of doing this, they would point to mottoes by Pearse or McSwiney on their cell walls. The republican hunger-strikers sought to escape their actual paralysis by realigning their plight with a mythico-religious tradition of *renewal-through-sacrifice*. [. . .]

The invocation of this sacrificial rhetoric was to become a conspicuous feature of the Long Kesh campaign. But it was something which operated largely as a pre-reflective password of the tribe, frequently escaping critical analysis. The IRA's ideology of martyrdom inverted what went by the name of normal political logic (at a parliamentary or military level); it subscribed instead to a mythic logic which claimed that defeat is victory, failure is triumph, past is present. [. . .]

The IRA's ideology was sacrificial to the degree that it invoked, explicitly or otherwise, a 'sacred' memory of death and renewal which provided legitimation for present acts of suffering by grafting them onto paradigms of a recurring past. It thus afforded these acts a timeless and redemptive quality. By insisting in 1978 that their prison campaign was 'not ten years old but sixty years old', the IRA were clearly identifying with the long nationalist tradition of the 1916 and Fenian martyrs. On the one hand, to be sure, the Provisionals presented themselves as a highly modernised and pragmatic paramilitary movement. But on the other, they confessed to taking their 'inspiration and experience from the past', that is, 'from the native Irish tradition' founded on 'our Irish and Christian values'.

[. . .] Hunger-strikes were better recruiters than bomb-strikes.[18]

A final point about myth as an energising force is illustrated by a warning of Kearney that reliance upon myth as a motivating and legitimating element may help the process of emancipation, say, when it is related to the myth of a mother-land (to be defended at all costs), yet it may also lead to a hyper-defensive reluctance to engage in dialogue and contemplate concessions towards others. This seems a possibility where so many outside observers deplore and condemn what seems to be the obduracy of Sinn Féin or of the hardline Protestant factions to 'give up the gun'. Those who maintain unwavering loyalty to particular myths tend to exclusive rigidity of outlook and behaviour and this excludes dialogue:

Myth is a two-way street. It can lead to perversion (bigotry, racism, fascism) or to liberation (the reactivation of a genuine social imaginary open to universal hori-zons). If we need to demythologise, we also need to remythologise. And this double process requires a discrimination between authentic and inauthentic uses of myth. For if myths of motherland are often responses to repression, they can also become repressive in their own right. That is why it is necessary to see how myth eman-cipates and how it incarcerates, how it operates as an empowering symbol of identity and how it degenerates into a reactionary idol. At best, myth invites us to reimagine our past in a way which challenges the present status quo and opens up alternative possibilities of thinking. At worst, it provides a community with a strait-jacket of fixed identity, drawing a *cordon sanitaire* around this identity which excludes dialogue with all that is other than itself.

Without mythology, our memories are homeless; we capitulate to the mind-less conformism of fact. But if revered as ideological dogma, and divorced from the summons of reality, myth becomes another kind of conformism, another kind of death. That is why we must never cease to keep mythological images in dialogue with history. [. . .][19]

TERRORISM AS A LEGACY

Arthur also has in mind the generative force of memories, myths and symbols in deepening the attitudes and the resilience of sectarian combatants and the mainly passive, wider society supporting them. For him the length and intensity of this civil strife suggest that history 'has been fashioned as a weapon' and that it represents a 'culture of violence':

This has not been simply a low-intensity 'war' but also a campaign of attrition visited primarily on civilian communities conducted often by their *soi-disant* defenders (and often with the complicity of the community). But they also mask the degree to which the violence is 'controlled' as if it operated under strict rules of the game – unlike Lebanon from the 1970s or former Yugoslavia where ethnic conflict had been kept under artificial wraps for a generation or more and then exploded with an intense ferocity.[20]

Thirty years of sectarian divide and violence in Northern Ireland have caused most observers to ask: 'why does it go on?' For Townshend, at least, this three-decades-long persistence of 'latent civil war' calls for continuing investigation and he suggests that political violence persists because public perceptions come to regard it as an end in itself. It conveys a message and a clearly understood one, more within Ireland than outside. Yet, the configurations of the conflict are never entirely clear and there is a mesh of relationships between explosive militarism and cautious political moves which probably begs the question of how effective terrorist violence really can be. Some of the momentum is carried forward often in a loose and episodic fashion by paramilitary elements on both sides of the divide. Townshend's question in conclusion is a troubling one: has terrorism assumed a 'normality' in Ulster that seems in some respects permanent without ever offering a solution?:

Political violence persists because it is effective. Its efficacy is the primary condition of its adoption, readoption, legitimation, and containment. This is not to deny that at certain periods or levels of conflict there can emerge what has been called a subculture of violence, in which for organizational or psychological reasons violence becomes self-validating, or autotelic. Walter put the distinction with typical lucidity: 'As long as terror is directed to an end beyond itself, namely control, it has a limit and remains a process. [. . .] Under certain conditions, terror becomes unlimited and therefore no longer a process but an end in itself. [. . .]'

So the crucial question about the process of terror is not How much damage was caused? but What message did the damage convey? The message may or may not approximate the one intended by the terrorists. A longish list of possible messages could be drawn up without much difficulty: it would include We are strong enough to do this; We mean business; Our opponents cannot protect you; and so on. In the case of the IRA it is evident that all these kinds of statements made by acts of violence were grasped at quite an early stage, certainly by 1921. Despite many vicissitudes in the intervening years, the IRA has never lost sight of this deliberate application of harm as communication. Most important, such messages were on the whole clearly understood by their principal audience, the Catholic community in the six counties.

By contrast, these acts have communicated radically different messages to their secondary audiences, the British public and the northern unionists. [. . .]

The theoretical capacity of terror to fracture the state as the symbol of public order and clamorously to break the monopoly of legitimate coercive power (which organized criminals also break, but quietly) has been effective only within ethnic limits. Outside them the paradoxical outcome has been, if anything, reinforcement of the attitudes and policies the IRA needed to undermine. This has been as clear at the practical, administrative level – where the suspension of the devolved Northern Ireland legislature and its replacement by direct British rule in 1972 looked at first like a republican success but has come in time to be a larger obstacle to their aims – as at the attitudinal level, where an ingrained British reaction has been the refusal to 'give way to force' whatever its cause.

[. . .] Any complacent notion that the level of violence has become 'acceptable' to either the authorities or the communities is soon ruptured by periodic outrages, but sheer force of habit has made many of the trappings of guerrilla terrorism practically invisible. It is possible that basic assumptions about the nature of normality have altered over the twenty years of irregular warfare; certainly nobody in Britain in 1969 would have believed it possible for troops to maintain public order for more than a few months at most. Force of circumstance may be driving the six counties to a form of political life that is permanent and yet in no sense a solution.[21]

THE PEACE AGREEMENT

In the wake of thirty years of terror, April 1998 brought a breakthrough in the shape of all-party consensus. This was the so-called April Agreement which is summarised by Whittaker (1999):

The April Agreement has three strands: a democratically elected assembly with executive and legislative authority protecting the rights and interests of all; a North–South Ministerial council for consultation, cooperation and action on matters of mutual interest; a British–Irish council representing Belfast, Edinburgh and Cardiff. Human Rights are to be protected through a possible Bill of Rights. Arms are to be decommissioned within two years. Provision is to be made for improved security liaison and for prisoner release.

Throughout Great Britain the settlement of April 1998 was greeted with immense relief. Was the conflict of thirty years now brought to an end? Apart from understandable hyperbole there remained areas of concern and controversy. As in all moves towards conflict settlement, it is difficult for negotiating participants to encourage their followers to accept the compromises and concessions they feel bound to make.[22]

Given that the April Agreement remains in the fullest sense unratified two and a half years later, the opinion recorded above seems something of an understatement. There is general dismay, markedly in all sections of Northern Ireland's society, that the promise of settlement and of reconciliation remains uncertain. There is an ominous shadow unless arms are finally 'decommissioned'. There is the suspicion that the handgun rules.

THE PROBLEM OF DISARMAMENT

The prospect of an end to terrorism in Northern Ireland raises many debatable issues in regard to timing, intentions, and the extent to which a final and pacific laying down of arms can be guaranteed. Three questions, especially, seem difficult to answer. First, which sectarian groups can be relied upon to bring objectivity and consistency to the implementation of peace? Second, what is the extent of the usable weapon stocks held by rivals in conflict? Third, how far is general disarmament likely to be successful?

First of all, it is very clear that the sectarian divide is fragmented. Catholic Sinn Féin's militarists in the Irish Republican Army (IRA) have broken away into such groups as the Dissident IRA, the Real IRA, and the Continuity IRA or Continuity Army Council. Then there is the Irish National Liberation Army (INLA). Recently, members of Catholic Reaction Force have been associated with arson and targeted killings. Altogether, these groups account for possibly 600 well-armed men with doubtless many hundreds of tacit supporters in Catholic areas. On the Protestant Unionist flank there are half a dozen identifiable groups, by no means all committed to violence – the Ulster Unionists, the Ulster Democratic Party, the Ulster Volunteer Force (UVF), the Loyalist Volunteer Force (LVF), and the Ulster Defence Association or Ulster Freedom Fighters. Numbers may approximate those of their Catholic rivals. Again, there is a tenuous observance of the cease-fire by the vigilante elements in the two last-named bands. (A much more liberal (and pacific) Third Force is made up of the Labour Coalition, the Socialist and Democratic Labour Party (SDLP) and the Alliance Party.) What is unpredictable and, of course, worrying is the degree to which latent terrorism is, as it were, under wraps. While all parties declare that it would be inadmissible to reject disarmament, few seem ready openly to give up their arms. Even if terror is completely dispelled, embittered extremists may step up violence.

Second, the resumption of terrorism is always a possibility so long as considerable weapon stocks are covertly kept in being. Dependable figures are hard to come by, at least in public revelations. There is every reason to credit the existence of many thousands of assault rifles, handguns, machine-guns, several tons of Semtex and other plastic and commercial explosives, mortars, grenade launchers, flame throwers and large amounts of material for Molotov Cocktails. Reportedly, the IRA has fair supplies of anti-tank weapons and several rocket launchers.

Third, there is the problem of disarmament or 'decommissioning'. This has been a complex affair despite the loudly voiced statements of numerous Ulster politicians putting the situation in simple, non-negotiable terms. Sinn Féin's wish has been to put the arms matter to one side until they were allowed to sit in the new power-sharing executive the April Agreement envisaged. Unionists would have No Truck With Armed Terrorists. Neither party was comfortable with the British Government's compromise suggestion in 1998–99 that talks about disarmament and representation could proceed in tandem. There has always been an element of the zero-sum game in the rhetoric: 'If it's good for them, it must be bad for us'. Certainly, for paramilitary activists, the IRA and the Unionists any handing in of arms, without firm guarantees by others, represents 'surrender'. There is little understanding of the position taken by South African and Israeli guerrillas, who realised they had to make sacrifices for the sake of peace.

Already in January 1996 there were firm recommendations from the Mitchell Commission set up in Belfast to frame proposals for disarmament. It was a three-man body, composed of United States senator George Mitchell, Canadian general John de Chastelain, and former Finnish premier Harri Holkeri. Their advice was that the British Government abandon the demand that paramilitaries give up their weapons before all-party talks could begin. Unequivocal negotiations and independent verification would call all bluffs.

Two years later, in April 1998, no discernible progress had been made in getting rid of weapons. The Mitchell requirements for the laying down of arms were made very clear in their contribution to the sixty-seven page text of the April Agreement, that 'Moment of History' as the Irish press saw it:

All participants reaffirm their commitment to the total disarmament of all paramilitary organisations. They also confirm their intention to use any influence they have to achieve the decommissioning of all paramilitary arms within two years following endorsement in referendums north and south of the agreement and in the context of the implementation of the overall settlement.

The Independent Commission (the Mitchell Commission) will monitor, review and verify progress in the decommissioning of illegal arms, and will report to both governments (London and Dublin) at regular intervals.[23]

POSTSCRIPT

The position about decommissioning is still one of waiting for things to begin. Ulster Unionists partnering Republican Sinn Féin in a new Northern Ireland executive temporarily left the executive in February 2000 since complete IRA decommissioning had not been started by February 2000 and would not be completed by May 2000. Whitehall and Dublin prefer the term 'putting the weapons beyond use' to 'decommissioning' as a spur to convincing terrorists on all sides that laying aside weaponry is a voluntary and trustworthy act. In May 2000, two independent 'inspectors', from South Africa and Finland, were to inspect IRA arms dumps, sealed but not finally destroyed. For the first time in thirty years tension in Ulster is dramatically lower and British army numbers have been much reduced.

Sanguine expectations and plain speaking were to rid Northern Ireland of terrorism. They have not done so at the time of going to print. One suspects that memories and myths have some consequence in this failure. United States Senator George Mitchell in 1999 finished a five-year term in Belfast as mediator. His patience and diplomatic ingenuity are now legendary. In April 1996, when terrorism was still rampant in Northern Ireland, he spoke of the violence around him in very direct terms:

There is a powerful desire for peace [. . .] that desire creates the present opportunity. [. . .] All sides must forget their vast inventories of historical recriminations. [. . .] What is really needed is a decommissioning of mind-sets.[24]

Chapter 8

Argentina

THIS CASE-STUDY OF TERRORISM in Argentina describes an experience which, for most Argentinians today, has been enigmatic and macabre. For almost forty years they have had to live in an atmosphere of uncertainty and danger where hopes have been raised through the promises of charismatic politicians, where the collapse of those promises led to frustration and bitterness and when, as regimes elbowed one another out of the way, bewilderment and alienation divided class, families, and friends. Outrage focused hostilities, enmity sparked violence. Worst of all, the free-for-all became a combat zone for all sorts of terrorists, individuals bent on vengeance, political activist groups settling old scores, and state-sponsored killers on the rampage.

The subject of this study, the group called the Montoneros, originated in 1968 as a small-centred and unarmed response to a perceived need for revolutionary change. Circumstances were such that the scenario became in time a paroxysm of indiscriminate violence. The story of how it developed in that way is an intriguing and disconcerting one.

THE ONSET OF POLITICAL VIOLENCE

Argentina is South America's second largest country, one million square miles altogether. Of its 34 million people, one in five came from Europe as immigrants between 1850 and 1940. Some 92 per cent claim to be Roman Catholic. There are 80 per cent who are townspeople and one in three live in or around the capital, Buenos Aires. Richard Gillespie (1982) describes the onset of Argentina's violence:

Argentina's history has been marked by considerable violence since the country emerged as an independent state early in the nineteenth century. Conflict between unitarians and federalists was prevalent in the early decades of nationhood, and in the twentieth century military interventionism and popular rebellion have contributed to political instability. However, explanations of the 1970s violence that rely heavily on the country's political culture are unconvincing, since there are other Latin American countries – such as Mexico – that have distinctly stronger traditions of political violence yet failed to generate a significant guerrilla or terrorist movement in that decade, in part because they possessed a more effective political system.

Since the Second World War, Argentina had experienced extreme political polarisation, which still greatly affected political outlooks and behaviour in the 1970s, militating against the democratic spirit of compromise. The perception of Argentina as a 'dependent' country encouraged nationalists to see problems in terms of a crude imperialism-versus-nation dichotomy; and for some of them, the rise of popular nationalism in the twentieth century led to further reductionism, with the nation identified with the people and imperialism with the oligarchy.

The military overthrow of [President Juan] Perón in 1955 produced much greater polarisation not only because force was used to remove the first Argentine government to be elected on the basis of universal suffrage but also because the ensuing Aramburu government was vindictively and violently anti-Peronist. It sought to completely eliminate Peronism from Argentina, even to the extent of outlawing public reference to Perón and removing Eva Perón's mortal remains from the country. When the Peronists attempted a halfhearted and badly coordinated civilian–military uprising themselves in 1956, Aramburu authorised the execution of twenty-seven rebels after their surrender, thereby showing his contempt for half the population. Between 1955 and 1973, Argentina's major popular movement, Peronism, either was prevented by proscriptions from participating in the political system or, when allowed to win elections (as in 1962), saw the results nullified by the military.

Besides profound political polarisation, there was broad disillusionment with political democracy. Representative democracy had been introduced only in the twentieth century and had been subverted repeatedly by military interventions since 1930. Moreover, its quality under the early Perón governments of 1946–55 upset part of Argentina because of Peronism's less liberal facets. The fact that democracy never became consolidated engendered a broad cynicism that affected attitudes towards political parties, as did the corruption associated with previous Radical and Peronist governments. By the late 1960s there existed among the middle classes considerable scepticism concerning constitutional-party political activity, as well as an awareness that the post-1966 military regime headed by Onganía was not going to allow a return to even this limited type of activity – at least, not unless obliged to do so by popular pressure.

Sociologically, most of the violence of the 1970s was the product of a middle class that had become deeply fragmented. A modernisation process that had begun in the 1950s had not succeeded in preventing precipitous national economic decline but had affected the cultural climate. Traditional institutions such as schools, the family, and the church were losing their effectiveness as socialising agencies. The middle class had lost much of its cohesion, and intransigence grew among its competing fragments. While the established sectors of the middle classes still tended to look to traditional values and institutional supports (ultimately the military), the young generation was swept by new cultural influences. Argentina's youth turned in great numbers against an older generation they blamed for their declining career prospects and the lack of effective political participation. Thus, there was an important element of children rebelling against parents in the rise of the guerrilla units, most of whose recruits were in their twenties; for them, 'violence became the predominant communication strategy'.

The appeal of violent forms of radical action was enhanced by the apparent effectiveness of armed struggle (and more generally of voluntarism) in Cuba, a country altogether different from Argentina yet a country that had experienced a student revolution and was linked to Argentina through the presence of Che Guevara in the revolution and through the subsequent efforts of revolutionary Peronist, John William Cooke, to implant [Guevara's] *foquismo* at home. Guevara's most influential contribution lay arguably in helping to export the myth and mystique of the *guerrillero heroico*, which encouraged many young Latin Americans to risk their lives in the name of a superior morality.

In contrast with this new Latin American revolutionary current inspired by Cuba, the traditional Argentine Left held little attraction for young people. The Communist party's working-class following, which had been substantial in the 1930s, had been lost since the rise of Peronism, and the Socialist party had embarked upon a course of terminal fragmentation in the 1950s. The traditional Left collectively had made the mistake of equating Peronism with fascism and as a result became isolated from the mass movement. Peronism's continuing hold over the working class after 1955 produced great frustration for the classical Left, whose youth groups responded by turning to armed struggle or by reconsidering the merits of Peronism, or both.[1]

THE BIRTH OF THE MONTONEROS

A small group of students, a dozen or so, met in 1968 to call zealously for a new Argentina, one based on egalitarianism and one shorn of ultra-conservative élitism. Crassweller (1987) has described their beginnings:

Unknown as individuals, they still numbered in June 1970 only the original twelve, now hardened by their two years of preparation. Of the founders, few had come to maturity as Peronists and there had been little or no leftist influence on their development. Their political origins were in conservative and traditional Catholicism, and in the organisation known as the Tacuara, an action-oriented right-wing organisation of the firmest persuasion, coloured by Falangist principles. But ideology in a pure sense was secondary in the development of these militants. Nationalism was a more potent driving force, and so was the psychological commitment to violent and direct action. These were the two constants in their evolution, and it was a coincidence of the times, in the form of their encounter with radical Catholicism and the indoctrination offered by left-wing priests, that gave precise contours to those two forces. Nationalism and direct action were now blended with radical Catholic notions of social justice, and the progression to revolutionary Peronism came naturally.

That transition was immeasurably facilitated by the Creole personality that the early Montoneros cultivated, doubtless sincerely: 'a union of men and women who are profoundly Argentine and Peronist', in the words of the early Montonero communiqué. Resistant to Marxism, as others of the extremists were not, the Montoneros drew upon historic imagery and legend. Their very name revived old deeds now embellished with myth, for the original Montoneros were the bands of rough gaucho horsemen who had fought behind their *caudillos* in the era of independence. In their field operations that were soon to come against banks, military posts, and similar targets, the reborn Montoneros were sometimes garbed in the blue of the national flag. Their interviews and pronouncements invoked the metaphors and symbols of the national past. Their motto was itself an affirmation of the extremism and the resistance to compromise that was so striking [. . .] [it was] 'All or Nothing'.[2]

Writing some years earlier, Gillespie (1982) has looked closely at the origins of the Montoneros:

The Montoneros arrived on the Argentine political scene during some of the stormiest years of social conflict ever experienced by their country. Founded two years after the 1966 usurpation of power by General Juan Carlos Onganía and the Armed Forces, they devoted two years to preparatory training and the accumulation of resources before announcing their existence to the world in May 1970.

An initial glance at the political backgrounds of prominent early Montoneros presents the observer with an enigma: many of the young men and women who took up arms in the late 1960s and early 1970s in pursuit of popular nationalist and socialist ideals had gained their political baptism in branches of the traditionally-conservative Catholic Action (AC); some had even started out in the Falange-inspired Tacuara; very few originated on the Left, and hardly any began their political lives as Peronists. Later they were to paint a retrospective self-portrait which presented the birth of their organization as a synthesis of Peronist and Guevarist currents. The portrayal was ideologically ahistorical, but highly revealing nevertheless: its rationale was that the Montoneros set out to fuse urban guerrilla warfare, an adaption of Che Guevara's *foco* theory, with the popular struggles of the Peronist Movement, in other words to unify vanguard and mass activity. They thus characterized themselves in a manner which emphasised strategies and methods rather than political and ideological definitions and, in passing, through omission, sought to obscure the fact that most Montonero pioneers were initially anything but revolutionaries.[3]

Fundamentally, it was the exciting promises of Perón that brought a flood of young people into the Peronista movement in 1970–73 and many of them to rally to the banner of the Montoneros – the spearhead of *Tendencia Revolucionaria*, the revolutionary advance. Gillespie (1982) describes how, from diverse backgrounds, they saw themselves championing the cause of social justice and national unity:

The radicalization process of the late 1960s and early 1970s, more often than not accompanied by 'peronization', was thus quite extensive, most directly a product of political and cultural factors, and greatly stimulated by the authoritarianism of the military regime – a regime whose repressive methods were at times brutal, always unsophisticated, but never efficient. For many, Peronism was perceived merely as a popular alternative; tens of thousands, however, came to take Perón's radical rhetoric at face value and embrace Peronism as a genuinely revolutionary alternative. Their naivety, their readiness to accept the Movement's myths, was not merely a matter of youthful romanticism but of the need of people from liberal or reactionary backgrounds to *prove themselves* as Peronists. It was their way of atoning for the past, their way of establishing their credentials in a Movement which has always emphasized loyalty to the leader and doctrinal orthodoxy as virtues. At the same time it should be remembered that those of Montonero orientation were defining or redefining themselves within the confines of a long-standing strain of Argentine political culture, and that which was arguably the most authentically national and Latin American: they conformed to the tendency to support and trust personalities rather than policies, leaders rather than organizations; and they shared in their political methods the individualism of an immigrant society, and the preparedness to use violent direct action to achieve political objectives, especially when the political force of anti-Peronism rested primarily upon the armed force of the Argentine military. In drawing together radical Catholicism, nationalism, and Peronism into a populistic expression of socialism, the Montoneros brought together a whole wealth of historical legitimacy into something which attracted civilians of diverse political denominations: Catholic militants, popular nationalists, authoritarian but populistic nationalists, recruits from the traditional Left, combative Peronists. The original group contained no outstanding theoretician, yet its very pragmatism was as often a source of strength as of weakness in the early years, facilitating tactical flexibility and the forging of political alliances. Emphases differed: some members saw the goal as a national variant of socialism; others envisaged it as a socialist form of national revolution. All, however, saw the 'principal contradiction' affecting Argentina in terms of imperialism versus the nation, and the latter's interests as represented by a popular but multi-class alliance. Indeed, due to their relegation of class struggle to a secondary plane and their devotion to a leader who had in power sponsored class harmonization, it can be said that the Montoneros were less 'leftist' to the extent that they were Peronist, and vice versa. They presented their organization as a champion of the people, *el pueblo*, because they were not working class themselves; and, rather than seek the 'workers state' aspired to by the non-Peronist revolutionary Left, their central commitments were to national development, social justice, and 'popular power'.[4]

THE APPEAL OF ARMED STRUGGLE

Were those who founded the Montoneros practitioners of terrorism from the beginning? Gillespie in 1982 finds no straightforward answer to this question. In the first place, their early position was that of a peaceful and essentially defensive polemic:

At no time during the 1970s did the Montoneros appear capable of leading a popular revolution or of seizing State power by military means: indeed, they themselves classified much of that decade as phases of 'defensive' struggle. Their relevance lies not in political triumph, but rather in their serving as an illustration of both the potential and the limitations of a strategy which numerous left-wing and national liberation movements have experimented with in recent years. No account of the Montonero experience would be complete, however, if it merely discussed the trials and tribulations of an organization of urban guerrillas. The Montoneros started out as such, but rapidly developed into a radical nationalist movement which, when permitted openly and legally to mobilize political support, did so, and did so impressively. Tens and even hundreds of thousands of Argentines rallied behind their banners in the heady months of 1973–74.[5]

Second, the violence that was breaking out in Argentina in the early 1970s was sporadic and multifaceted:

The insurgent forces included dozens of tiny groups that attempted to initiate guerrilla warfare in the late 1960s. Among them, five grew to become the most significant organizations of the early 1970s, these being the People's Revolutionary Army (ERP), the Montoneros, the Peronist Armed Forces (FAP), the Revolutionary Armed Forces (FAR), and the Armed Forces of Liberation (FAL). The picture became further simplified around 1973, when some guerrillas decided that changed circumstances counselled the termination of their armed struggle. With the military relinquishing office, free elections being held, and Perón returning to Argentina, some Peronists, chiefly associated with the FAP, responded to new opportunities for open political activity. Meanwhile, those who held on to a perspective of armed struggle became polarized around the leading Peronist guerrilla organization, the Montoneros, and the Marxist ERP.

Third, the differing perspectives of insurgent groups steered some of them, in particular, the Montoneros, to embrace Che Guevara's theory of foquismo, the notion that armed struggle was the most effective way of bringing about revolutionary conditions, a climate of change achieved for the waiting masses. The Montoneros did not hesitate to prime their weapons:

Influenced by Guevarism, the Montoneros initially saw themselves as a 'politico-military organization', whereas under the influence of the Chinese and Vietnamese models, the originally Trotskyist ERP envisaged itself as the embryo of a people's army under the direction of the Workers' Revolutionary Party (PRT), although in practice the membership of the PRT–ERP remained undifferentiated. Cuban and Asian influences were combined in both cases, although the nationalistic Montoneros never made international acknowledgements in public. As they grew, the Montoneros became more interested in Mao's writings on warfare and set about constructing a Montonero army directed by a Montonero party, and the ERP's admiration for Cuba was reflected in its decision to launch a rural foco in the province of Tucumán in 1974.[6]

It is the term 'terrorist' when applied to the Argentinian scenario that Gillespie, writing in 1995, views with caution:

The propensity to view these organizations as 'terrorist' was always greater outside Argentina than within. Certainly the organizations did not conceive of themselves as 'terrorist'. They associated terrorism with former anarchists of the 'propaganda by the deed' school, contemporary neofascist groups and the extreme left-wing European groups that resorted to violence after the collapse of the 1960s student movements. Their differences with these groups were not just ideological but concerned methods. While others sought to effect change through their own initiatives, even where the initiatives were designed to detonate a social explosion, the Argentine insurgents saw themselves as forming part of a popular movement and developing therein a people's war strategy in the belief that the movement could not triumph without its own armed forces. Only when the attempt to involve the masses in their strategy was clearly foundering, in the mid-1970s, did the Montoneros confront the state in a more conventional military fashion that involved substituting themselves for the masses far more consciously, yet even then their refusal to target innocent civilians set them apart from modern European terrorists. The Argentines' use of violence became less discriminate, but they never viewed the bombing of crowded public places as productive.

Nor did the Argentine public generally regard the insurgents as 'terrorists'. In the context of mounting popular opposition to a discredited and repressive military regime established by General Onganía in 1966, there was considerable reluctance to condemn the rebels, especially since many of their early deeds involved only symbolic violence, aimed against property rather than people. Public perceptions changed somewhat as the violent campaigns were stepped up, but the ERP's ill-fated adventure in Tucumán at least helped reinforce their 'guerrilla' image. For some observers the Montoneros' resort to less discriminate violence after 1974 was at least 'understood' in view of the activity of the Triple A death squad established by right-wing Peronists in 1973. For some, the violence of the Triple A and the 'dirty war' initiated by the armed forces in 1975 (first in Tucumán and then nationally) made greater guerrilla violence, including attacks on civilian political opponents, seem more legitimate.

Analytically, a distinction between terrorist, referring to terror-inspiring methods and agents, and urban guerrilla warfare, 'a form of unconventional war waged in urban and suburban areas for political objectives' and seen within the broader perspective of a people's war, is essential for any understanding of the guerrilla movements of Argentina and Uruguay.[7]

Guerrilla warfare in rural areas, as Guevara had called for and as the Cubans had practised, was a form of armed struggle that did not much appeal to the Montoneros – at any rate, in the beginning Argentina had a distinctive, significantly urban geography:

Efforts to apply *foquismo* after 1959 in mainland countries had ended in calamity. Guevara's own 1967 death in Bolivia had demonstrated how much better prepared US and Latin American counter-insurgency agencies were to rapidly respond to guerrilla activity in the countryside, and persuaded many revolutionaries of the need to take greater cognisance of the peculiar characteristics of their own countries when devising strategies.

In looking to urban guerrilla warfare in 1968, the Montoneros acknowledged the geographical isolation of the rural pioneers. Of Argentina's 23 million inhabitants, about 75 per cent were urbanites, living in towns of over 2,000 residents. Virtually half the population was concentrated in the City and Province of Buenos Aires, and two-thirds in this region plus the adjoining provinces of Santa Fe and Córdoba. The remaining one-third populated nineteen out of the twenty-two provinces. Yet, while avoiding geographical isolation, the Montonero strategy militated in favour of social isolation. Experience had suggested to most working-class activists that their strength lay in collective industrial muscle rather than in firearms. Economic constraints upon working-class involvement with the guerrillas were, moreover, often prohibitive. Workers might collaborate or sympathize with the guerrillas, but few could afford to go underground as 'professional' combatants, especially when married and with their wage as the sole financial support of themselves and their dependants. Middle-class radicals had considerably greater economic independence here, and students, whose university studies normally lasted five or six years, had much more time available for the demanding life of the *guerrillero*. Not surprisingly then, urban guerrilla warfare in Latin America prospered most in Argentina and Uruguay, both highly urbanized countries with huge, culturally sophisticated middle classes, increasingly affected by the curbing of political and cultural liberties as governments in each country introduced authoritarian controls along with unpopular economic measures.[8]

To be effective a Montoneros struggle, if an armed one, had to be an urban guerrilla campaign:

The ERP and Montoneros' urban guerrilla strategy did not rule out some of the activities associated with European terrorist groups, such as bank raids and kidnappings of business leaders, especially those representing foreign corporations. However, the proceeds from such activities were put to a much more ambitious use by the Argentines – the building of an army capable of eventually defeating their country's standing army – instead of being used simply to finance and escalate a campaign of terror. The guerrillas became more 'militaristic' as their vision of fomenting a people's war faded, and they were drawn increasingly into the reactive violence of vengeance killings as the conflict developed. None the less, the objects of their violence were well-defined political enemies, and about 70 per cent of their victims were men under arms. The eventual wearing of uniforms by both the ERP and the Montoneros in their guerrilla operations symbolically reinforces the view that their violence essentially belonged to the domain of warfare, though to a strategically disastrous urban-guerrilla variant of it. In the case of their attacks on foreign businessmen, they may perhaps be regarded as having employed terrorist *tactics*, or as having entered a penumbra separating urban guerrilla warfare from terrorism, but these attacks were subordinate to an overall politico-military strategy.[9]

The Montoneros leadership, certainly in its early days, was quick to realise, as Gillespie puts it, that their political objectives would not be secured solely through the force of their own firepower:

Their ambition to develop into people's armies ensured that in the early phase of warfare the careful cultivation of popular sympathy and support was paramount. Thus, the early guerrilla actions were predominantly acts of 'armed propaganda': the hijacking of food-delivery vans for distribution in shanty towns, the bombing of buildings and monuments to mark Peronist and Guevarist anniversaries, the destruction of élite country clubs and the premises of foreign multinationals, brief commando-style occupations of small towns near to Buenos Aires and Córdoba, and so on.

However, even in this early phase there were some actions that were closer to the domain of terrorism than to urban-guerrilla warfare, the targets being civilians. Trade-union leaders Vandor and Alonso were assassinated; there were several Montonero attacks on enemies within the Peronist movement; and a number of foreign business executives were kidnapped and a few killed (although the level of business abductions was far lower than in 1973–75). Yet even these acts of violence were not universally condemned.

Evidently, during the early phases of guerrilla warfare, some acts of violence were repudiated by the social groups whose support the guerrillas were seeking to cultivate. Yet the incidents most likely to cause outrage were greatly outnumbered by the kind of Robin Hood actions and spectacular stunts that had already endowed the Tupamaros in neighbouring Uruguay with something of a romantic image. And sympathy for the guerrillas was rekindled periodically by illegal repressive actions on the part of the state.[10]

THE MONTONEROS DEVISE A STRATEGY

The Montoneros appear to have been influenced by contrasted strategic influences: the one, the revolutionary urgings in the 1960s of a Spanish Civil War veteran, Abraham Guillén; and the other, the classical theories of Carl von Clausewitz (translated for Argentina in 1976). This is the opinion of Gillespie in 1982:

Apart from advocacy of the urban setting, much of Guillén's writing simply publicized classical formulae for guerrilla struggle. Hence: 'Operations should consist of scattered surprise attacks by quick and mobile units superior in arms and numbers at designated points but avoiding barricades in order not to attract the enemy's attention at one place. The units will then attack with the greatest part of their strength the enemy's least fortified or weakest links in the city'. The struggle would be 'prolonged', consisting of 'many small military victories which together will render the final victory', but it would not be an exclusively military affair. Without a positive orientation towards working-class and popular struggles, without a conscious effort by combatants to coordinate their activities with these and progressively incorporate the masses at large into an eventual liberation army, revolutionary warfare would degenerate into terrorism. Guillén therefore urged a 'total war: economic, social (strikes), demonstrations, protests against the cost of living, isolated violent actions, well-directed propaganda, [and] a coherent international policy, but all combined with the liberation army and the guerrillas (located at the enemy's back)'.[11]

Was Guillén's concept of 'total war' likely to bring the Montoneros to outright terrorism after all? Gillespie (1982) stresses in a note what is for him an important distinction:

The terms 'terrorism' and 'terrorist' refer to terror-inspiring methods and agents, and, though often used loosely in political invective, do not properly characterize the Montoneros. Political terror is concerned with 'the use of coercive intimidation by revolutionary movements, regimes, or individuals for political motives'; 'Political terrorists always resort to political murder in order to induce the psychic state of terror' (Paul Wilkinson, *Political Terrorism* (London: Macmillan, 1974), pp. 11–12). Anti-State terrorists set out to intimidate and to show that the State is incapable of guaranteeing public security and order. The more indiscriminate and unpredictable their violence, the more likely they are to succeed in their objectives. But those who engage in urban guerrilla warfare – 'a form of unconventional war waged in urban and suburban areas for political objectives' (Idem, *Terrorism and the Liberal State* (London: Macmillan, 1977), p. 60) – are after the conquest of State power by means of a politico-military strategy which demands considerable public support and involvement. Their violence therefore tends to be both discriminate and predictable, though it often provokes a far less discriminate backlash. Whereas terrorists may regard innocent civilians at legitimate targets, urban guerrillas generally limit their attacks to State agents (especially military and police personnel) and clearly defined political enemies (often associated in some way with State or right-wing violence). Since their activities were guided by aims to incorporate rather than terrorize ordinary people, the Montoneros and Tupamaros should properly be regarded as urban guerrillas. However, urban guerrilla warfare and political terrorism are not always mutually exclusive phenomena. Whether or not individual acts of violence should be classified as instances of terrorism depends greatly upon specific circumstances, for terror is 'a subjective experience' (*Political Terrorism*, p. 11). And terrorism may be employed by urban guerrillas as an 'auxiliary weapon' (ibid., p. 38) especially when they are weak and socially isolated. Nevertheless, it must be stressed that insurrectional partisan violence in Argentina has been devoid of the random terrorism (bombs in crowded public places) witnessed in recent years by Europeans.[12]

As for von Clausewitz, his thesis for the Argentinians was that 'the defensive form of warfare is intrinsically stronger than the offensive'. Well-directed strikes, then, might put decisive punch into a total, revolutionary war. Fatefully, though, as Gillespie suggests, these twin influences failed to achieve the extent of military and political success for which Montoneros enthusiasts were waiting:

As the guerrillas saw it, the Armed Forces had launched an offensive against the Argentine people in 1966, but one which could be contained by a defensive campaign of exhausting the enemy, prior to a counter-offensive by the popular forces. Clausewitz had never advocated pure defense, since war by definition has to be waged by both sides. Rather, his was a relative concept of defense, one which included offensive battles, for 'the defensive form of war is not a simple shield, but a shield made up of well-directed blows'. The analogies were of course far-fetched, but just about sustainable: they involved the application of vintage discussion about the advisability of waiting and parrying when an enemy advances (on the basis that 'it is easier to hold ground than take it') to a situation where the enemy had, in a sense, already triumphed, through seizing State power, and where its 'attack' now took the form of military decrees.

The Montoneros envisaged a popular war, Guillén class warfare in its fullest sense, yet in practice this war was neither decreed by the people nor by the working class: only by a handful of combative middle-class youths, so few in number that their attempts to apply Clausewitz to the concrete jungles of Buenos Aires, Córdoba, and Rosario would seem with hindsight patently ridiculous had the outcome not been so tragic. What was valid was the advice only to strike when possessing tactical supremacy, and not to over-commit one's forces through over-ambition, but this was surely only common sense for any insurrectionist. Nevertheless, it was the writings of Guillén and Clausewitz which shaped the discourse of Montonero strategics, with [. . .] Clausewitz in time totally overshadowing Guillén. As the Montoneros developed, the more their military pretensions became guided by considerations of regular warfare, and they rapidly forgot the lessons which Guillén drew from the Tupamaro decline in Uruguay: chiefly, avoid the establishment of fixed urban bases which jeopardize guerrilla mobility and security; do not build a 'microstate'; discard the use of 'people's prisons' the existence of which focuses 'unnecessarily on a parallel system of repression'; and — most important of all — remember that 'to be victorious in a people's war, one has to act in conformity with the interests, sentiments, and will of the people. A military victory is worthless if it fails to be politically convincing'. The Tupamaros [in Uruguay] had become fatally 'overly professionalized, militarized, and isolated from the urban masses', and the Montoneros, invoking the authority of Clausewitz, were to share their fate.[13]

THE MONTONEROS AND THEIR IDEOLOGY

Remarkably, Argentina has failed to produce a significant guerrilla ideologist despite the growth of urban guerrilla organisations and the articulacy and talents of the public in general. With its emphasis on immediate action and visibly derived returns, Gillespie believes that *foquismo* may have displaced a broader ideological approach:

To quote one of the early pioneers, *foquismo* served as a kind of 'super-ideology' that attracted groups emanating from the Left, Right and Centre on the basis of a method and an image. What was originally put forward as a politico-military strategy became for its adherents the main issue separating revolutionaries from non-revolutionaries; one became a revolutionary only through armed struggle.

The appeal of *foquismo*, which overwhelmingly attracted people in their late teens and twenties, lay in the immediacy of its promised impact. There was no need to wait until 'objective conditions' for revolution or a 'revolutionary consciousness' among the masses matured; small groups of revolutionaries could contribute to the development of these conditions by initiating an armed struggle. The thesis was particularly appealing in view of the perennial weakness of the Argentine Left and in view of Peronist control of the labour movement. The working class had demonstrated militancy on many recent occasions and thus seemed to possess real revolutionary potential, yet it appeared to the *foquistas* to be held back by a lack of politico-military organization and by the dead hand of a trade-union bureaucracy that often sought to collaborate with the government of the day. Violent action was seen as a means of transforming this situation: by demonstrating the vulnerability of the state, it would encourage people to collaborate with or join the guerrillas.

Certainly, in terms of publicity, *foquismo* did achieve an immediate impact, which was interpreted as progress by its adherents. Of course, its high profile attracted repression as well as media attention, but early guerrilla losses proved no great deterrent to violent activity.[14]

THE ORGANISATION OF THE MONTONEROS

Gillespie (1982) shows that two characteristics were evident in the shape of this small proto-terrorist group: first, bureaucratism with authoritative trappings, and, second, a compartmentalised and cellular organisation. It might be thought that leaning the first way (termed *aparatismo*, undue emphasis on a grandiose structure) might be incompatible with flexibly developing a mass 'workers' front. However, the command echelon was able to pull the Montoneros together by exercising strict disciplinary control over each *aspirante* (guerrilla trainee) and by ensuring that no activist knew too much about either the hierarchy or the operational units made up of 5,000 or so recruits:

The basic fighting units were the military commands, the *comandos*. [. . .] Cross-cutting this structure were functional subdivisions of the organization: Córdoba police reports of mid-1970 spoke of there being a 'maintenance department' (responsible for acquiring vehicles and the logistical side of operations), a 'documents department' (providing counterfeit military and police papers, facilitating freedom of travel), a 'war department' (which planned kidnappings, holdups, etc.), and a 'psychological action department' (in charge of the preparation of declarations and communiqués).[15]

Certainly, the organisational structure was elaborate. After 1973 and aside from the functional subdivisions there were cadres with specific areas of responsibility – Peronist Youth for city work, Peronist University Youth for campus activity, Peronist Working Youth to infiltrate the trade unions, Peronist Shanty-town Dwellers Movement to invigorate the slums, a Peronist Tenants Movement for high-rise tenements, a Secondary Students Union for schools activities, a Women's Section (named after the charismatic Eva Perón).

Montonero leaders took positive steps to maintain morale after 1975 by issuing medals for heroism and three years later they ordered uniforms to be worn. If iron discipline was regarded as underpinning morale, a code providing for severe penalties discouraged infringement of the movement's ethic, as Gillespie (1995) relates:

Once a recruit had graduated from the periphery (*milicianos*) to the organization proper (*aspirantes*, *oficiales*), there was no easy way out of the Montoneros. Members were expected to 'resist until death' if cornered by the security forces or taken captive, and any failure to do so was punishable. Those who committed suicide when trapped, by taking their regulation-issue cyanide capsules, were sometimes posthumously awarded medals by the leadership. One member was promoted and decorated for helping his wounded girlfriend commit suicide. But some of those who deserted, or who gave away important information when tortured by their captors, were shot later by their own comrades.[16]

THE MONTONEROS AND THE PUBLIC

Already in 1970 the Montoneros set out to become the Armed Wing of the People. This was the way forward, to be the broad political-cum-military vanguard of a popular revolution:

They [the Montoneros] looked to the outbreak of a 'popular war', rather than a mere confrontation between military apparata, and insisted that 'our struggle and the mass struggle must go together, mutually feeding and maintaining each other'. However, while the Montoneros aspired to form part of an 'integral' strategy, involving political, trade union, and student activity as well as the armed element, they were clearly content to promote the guerrilla aspect themselves and to leave the remaining complementary activities to other sectors of the Movement.

More radical than the Peronists, the Montoneros regarded the destruction of a capitalist state and its army as preconditions for the taking over of power by the people. This note of solidarity with Third World liberationists was to sound little resonance in Argentina's cities although:

[the Montoneros . . .] attracted an increasing number of lower-middle-class youths, unwilling to entrust their interests to a working-class leadership, but held little appeal for the industrial workers. A small minority of the latter, principally located in Córdoba, rejected the Montoneros' views from a more revolutionary standpoint, whereas the economistic majority [sic] looked upon armed strategies as alien to their experiences, struggles, and needs. They did not, for the most part, respond to the Montonero example of taking up arms, relying instead upon their labor unions to effect an improvement in their living standards. The Montoneros demanded too much of these workers and promised them too little. While offering them no greater material benefits than did orthodox Peronism for the duration of their 'national liberation' stage, the Montoneros were calling on the workers totally to subordinate their own traditional, tested, means of struggle to a new, unproven, politico-military strategy. Rather than just collaborate with guerrilla units, the masses were urged by the Montoneros to themselves adopt 'the organizational forms and methods of struggle typical of an armed organization', as a first step towards the 'gradual and organized incorporation of the people into the armed organizations' and their transformation into a popular army.[17]

People's frustration and resentment welled up as the newer horizons of which Perón had spoken vanished and there crumbled into dust the Montoneros' confident forecast of political and economic freedom for all. Hodges (1976) put it this way:

The program of national liberation was an evidently populist one, predicated on the establishment of a popular state which would control and plan the economy as a necessary condition of political and economic independence. This would be achieved through the expropriation of the property of the landed oligarchy and big foreign enterprises in Argentina, and the transformation of the professional army from an occupation force in the service of the monopolies into a force for national liberation. The liberation of the people in an immediate sense was to be accomplished through provisions regulating matters of health, housing, and employment; through the abolition of repressive laws and the granting of amnesty to political prisoners who had fought the dictatorship; and through the participation of the people in government through their political, trade union, and youth organizations. This was the Peronist programme for which the people voted in the March elections – a programme of revolutionary nationalism aimed at overcoming Argentina's condition of dependency. [. . .] But it was not long in being betrayed.[18]

With the death of Perón in July 1974, after only twenty-four months of renewed promise-and-hope the consequence was foreseeable: the mayhem of right and left posturing, then fighting for advantage, the confusion and the ugly vendettas in the towns and, waiting in the shadows, a junta assembling a security force to put an end to dissidence. Protest had to flame into violence and Argentina now had rampant terrorism in its midst.

THE STATE RESPONDS TO TERRORISM

During the first years of urban guerrilla activity, state response was constrained by the realisation of the military junta of 1966–72 that their days in power were numbered. Nevertheless, they saw that Perón's triumphant return from exile in 1972 was not to head a united community but one deeply divided between belligerent left and right wings. Why should they not wait until the violent ones, the 'terrorists', eradicate each other? Undoubtedly, counter-terrorism became quite out of hand with Perón's henchmen hitting out mercilessly at those on their left flank and the state hunting anyone considered 'subversive'. There are a number of grounds for Gillespie's criticism of these policies:

First, they were never applied evenhandedly and thus lacked legitimacy. Far from representing a serious effort to put an end to political violence, the measures were little more than right-wing attacks on militant labor and the Left, and they affected the whole of the Left and not only the proponents of violence. Second, the banning of various front organizations, such as the PA [Authentic Party] destroyed any possibility of reintegrating elements of the guerrilla movement into conventional politics and thereby dividing the rebel organizations and weakening their capacity for violence. Third, the use of crude censorship helped undermine the democratic pretensions of the government while encouraging the guerrillas to resort to spectacular attacks that could not be hidden from the public eye. Fourth, many of the new laws whose draconian punishments alienated sectors of public opinion were in fact rarely applied to guerrilla detainees. Captured Peronist guerrillas mainly faced imprisonment without trial, and ERP contingents captured during combat appear to have been massacred on at least two occasions. Fifth, the governmental tactics resorted to by the Peronists played into the hands of the military, who were restored to prominence and flattered as if they did not themselves constitute a threat to democracy. And finally, the attempt at a legal response to insurgency was entirely vitiated by the government's coincident and extremely transparent sponsorship of illegal violence in the form of the Triple A death squad [Perón's Right Wing gunmen].[19]

The methods resorted to by the Argentine army in order to eradicate terrorists seem to have taken the Montoneros by surprise. Gillespie describes it thus:

They expected fierce armed confrontations in the streets, vehicle checks, raids, house-by-house searches, and mass detention, but assumed that the latter would be as before: about ten days to endure torture before the detention was legalized, followed by the re-establishment of contact with one's family and organization. Only slowly did they detect the new repressive infrastructure and methods: officially sanctioned but clandestine concentration camps and torture centres, plus special units based on the military services and police whose function was to abduct, interrogate, torture, and kill. Under the new regime, not only was torture more savage: the detainee was now at the disposal of captors who had all the time in the world, were unmolested by judicial interference, could totally isolate the prisoner from society, and had no need to produce a living person at the end.[20]

THE DEMISE OF THE MONTONEROS

Three things chiefly brought about the collapse of the Montoneros movement: internal dissension and desertion; external harrying by rightist elements loyal to Perón; and a vicious programme of extermination carried out by government security forces. First of all, through 1979 and into 1980 six at least of the principal Montoneros lieutenants were losing heart – they were 'in retreat' according to Gillespie (1982):

[They criticized] the *foquista* nature of the counter-offensive, and acknowledged that a genuine popular counter-offensive could only have been 'promoted' and not 'launched' by an organization such as their own. Above all, they isolated the roots of original Montonero sin in a 'Clausewitzian reductionism' which presented 'the complex social struggle as movements of conventional military forces', and which had condemned experienced leaders to be lost in a 'confrontation between two apparata and not between two social forces'.

Moreover, numerous Montoneros, when rounded up by pursuers, were accepting readily the alternative of 'collaborating' rather than the certainty of barbarous methods of 'inducement'.

Taken chained and hooded to the torture chamber most of them cooperated, soon concerned solely, but hopelessly, about their own individual survival. 'Without the Montoneros, the Armed Forces would not have been able to destroy the Montoneros', the testimony records. Prompted by pain, Montoneros talked because of the political bankruptcy of their organization and its military decline; they talked because they knew their friends were talking; because their leaders had taken off and abandoned them.[21]

Second, there were many in the Peronist camp seeking vengeance against those who had, as we have seen, 'betrayed' Perón's orthodoxy, or moved too far to the left, and resorted to guns and explosives. The traitors would now be given some of their own medicine. Death squads killed in the streets and tenement blocks and hauled thousands away to oblivion as *desaparecidos*, the 'disappeared'. Third, the military government, reinstalled securely by 1976, set out on a Draconian hunt-and-kill witch hunt to extinguish subversive militancy. Gillespie considers that the Montoneros were quite decimated by 1980:

Militant workers were often referred to by the junta as 'industrial guerrillas'. So many ended up dead because the junta not only saw subversion in virtually all who disagreed with them but also regarded 'subversives' as irredeemable. The military chiefs were authoritarian personalities full of self-righteousness, and when the guerrillas began to target members of the armed forces, their response was one of fury.

Besides being indiscriminate, the violence used by the state was terrorist in the sense that it sowed widespread fear in society. This found reflection in the high degree of self-censorship accepted by the Argentine press during the 'dirty war', the reluctance of the judiciary to act on human rights abuses, and the silence (when not the complicity) of the Roman Catholic Church. Given the military regime's full involvement in the violence, it is accurate to speak of state terror and not simply state-sponsored terror.[22]

It has also been suggested here that state terrorism left a more damaging legacy than did urban guerrilla warfare. The former was more devastating because, unlike the guerrilla warfare, it operated with the full resources of the state behind it, and with impunity, at least while the military regime lasted.[23]

The tally of political violence in Argentina between 1970 and 1980 is hard to calculate in retrospect. In 1977 the Argentine Commission for Human Rights set up in Geneva by the United Nations was already blaming the military regime of General Videla for instituting a policy of state terror. It was estimated that the consequences of the terror were at least 2,300 political murders, 10,000 summary arrests and no less than 20,000 to 30,000 'disappearances'. Elsewhere, Amnesty International was declaring that Argentina's savage dismembering of a civilised society violated almost every basic human right and that the list of accounted for victims and of unaccounted for others was endless. Undeniably, most Argentinians were sickened and saddened by their experience even when they did not pay for it with their lives.

Chapter 9

Spain

SPAIN DIFFERS FROM ALL other Western democracies, not only in strength of provincial nationalism, but also in the level of violence brought about by conflict between Madrid and the provinces. This case-study looks at the ETA movement in the Basque homeland of north-west Spain which has led to forty years of violence. Although the Basques have only a weak and recently conferred political identity, they are nevertheless an ancient nation with a unique non-Indo European language. The proud traditions and customs of former times have, however, been drastically affected as subsistence farming in the hills gives way to large-scale mechanised agriculture in the southern plains and sleepy seaports and inland market towns have been transformed by the introduction of shipyards and steel plants, magnets to immigrants from lower Spain.

OVERVIEW

At the time of writing (December 2000) a cease-fire tentatively arranged in late 1999 shows little sign of permanence. As an example of terrorist campaigning, what has happened among the Basques of Spain (and may happen still) poses a number of intriguing questions as Shabad and Ramo (1995) relate:

ETA [*Euzkadi ta Askatasuma* – Basque Homeland and Freedom] was founded in 1959 by a coalition of radical youth groups, one of which had split from the historic Basque Nationalist Party. Its primary aims from the beginning have been Basque independence and recuperation of Basque culture and language. These objectives continue to be at the centre of ETA's ideological program, the five-point KAS Alternative, which it set forth in the mid-1970s as the minimum conditions to be met by the Spanish state in exchange for ETA's abandonment of political violence.

Most of the five points are radical nationalist demands. The first of these is reform of the 1978 Spanish constitution to accept the right of self-determination; a second is the assertion of the territorial integrity of all Basque provinces in Spain, which means the revision of the 1979 Basque Autonomy Statute to allow for the incorporation of Navarra into the Basque Autonomous Community; a third is the demand for the institutional predominance of Euskera (the Basque language); the fourth point calls for the unconditional amnesty for all political prisoners and the withdrawal of all Spanish police and armed forces from Basque soil. The last refers to the conditions of labor and expresses solidarity with the working class. Apart from this, no other mention is made of leftist ideological principles.

ETA's strategy of armed struggle was adopted in 1962, but in the 1960s and early 1970s ETA engaged in only sporadic acts of violence against the authoritarian and ultra-Spanish nationalist Francoist regime. The most dramatic and consequential of these was the assassination in 1973 of Prime Minister Carrero Blanco, heir apparent of Franco, an event that helped to bring about the demise of the authoritarian regime. After Franco's death in 1975, ETA violence increased dramatically, particularly during the transition to democracy and the granting of regional autonomy to the three Basque provinces (Alava, Guipúzcoa, and Vizcaya) in 1979–80. Of the more than 600 deaths attributable to ETA between 1968 and 1991, about 93 per cent occurred after Franco's death; about 27 per cent took place in 1979 and 1980 alone, during which time the Basque Autonomy Statute was being negotiated and elections to the first Basque regional government were being held. Thus, despite the rebirth of democracy in Spain and the achievement of autonomy for the Basque region, ETA continued to act as though 'nothing had changed'.

But things had changed. Civil liberties were restored, political competition became legitimate, autonomous trade unions were permitted, and open expression of ethnic nationalist sentiments – even of demands for territorial independence of ethnically distinct regional populations – was allowed. Why then did ETA violence not only persist but escalate after the restoration of democracy? Was this part of its original plan? Did political and social circumstances in the Basque Country make possible a continuation of ETA's activities? Or 'are members of terrorist organizations, once assembled, like the sorcerer's apprentice who, unwilling to be dismissed when the job is done, continues the violence?'

The endurance of ETA in the context of the rebirth of Spanish democracy and the granting of autonomy to the Basque Country presents an interesting puzzle. Why did the armed struggle go on, and what were the effects of ETA violence on the new democracy and on Basque society and politics?

First, however, we should specify the geopolitical limits of our research. According to Basque nationalists, Euskadi – the Basque Country, or the Basque nation – is composed of seven territories or provinces: four in Spain and three in France. Thus conceived, Euskadi has about 2,900,000 inhabitants living in an area of 20,644 square kilometres. But this notion of the Basque Country, which originated in the late nineteenth century, conflicts with a more complex reality. On the administrative level, the three French provinces (8.2 per cent of the whole Basque population and 14.3 per cent of its territory) are little districts of the larger so-called Pyrenees Atlantiques region. The four Spanish provinces are presently divided

into two autonomous, or self-governing, regions, each having different social structures, institutions, and party systems: on the one hand, there is the unprovincial
autonomous community of Navarra with 17.6 per cent of the Basque population
and 50.5 per cent of the territory; and on the other, there are the three provinces
of Alava, Guipúzcoa, and Vizcaya, which make up the autonomous community of
the Basque Country, or Euskadi. Neither Navarra nor Euskadi, it is important to
note, is ethnically homogeneous. In the latter, about 30 per cent of the population
were born outside of the region and an additional 11 per cent are first-generation
Basques. The frame of reference for our analysis is the Basque Autonomous
Community, in which Basque nationalist parties are dominant and ETA has drawn
most of its militants, focused most of its violent activities, and received its greatest
popular support.[1]

BASQUE NATIONALISM: THE SOCIO-ECONOMIC CONTEXT

Basque nationalism, as an ideology and movement, emerged during the 1890s mainly
as a result of various social developments associated with rapid industrialisation.
Shabad and Ramo survey this regional transformation and see it as promoting ethnic
solidarity:

Explanations of Basque nationalism and of ETA violence, in particular, focus on
the interaction of several distinct, but related, characteristics of the Basque Country
and of its relation to the Spanish state. These range from structural characteristics,
to the cognitive, evaluative, and affective orientations of different groups involved
in a centre–periphery conflict, to the ideological views and personal motivations
of those who choose to engage in violence rather than pursue more 'normal' political activities.

During the course of its economic transformation, traditional Basque society,
founded on small-scale agriculture and commerce, was changed to a society based
on mining, heavy industry, shipbuilding, and banking. Between 1842 and 1868,
industrialization was first localized in the provinces of Vizcaya and Guipúzcoa where
the resultant dramatic growth in population size and urbanization provided
favourable conditions for the later rise of Basque nationalism.

Two other developments associated with industrialization were also of great
importance for Basque ethnic mobilization. Industrialization created a different
system of social stratification in which a new class of Basque industrialists and
financiers became dominant and were soon incorporated into the Spanish oligarchy.
Efforts by this group to integrate the Basque provinces economically and politically
with Spain provoked intense hostility from the traditional *petite bourgeoisie*. In addition to the emergence of a new financial and industrial oligarchy, a working class
also developed, as thousands of farmers from impoverished areas of Spain moved
to urban areas in the Basque Country. With the rise of this new immigrant working
class, Spanish trade unions and anticlerical leftist parties became major social and
political protagonists in the Basque Country. These changes in class formation and
their political expression posed serious threats to the socioeconomic and political

status of the traditional urban middle class and to the hegemony of Catholic and rural Basque culture. It was among these segments of society that Basque nationalism developed and flourished.

Another period of rapid social and economic transformation occurred during the so-called economic boom between 1960 and 1975. The population of Euskadi increased by 44 per cent, and this time all three provinces experienced growth. Once again, immigration from other parts of Spain was an important factor contributing to population growth (40 per cent in the 1950s and 48 per cent in the 1960s). By 1975 only 51 per cent of those living in the three provinces were natives born of Basque parentage; 8 per cent were of mixed parentage; 11 per cent were first-generation Basques; and 30 per cent had been born in other parts of Spain. Sixty per cent and 40 per cent of residents of urban and metropolitan areas, respectively, had some Basque ancestry; this compares with 85 per cent of the rural population.

As a result of this 'second' industrial revolution, the active population in Euskadi increased by 25.2 per cent between 1960 and 1975; the increase in Spain as a whole was only 9 per cent. The sectoral distribution of this expanding work force once again radically altered Basque society and had important implications for Basque nationalism in the late Franco period and the transition to democracy. The native Basque population became increasingly middle class and urban, and in time the political and social influence of this nationalist bourgeoisie supplanted that of the Basque, but Spanish-oriented, oligarchy. The nationalist movement itself became increasingly interclassist.

The immigrant proletariat remained a distinct, but increasingly substantial, segment of Basque society. Rather than undermine ethnic solidarity, these major social and economic changes helped to promote it. They did so not only through the creation of modern infrastructures for ethnic mobilization but also by the very threat they posed to the declining, but increasingly idealized, traditional Basque culture. Indeed, during the 1950s and 1960s it was primarily traditional institutions, like the church and family, that sustained ethnic solidarity.

The transition to democracy coincided with an economic crisis in Spain. Because the Basque Country was a region of early industrialization and heavy industry, this economic crisis was felt most acutely in Euskadi. Policies of industrial restructuring, combined with ETA actions against Basque industrialists (in the form of assassinations, kidnappings, and the imposition of a system of 'revolutionary taxation'), resulted in high levels of unemployment, particularly among the young. This provided additional fertile ground for complaints about economic exploitation of the Basque Country by Madrid, as well as for recruitment of new ETA members.[2]

BASQUE NATIONALISM: THE POLITICAL CONTEXT

Politically, relations between the Spanish capital and the Basque Province have been those of conflict for centuries. Franco sought to eradicate Basque distinctiveness by removing what autonomy they had achieved. This and Madrid's reluctance to loosen its grip after the 1936–39 civil war was seen as justifying a Basque resort to violence, as Shabad and Ramo relate:

Although Spain was an 'early' state, the political, social and cultural integration of its territorial components – nation building – was not fully accomplished. Several provinces (including those of the Basque Country and Catalonia) had for lengthy periods of time enjoyed considerable political autonomy from Madrid. This in turn allowed regional minority cultures and languages (like Euskera and Catalan) to persist despite efforts by the centre to promote a single Spanish (or Castilian) language and national identity.

To preserve their traditional culture and historic political rights (the *fueros*), Basques figured prominently in the two nineteenth-century Carlist struggles against liberal and centralist governments in Madrid. The Carlists were defeated, and seven hundred years after they were first established, the Basques lost their *fueros* in 1876. The Basques' struggle against centralism and their ultimate defeat coincided with the dramatic changes associated with industrialization. Thus, in the late nineteenth century numerous segments of Basque society perceived threats to their collective identity coming both from Madrid and from new groups within the Basque Country itself. It was at this time that Basque nationalism as an ideology and a movement arose.

Just as the civil war was about to erupt, the Second Republic granted political autonomy to the Basque provinces. Basque nationalists, despite their religious and conservative views, allied themselves with the Republican forces against Franco. Once again they were on the losing side. Franco branded Vizcaya and Guipúzcoa 'traitorous provinces' and, in the process of creating a highly centralized regime, abrogated the last vestiges of their autonomy, the *conciertos económicos*.

In order to eradicate Basque distinctiveness once and for all and to create 'a single personality, Spanish', the Francoist regime engaged in physical and symbolic repression of any outward manifestation of Basque cultural and political identity. As a result, Basques, and particularly nationalists, came to view their territory as suffering 'military occupation' by an illegitimate Spanish state. Thus, the duality of 'us' (Basques) versus 'them' (Spain) became even further entrenched as a part of Basque political and cultural reality.[3]

Post-civil war generations of Basques grew up in a climate of physical and symbolic violence and repression, in which all things Basque were labeled by the authorities as 'traitorous' and as falling within the realm of social transgression. This climate was reinforced by the transmission from older to younger generations of historical memories of earlier periods of violence against the Basque Country, as had taken place during the Carlist and civil wars. The choice made by a segment of the Basque community to engage in violence against the violence of the 'occupying forces' of the Spanish state – a choice understood, if not wholly supported, by others – contributed further to the rise of a 'culture of violence' in Euskadi.[4]

Furthermore, by placing all expressions of Basque identity into the category of social transgression, the Francoist regime helped to make the formerly impermissible – including violence – permissible. More important, it made the resort to violence, in the minds of many Basques, a morally justifiable response: If the situation is to be defined in terms of violence, there is already an ever present institutional violence; any response to it, even pacifism, is violence. Violence, therefore, is the basic agent of social change; and whoever refused to participate in it lacks personal commitment.[5]

THE CALL TO ARMS

It was in 1962 that student activists in ETA, increasingly dissatisfied with the moderate nationalism of the rather conservative Basque Nationalist Party whose rhetoric they contemptuously referred to as 'possibilism', took a more vigorous stance defining ETA as the 'Basque Revolutionary Movement of National Liberation'. This signalled the taking up of a position of insurgency against Madrid's government. In 1963 ETA made its first contacts with the Spanish Communist party and suffered the consequences of police repression in the aftermath of workers' strikes. The following year, at an ETA assembly, a significant shift in ideology was announced and, again, Shabad and Ramo describe developments:

It was at this assembly [in 1964] that ETA approved 'Insurrection in Euskadi', a document written in exile in France for the political education of its militants. It was at this meeting, too, that the strategy of armed struggle began to take on sacral overtones and to be sublimated into the idea of messianic liberation led by a vanguard of the enlightened. With ETA's growth after 1964, three distinct, but often overlapping, tendencies emerged within the organization. The first, promoted by the founders of ETA in exile in France, stressed ethnolinguistic principles and was virulently anti-Spanish. The second had as its model anticolonial struggles and emphasized the importance of guerrilla warfare. The third was pro-worker in its ideological thrust. French actions against the first group and police repression in Spain against the second resulted in the dominance of the third faction in 1965 and 1966. This group replaced the strategy of national liberation with that of 'class struggle', to be based on Marxist–Leninist principles and collaboration with the burgeoning workers' movement (including 'Spanish forces' both in Euskadi and in Spain as a whole).[6]

ETA, in the late 1960s, was a fragile coalition in many respects uneasily expressing the aims of neo-Marxists, national liberationists, and extreme militants who modelled themselves on Third World anti-imperialist guerrillas. By degrees the split between 'the men of the gun' and the more 'intellectual' Marxists became impossible to bridge, the former accusing the latter of Spanish 'infiltration'. The idea of popular revolution was torn two ways with a growing tendency towards sporadic terrorism. Shabad and Ramo put ETA's internal dissensions in these terms:

Throughout its history, the sources of ETA's factionalism and instability have been intense conflicts over four main issues: the priority to be given to national versus social liberation; the emphasis to be placed on mass political activity and, after Franco's death, on participation in democratic institutions versus armed struggle, and how best to reconcile these two strategies; the relation between the political and military branches of the organization and the degree of autonomy to be permitted to the latter; and, finally, the desirability of links with 'Spanish' political forces. Divisions over these issues have never clearly demarcated one group from another. Rather, depending on time and circumstances, views on these issues have overlapped in different ways and have thus resulted in unstable and temporary coalitions among ETA factions. But differences over ideology and strategy have not been the sole sources of internal conflict and instability. Power struggles among leaders have played their part as well, and divisions among the rank and file have often been determined less by differences over ideology and strategy than by friendship patterns and personal ties to one or another leader.[7]

Michel Wieviorka (1997), on the other hand, has no doubt about the extent to which ETA leaders decided to turn theory into practice:

Faced with a dictatorship which was itself violently repressive, which resorted to imprisonment for political reasons, torture and execution, faced with state violence which went far beyond straightforward repression of political activists and was aimed at prohibiting any expression of national sentiments, armed struggle appeared as the only possible response, one which had proved itself over time with the Algerian FLN or Mao Zedong's Long March, and one which was exemplified in many national liberation struggles and guerrilla movements all over the world.

However, like other left-wing activists in western Europe, for a number of years ETA did not put this principle into practice. Armed struggle was an objective, an idea, an aspiration, the subject of heated discussion and childish squabbles, not a practice.[8]

Wieviorka regards ETA's reliance on terrorism as counter-productive and as an inappropriate response to social problems in a region becoming increasingly prosperous:

Hence the movement relies more on violence to keep itself alive. The increasing use of terror is its chief characteristic. Yet such reliance on terrorism has changed the character of the movement itself. Indeed, it has become counter-productive. For as a method terrorism has become blind where it was purposeful. It confuses means and ends. It bears little relation to the expectations and experiences of the people in whose name it is carried out. Terrorism has in fact broken up the original 'synergistic' qualities of the three dimensions mentioned above. Basque nationalism then is increasingly dependent on violence for its own sake. The movement has lost its original meaning. As already indicated, when the principle of armed struggle was adopted by the first militants of ETA, they were neither desperate nor poor. The Basque region was neither an economically exploited region nor the victim of a centre which pillaged its wealth. On the contrary, industrially and financially, it was a major centre. It was indeed a key to economic growth in Franco's Spain. It was critical to the more over-all modernization process. Indeed, it attracted large-scale immigration. The recourse to violence, at least in its initial stages, was not therefore the result of crisis or poverty but rather prosperity and growth.

Precisely because of such prosperity there was a well-defined proletariat. What gave Basque nationalism its originally revolutionary appeal and impetus was its attractiveness to those who saw the future in terms of a radical 'repossession' of wealth by the proletariat. The revolutionary class, the class with radical 'brains', was neither poor nor excluded. The chief agent of nationalism was a strong labor movement capable of aspiring to the leadership of an already well-established industrial society. ETA's activities had always been based on strong nationalism. It was able to hitch this nationalism to the star of the labor movement.[9]

A point raised by Shabad and Ramo is that ETA did not neglect to build up an international dimension: there was nearby France as a refuge for terrorists on the run, and beyond, there was sympathy and weapons:

As for ETA's connections to other terrorist organizations, some members have been given training in Third World socialist countries, such as Yemen, Algeria, Libya, and Cuba. Available data suggest that ETA's arms come from the Middle East, and some of its funds have been provided by the Libyan government. Purchase of weapons, mostly from Communist Czechoslovakia and the former Soviet Union, was coordinated with other European terrorist groups. Since the 1970s, the closest and most continuous links with foreign terrorist organizations have been with the IRA.

The international dimension of ETA violence has also been reflected in its various efforts to ally itself ideologically with and to model its strategy on Third World anticolonial insurgent movements. As it turned out, these foreign models were largely inapplicable to Basque society. ETA was never able to create a broad-based insurrection movement or to engage in full-scale guerrilla warfare. None the less, the adoption of anticolonial models of armed struggle in the early 1960s had significant repercussions for ETA and for Basque nationalism and society.[10]

THE NATURE OF ETA'S VIOLENCE

An account of Basque terrorism raises a number of issues as we have seen earlier. Cyrus Zirakzadeh (1991) believes that some discussions of this terrorism employ inadequate perspectives and so prove less than helpful to understanding of motive and development. In his detailed account of that 'rebellious people', the Basques, he argues that many writers focus too narrowly on armed struggle and neglect to consider the wider, non-violent areas of social interaction leading to various forms of protest. To refer to all ETA members as terrorists-in-the-making clouds the picture and the result is a 'negative characterisation' of Basque political violence. Zirakzadeh's conclusions provide scope for discussion about some of the reasons for terrorist behaviour and the shape it may eventually take:

We began our reflections on the causes and characteristics of Basque political violence by recounting a common view of the subject, that we have called the modernization interpretation. According to this position, the violence was primarily an expression of Basques' intense feelings of cultural dislocation and personal stress brought about by unusually rapid and widespread social changes, including secularization, urbanization, and industrialization. Popular feelings of distress were also reflected in and reinforced by the antimodern ideology propagated by the Basque

Nationalist Party, which strongly criticized the values and structures of industrial, urban and commercial society, and celebrated those of preindustrial times. Culturally uprooted, persons from rural and small-town backgrounds lashed out at the agents and symbols of modernity, but without specific grievances in mind and without thoughts of achieving particular goals. Violence principally resulted not from economic concerns and political calculations but from cultural unfamiliarity and acute personal pain. The expressive political violence in turn antagonized Spain's armed forces and thus indirectly endangered Spain's open, pluralistic political system.

This study has presented an alternative interpretation that places great emphasis on economic problems and grievances, the mediating influence of local social movements and political struggles, and the adaptation and modification of non-Nationalist as well as Nationalist ideologies to a complex political and economic situation. The book has viewed the members of ETA as rational actors who consciously gave meaning to their circumstances, and who adapted, refined, and readjusted ideas according to constantly changing political circumstances. Etarras' (ETA members) ideas, such as the spiral theory of violence [contra-violence begets violence], were not simply expressions of rage but attempts to calculate under complex, local circumstances how best to respond to economic crises. [. . .]

[Basque political violence] was not solely a consequence of intense nostalgia generated by rapid social change. It was also a consequence of strategic choices by a set of political activists enduring economic crises who believed they could launch a spontaneous social revolution from below through the calculated use of violence. The hope of ending (or at least greatly reducing) economic suffering, of course, does not absolve the activists of moral responsibility for their acts. Murder and kidnapping, even when undertaken for purportedly humanitarian ends, are still murder and kidnapping. But this book modifies the current modernization interpretation by emphasizing the purposefulness and intended effectiveness behind violent acts, and raising questions about the material interests, local social institutions, and theoretical reasoning that led to the violence.[11]

THE TALLY OF TERRORISM

Statistics of lethality and abduction by ETA terrorists have been compiled by Shabad and Ramo:

During the more than thirty years of its existence, ETA has been responsible for more than 500 assassinations, more than 1,000 injuries, 60 kidnappings, innumerable bombings, armed assaults, and robberies, and an extended regime of 'revolutionary taxation'. ETA has been responsible for more than 70 per cent of all people killed in terrorist actions in Spain during the last twenty years.

Basque industrialists were also the target of nearly 500 attacks (bombings, sabotage, robberies and armed assaults) between 1972 and 1983. The second prime targets of attack have been banks, firms in crisis or in the midst of strikes, and, since France's decision in the late 1980s to cooperate with Spanish anti-ETA efforts, French firms.

In recent years there has been a qualitative change in the kind of violence practiced by ETA. Violent actions have been more indiscriminate and fatal, more frequently directed against collective targets (e.g. supermarkets, police headquarters), more often staged in the largest Spanish cities (Madrid, Barcelona, Zaragoza), and more sophisticated in the use of weapons. One can only speculate, but such changes tending toward more extreme, albeit less frequent, violent activities may have been the result of a loss of support for ETA among the Basque public in the late 1980s and hence the result of the erosion of the ties between ETA and the community it purports to represent.[12]

The militants of ETA itself have borne serious loss: 100 of them have died, 20,000 have been arrested with 600 of them lingering in Spanish gaols and 700 of them in France.

TERRORISTS AND INTERNAL SECURITY

Something that continues to arouse violent dissent among Basques today is the largely unsolved question of who controls internal security in Euskadi (also known as Euzkadi) after the autonomy granted in 1979. Should it not be the Basques themselves with their own carefully recruited and trained police personnel, one lightly armed protector of the peace for every 500 inhabitants? Or should it be officers from the Civil Guard and the National Police, successors to those sent by Madrid in the 1960s to enforce a harsh state of emergency? That repressive contingent sent one officer for every 600 or so inhabitants and their operational orders and legal codes were rigorous. In the light of those circumstances, a 'terrorist' response by quick-triggered ETA guerrillas was to be expected as Jose Trevino (1982) relates:

By far the typical ETA assassination however involves rank and file policemen. Most killings occur in broad daylight in the streets. On other occasions the terrorists calmly walk into a bar or cafeteria serving policemen on breaks from their duties. Often without even bothering to conceal their identities, the terrorists single out their targets and 'execute' them in front of scores of onlookers. Yet, when police investigators try to ascertain the facts, witnesses are almost impossible to find.

The reluctance of Basque citizens to cooperate with the investigators comes mostly from fear or apathy, although there are those who are truly sympathetic to ETA's cause. The fear of associating or collaborating with the police is well founded. There is little doubt that ETA has an effective intelligence network which pervades almost every segment of Basque society. Further, ETA has repeatedly demonstrated its ruthlessness against informants and 'collaborators'. Besides, the ordinary citizen is generally noncommittal. He wants to live in peace in his homeland. The policemen are almost all outsiders, recruited from other regions of Spain. They are largely unfamiliar with the local culture and customs and within a year they are normally reassigned out of the Basque region.

Consequently, in Euzkadi, a vicious circle sets in. The inability of the police to cope with terrorism undermines the already shattered confidence in the police.

The public's reluctance to cooperate further undermines the police forces' ability to fight terrorism effectively.[13]

Today, twenty years later, ETA has agreed to a cessation of its terrorist activities under the terms of a cease-fire. The question of who supervises internal security, an external or internal force, remains a severe irritant and so a further explosion of violence at some stage cannot be ruled out despite, as we have seen, a general Basque hostility to continued terrorism.

THE WANING OF ETA

The death of the Spanish dictator Francisco Franco in 1975 ushered in a transition to democracy that was fairly rapid with the legitimising of political parties in 1976, a new constitution in 1978, autonomy granted to the Basques in Euskadi in 1979, and elections for the Basque parliament in March 1980. Transitional developments did not dissipate tensions. Much opinion in Spain, in the parliamentary debates in the Cortes, in the Spanish press and generally among the public continued to describe Basque separatists as 'crazy' or 'criminal'. Most Basques revered their leaders as 'patriots' and 'idealists' whose right to bear arms in defence of Euskadi was a sacred duty. Beyond, though, the strident rhetoric of both sides and the drama of terrorist incidents, the 1980s opened with cautious feelers about an end to intolerance, fanaticism and violence and the chance of a defined and negotiated settlement. By 1985 even the Basque government was ready to condemn for the first time the terrorists in their midst who were responsible for indiscriminate violence in which many innocent citizens had lost their lives. ETA members, their supporters, and their tactics were now seen as inimical to democratic freedom and progress. Hundreds of thousands of Basques flooded the streets to demonstrate an appeal for an end to ETA's terrorist actions. Cooperation between the governments of Spain and of France had, in any case, started to blunt the edge of militant ardour. ETA began to turn in upon itself with fragmentation and quarrelling:

ETA's behavior in the late 1980s was reflective of its changed circumstances. On the one hand, the willingness of ETA to cast aside its conditions regarding talks with the Spanish state indicated that the organization's leadership had come to realise that ETA's position had deteriorated in terms of its ability to recruit new members, to carry out sustained effective actions, and to enlarge, let alone maintain, its degree of popular support. Thus, it was best to 'negotiate' while ETA could still do some damage and extract some concessions from the state. But along with this changed stance toward talks, what the simultaneous acts of violence and abrupt withdrawal from negotiations also suggested was that ETA had become increasingly divided between hard-line and moderate elements. It was with the latter that the government pursued its discussions. [. . .] What might such talks accomplish were they to take place? Most likely, ETA would be reduced to its most violent core, a group of militants concerned primarily with the very survival of the organization.[14]

POSTSCRIPT

There does not appear to be a readily acceptable explanation of ETA's enduring violence following the rebirth of democracy in Spain after 1975. Was it a consequence of a 'culture of violence' (political violence, that is) married to an idealised, romantic view of traditional Basque values, aspirations and mores? This seems to be a conventional summation by many writers on Basque terrorism. Few of them go on to attempt a definition of such a 'culture'. In the early days of ETA, impulses that were part-nationalistic, part Communist, spurred on a clandestine élite to work for revolution undaunted even when the support of most Basques visibly drained away as autonomy became more credible. Euskadi was not relishing the prospect of another string of decades of conflict. That a democratic regime succeeded an authoritarian one in Spain did not make it easier to deal with ETA's overt terrorism and with the lingering suspicions and dissatisfactions of so many Basques.

Did terrorism among the Basques bring them a brighter future and do much to advance or retard the onset of liberal democracy? A tentative response to this question is that of Shabad and Ramo, writing in 1995:

What can be concluded about the effects of ETA violence? Two primary goals of terrorist organizations, whether they be ideologically left or right, religious or nationalist, are to undermine the legitimacy and the stability of the existing regime. How effective such organizations are in achieving these goals depends on a number of factors. One of these is the nature of the regime itself, although the impact of regime type is itself conditioned by other variables. Authoritarian regimes, such as Francoist Spain, are by their very nature far less inhibited by legal and normative constraints from countering the violence directed against them. Moreover, clandestine organizations have fewer opportunities, particularly in more repressive periods, to get their message across to their intended targets and to acquire essential resources such as militants, weapons, funds, safe houses, and so on. But at the same time, grievances provoked by repression of class interests or of religious and ethnic sentiments may foster growing and increasingly radical popular discontent with existing rule. This, in turn, provides a favorable climate for oppositional violence.

Democratic regimes, on the other hand, have a greater ability to lay claims to legitimacy and loyalty. They provide opportunities for voicing demands and expressing dissent through peaceful means. But should political violence occur, democratic governments, unlike authoritarian regimes, are faced with an unenviable choice. They may choose to act within the boundaries set by the constitution – and risk failure and being made to appear ineffective in the eyes of the public and the military – or they may resort to extralegal means to combat threats to the regime; this would not only undermine democratic rule itself but also provoke that segment of society in whose name the terrorist organization acts. Either extreme – failure of democratic means, or state violence – may achieve the terrorist organization's goals of delegitimation and instability.

The choices made by democratic governments for countering political violence are conditioned by a number of factors. One, of course, is the particular mix of values of governing élites themselves, their assessments of the circumstances they face and the likely outcomes of differing strategies, and their perceptions of the pressures placed on them from rival political élites. These normative, cognitive, and affective orientations may, in turn, be influenced by other variables, such as the actual scope and frequency of violence wreaked by antisystem forces and the patterns of opinion of various segments of the population.

Another factor, which we have emphasized here and which differentiates democratic from authoritarian regimes and hence their possible responses to political violence, is the embeddedness of terrorist organizations in a pluralistic political environment. The interaction between the terrorist group and more moderate 'alegal' or prosystem political forces that also represent the relevant social group may have an effect on public opinion, the severity of political violence, and ultimately the decisions made by governing élites on how to combat terrorism. We have argued here that it is too simplistic to view the interaction between these two kinds of groups as one of rivalry alone. Although it is true that the existence of legal channels for the expression of group interests may undercut frustration and support for organisations like ETA, the presence of extremist groups willing to use violence may be implicitly encouraged and overtly manipulated by more moderate forces to strengthen their bargaining position vis-à-vis the state. The relation between the two, therefore, is apt to be one of conflict *and* collusion, and both types of interaction potentially serve the interests and objectives of each group.

Thus, there is a complex array of factors that determine the effectiveness of oppositional violence at any given time and under a particular type of political rule. It is difficult to say, based on the Spanish case alone, whether terrorism is more effective under authoritarian or democratic rule. The Francoist regime did not end because of ETA, nor did democracy fail to consolidate because of ETA violence. At the same time, ETA violence did hasten the demise of Francoism, if only through its assassination of the dictator's heir apparent, Carrero Blanco. And it did jeopardize the transition to democracy by reinforcing or provoking hostility to the evolving rules of the game in two different quarters. Basque nationalists refused to endorse the constitution and only gave it 'backward' and ambiguous legitimacy through subsequent support of the autonomy statute. And a segment of the military came very close to toppling democratic rule in its February 1981 coup attempt. Although ETA activities did not lead to the destruction of democracy, they did help to change the rules of the game in another way. As Basque nationalist leaders have argued, without the constant pressure exerted by ETA violence, political élites in Madrid may not have felt as impelled to grant concessions to demands for Basque autonomy and for a fundamental restructuring of the centralised state. Ironically, without such concessions, democratic consolidation may not have been possible.

To say that ETA did not prevent democratic consolidation is not to conclude that ETA had no serious negative consequences. But these were primarily confined to the Basque Country. The persistence of ETA after Franco's death helped to sustain a culture of violence and, in so doing, placed major obstacles to the evolution of more rational and secular patterns of social and political interaction. It polarized and radicalized public opinion in Euskadi and called into question the legitimacy of the new regime. And it significantly affected the behavior of other, more moderate nationalist groups, thus making the resolution of centre–periphery conflicts more difficult to achieve.

Given these negative effects, it is fortuitous that separatist violence did not occur in other ethnically distinct regions of Spain, such as Catalonia and Galicia. Had it spread to other areas and not been confined primarily to the Basque Country, Spanish democracy might have been stillborn.[15]

Recent developments in Euskadi, the Basque homeland, to some extent echo what has taken place in Northern Ireland. In London and in Madrid early government insistence on terrorist disarmament before admission to a legislature has given way after prolonged discussion to conciliatory gestures – a phased 'handing-in' of all weapons, and the freeing of prisoners. ETA's peace resolve in September 1998 announcing a 'total and undefined cease-fire' must have taken account of growing public hostility to continued and profitless terrorism. Unfortunately, ETA's peace negotiators are still unable to rein in extremists on the flanks of the movement.

Chapter 10

Algeria

THE BITTERNESS AND BRUTALITY of terrorism in Algeria have made world headlines for almost fifty years. To understand the origins and development of turmoil in that country it is necessary to look rather closely at its political landscape. The lethality of the struggle there owes much to feelings of failure and futility among Algerians. The ending of the Second World War in 1945 brought for many colonial territories expectations of increased self-determination. In Algeria the French colonial administration failed to pay attention to articulate demands from the non-French population for social and economic reform. The liberation movement failed to frame a convincing popular campaign and to communicate it to a wide, eager constituency. Successive administrations, largely French but with Algerian membership, failed to address political, social and economic issues and to establish any legitimate authority acceptable to those who felt disenfranchised. They fell short of building any tolerance between secular governance and the Islamic observance of the majority of the population. Failure to deal with manifestations of protest and to use the possibilities of discussion and compromise led to irrepressible frustration and growing violence. Lack of leadership, irresolution, disunity and confusion resulted in widespread lawlessness and a recourse to terror tactics among malcontents. These latter are organised in a number of groups: the FLN (Front de Libération Nationale), the FIS (Front Islamique de Salut), the GIA (Groupe Islamique Armé), and the MIA (Mouvement Islamique Armé).

THE POLITICAL BACKGROUND TO ALGERIA'S CONFLICT

There are many written accounts of the origin of Algeria's chaos and a useful outline is to be found in the report of a visit to Algeria by a panel of 'eminent persons' who were appointed by the Secretary-General of the United Nations in June 1998. The panel report contained the following historical account:

On 1 November 1954, the principal Algerian nationalist movement, the FLN, began a struggle for independence. A ceasefire was agreed to in March 1962 and independence was declared in July 1962.

In August 1962, the Algerian provisional Government transferred its functions to the Political Bureau of the FLN [the Front de Libération Nationale] and in September a National Constituent Assembly was elected from a single list of FLN candidates and the Algerian Republic was proclaimed. A new government was formed with Mr Ahmed Ben Bella as Prime Minister.

A draft Constitution providing for a presidential regime, with the FLN as the sole party, was adopted on 28 August 1963. In September 1963, the Constitution was approved by referendum and Mr Ben Bella was then elected President. In June 1965, the Minister of Defence, Col. Houari Boumedienne, deposed Ben Bella in a military coup. Former President Ben Bella was first imprisoned and later allowed to go into exile.

In June 1975, Mr Boumedienne introduced plans for: creating a socialist system, maintaining Islam as the State religion, the drafting of a new Constitution, and the holding of elections for a President and National People's Assembly. A National Charter was adopted by referendum in June 1976, by 98.5 per cent of the electorate. In November, the new Constitution incorporating the principles of the Charter was approved by referendum.

Following the death of President Boumedienne in December 1978, Col. Chadli Ben Djedid, commander of the Oran military regime, succeeded him. Within two years, President Chadli and his government began to gradually reverse the socialist economic policies pursued by President Boumedienne.

Liberalization of the economy and an overhaul of State machinery gained pace in the period after the oil price crash of 1985/86. In 1987, in response to the decline in the price of petroleum and the increase in Algeria's external debt, the Government introduced austerity measures and began to remove State controls from various sectors of the economy. The acceleration of efforts to open the economy to the free market was accompanied by steps towards political pluralism. The country remained a one-party State until 1989.

After his re-election in 1984, the Chadli presidency had been marked by periods of unrest especially in 1986 and 1987. Severe unemployment, high prices and shortages of essential supplies, resulting from the austerity measures, provoked, in 1988, a series of strikes led by the Union Générale des Travailleurs Algériens (UGTA) and in October of that year riots erupted in Algiers, spreading to Oran and Annaba. A six-day state of emergency was imposed and according to official sources, 159 people were killed and 3,500 were arrested during confrontations with the government forces.

In response to the unrest, President Chadli proposed constitutional amendments allowing non-FLN candidates to participate in elections. These reforms were approved in November 1988. A new Constitution signifying the end of the one-party socialist State was approved by referendum in February 1989, allowing the formation of political parties other than the FLN.

Other legislation adopted in July 1989 further reduced State control of the economy, allowed the expansion of investment by foreign companies and ended the State monopoly of the press. Despite these changes, strikes and riots continued during 1989, in protest against alleged official corruption and the Government's failure to improve living conditions. A programme of economic liberalization was announced and the first multiparty municipal and provincial elections scheduled for December were postponed to June 1990.

In April 1991, President Chadli announced that the first multiparty general elections would take place in June. The FIS argued that a presidential election should be held simultaneously, or shortly after, and in protest against the electoral law proposed by the Prime Minister, Mr Mouloud Hamrouche, the FIS incited an indefinite strike and demonstrations, demanding the resignation of President Chadli. Violent confrontations occurred, and in response President Chadli declared a state of emergency and postponed the general elections.

The National People's Assembly was dissolved by presidential decree on 4 January 1992 and on 11 January President Chadli resigned. The High Security Council cancelled the second round of voting and on 14 January a five-member High Council of State (HCE) was appointed to act as a collegiate presidency, until the expiration of Chadli's term of office in 1993.

Amid sporadic outbreaks of violence and terrorism, the security forces took control of the FIS offices in early February 1992, the High Council of State declared a 12-month state of emergency and in March, following a court decision, the FIS party was formally dissolved.

On 26 August 1992, a bomb explosion at Algiers airport indicated a shift in terrorist methods: from then on, violent acts were directed not only against the security forces or Government officials and civil society figures, but against people who were not specifically targeted.

Political efforts and attempts at reconciliation continued against a background of escalating violence throughout the country, and in December 1992, against a background of severe economic and social problems, a curfew was imposed in the capital and in the six neighbouring departments. In February 1993, the state of emergency was renewed for an indefinite period.[1]

THE ERUPTION OF VIOLENCE

As a consequence of so much political volatility, contemporary Algeria is a 'state in agony' according to Martin Stone (1997). Islamic insurgents target state employees and supporters, even foreigners. Algeria's military-backed regimes, unable to cope with their citizens' economic and social distress, continue to lash out savagely at all dissenters, many of whom are being recruited by the FLN as guerrillas. Thus, terror tactics have had a long history whether they are the result of political extremism or of clan vendettas:

3.30 p.m. Monday 30 January 1995: a car loaded with TNT explodes in front of the Algiers headquarters of the Sûreté Nationale on the boulevard Amirouche. At this time of day carnage is inevitable. An overcrowded bus passes in front of the car at the moment of detonation, and the street is crowded with shoppers buying food for the start of the holy fasting month of Ramadan, which starts later in the evening. Blood, limbs, clothes and papers litter the pavement; severed limbs have to be removed from the roofs of nearby buildings. Forty-two people are killed, more than 250 injured. Although this is the worst single bombing in the history of independent Algeria, it has taken place in an unexceptional week: in addition to at least thirty members of the security forces being killed, gunmen have kidnapped and killed the four children of a hero of the war of independence and murdered a French resident in Algiers.

Algeria in the mid-1990s was in a desperate condition. Between 1992 and 1997 some 120,000 people were killed in a terrorist insurgency characterised by staggering cruelty on both sides. Fanatical Islamist insurgents pursued a dirty war to topple the state, fighting fearlessly against their numerically superior foe and literally terrorising the population. In the mountains and the countryside, an informal guerrilla army laid ambushes for a security apparatus reliant mainly on conscripts; in the cities and towns killers, some in their teens, assassinated thousands of 'liberals' who were considered supporters of the state: schoolteachers, doctors, lawyers, journalists, academics, civil servants and former fighters in the war of independence against France. More than 100 foreigners were killed, mostly French, of whom more than thirty were men and women of religion – priests, nuns, monks. The Bishop of Oran was among them.

Algerians grew accustomed to unexplained explosions and bursts of gunfire at night; to news of yet another colleague or relative being knifed to death or gunned down while on the way to work or out shopping; to constantly coming across security force roadblocks and checkpoints that could always turn out to be a dreaded *faux barrage*, a 'false checkpoint'. Across northern Algeria, guerrillas raped and murdered women, some merely for refusing to wear the veil. In certain villages guerrillas even tried to enforce the highly questionable practice of *muta'* (temporary) marriage, which is tantamount to legalised prostitution. Individuals who considered themselves at risk were forced to live the life of a fugitive, furtively staying with friends or in protected compounds surrounded by the security forces. Those who could afford it left to live and work abroad, mostly in France.

Algerians had learned to read between the lines of the terse reports of security encounters published in the government-monitored press. They had become accustomed to reports of startling military successes against the guerrillas in the mountains and of 'key' terrorist leaders being killed in raids, understanding that, in reality, summary justice had been meted out. Many Algerians, even members of the security forces, accused members of the state itself of being behind the terrorist actions as a means of prolonging the violence for their own ends. Policemen secretly complained of being ordered to participate in death squads, shoot-to-kill raids and the torture of suspects.

The factors that underlie this appalling situation are complex and hotly disputed. Having lost virtually all legitimacy, Algeria's military-backed regime clung to power in the face of a savage terrorist war. Thirty years of rural depopulation had resulted in overcrowded cities where unemployment was rampant and the living conditions of the majority were intolerable. From being an elegant colonial port in 1962, Algiers had developed into a sprawling overcrowded metropolis. Most of the population were under thirty years of age, their parents having moved from the more socially conservative rural areas to the city in the 1960s and 1970s. Thousands of families were crammed into crumbling old apartment blocks or into modern soul-less high-rises, with children often forced to sleep in beds by shifts. Unemployment and under-employment were high; the quality of life poor for most; and a sense of hope absent. The pattern was repeated in most towns across northern Algeria – Blida, Medea, Constantine, Skikda. Economically Algerians were paying the price for the mistakes of the past: the grand industrialisation schemes of the 1970s; over-reliance on oil and gas revenues; and the effects of a crippling foreign debt. [. . .]

A nation-state in Algeria as defined in European terms came into being during the latter half of the nineteenth century. In the first six decades of the twentieth century the indigenous Muslim populations re-evaluated their own societies and over time determined to suppress their inherent divisions and coalesce together to eject the occupying colonial power. This suppression of social segmentations spawned new factions and frictions within society that re-emerged immediately after independence in 1962, only to be swept aside as a small westernised élite seized power.

This élite used the imperatives of nation-state building, the assertion of polit-ical independence, national development and stability to suppress debate about the political, cultural, religious, social and even linguistic identities and directions of the independent state. One of the key questions left unaddressed in the early 1960s was the religious orientation of the Constitution. The regime's adoption of a blend of Third World socialism, Western European social democracy, pan-Arabism and Islam was a compromise designed to appeal to all sectors of society, but which in fact was rejected by all.[2]

RELIGIOUS AND SECULAR RIVALS IN CONFLICT

Ever since independence was won from the French in 1962 government opponents, religious and secular, have remained bitter rivals with divided allegiances in the view of Martin Stone (1997). Stone emphasises that Islamic fundamentalism in Algeria and elsewhere is not in itself disposed to using violence though frustrated zealots may feel bound to adopt it:

Since independence, Algerian politics has been dominated by the interaction between various factions, clans, interest groups and ideological tendencies. Until 1989 the official ruling organisation, the Front de Libération Nationale (FLN) was merely a political façade behind which these various groups vied for power and influence. Although the one-party state was formally demolished in 1989, the four main political tendencies within the FLN – the dirigistes, the liberals, the secular-ists and the Islamists, each of which held conflicting conceptions of Algerian society – became locked in a bitter rivalry. This dangerous interplay grew apace with the introduction of political pluralism and the legalisation of the Front des Forces Socialistes (FFS) and the establishment of the Front Islamique de Salut (FIS) in 1989. As with previous groups, there was considerable blurring and flexibility of the groups' memberships and ideologies, with some public figures considering them-selves as belonging to more than one camp. Although the FFS and FIS had supporters in government and in the political parties, their efforts were principally directed at gaining the ear of the ultimate power in Algeria, the military. The military was itself divided over the Islamist 'problem', broadly forming two camps – the 'erad-icators', who favoured liquidation of the Islamists, and the 'conciliators', who sought to bring them into the establishment. [3] [. . .]

Algeria's struggle for independence lasting eight years was one of the most bitter and bloody wars of self-determination in history. To describe the war as merely a struggle between colonisers (the French) and colonised (the Muslims) would be misleading and incorrect. Parallels with South Africa are more appro-priate as the conflict was principally between the *pieds noirs* (Algerians of French descent) who wanted to remain in their native land under French protection, and the indigenous Muslims, who demanded initially an end to their second-class status but ultimately full statehood and complete control over the reins of power. The war also involved feuds and disputes between rival Muslims and between the *pieds noirs* and the French authorities. Acts of barbarism were committed on all sides. [. . .] Thus it was that the population of newly independent Algeria was over-whelmingly disoriented, bewildered, displaced and hopelessly ill-equipped for the task ahead.[4] [. . .]

Muslim activists often turn to violence out of desperation as so-called modernist regimes seek to suffocate the evolution of political Islam to protect the interests of the ruling élite. Sometimes the regimes themselves create and protect activist groups in order to besmirch the reputation of more mainstream Islamists whom they perceive as representing a greater threat.[5]

There were around sixty Islamic extremist groups active in Algeria in the mid and late 1990s. They ranged from tiny cells operating in cities to militias boasting as many as 50–60 armed guerrillas active in remote mountainous areas. The Algerian regime was anxious to present the groups as posing a serious though not terminal threat, and thus the Algerian media often distorted reporting on their activities and composition. Such distortion also characterised the greater part of contemporary foreign, and particularly Western, reporting on Islamic extremism in Algeria. By July 1997 at least 100,000 people had died in terrorist violence over the previous three and a half years, though the real figure may have been as high as 120,000. The inclusion in this figure of at least 115 expatriates killed during this period rendered Algeria statistically the most dangerous place in the world for foreigners, most of whom were murdered by the GIA [Armed Islamic Group] or its allies. However, the blood feud and the vendetta have traditionally played a major role in Algerian society and a considerable proportion of murders and other attacks ascribed to terrorists in fact represented the settling of scores originating in times of greater security and stability. [. . .]

The phenomenon of Islamic extremism in Algeria should be considered against the wider background of the Muslim world and the non-Muslim world's percep-tion of it. Violent Muslim groups stepped up activities in several Islamic states in the early 1980s as the Iranian revolution and the Lebanese civil war increased the non-Muslim world's awareness of the growing importance of political Islam. Indeed, Western observers have found it difficult to distinguish extreme Islamism from its merely political or fundamentalist manifestations. As in other Muslim countries, the vast majority of Islamists in Algeria vigorously reject the use of violence to achieve their aims. A comparative study of countries where Islamic extremism has developed would produce a number of common factors. In Algeria, as in Egypt and Tunisia, extremism grew in an environment where the regime simultaneously rejected radical Islamism on one level while adopting parts of its agenda on another. At times these regimes appointed Islamist figures to government posts as a means of opposing leftist influence, particularly among students. [. . .]

Broadly there are two strands of Islamic extremists in Algeria: religious zealots and frustrated Islamists. Religious zealots were active in the 1960s but only rarely in the 1970s, and the first significant attacks did not begin until political Islamism was gaining momentum in the early 1980s. [. . .]

The distinctions between the FIS [Front Islamique de Salut] and the extremist fringe became increasingly blurred as the violence worsened throughout 1992 and 1993. Even allowing for the regime's readiness to ascribe almost every act of violence in Algeria to Islamic extremists, many party members and officials within and without Algeria were directly or indirectly involved in extremist activities. In the first six months of 1992 the organisation grew rapidly as thousands of frustrated FIS supporters went underground in the weeks after the cancellation of the elections. The sight of relatives and friends rounded up and transported to the Saharan internment camps was a major incentive for many to join the MIA [Mouvement Islamique Armé]. Official reports of 'terrorist' trials frequently mentioned the alleged perpetrator's former – or in some cases – current membership of the FIS.[6]

ALGERIA'S GUERRILLAS: ORGANISATION AND FOREIGN SUPPORT

Martin Stone continues his account:

The MIA was organised on the triangle system developed by FLN guerrillas during the war of independence. Under this system each member of the cell knows only two other members of the network, though not their rank or status within the organisation as a whole. If detained and tortured an activist's objective is to remain silent for at least twenty-four hours to allow the other members of the cell to go to ground and inform the network. This allowed the network to continue functioning effectively even when the presumed leadership of the organisation had been arrested or temporarily incapacitated. The network was highly decentralised: cells were based on apartment blocks or *quartiers* and no activist ever came into direct contact with the leadership. Although there is strong evidence to suggest that the leadership took policy decisions on strategy and targeting, the cell commanders themselves made the day-to-day decisions. [. . .]

There is no reliable data on the numerical strength of the Islamic extremist groups. The authorities in April 1993 claimed that there were no more than 175 active guerrillas (most of whom were members of the MIA) with a network of 925 supporters. These figures were almost certainly gross underestimates, and the true number of active guerrillas was more likely to be as high as 10,000 or even 15,000, with perhaps as many active supporters. The estimated strength of the GIA's [Groupe Islamique Armé] armed forces was some 2,500. Guerrillas were predominantly under twenty-five, unemployed and lived in towns or cities, though many were older and had long criminal records. The groups raised money among Islamist supporters in emigré Algerian communities in Europe and North America, particularly from wealthy Algerian businessmen with Islamist sympathies. Armed robbery of banks was an additional source of finance; in March 1993, for instance, there was a five-day siege of a bank near Blida. [. . .]

Iran and Sudan have often been demonised as the grand international patrons of Islamist organisations, and Algeria has repeatedly singled out the two countries as foremost among foreign governments that support its extremist groups. In March 1993 Algeria severed diplomatic ties with Teheran. Although the extent of Iran's support of Algeria's extremists has probably been exaggerated, there is considerable evidence pointing to official Iranian support as part of its policy of exporting the Islamic revolution throughout the Muslim world. There is reason to believe that Iran was involved in the Algiers airport bombing of August 1992 and there were occasional reports of Iranian 'agents' being deported from Algeria. The Algerian press described the Iranian embassy in Algiers as a 'nest of spies' and claimed that Iran paid for a group of Algerian Islamists to travel to Lebanon to receive military training in Hezbollah camps. Evidence of Sudanese involvement, however, is less convincing and rests mainly on the established links between Islamists in Teheran and the Sudanese capital, Khartoum. Sudan's Islamist-backed military government has earned a reputation as a haven for numerous foreign Islamist groups, particularly Egyptians, and the Algerian authorities probably feel compelled to denounce Sudan as well as Iran. [. . .]

ALGERIA'S GUERRILLAS: THE PATTERN OF TERRORISM

Remote mountainous regions provided the ideal terrain for the extremist groups, as they did for the FLN and the followers of Bouyali before them. Both the MIA and GIA formed *maquis* groups in the mountains of the Tellian Atlas, from where they could mount ambushes on the security forces along roads and in nearby population centres. Official figures for terrorist-related incidents in the period February 1992 to April 1993 showed that of approximately 860 casualties, 315 were security-force personnel and soldiers; 370 presumed Islamic extremists; and 170 were civilians. The guerrillas would often terrorise the local population into concealing their whereabouts from the security forces. An operation in May 1992 provides a good illustration of the size and organisation of a typical guerrilla force. Five army battalions were mobilised against armed extremists who had installed themselves in the remote mountainous region near Lakhdaria, south-east of Algiers. The MIA-linked group had planned to use its remote base on Mount Zbarbar to attack the security forces and symbols of state authority in the area. Abdelkader Chebouti was also reported to have established a training camp on the mountain to shelter a number of Islamist army deserters. At least 150 would-be *maquisards* were arrested in the operation.

In the autumn of 1992 the extremists began an assassination campaign against their enemies. The motives behind the killings were a combination of classic terrorist tactics ('kill one to scare a thousand') and religious zeal. As Francis Ghilles has observed, the killings were often redolent of sacrificial acts. 'Honour can only be washed with blood, [and] witnesses must be present at the sacrifice'. Cassette tapes of sermons in which extremist imams ordered the faithful to kill anyone collaborating with the authorities began to appear in September 1992. Those under threat ranged from members of the government to civilians perceived as supporters of the regime in a wide range of professions and who were therefore enemies of the Islamist movement. This included civil servants, local government officials, *mudjahidine*, party politicians and officials of state-run authorities. The assassinations were usually well planned and executed, and the periodic waves of attacks on particular targets were intended gradually to increase pressure on the regime. By 1995 most politicians and senior civil servants had been forced to flee their villas on the hills above Algiers to take refuge in the well-guarded seaside resort of Sidi Fredj to the west of the city, from where the most important travelled to work by helicopter. [. . .]

In 1993 the extremists broadened their interpretation of their enemies to include relatives of government officials and 'anti-Islamist' civilians. While many victims had some family connection with the security forces, such as fathers or uncles in the gendarmerie or police, others had no apparent reason for being targeted. Scores of merchants, shopkeepers, engineers and labourers were knifed or shot to death. The assassins also struck at minor employees in local or central government. Although they were technically civilians, the MIA singled them out because of their vulnerability and their connection to the state. In March 1995 the GIA issued a warning that it would kill the wives, sisters and daughters of state functionaries, and followed it up with a spate of murders of women. In one such incident, a young secretary in a state-linked institution was shot in the back of the head as she entered her apartment. She died in her brother's arms. The extremists later imitated the tactics of the FLN by carrying out random bomb attacks in public places. In 1994 the GIA began to plant bombs with the aim of terrorising the population into pressing the authorities to negotiate with the Islamists. Among the most serious of these incidents was the blast outside Algiers central police station in March 1995, in which more than forty people lost their lives. In June 1995 the GIA began a campaign of suicide car bombings in Algiers.

The zealots also struck at journalists writing in 'anti-Islamist' publications and working for the state broadcasting corporation. [. . .]

Infiltration of the armed forces was an important element in the extremists' armoury. Scores of incidents were planned with the knowledge and assistance of security-force personnel, acting either voluntarily or through direct or indirect intimidation. [. . .]

In September 1993 the GIA began to murder foreigners, and by mid-1997 more than 115 had died in Algeria, though, as with all other aspects of the post-Chadli crisis, there was a large degree of falsification in the reporting of the murders. [. . .]

The GIA staged more attacks on foreigners across Algeria over the years that followed. The incidents were a combination of opportunism and sophistication. Most victims were long-term expatriates with no security and thus easy to target. Other victims were nationals of socialist or former socialist countries (such as Vietnam) with which Algeria had cemented cooperative alliances. [. . .]

By 1995 the leading Western countries, particularly the United States, had identified Islamic extremists as the most significant threat to Western interests worldwide, citing Algeria as the most visible 'proof' of this development. The threat of terrorist attack decimated Algeria's foreign business community, and those expatriates who remained did so from the safety of a guarded company compound, or were likely to be long-established residents who refused to leave Algeria and were unable to afford any protection.[7]

COUNTER-TERRORISM MEASURES

In 1998 the report of the United Nations 'eminent persons' was to acknowledge that terrorism in Algeria had passed through four stages. The report went on to describe the counter-terrorist measures being put into effect by the Algerian Government:

In the first stage it was aimed at security forces and government employees; in the second stage it was aimed at intellectuals, journalists, lawyers, artists and foreigners; in the third stage it was aimed at the general infrastructure of the country, e.g. bridges, schools, railways, and electricity supply; and in the current stage, it is aimed at the entire population. [. . .]

The authorities, on 30 September 1992, had created 'special courts' to try cases of terrorism. A terrorist act was defined as 'any violation of State security, the territorial integrity of the country or the stability and normal functioning of institutions by any act having the object of sowing terror among the population and creating a climate of insecurity by attacking persons or property.' [. . .]

Between October 1992 and October 1994, 13,770 persons had been judged by the special courts and 3,661 of them, or 25 per cent of those appearing, had been acquitted. There had been 1,661 sentences of death, 1,463 of which had been passed *in absentia*, and 8,448 sentences of imprisonment. [. . .]

In the light of experience with the struggle against terrorism at the judicial level, judicial procedures had been standardized in February 1995 through the abolition of the special courts and abrogation of the decree on terrorism and subversion. 'Terrorist and subversive crimes' are now legally defined and are to be dealt with by the ordinary courts. However, some lawyers with whom we met told us that some of the features of the special courts had been passed on to the regular courts. This allegedly had the effect of qualifying many acts as terrorist acts, although this might not always be the case. [. . .]

We were told that with the rise of terrorist violence, the civilian population, especially in the remote rural and mountainous areas, had been increasingly exposed to wanton acts of violence and brutality. The population of these villages and communes had requested that they be allowed to possess and retain arms and ammunition for their self-defence. Accordingly, legislation had been passed providing for the establishment of self-defence groups in villages and communes. The legislation authorized each household to have a gun and some ammunition. The self-defence groups operated under the control of the army or the gendarmerie, whichever was nearer. Ammunition provided to a household had to be accounted for and was intended to be used only for self-defence.

The Government had been able to reverse terrorism and to bring it to the stage where it had almost been eliminated largely because of the existence of these self-defence groups. The Government estimated that about 3,600 terrorists remained in widely scattered isolated areas. The Head of the Armed Forces, General Lamari, told us that wherever self-defence forces had been established, attacks by terrorists had stopped in 99 per cent of the cases. It was pointed out that the back-bone of the self-defence group was represented by former fighters in the independence struggle, 'the patriots'.

We were told that the self-defence groups had indeed played a decisive role in the fight against extremist violence; however, it was alleged that they were also sometimes responsible for excesses committed against the civilian population. Bearing in mind the atmosphere prevailing in Algeria, in which there is simulta-neously a transition to an open society and a fight against terrorism, we asked about monitoring arrangements and procedures to ensure that the self-defence groups did not commit excesses. The authorities told us in response that the self-defence groups came under the authority of the gendarmerie or the army, whichever post was nearer.

Some of those with whom we spoke told us that the Government needed to improve the ways in which it responded to terrorism and in which it dealt with charges that excesses are committed by security forces. We asked repeatedly about the arrangements in place for preventing excesses from being committed by these forces, about how they were implemented and with what results. For the most part we received only general answers. The authorities did, however, provide us with lists of around 140 cases in respect of which action had been taken against members of the security forces. We think that this is an area where the Government should be more open.

We met one of the self-defence groups when we visited the village of Igujdal in the Kabyle region. Officials, members of the self-defence group and the population of the village were present. In our discussion with members of the self-defence group, they informed us that they had had to face extremist violence for six years. Their village had been attacked and they had had to defend it with their own arms. After they had repulsed the attacks, the authorities had come and offered help. They had then organized a self-defence group in the village. The self-defence group was headed by a committee, and every night some members of the group kept guard over the village.

Asked whether they were united in agreement on the organization of the self-defence group, they answered in the affirmative. However, a member of the group said that whereas the vast majority had served on it for almost six years without any recompense, they had discovered that some members were being paid clandestinely by the authorities. When we asked how payments were made, the answer given was that they were made through the regional office. The President of the Regional Assembly, who was present, acknowledged that when the regional assembly had voted funds for the budget it had decided against a provi-sion for such payments; however, the Minister of the Interior had reversed that decision.

Asked whether they felt that their security would be threatened if the self-defence groups were abolished, they answered that the villagers did not know what would happen if extremist violence continued. One speaker stated, 'We are fed up with extremist violence. [8] [. . .]'

The 'eminent persons' report concludes with a direct recommendation to the Algerian authorities:

It is crucially important, at the same time, that the Government give serious consideration to programmes of social reform that would reduce the sense of hopelessness that we were told was very widespread among large sections of Algerian youth. Unless these pressing social problems are tackled urgently and effectively, Algeria could experience more social dislocations and tension in the future.[9]

POSTSCRIPT

There are a number of disquieting circumstances in the case of Algeria's terrorism. In the first place, the scale of violence has led to frenzied butchery as referred to above where terrorist targeting has been superseded by wholesale slaughter chiefly of villagers. One estimate is that 75,000 lives have been taken during the period 1992–98 alone. Another 20,000 or so Algerians have 'disappeared'. Second, the Algerian Government has rebuffed all help from the outside for the homeless and the traumatised. As we have seen, a panel of United Nations visitors was allowed some freedom to survey and report but Algeria has not been ready to facilitate monitoring of a destabilised situation and offers of help from any other quarter. Terrorism in Algeria is to be dealt with by Algerians alone. Third, and doing nothing to reduce the impression of failure on all sides, is the apparent existence of a logistical network of sympathisers among expatriate Algerians elsewhere in Europe, chiefly in France. Fourth, there is the determination of armed Islamic groups – much splintering has taken place – never to enter into dialogue or truce with the force for law and order in an all-out struggle against an illegitimate and secular Algerian government. And fifth, there is the suspicion, aired in the Western press from time to time, that a defeatist government often turns a blind eye to the brutal activities of rebel groups. There is, indeed, much about the Algerian scenario that prompts the question whether we have here the twisted possibility that the means is becoming the end.

Chapter 11

Peru

CONSIDERED BY MANY TO BE the most dangerous and violent terrorist organisation in the world, the Shining Path group (Sendero Luminoso or Sendero) of Peru is unique in many ways. After twenty years of violent disruption of civilised order it remains today a menace to Peruvian society despite the attempts of successive governments to defeat it and despite a general revulsion at its message and its methods. Christened by Marxists as 'a shining path to the future' it represents for most Peruvians something that is archaic and destructive. Originating as an educational enterprise in the Indian-settled lands of Peru and directed by academics anxious to reinvigorate a community, it has twisted away into authoritarian rigidity, contemptuous even of the poor it set out to benefit. Insurgency, as a thrust for liberation – power to the people – is not hard to understand where it has arisen in many other countries: in Peru it has broken down into an illiberal, obsessive reliance on violence. There is a messianic insistence on the part of a leader and acolytes on power (only) for the Party. 'Everything other than power (for the Party) is illusion', is Sendero's apocalyptic claim. Peru has been lacerated by the toll of 18,000 dead, 3,000 'disappearances', and well over 2,500 terrorists captured. Violence continues. This case-study will attempt to throw light on the origins and development of a vicious form of terrorism. Following that, the question will be put: 'What can contemporary Peru do about its "time of terror", now two decades old?'

THE ORIGINS OF SENDERO

A detailed and very systematic account of the birth and development of Peru's terrorism is provided by David Scott Palmer (1995). He isolates a number of key factors in the context surrounding the rise of Sendero.

First, we should use the label 'terrorist' advisedly – the group would disown it:

Sendero does not see itself as a terrorist organization, but rather as a revolutionary movement fully engaged since 1980 in a people's war. Actions that others call terrorist, Shining Path militants justify as a necessary part of a long-term struggle to take power in a country in which the élites have always violently exploited peasants and workers. By labeling the movement terrorist and by emphasizing counter-terrorism in its response, the government may well be playing into Sendero's hands. Its actions make the peasantry more fearful of authority; provoke local, national and international revulsion against the government; and foster conditions that contribute to the generalization of violence in Peru by provoking others on the Left and the Right to carry out their own terrorist actions.[1]

Second, Sendero began in a small provincial university in the 1960s:

[They were] one more group on the Marxist Left within a pluralistic Latin American academic context. In 1963 and 1964 there was no reason to believe it would ever be anything more than that. The activist young professor who led this particular 'study group', Abimael Guzmán Reynoso, was one of several at the university at the time who covered the political spectrum from radical to government supporters to conservative. Like the others, the university group identified with Guzmán, developed ties with national political movements in the 1960s and competed for influence in universities and unions around the country. Guzmán's organization was affiliated first with Castroite groups and then with the Maoist party breakaway after the 1963 Sino-Soviet split.

Sendero did not grow out of a national context of systemic and official repression or a systematic thwarting of opportunities for access to national politics. Shining Path in a real sense made the revolution in Peru. Inappropriate government responses then contributed to creating the conditions that Sendero had already posited to justify its actions. The terrorism engendered by Guzmán's organization was one component of its deliberate action to force a repressive state response that would alienate the populace and make them more receptive to Sendero's message; it was not a reaction to standing state-terrorism practices.[2]

Third, the place where the movement began was an inauspicious locale:

Sendero got its start in one of the most isolated and poorest regions of Peru, where central government access had been historically intermittent, communications difficult or virtually impossible, poverty generalized, and Indians and Indian communities very predominant (the region of Ayacucho).

Fourth, the university where it all started was launching an innovative extension movement (after closure for some years):

Most significantly, the University of Huamanga was designed to serve as a catalyst for social and economic change in the region by offering to local youth an array of specializations most needed to address the problems of the Ayacucho area. Instead of the traditional schools of law, medicine, and engineering, there were programs of education, applied anthropology, rural and agricultural engineering, and nursing. Instead of immediate specialization upon entering the university, students spent their first two years in 'basic studies', a type of interdisciplinary liberal arts education, to broaden their knowledge of the world around them. In another major departure from previous higher education practice in Peru, the faculty was contracted on a full-time basis with salaries set high enough during the first few years to attract some of the country's best academics.

Furthermore, a specific mission of the university was to reach out to the wider community with an array of services in health, education, and local development [. . .] . the distinctive contribution of Peru's first 'new' university – active participation in various aspects of local development in one of the poorest regions of the country – was gradually infused with a radical, sectarian political content. Under the leadership of Professor Guzmán, first as education-program teacher, then as director of the teacher-training school, and finally as director of personnel of the university, the goal of forging an institution committed to the teaching and extension of Marxist principles in all of the university's activities was realised between the mid-1960s and the mid-1970s.[3]

Fifth, the region of Ayacucho had been a field for an array of government development programmes since 1963 which had materially improved the local economy, the infrastructure of settlement and housing, public health, and literacy. Inevitably, though, overlap in provision and some disagreement was sure to occur:

The growing sectarianism of the University of Huamanga's extension activities in the late 1960s and early 1970s was counterbalanced for a time by this array of government programs, with generally positive consequences for the local, mostly peasant population. University students were active with their political agenda in some communities, while the government and its affiliates were involved with theirs in many others. By the early 1970s, however, the dynamic shifted markedly, largely due to inappropriate new government programs. The resulting decline in the well-being of many Ayacucho peasants made it even harder for them to cope after the earlier improvement in their situation, however modest. It set the stage for Sendero more easily to expand its access to and influence with a peasantry increasingly disquieted, disillusioned, and discontented.[4]

Sixth, and again perhaps inevitably, the academics in the University of Huamanga began to pull away from any state enterprise towards their own ingrained philosophical stance that no better deal for the peasants could be anything less than a revolutionary transformation of society and that the ideology sustaining that must be principally Maoist:

They were advancing their Maoist vision of Marxism by action as well as by study instead of being satisfied by merely talking about it. The emerging conviction that they alone had discovered the keys to Marxist theory and practice by years of diligent study, conscientious application in the field, and the building of close ties between some Ayacucho peasants and the intellectual vanguard gradually produced a virtually unshakable faith in their uniqueness, even within the larger Marxist revolutionary community. They saw themselves, if you will, as the equivalent of the reborn Christian, the true carriers of the faith and, therefore, destined to eventual triumph no matter how daunting the odds.[5]

Seventh, the pinnacle of responsibility must be that of the Leader (Guzmán):

Professor Guzmán went on to hold key positions in the university. The directorship of the teacher-training school permitted the introduction of a more partisan political criterion and the use of his considerable academic and personal skills to attract and radicalize many enterprising students of humble origins. The patronage and influence involved with this position enhanced his already demonstrated ability to attract a substantial number of the most able students and faculties in the university and commit them to his radical course.

Though already a Communist party member, part of his militancy and revolutionary conviction, like that of his closest circle, might have been derived from the impact of the poverty and isolation of Ayacucho, with which he had daily contact through his students, the extension programmes to outlying communities, and the city itself. Another key element is the personal magnetism Guzmán projected, his dedication to the study of Marxist writings, and his ability to synthesize his insights in a pedagogical way that made everything seem so clear and correct. In a university in which the student body had grown enormously by the early 1970s and in which most of the outstanding Peruvian intellectuals originally attracted to Huamanga had departed, Guzmán's talents stood out even more.[6]

Eighth, and very significantly, Sendero's initiators waited for the government to make a move. What turned out to be a long-term military regime (1968–80) focused on the need to change the country in order to save it:

The government [military, 1968–80] adopted an aggressive Third World stand. A number of large private corporations, both domestic and foreign-owned, were nationalized. The state expanded dramatically in size, from being one of the smallest in Latin America to one of the largest. The Marxist Left was legalized and legitimated, particularly labor unions, which proliferated at historically unprecedented rates even as the government was attempting to construct a competing social-property structure combining workers and management in industry, mining and agriculture. A major agrarian reform was undertaken, starting in 1969, that over the next ten years dramatically restructured Peruvian agriculture.

However well intended and however significant their benefits for some sectors of Peru's population, the changes introduced by the military government also facilitated the rise of Sendero in a number of ways. Encouraging Marxist groups provided alternatives to Shining Path on the Left, on the one hand, which proved to be a major obstacle to the advancement of Sendero's guerrilla war. But on the other hand, by letting the political dynamics within the universities largely take their own course in the 1970s, the military regime allowed the Sendero centre at the University of Huamanga to become much stronger than it would have been had it been subject to closer review. The reformist phase of the military government, 1968–75, coincided with the period of Sendero control of the university and the concomitant expansion and deepening of radical study groups there.

In addition, the application of the agrarian reform in the Ayacucho area proved disastrous. This was mainly because this region had a much higher proportion of Indian communities to private haciendas than most other parts of the country, and the haciendas were both smaller and poorer for the most part. As a result, the agrarian reform broke down the old system without providing an alternative that would generate new resources in its place. Historic animosities and tensions, previously moderated by the weight of the status quo and government mediation, increased, and most of the peasantry wound up worse off as a result.

The overall effect was a substantial decline in production and peasant well-being in the area even as alternative avenues of recourse were also being reduced. Shining Path's ongoing activities in the communities became more and more important, partly as a direct consequence of the application of central-government policies in the Ayacucho area.

Sendero, given its years of preparation and expanding presence in the area, was particularly well positioned to take advantage of the government's problems and the growing distress of the local population. Sendero Luminoso's historic decision to launch the people's war in early 1980 was, thus, far from fortuitous.[7]

SENDERO'S STRATEGY

Scott Palmer (1995) has traced the evolution of Sendero's strategy as a response to the opportunities outlined above:

The Sendero strategy is, at root, a prolonged war of attrition over an increasing expanse of the national territory, a war that is intended to force the government to increase its expenditures on military actions, thus making it less and less able to satisfy basic popular demands. In addition, militants work to create an increasingly chaotic situation in the cities that authorities will eventually not be able to control. Over time, the population, especially the third that lives in Lima, will lose its capacity to cope and will see in Sendero 'the only authority capable of restoring order'. Military success is not Sendero's goal, according to some analysts. Rather, it is to paralyze the economy, destabilize the government, and force authorities into making unpopular decisions.

However, the organization does pursue a long-term military strategy designed to take military advantage of the government's growing inability to manage the country. Following Mao, Sendero's prolonged people's war is to develop in three strategic phases in its relation to government forces: defense, equilibrium, and offense. Each is determined by the relative size and operational capacity of Sendero forces vis-à-vis those of the government. In the 'strategic defensive' phase Sendero wages 'guerrilla war' with small armed units; in the 'strategic equilibrium' phase the armed struggle becomes a 'war of movements' with much larger military forces, up to battalion size, capable of engaging government forces on equal terms.

Given this strategic assessment, for Sendero the role of terrorism is central to attaining its objectives. [. . .] Terrorism for Sendero has the specific objective of reducing the scope and capacity of government authority, thereby causing the centre to lose legitimacy in the minds of the population.

SENDERO'S ORGANISATION

To work towards its objectives, Sendero has constructed an elaborate political and military structure:

The basic unit is the cell. Each cell has five to nine members, including a leader, called the *responsable político*, as well as two explosive experts, a physical training instructor, and a person responsible for ideological training. Cells do not normally operate in their home regions, and members are not apprised of orders given to other cells, or of the identity of other members. Only one member, usually the *responsable político*, has direct communication with the next higher level of leadership. There is also a hierarchy of commitment and responsibility broken down into five distinct groups – premilitants, militants, military personnel, organizers, and leaders – of which the first three operate in separate cells. These cells are, in turn, coordinated by the leader of the subsector who answers to a zonal director responsible to a regional committee. Planning and coordination between zones is carried out by a coordination committee, ultimately answerable, along with its regional counterpart, to the National Central Committee, the ruling body of Sendero.

The country is divided by the Shining Path leadership into six regional committees. In the Metropolitan Region there are also four 'special squads' with specific and distinct duties related to 'annihilation', 'assault', 'containment', and 'razing', which carry out selected terrorist operations in a coordinated sequence.

Much of the responsibility for the selection and implementation of specific operations rests with the regional committees and their commanders, giving the organization a substantial degree of local autonomy. This means that the dynamic of Sendero activities in one part of the country may in many cases bear little relation to that in another. It also gives to the movement a flexibility that rests with those who presumably know more about local situations than those at the top.

Overall control remains firmly in the hands of the National Central Committee and, before he was captured, most particularly in those of Guzmán himself (whose *nom de guerre* was Comrade, then President Gonzalo). In addition, there are periodic party congresses (believed to have been held in 1979, 1982, 1985 and February 1988) to assess and critique the movement's progress.[8]

Sendero organisational capacities have been improved by carefully tailoring strategies to peasants' concerns about personal security and economic survival, a risky way of proceeding in view of government counter-insurgency and the fragile nature of any alliance with frightened *campesinos*. Cynthia McClintock (1984) has this to say about Sendero methods:

In tailoring its strategies to the peasants' concerns about personal security and economic survival, Sendero has been a much more calculating guerrilla organization than its predecessors. The movement has reduced its risks in various ways. Most Senderista militants are indigenous to the region and thus do not stand out physically from the rest of the population. Also, members' identities are carefully concealed. All members use aliases, and during terrorist activities they are masked with large woolen hoods. Few Senderistas know more than four others: each guerrilla cell has a maximum of five members; one is the leader, joining the committee at the next higher level.

Sendero has also reduced risks to the peasantry by restricting the presence of governmental authorities in the Ayacucho region. As early as the 1970s, officials who sought to enter Senderista territory were shot. Since 1980, Sendero has targeted civilian authorities assiduously. Between 1980 and August 1983, eighteen civilian officials were assassinated, and many more wounded or threatened. As a result, virtually none are left in the area.

Sendero has provided significant benefits to its supporters. Of course, it promised a better life. But the movement has also taken action – violent action – to benefit the peasants materially. After blacklisting relatively well-to-do landowners, shopkeepers, and intermediaries, and either killing them or causing them to flee, Sendero distributed their property among villagers, and cancelled debts to them. To recruits, Sendero has offered basic subsistence (probably possible as a result of Sendero's economic levies on the drug trade). Sendero's terrorist actions are also apparently perceived as daring by some Sendero recruits, a disproportionate number of whom are mere adolescents.

Since January 1983, with the onset of the government's counter-insurgency offensive, the political cost–benefit equation has blurred somewhat. Sympathy for Sendero has become much more dangerous. The toll of the struggle has mounted. By early 1984, the government admitted that about 3,500 people had been killed; 1,500 'disappeared'; and 4,000 had been arrested. Although the government reports most of the dead as Senderista militants, it is known that villages considered sympathetic to Sendero were raided and even bombed; Amnesty International and other independent observers believe that most of the dead were civilians.

Sendero's own actions during this period may have alienated the peasants. It has been reported that Sendero became more ruthless and wanton in its attacks, and that the guerrillas tried to reduce agricultural production and to stop weekly markets. Probably most important, Sendero was unable to protect its peasant allies from counter-insurgency offensives; when Ayacucho's pro-Senderista villages were assaulted, the guerrilla leaders fled elsewhere. At the same time, Sendero's ranks have become less disciplined and coordinated, and may even have been infiltrated by 'pseudo-Sendero' criminals.

Yet, it does not appear that the security forces won many peasants to their side during 1983. As we have seen, the subsistence crisis in the southern highlands was worsening at this time, and peasants were especially angry at the government. Moreover, the behavior of Peru's security forces in Ayacucho, like the behavior of most militaries amid such conflicts, was generally reported to be poor. The counter-insurgency personnel were regarded by many as arbitrary, brutal, and corrupt. While the security forces did attract some peasants to their side – most clearly,

the Iquichanos – economic inducements were rumored to be of considerable importance to the peasants' decisions.[9]

Scott Palmer (1995) has attempted an estimate of Sendero growth over the years
1980–92 and also a tally of reported incidents and casualties for which the guerillas
have been held responsible:

Although estimates vary widely, Sendero is believed to have grown from about 100
militants in 1980–81, to 3,000 to 10,000 in 1987–88, to 3,000 to 4,000 armed
cadres, as many as 10,000 militants, and some 50,000 premilitants (sympathizers
and occasional contributors or members of front organizations) by mid-1992.
Guerrilla casualties, mostly Sendero, have been high: the number of 'presumed
terrorists killed' through 1992 was 10,655. Among the casualties are many important Sendero figures, including entire cells, regional committee members, and
members of the Central Committee. Even so, the number of reported incidents
exceeded the thirteen-year average of 1,814 every year between 1985 and 1992.
The ratio of deaths per 100 incidents also rose sharply during the four-year period
beginning in 1989, even though both incidents and deaths declined by 30 per cent
through 1992, after both hit historic highs of 2,779 and 3,745, respectively, in
1990. Over 62 per cent of all police and armed-forces political-violence casualties
have occurred since 1989 (1,420 of 2,278). These gruesome data make abundantly
clear that Sendero as an organization has clearly been capable of maintaining its
destructive course in spite of increased pressure from government forces.[10]

THE GROWTH OF SENDERO EXPLAINED

Once again, Scott Palmer has listed what he considers are crucial factors, both
inside and outside Sendero, which help to explain the movement's growth. First,
there is the ideology:

A complete system of values and beliefs from a basic Marxist conception of the
class struggle (Marx), the dictatorship of the proletariat (Lenin), rural revolution
(Mao), and nationalistic domestic Third World revolution (Mariátegui), with
Guzmán as the living guide. The Sendero ideology provides a recognizable alternative value system in a group-solidarity setting that, when combined with actions,
enhances one's self-worth.
   It may be compared with a religious experience, an alternative to Catholic or
Protestant activism, because of which the individual 'convert' changes personal
behavior and feels much better about himself or herself. It can also be an alternative to activity in a more moderate Marxist party or union, which Shining Path
leaders view as a violation of radical orthodoxy because these parties or unions
stoop to participating in what SL militants believe is a totally corrupt system. The
myth of invincibility and of the inevitability of eventual triumph that SL training
and flyers espouse appeals to an idealistic youth's inclination to self-sacrifice for the
larger and longer cause. Purity is achieved and maintained by aloofness, discipline,

intense training, spartan living, following the lead of the superior, and putting the movement ahead of self. Ideology is inculcated through the 'popular schools' or through militant teachers trained at the University of Huamanga while the education programme was under Sendero influence, teachers who are now working in other teacher-training programmes or in public schools [state schools].

Second, there is an array of supportive fronts and organisations:

[These are] designed to support and publicize Sendero activities at the grass roots or to defend, protect, and help militants or family members.

Third, recruitment of sympathisers has been taken in hand most efficiently:

From among the most able of these activist Sendero sympathizers can come the replacements for the premilitant and militant cells of the party. A third important factor, then, is that a recruitment hierarchy begun with this group of legal (until 1988) organizations at the base has been capable so far of keeping a flow into the clandestine cell structure and so on up the ladder to the top.

Fourth, a factor helping to explain why the movement was able to sustain its violent momentum through 1992 despite government pressures is the large number of women involved:

[Women appeared] at all levels of the organization, right up to the top positions in both the regional commands and the National Central Committee. Sendero's MFP [Women's Popular Movement] was formed in 1975. During the early 1980s all the known secretaries of the Lima Metropolitan Committee were women, along with at least half of the leadership of the other regional committees. Large numbers of women participate in Sendero's major military operations, and a woman is frequently charged with responsibility for delivering the fatal shot in the assassination-squad operations. In 1987 alone, 491 women of the 790 captured were charged with 'terrorist crimes'. It is speculated that women overcome the subordinate role and status historically ascribed to them in Peruvian society when they participate as equals in the Shining Path apparatus and lead many of its initiatives.

Fifth, Sendero has made a deliberate effort to recruit very young people as 'iron militants':

Militants in rural areas are often only fourteen or fifteen years old. The youth are perceived by the leadership as more idealistic and more easily formed. Without the outside commitments and experiences of their elders, they are also more easily and more completely committed to the Shining Path cause. Sendero thus secures strong and unquestioning supporters by attracting and educating them while their personal perceptions and values are still in flux. Older people are considered to be much harder to work with, less predictable in their commitment to the organization, and less trustworthy. Today's fifteen-year-old militant, if he or she survives, will be tomorrow's twenty-two-year-old commander, organizer, or leader.

Sixth, there is the overarching importance of the leader:

In Guzmán, the Communist Party of Peru had from 1963 until 1992 [his time of capture] a very special combination of intellectual and tactical ability. The image projected was that of an aloof but charismatic individual of remarkable powers of comprehension, interpretation, and capacity for prediction, totally sure of himself and of the rightness of the cause. His analysis of Peru and the revolution is considered by his colleagues to be the equal of the great Marxist leaders, Marx, Lenin, and Mao, and thus worthy of elevation as 'the fourth sword of Marxism'.

What impressed many observers of Sendero's development in Peru was the total dedication of members to the leader.

A seventh and final factor strengthening Sendero's operative capacity is a profitable connection with certain aspects of the drug trade in Peru and in particular:

[. . .] access since the mid-1980s to a portion of the significant resources generated by coca and cocaine paste production and trafficking, largely in Peru's upper Huallaga valley. Though not conclusively proved, it is believed that Sendero garnered a minimum of $10 million a year (some estimates range as high as $100 million) between 1987 and 1992 from 'taxes' on a large portion of the valley's 80,000 coca growers and from levies of up to $15,000 a flight on the mostly Colombian traffickers as they landed on the scores of clandestine runways in the valley to pick up their cargoes of cocaine paste. Many analysts have concluded that this income is used to pay salaries to Sendero militants, provide financial support to families of cadres killed in combat, and to pay for arrested comrades' jail maintenance and legal fees for court trials.[11]

In any case a key factor making for Sendero strength, apart from the secrecy of gathering and movement, was its self-sufficiency deriving what was needed from the locality:

Food and sustenance came from the peasants who supported them, arms from the military and police by taking them, and dynamite from the mines and road building crews. In this fashion the revolution did not become dependent on outside sources, with their own agendas and objectives, which might subvert the local dynamic of the revolutionary process.[12]

Finally, in Peru, a progressive erosion in economic opportunities as a result of gross inflation, unemployment, and increasing poverty presented Sendero as a radical and desirable alternative to what was not being afforded by the state:

[There was] a certain appeal – employment, restoration of self-respect, a coherent, fully defined belief system, and specific solutions to Peru's current problems.[13]

SENDERO LUMINESCENCE BEGINS TO FADE

Despite the receptiveness of peasants, the *campesinos,* and of poor urban workers to the revolutionists' promises and plans, Sendero momentum has been uneven and halting since 1990 though its menace is always in the shadows. Frustration on all sides has led to much appalling violence. Mayors have been assassinated, government cooperatives destroyed, *hacienda* (estate) owners and government officials ambushed, altogether a cycle of disruption seemingly without much object. Sendero appears to have taken little account of the insight and common sense of the *campesinos* as a Peruvian sociologist, Carlos Izaguirre, commented in 1996:

Guzmán underestimated the resilience of the survival mechanisms that the Peruvian people have developed over decades, and the faith in progress that underscores their Sisyphean efforts. He failed to appreciate the true dimensions of this age-old game of resistance and adaptation, of scepticism and expectations, and of simultaneous rejection and acceptance of the rules and the predominant institutions.

The idea of radical rupture is profoundly alien to Peruvians. Shining Path sought to implant it through the use of terror. They killed hundreds of *campesinos* for bettering themselves as traders and sellers, for serving as state officials, for voting in elections, and for being mayors or grassroots leaders opposed to the armed struggle. They tried to boycott elections, development projects, and the markets where *campesinos* sold their products. They wanted to turn every protest march into a general 'armed strike'. They tried to impose the fiction of their own authorities and popular committees. Shining Path had some success, but it was precarious. In the end, they invited military repression and intervention in the areas where they organized.

In this way, the spiral of terror grew from both sides. But the pragmatism of the *campesinos* eventually led them to forge an alliance with the army, since it had both more power and the representation of the state. Despite the military's record of brutality, tens of thousands of *campesinos* began forming, under military tutelage, civil-defense patrols to fight off Shining Path.

Shining Path's insurrection thus became a revolution of *campesinos* against *campesinos* — a popular war against the people. Shining Path had most appeal among social groups located on the periphery of productive activity: students, teachers, unemployed young people from the shanty towns. With this membership, Shining Path developed more as a sect than as a movement with a popular base of support. This lack of consistent social support would prove to have dire consequences for the Party.[14]

GOVERNMENT RESPONSE TO SENDERO TERRORISM

Between 1989 and 1992 Sendero stepped up its terrorist activity in and around the Peruvian capital, Lima, badly shaking the government's confidence as Izaguirre relates:

During this same period, after several years of striking out blindly against the population, the state began to reformulate its counter-insurgency strategies. Even though the police and the military did not coordinate their efforts – indeed, there was a great deal of rivalry between the two institutions – these shifts hastened Shining Path's demise. Through stepped-up intelligence efforts, the police were able to arrest a number of key intermediate-level leaders, weakening Shining Path's internal organization.[15]

Government response to the challenge of political violence and terrorism begun by Sendero and emulated to a lesser extent by other groups has taken a variety of forms since 1980. The haemorrhaging of economic growth, hyperinflation, spiralling unemployment, and industrial strikes all diverted ministerial attention in the earlier years away from acts of violence and denied the security battalions the personnel and funds they needed. Counter-terrorist measures lacked force and coordination and were marked by indiscriminate search and arrest, summary interrogation, even torture, means of repression which often led to numerous casualties among bystanders.

By 1985 the Peruvian government was rooting out internal problems of corruption, maladministration, and human rights violations within its own security department. A National Agency against Terrorism was set up, a state of emergency was proclaimed and intelligence work made more sophisticated. In 1990 a political newcomer and professor of mathematics, Alberto Fujimori, surprised Peru by winning the presidency. Fujimori introduced a neoliberal reformist programme and a determined long look at the nature and extent of terrorism. By 1992 Guzmán himself had been arrested along with 300 sector leaders in that year alone. Two years later, from his cell in a specially built impregnable prison, Guzmán put a peace proposal to Fujimori. There might have been some negotiating room here had not the leaders of Sendero still at large vociferously proclaimed their disassociation from any peace feelers and cessation of their terror campaign. The only course the government felt feasible was to try to turn the edge of terrorist ardour and recruiting by enlisting the support of *campesinos* for a policy of rural reinvestment and land reform. Security in the towns and the countryside was to be improved through mustering civil-defence patrols made up of volunteers and military advisors. Measured by the number of incidents and deaths, terrorism began to wane after 1995. Yet, as Scott Palmer sees it, the government of Peru has, year by year, frequently played into the hands of Sendero's strategists:

First it gave the guerrilla cadres time and space to grow. Then it applied military force in an often indiscriminate manner, thus alienating local, usually peasant populations. When the government finally began to get things right on counter-insurgency policy in 1985 and 1986, the momentum could not be sustained, due to disastrous macroeconomic policies that impoverished millions with runaway inflation. Government human rights violations multiplied as well. The drastic economic measures required to undo the damage at the macro level further increased human misery at the micro level, besides virtually guaranteeing two or three years more without economic growth.

Sendero took full advantage of the opportunities presented it. They expanded the organization and recruitment, especially in Lima. They increasingly invoked citywide armed strikes in urban centres around the country. They continued to damage the country's infrastructure as well as, and sometimes simultaneously, set off car bombs for maximum psychological effect. And their agenda of highly selective assassinations and intimidation, in Lima shanty towns especially but also in other sensitive locations around the country, moved inexorably forward.

The result of government errors, on the one hand, and Sendero's adroitness, on the other, was, not surprisingly, an erosion over time of government capacity and legitimacy, particularly in those provinces and urban slum areas where the Shining Path converts had been most active. As the central government became more and more bogged down by severe economic constraints, more and more opportunities opened up for Sendero to advance, even though the guerrillas themselves lacked the installed capacity to take full advantage of them. Government authorities were further hampered by continuing the long-standing practice of focusing attention on the provinces, which frequently resulted in inappropriate or even counter-productive policy formulation and implementation. Bureaucratic rivalries among different government agencies and political parties that put narrow partisanship and short-term gain above the country's interests complicated the process still further.

Democracy should have been a major bulwark against the advance of Shining Path in Peru, but as it was practised in the 1980s, it contributed significantly to the generalization of violence and to its own erosion.[16]

POSTSCRIPT

After twenty years of furious campaigning in Peru, that bright, articulate message, Sendero Luminoso, Shining Path, is in most respects a dark and dangerous quagmire. Its premises and promises have opened few doors and slammed most of them shut in the estimated 80 per cent of Peru in which its desperate advocates operate. Terror and intimidation are the chief mechanisms to manipulate for influence and control, mechanisms that are counter-productive and destructive. Sendero, in common with other terrorist factions (especially in Germany and Italy), has to a significant extent become a prisoner of its own ideology. It was in 1996 that Izaguirre, with a sociological perspective, detected a movement ideologically pinioned and divided:

The cycle of political violence begun in 1980 came to an end during the brief period framed by two watershed events: Guzmán's arrest in September 1992, and the declaration by Shining Path leaders still at large of their opposition to Guzmán's peace proposal in February 1994. 'It is a norm of the Communist movement that Party leadership cannot be exercised from prison', said the dissident faction in direct allusion to Guzmán. The play's final scene is the division of Shining Path into Guzmán's pro-peace faction, and the faction that continues to wage war.

Both factions are trying to resolve the same problem: how to keep Shining Path alive and relevant after the many defeats the Party has suffered. For Guzmán, saving the Party requires halting all sabotage and guerrilla activities and engaging in unarmed political activities for several years. Those who oppose him, led by Oscar Ramírez Durand ('Comrade Feliciano'), believe the Party's only salvation lies in continuing its armed activities, though with less intensity than before, and emphasizing the reconstruction of its grassroots cells via the classic ant-like work of its clandestine militants.

Despite their opposing prescriptions for action, both sides perceive that Shining Path has entered a new phase of its existence. Guzmán has even said so explicitly in his new manifestos. Feliciano and his comrades, by reducing their activity and prioritizing underground political activity, recognize implicitly that times have changed. Aware that Shining Path has lost the leading role that it held in the early 1990s, both groups share the common goal of remaining in the wings, like understudies, in anticipation of better times.

It is unlikely that Shining Path will disappear from Peru's political stage any time soon. But given the reduced size of both factions, the violence will be low-key and will take place mainly in parts of Peru that are of little political or economic importance, such as shanty towns in Lima and towns in the jungle or Andean highlands.

Shining Path is no longer proclaiming – to audiences in Peru and the rest of the world – the existence of their popular committees or their impending overthrow of the state. Rather, they are hoping to exercise a combination of political hegemony and terror at the local level. Occasionally, they will carry out a spectacular act of sabotage or ambush a military patrol. These activities will not endanger the stability of the state or even cause foreign investors to leave Peru in search of safer pastures. The principal aim of such activities is to remind everyone of their continued presence on the political stage. Shining Path poses few risks to Peru's stability in the short term, but the risks may grow as time marches on.[17]

Are there any certainties at all as to security in contemporary Peru? Scott Palmer's conclusion in 1995 is sombre and entirely relevant today:

Since 1980, terrorism has become institutionalized in Peru, some without question state-sponsored, but mostly guerrilla-provoked. The consequences in human and material terms have been devastating for society and the country at all levels. Sendero may not win, but through its systematic, selective, and methodical terrorism, Peru is certainly the loser.[18]

Chapter 12

Colombia

BETWEEN 1946 AND 1966 the Republic of Colombia was the scene of one of the most intense and protracted instances of widespread civilian violence in the history of the twentieth century. Known in Colombia simply as *La Violencia* this episode claimed perhaps 200,000 lives including 112,000 at its peak in 1948–50. Colombia, later, in 1960, had the highest violent death rate in the world.

The Colombian case-study differs from the others in that here we have an entire nation torn by the horrors of twenty years of political strife. Nobody was able to escape the tensions and dangers. More than in other Latin American states seared by violence, such as Peru and Argentina, in Colombia terrorism took hold of all sides of the conflict. The state of Colombia has recovered from two decades of turmoil and there is an appreciable measure of reconciliation among those formerly at each other's throats. Unhappily, though, contemporary Colombia is struggling with an immense drug problem of production, addiction and trafficking – with, of course, its own component of violence.

This case-study begins by examining the context within which protest, conflict and violence built up. Some explanations will be offered for causes and development of the terror, particularly in regard to the struggle with guerrilla forces. There will eventually be a close look at the peace process as it cautiously began and as it has gathered credibility and reliability. What this case-study will not do – the point is stressed in conclusion – is to settle back on simplistic, cause-and-effect discussion. Colombia's terror was always too multifaceted for that. For the reader the facts of this terror will beg a good number of questions.

THE COUNTRY OF COLOMBIA

Colombia is the fourth largest of the Latin American states and the third most populous. It is the only one of those states to have coasts on the Caribbean and the Pacific, otherwise it is landlocked with Panama to the north-west, Venezuela to the north-east, Brazil to the south-east, Peru to the south, and Ecuador to the south-west. There are 31 million Colombians, 58 per cent of whom are *mestizos* (mixed Spanish and Indian), 20 per cent owe their origin to other parts of Europe, and 14 per cent are *mulatto* (black–white mixture). Spanish is the language of the majority and 96 per cent declare allegiance to Catholicism. Seven out of ten live in towns, the largest of which are Bogotá (the capital and a megacity of five million people), Medellin, Cali, and Barranquilla. Even so, there are vast areas of rainforest (*selvas*) and plains (*llanos*). Colombia is rich in natural resources such as hardwood forestry, mining for gold and precious stones, petroleum, and coal. Agriculture provides a living for 30 per cent of those employed, 24 per cent are in manufacturing, and 17 per cent in commerce. Great strides have been made in building a diverse and vibrant economy despite the boiling over of social conflict for many years.

TWO COLOMBIAS: ONE TERROR

Colombia, as a context for sustained political violence, is often described as having two faces – the 'formal' Colombia, the constitutional state, and the 'informal' Colombia, a 'real' and very different polity.

Jenny Pearce (1990) has written at length about the two-in-one labyrinth that Colombia presents:

There is a Colombia which is constitutional and legalistic, which boasts all the trappings of a modern polity. This is the Colombia which is often described in the world's press as the most democratic country in Latin America. But there is also a 'real' Colombia of the people, where the rule of law barely holds, deprivation and poverty are the norm and democracy is just a word on a historic document.

Loyalty to two traditional political parties for many years was the link between the two worlds; the people fought out the bitter party conflicts on behalf of the ruling oligarchy and their own allegiances to the two parties which divided that oligarchy were sealed through generations of bloody vendettas. A tradition of party political violence was established which culminated in the late 1940s and 1950s in the last great civil war between the parties: *La Violencia*. The final phase of *La Violencia* was one of social banditry and lasted until 1965.[1]

The same élite that had been in charge before *La Violencia* emerged, in full control, after it. The challenge from below had been defeated before it took hold, and this enabled the economy to function and prosper through most of it. The peasants, meanwhile, rather than concentrate on their own class interests which might have turned them against the ruling élite, instead killed each other on its behalf, fighting its party battles and other parochial conflicts that divided them from one another.

No expression of social conflict was permitted outside the control of the two traditional parties. The state could play no role in the mediation of such conflicts and, indeed, had no independent role of its own to enable it to look after the interests of society as a whole.[2]

The economy came to mirror the duality of the political order, between the formal and the real.

At one level it modernised over the years and enjoyed growth rates which made it one of the most successful examples of economic management in Latin America. At the other level, a 'people's economy' emerged, in which the majority of the population live and work, the so-called 'informal sector'. These two economies are by no means separate, but are distinct in many ways.[3]

The formal economy resembled that of every other civilised and sophisticated state with its bourse, its banks and insurance firms, its real estate, its industrial and service sectors. This was the arena of pensioned employment, career build-ing, management strategies, and a wide array of responsibilities, loyalties and reasonable expectations. It was not the arena, generally, of hire-and-fire, of under-employment and unemployment, of seething conflict and proneness to vio-lence. The contrast with the informal sector was gross and unsettling, in the view of Pearce:

The informal economy covers a wide range of activities, both legal and illegal, all unregulated by the state. By 1984, 56.6 per cent of employment in the urban areas was in the informal sector, involving 3.5 million people compared with 2.7 million in the formal sector.

The informal economy includes workers who earn their living on the streets doing odd jobs, washing cars, shining shoes, collecting rubbish for resale, the hopeful providers of services who will leap out at a traffic light to wipe car windscreens. It includes casual sellers of artefacts, cigarettes, newspapers and flowers and also prostitutes and thieves.

Also belonging to the informal sector are those employed in small enterprises outside the ambit of government control and regulation. About half the construc-tion industry is in the informal sector. All are characterised by the precarious nature of existence. Long-term employment contracts, employment- and social-protection schemes, safety and health provisions are all absent, as is the payment of taxes to the authorities.

The sector operates at the margin of the formal economy of modern capitalist production and state provision.

But the low incomes generated in the sector make it difficult for informal workers to earn enough to provide the basic elements of life.[4]

The formal economic realm was the place of power, affluence and privilege, largely town centred, with a central core which remained exclusive and unready to admit any reform. Even so, in the Colombia of the 1950s there was a large increase in the eighteen to thirty-five age-group with growing uncertainties, a scramble for jobs, and much dissatisfaction. The frontiers of the informal economy encompassed thousands of acres devoted to large-scale beef raising and coffee growing where the *campesinos*, peasants, eked out a life of grinding poverty. Illegal activities flourished – embezzlement, bribery, tax evasion, smuggling for a black market, petty theft, drug trading. Characteristic of urban squalor on the other hand were appalling slums, delinquency, prostitution, malnutrition, and the scrambling for survival of the *gaminismo*, the street children in their ragged thousands. As was to be expected here was the seed bed of eventual rebellion.

If this was the nature of the 'real' Colombia several decades ago, a third sector of the economy, very much an informal one, has developed, namely the narcotics sector. By the late 1970s marijuana was going out of fashion to be replaced by cocaine. Growing the coca leaf (imported from Peru and Bolivia) represented for the peasant an undreamed opportunity to improve his livelihood. The opportunities were a magnet for thousands of unemployed to leave the capital, Bogotá, and other cities; there were opportunities also for a few with cash and little conscience to 'muscle in' and amass great fortunes as 'drug barons'.

Thus, for Pearce, there are two Colombias, for most of half a century a society cut down the middle with discordant elements manipulating for survival and space and with a succession of governments, twin party or coalition, quite unable to adapt to destabilising circumstances or handle processes of inevitable change. *La Violencia* was inescapable.

LA VIOLENCIA: SOME EXPLANATIONS

Paul Oquist (1980) takes a broad view of this phenomenon and argues that there are clear social–structural explanations, at least four chief ones, namely, political rivalries, socio-economic causes, institutional aspects, and psychological/cultural factors. In outline they are as follows.

First, political discord:

The 1946–66 violence occurred in a country whose historical context includes the Spanish conquest, the wars for independence, and the multiple civil wars that took place throughout the nineteenth century. Since the 1850s, social violence in Colombia has been closely associated with partisan rivalries between the two traditional political parties – the Liberals and the Conservatives – but, although party competition is an important element in the analysis, it cannot be stated that this factor alone caused the violence.

The immediate twentieth-century antecedents of the 1946–66 violence stem from the electoral violence that surrounded the 1922 presidential campaign, the transference of the presidency from the Conservative to the Liberal party in 1930, and the various manifestations of socioeconomic violence in the 1920s, 1930s and 1940s.

Forced abandonment of agricultural plots and coerced land sales at under-value prices spurred the political conflicts. Violence reappeared in 1946 during the electoral campaign. However, the most intense violence centered precisely in those areas that had been most affected by the partisan violence of the 1930s.

This local partisan violence soon became the overriding national political issue. Charges and countercharges of responsibility for the killing escalated the friction between the two political parties. An accelerated rate of inflation and numerous strikes also contributed to the general social unrest.

In addition to the partisan battles, agrarian conflicts of various types, struggles for control of local power structures, revenge raids, and banditry were common.

The social fabric of Colombia seemed to have disintegrated. Although the civil wars of the nineteenth century with their positional, battlefield warfare carried high death tolls, they were not comparable to the horror and lack of security for the entire population that resulted from decentralized battles, raids, and killings in village after village, year after year.[5]

After the failures of government coalitions and the ever-present threat of takeover by a military junta, a *Frente Nacional* (National Front) administration was formed in 1958 ostensibly to try to bring an end to the ferocity of *La Violencia*. The exhaustion and revulsion felt by Colombians had to give way to agrarian reform, innovative development in the towns, a wider measure of political freedom and 10 per cent of the state budget to go to state educational projects. Liberals and technocrats in government would work in harness with organised labour. The dream, though, failed. The feud between rival interests, basically a defensive posturing, never vanished. It was a sour feeling of stalemate, *plus ça change*, as Oquist recalls:

Some important party leaders sought continued coalitions to defend basic common interests of the dominant classes and/or to avoid a civil war. The dynamics of party competition proved unabatable, however, and the party struggle continued at all levels of society.

In sum, a division in Colombia's *clase dirigente* ('ruling class') occurred as a result of nonpluralistic, mutually exclusive partisan politics under socioeconomic circumstances where neither side would admit banishment from state power. The result of this conflict was a partial collapse of the state in a society with numerous potential social conflicts. The deflation, inefficacy, and, in some cases, absence of state power led to the exacerbation of these conflicts, and frequently to their violent expression. Many of these conflicts were of an interclass nature. This combination of different social processes in *La Violencia* accounts in good measure for the intensity of the phenomenon. Its geographical distribution was generally concentrated in those areas in which there occurred both the partial collapse of the state and the maturation of social contradictions into acute conflicts.[6]

Second, Oquist considers possible socio-economic causes of the prelude to communal violence. Again, he discerns an element of defensiveness:

Antireformist forces used violence as an instrument of repression to the point that it became institutionalized. Certain sectors of the Liberal party responded to this violence in an attempt to topple the reactionary groups from power. This intraélite conflict was accompanied by a revolutionary popular uprising without ideology that proved to be emotional, cruel and unorganized.[7]

Oquist quotes a Colombian sociologist probing social causes and seeing:

[. . .] violence as the product of a counterrevolutionary strategy elaborated by the dominant groups in Colombian society to crush a mass movement that threatened the basic legitimacy of the prevailing institutions.

The dismemberment of popular movement took place in three stages:

1   The probing of the capacity to resist followed by an offensive against the most powerful unions, and popular organizations.
2   A systematic offensive by means of the massive unleashing of violence and an implacable annihilation of popular leadership, including the assassination of Gaitán [a prominent Liberal].
3   The establishment and consolidation of oligarchical support structures with the application of a formula of economic liberalism and political absolutism.[8]

Fundamentally, then, as one Colombian understands it, *La Violencia* incorporated three basic types of violence:

(1) the counterrevolutionary violence that used the state as the prime instrument of repression; (2) survivals of the traditional confrontations between Liberals and Conservatives; and (3) a confusing, conflictive process of combined popular resistance and social decomposition.[9]

Violence, to become terroristic in time, broke out into general sectarian warfare, once more as Colombian sociologists view it:

The political violence seems to have hidden class struggles but the latter, in reality, often assumed the form of the former. [. . .] The violence in the cities and in the rural regions might have had electoral ends in the beginning; but later the ends became more complex, and in this complexity it was possible to perceive, in some provinces, the war of the landlords against the sharecroppers, squatters, and poor peasants, and, in the agrarian exploitations of the capitalist type, the persecution of the owners against the labor organizations.[10]

Third, there are institutional aspects leading to grave disequilibrium:

[These were] attributable to an entire series of dysfunctional institutions. The roles of the society were deformed as part of widespread structural cleavages in Colombian society. For example, the police, rather than being the guardians of order, became the agents of disorder and crime.

The principal dysfunctions were the following: impunity in the judicial institutions, poverty and lack of land in the economic institutions, rigidity and fanaticism in the religious institutions, and ignorance in the educational institutions.[11]

Fourth, for Oquist there are psychological/cultural factors. Many who follow this line of consideration, Colombians and foreigners, regard *La Violencia* as an irrational phenomenon with a degree of sensationalism, perhaps, in their putting of the case where such terms are used as frustration or uninhibited political passion or a need for aggression or status deprivation. Oquist is guarded in applying such concepts as causative factors:

> Violence may be either rational or irrational. Violence is considered rational if it is a means utilized in the pursuit of potentially realizable goals. Conversely, 'irrational violence' is physical aggression or the credible threat of the same that is not oriented towards a goal, but that has violence itself as a goal (i.e. as in the case of psychological satisfaction derived from violence), or that does not have the potential to achieve the goal in question. Examples are a senseless killing, the elicitation of sadistic, masochistic, or cathartic satisfactions, violence employed in the pursuit of an impossible goal, or violence by which it is impossible to achieve a realistic objective. In sum, the violent conduct of psychotics, sadists, or *quijotes* ('rebels motivated by illusory causes') with tenuous relationships to reality constitutes 'irrational violence'.
>
> Most instances of widespread, protracted social violence are not characterized by irrational violence. However, irrational violence does tend to accompany rational violence and increase in intensity with it.
>
> In Colombia, the sociopolitical processes known as *La Violencia* were accompanied by much irrational violence. This is hardly surprising considering the intensity of *La Violencia* and the degree to which the repressive capacity of the state was deflated.
>
> [. . .] The irrational aspects of the phenomenon do not satisfactorily explain its origins or its intensity or its geographical distribution. To achieve an explanation of widespread, protracted, social violence, one must refer to the *social conflicts* that underlie such conduct and to the factors that condition whether a given conflict becomes violent or not.[12]

In Oquist's mind, whatever the significance of the factors outlined above, prime responsibility for Colombia's slide into chaos was the failure of its legitimate government:

> A partial collapse of the state occurred as a result of intense partisan conflicts. The political élite was divided to such an extent that state authority was deflated. This took place at the national, regional, and local levels. It is this partial collapse of the state that explains the nearly simultaneous evolution of numerous conflicts into violence. This dovetailing of various physically coercive struggles is what in turn explains the intensity of *La Violencia*. The duration is in part attributable to the difficulty of reasserting state authority in some areas.[13]

THE COURSE OF VIOLENCE

By 1950 a full-scale civil war was being fought in some of Colombia's provinces. There were Liberal guerrillas in the field taking on the left wing, there were Communist guerrillas fighting Liberals and anyone suspected of capitalist and entrepreneur leanings, there were Government counter-guerrillas mopping up those branded as 'disloyal'. On the peripheries of action there were bandits out for spoil. From time to time there would be a truce agreed and a short ceasefire. So fierce and frenzied was the momentum of violence that the age-old arguments about cattle pasturing and access to water and trails were now settled not with fist and stick but with arson and gelignite. Even the priests, it was said, carried pistols to dissuade the more aggressive members of their congregation. The nation was steadily engulfed with violence, the *La Violencia* that was to last a good fifteen years until its exhausted slackening in 1965.

The relentless, sad cycle of terroristic conflict has been chronicled and examined by Jenny Pearce (1990) who divides it into two phases, namely, 1949–53 and 1958–65:

La Violencia 1949–53

The first phase of *La Violencia* was its most violent. Three-quarters of its estimated 200,000 victims were killed between 1948 and 1953, more than 50,000 in 1950 alone. In these years the violence was generated mostly in the name of the parties; rural bosses mobilised their peasant clients in bloody vendettas against neighbouring villages; Liberal landowners organised peasant–guerrilla armies which engaged the Conservative forces of the state in 'hit and run' actions. A great mobilisation of peasant armies took place, with an inherent ambivalence. While they were led politically by sectors of the dominant classes through the traditional parties, the military leadership was in the hands of the peasants themselves.

Direct confrontation was rare; Liberal guerrillas carried out an act of sabotage and revenge exacted on any Liberal household. Paramilitary groups of civilians and police, such as the *aplanchadores*, the fearsome *chulavitas* and the infamous *pájaros* or assassins, carried out indescribable acts of violence which Liberals met with atrocities of their own. Decapitations, mutilations, sexual crimes and, with them, robbery and destruction of homes and land characterised *La Violencia* and earned it its name. Criminality and senseless violence intermixed with political and social violence. The barbarism unleashed was multifaceted and defies easy explanation. The army, reflecting the weakness of the state, was caught unprepared to deal with the guerrillas, but by 1951 it, too, was drawn into the conflagration.

La Violencia by no means affected all of rural Colombia but was confined to certain regions. It affected the coffee-producing regions with particular intensity, as well as Valle, the *minifundia* areas of Boyacá and the Santanderes (which had long histories of partisan violence) and also the cattle lands of the eastern *llanos*.

Within the coffee-producing departments, the region of Cundinamarca and Tolima became the centre of brutal partisan violence, as well as the place where landowners settled old scores against the local peasantry who had organised against them in the 1930s. The *chulavitas* spread terror and forced thousands to flee to the south of Tolima.

Elsewhere in the coffee-producing departments, complex developments took place. Many richer landowners chose to absent themselves. Liberals often fled on receiving the sinister *boleteo*, warning them to leave the region or face death. Thousands of poorer peasants, as well as richer landowners, were dispossessed of their land or forced to sell it very cheaply. Land changed hands in a variety of ways; peasants were dispossessed by other peasants as a result of party conflict and some peasants gained access to land abandoned by landowners as well as *vice versa*.[14]

In June 1959 a *coup d'état* erupted. A period of military rule seemed to many to be the only way of putting out the blaze and doing something to retrieve social and political order. Almost predictably and in devious ways the generals moved swiftly to break up the urban political movement and to curb independence of political expression. Relenting their harshness a little, the army command offered an amnesty to all past dissidents save for those known to be Communist. Again predictably, a measure such as this brought few rebels out of their sanctuaries, it was cynically received by townspeople and by *campesinos* being 'pacified' by riflemen and curfew. Nor were the ultra-conservatives in the army and police pleased at magnanimity which they saw as weakness.

La Violencia 1958–65

The formation of the *Frente Nacional* (mentioned above) as a life-support system did not achieve its objectives as Pearce relates:

Although the formation of the National Front officially brought *La Violencia* to an end, it did in fact continue in a different form, namely that of banditry, in which over 18,000 people lost their lives, 75 per cent of them in the departments of Tolima, Valle and Viejo Caldas.

The bandits of this second phase of violence were peasants who had been called guerrillas in its first phase, but who lost their political legitimacy in the new era. These bandit/guerrillas had either not accepted the amnesty offered by Rojas, or had done so and found themselves still under attack by the army. They had subsequently refused to accept either the amnesty offered by the National Front in 1958 or the party pact and peaceful coexistence which was then established.

They were joined by large numbers of revenge-seeking adolescents who had grown up during the terror and seen their homes burned down and their families brutally murdered. No longer dependent on national political leadership, they now looked to local bosses who began to use them for local political purposes. Banditry flourished in areas where official terrorism had been widespread but where the peasants had not developed their own forms of resistance – in the north of Valle, north of Tolima and in Viejo Caldas, mostly coffee-growing areas where small and medium property coexisted with large estates. Here there were ample mountainous regions in which to hide and rich pickings from the estates from which to live. Some day-labourers on the estates were 'part-time' bandits.

The local peasants gave active or passive support to the bandit chiefs. 'Chispas', 'Capítan Venganza', 'Desquite', 'Sangrenegra', 'Pedro Brincos' and others were mythical and heroic figures. Once in a while the bandits would identify with the social antagonisms of rural Colombia, as, for instance, when they even began to attack property belonging to landowners in their own party. Although potentially a radical social force, they mostly remained loyal to their Liberal Party affiliation. Their enemies were peasants of the other party as well as landowners, and they carried out violence against both. They accepted the patronage of local party bosses while standing out against the national political project of the ruling class.[15]

The government's failing grip on the security situation induced them to deploy all available resources in a counter-insurgency offensive. They appealed to Washington for aid and secured $60 million and useful equipment for dealing with riots. The United States had been grateful that during the Korean War of 1950–53 Colombia had set Latin America an example by sending a well-armed brigade to General Macarthur's expeditionary force. Thus, they willingly despatched 'security advisers' to Bogotá and there they established the first counter-insurgency training school in Latin America. Counter-insurgency met terror with terror. There was now every reason to expect a guerrilla struggle of remorseless intensity.

GUERRILLA STRUGGLES

A detailed account of Colombia's guerrilla struggle is to be found in Pearce (1990). She divides her account once more into two phases, the generation of 1964–mid-1970s and the generation of 1974–82:

The first generation 1964–mid-1970s

Only since the 1960s have independent guerrilla movements [the FARC (*Fuerzas Armadas Revolucionarias de Colombia*, the Revolutionary Armed Forces of Colombia) and the ELN (*Ejercito de Liberacion Nacional*, the National Liberation Army)] begun to challenge the domination of the traditional parties and propose an alternative structure of power.

The rupture with past struggles was incomplete. At least one guerrilla movement, the FARC, emerged directly out of peasants' experiences in certain regions during *La Violencia*. A handful of legendary guerrillas/bandits participated in the new movements – Fabio Vásquez, a founder of the ELN, was not the only guerrilla leader whose family had been wiped out during *La Violencia*.

But the new movements were primarily children of their times. As elsewhere in Latin America, but perhaps more so in Colombia where guerrilla warfare had been going on for ten years, the Cuban revolution made a big impact on the small group of left-wing students. They were impressed by the way in which, in little over two years, a tiny band of guerrillas had taken power in a small Caribbean island, and the belief that a revolutionary situation existed in Colombia soon took root among the urban radicals. Just under half the population still lived in rural areas and most believed that the revolution would start there.

Political exclusion had contributed to the rise of armed organisations that refused to form an allegiance with a political order that served only the interests of a profoundly conservative ruling class. Economic developments in the country-side, particularly in regions of colonisation or expanding commercial agriculture, encouraged peasants to turn to an option that offered defence against rapacious landowners and a political project in which they figured as actors and subjects.[16]

The FARC was born in the 1960s in the wake of army operations against peasants who had settled land during *La Violencia* and maintained their own armed defence under the leadership of the Communist Party. The party had organised the peasants and their armed defence, but as a party; 'armed struggle' in the rural areas was always subordinate to a broader political strategy, which included electoral participation, not armed struggle as a priority. This was the way they put their mission:

> Our party [. . .] nevertheless considers that there is no revolutionary situation in Colombia as yet. It does not consider armed struggle in cities because such a struggle can be little more than a series of isolated events accomplished by little groups [. . .] The guerrilla struggle is not at present the principal form of battle. [. . .]

Although it subsequently expanded its influence, the FARC remained for most of this period a defensive organisation, with roots among peasant colonisers for whom communism was less a political ideology than a strategy for survival. They faced the constant harassment of large cattle ranchers, backed by the army, only too ready to take over land the colonisers were forced to abandon through lack of resources and infrastructure. In these circumstances the FARC offered protection both from the ranchers and from unscrupulous middlemen, and also organised basic services.

In a number of areas the FARC took over the role of the negligent or absent state to become the governing authority for large numbers of peasants. Zones of self-defence became guerrilla fronts. In the Magdalena Medio, the FARC became a virtual rural civil guard, supported for a period by landowners as well as peasants as the only force to provide law and order. These roots enabled the FARC to survive the 1970s.[17]

A second group, the ELN, made its first public appearance on 7 January 1965. The ELN gained a great deal of publicity and sympathy when a radical priest, Camilo Torres, joined it at the end of 1965. Before taking up the armed struggle, Camilo had attempted to build a political movement, uniting all those hostile to the National Front. The 1963–66 period was one of recession and unrest. His programme, entitled 'A platform for a movement of popular unity', caused a great stir when it appeared in March 1965, bringing him into conflict with his religious superiors.

Camilo planned to build a United Front of popular movements to bring people with disparate political and religious beliefs together around a common revolutionary platform. He contacted the ELN in July of that year and began a long series of discussions. The ELN was interested in his work, recognising the need for a mass urban movement that might parallel the work carried out by the Cuban 26 July Movement in Havana.

Camilo's own charisma generated an initial wave of support. The first edition of his movement's journal, *Frente Unido*, cost about twice the price of a normal newspaper but sold 50,000 copies almost immediately. But the more Camilo spelled out his programme, the less unity it generated; too left-wing for some, such as the small Christian Democratic Party, and too liberal for the sectarian left, he abandoned the project at the end of the year. His decision to join the ELN caused a considerable stir, for he had won much respect for his political work, which was in fact more valuable to the ELN than his presence in the mountains. He was killed during his first action on 15 February 1966.

Many sought to follow Camilo's example; the ELN's military capacity grew and it extended its operations to the south of Bolívar. But it remained militaristic and did little organisational or political work among the peasants. Its authoritarian, vertical structure centred around a handful of key leaders. Tensions between them ran high and differences were often resolved through executions. Two basic conflicts emerged between those who began to stress political work in the urban areas, and those who stressed the military aspect and the peasantry. The urban work suffered a major blow in 1968 when the organisation's urban network was destroyed with the loss of many cadres.[18]

According to Walter Laqueur (1999) the FARC grew rich. Two-thirds of their wealth came from protection rackets among the growers of coca and opium poppy, and from extortion and robberies. These resources went to survival – buying weapons and refuge, bribing informers, and the forging of documents. Terror, for terrorists, is an expensive commodity. ELN activists hit out at Colombia's capitalist oil syndicates destroying their pipelines, refineries and offices.

The second generation 1974–82

A guerrilla movement with a difference, M-19 (Movimento 19 de Abril; the April 19 Movement) was founded in 1972 when there came together remnants of a popular national alliance (mainly urban middle class), a good many radical students, some enthusiastic Greater Colombia nationalists, and a hard core of Trotskyists whose extremism neither FARC nor ELN were prepared to tolerate. The recruits to M-19 quickly began to carry out a campaign of vigorous urban terrorism, for they felt rejected by a government which, on 19 April 1970, had defrauded a reform-and-trade union movement of a legitimate electoral victory. There was perhaps, in the beginning at any rate, something of a Robin Hood image, the robbing of the affluent to benefit the dispossessed. Pearce discusses M-19's distinctive approach:

M-19 never belonged to any left-wing tradition or Marxist orthodoxy. It is closer to what might be called 'armed populism', in which its folkloric leadership sought to build an anti-oligarchic and anti-imperialist mass movement with an armed wing.

The Leninist vanguard was rejected in favour of broad mass fronts with a multi-class character.

It was not until 1979, however, that it really hit the headlines when in January of that year it stole 5,000 weapons from the armed forces' main arsenal at Cantón Norte outside Bogotá. Although most of them were later recovered, the army never forgave the guerrillas.

Turbay Ayala became president in 1978, following the first national civic strike in 1977. Strongly influenced by the armed forces, his response was to establish the most repressive government the country had known, beginning with a draconian security statute. Imprisonment and torture, never absent in Colombia, became systematic. M-19 members were soon filling the prisons, being subjected to terrible tortures and emerging as heroes.

M-19 began operating in the rural areas, particularly in Caquetá, in 1979. This was a conflict-ridden region, with peasant colonisers protesting against the assaults of ranchers and the neglect of the state; in 1972, 10,000 peasants had occupied the capital, Florencia, for eight days. The FARC's already solid roots were reinforced by army and police repression of the civilian population. In 1978, Turbay Ayala declared the region a 'war zone'.

Both the guerrilla movements associated with the coca boom (M-19 and the FARC) took a pragmatic position on coca. The FARC established law and order in its areas of control and, in return, the producers and traders paid a percentage of their earnings to the guerrillas. It also protected the peasants from the traders (it stopped them paying them in *basuco* or crack) and encouraged the growers to grow food crops as well as coca. The FARC was authoritarian and harsh in punishing wrongdoers, but it established rules in a situation where the law of the jungle would otherwise reign. Its law of the mountain, as it was called, gradually won legitimacy and support. Corruption ran high within the army and police, further reducing their authority among a peasantry already deeply hostile after years of abuse at their hands. If the peasants did not pay the guerrillas, they might have to pay the army and it was usually more threatening and arbitrary in its behaviour than the guerrillas.

The FARC expanded its influence considerably in the late 1970s. At the end of 1979 it had nine fronts, by the end of 1983 it had twenty-seven. At its seventh conference in May 1982 it conceded for the first time that a revolutionary situation existed in the country, and added the letters EP (*Ejército del Pueblo*, People's Army) to its name. It also decided to adopt more offensive military tactics. These significant shifts were an indication that the armed struggle was on the agenda as never before.

Serious political mistakes and abuses of power accompanied the growth of the FARC's fronts, perhaps as a result of rapid recruitment with insufficient politicisation. The tactic of demanding protection money from landowners began to look more like criminal extortion than politics, particularly when it was used against the less prosperous landowners.[19]

FARC, in fact, went through such an expansion that its activists and their terror methods were welcomed among the rural poor in Venezuela, Panama and Ecuador.

THE POSSIBILITIES OF PEACE

After the general election in 1982 the new President, Belisario Betancur, a Conservative, had to cope with both severe economic recession and a crippling climate of insecurity. To bring about some degree of stabilisation he announced the formation of a peace commission on which all sectors of Colombian life would be represented. Even delegates from the Communist Party and from M-19 would be welcomed and all political prisoners would be offered unconditional amnesty save for those found guilty of atrocities. This brave attempt at national reconciliation never got off the ground. Army chiefs were hostile to any form of compromise. Ranchers and big business feared irreparable breaching of their exclusive domains. What agreement there was turned out contradictory and ambiguous. Meanwhile, it seemed as though the guerrillas were not losing face. The situation ended in disaster on 6 November 1965 when M-19 occupied the Palace of Justice in Bogotá. Hundreds of troops and tanks went in, the building was destroyed and twelve Supreme Court judges and their assistants, forty-one rebels and seventeen soldiers were killed.

After the Bogotá battle the army was the only state institution with the capacity for strong and decisive action. Colombians watched this with foreboding. The political parties were rent with factionalism, the drug mafia held sway in the towns and in huge tracts of coca growing land. The Catholic hierarchy had to wrestle with the daring radicalism of priests preaching 'liberation theology' and 'freedom' for the poor and oppressed. Would terroristic methods, if sustained, bring about constructive change or initiative a tumble into further anarchy?

THE STATE'S COUNTER-OFFENSIVE

Pearce is in no doubt that by 1986 Colombia's political crisis had become acute with power fragmented throughout the country. The 'formal' constitutional state was menaced, broken even, by the 'informal', unconstitutional initiatives of the violent. Was Colombia now becoming 'a democracy without the people', she asks.

Marginalised economically and politically, the state has reserved for the majority the 'state of siege' and all the exceptional repressive legislation and procedures that can guarantee order where other mechanisms fail. Even that sector of the middle class that has been included economically remains on the margins of the existing political system. By 1986 'official' and 'unofficial' repression dominated and the ruling élite was preparing to go on the counter-offensive against the many challenges that now faced the political order.[20]

On 27 January 1988 the President of Colombia introduced a 'Statute of the Defence of Democracy'. Pearce declares that not one of the seventy-eight articles in the statute referred, as one might have expected, either to drug trafficking or to extradition. To deal with 'political crimes' was the objective. Moreover, the wording of the statute struck an ambiguous note in places:

The statute defines a 'terrorist' so imprecisely that arrests can be made if an individual is under suspicion, or has participated in an act of civil disobedience which, in the judgement of the police, has provoked terror in the population or endangered lives or property. Radio broadcasts or articles about security problems can be taken as public or private incitement to participate in terrorist acts and penalised with up to ten years in prison.

Anyone suspected of participating in 'terrorist' activities can be arrested without a judge's order by a soldier or policemen and held for ten days before being brought to court – a period during which they are often subjected to torture or ill-treatment. The police and the military were given the right to search homes and arrest people without a judge's order. Two months later, after a wave of army searches without warrant, the Supreme Court declared it unconstitutional, but the practice continued in many areas.[21]

Habeas corpus provision was modified and civil trials now included personnel seconded by the army. Military operations regularly involved house searches, overt intimidation, torture, killings, and 'disappearances'. This continuous repression had much in common with the 'dirty war' practised by the government in Peru. As in Peru, the government's counter-terrorist measures included the arming of so-called self-defence groups as a means of legitimising paramilitary action.

Otherwise, counter-insurgency programmes sought out specific targets:

The government and the right all too frequently identified popular leaders with the guerrilla movements. Since counter-insurgency doctrine called for the isolation of guerrillas from their social base, 'draining the sea from the fish' as it was known, the government was able to justify the repression of all forms of popular protest. This kind of war bears heavily upon civilian populations – guerrillas are mobile and can more easily escape army operations.

The guerrillas and the popular movements therefore had a somewhat controversial relationship. The guerrillas could provide defence under certain circumstances, but in so doing implicated the popular movements in the armed struggle. The guerrillas supported the banana workers in Urabá and helped them improve their wages and conditions, but at the cost of the region being militarised. As they became more effective, though, the popular movements faced repression with or without the guerrillas' presence.[22]

REVOLUTION IN SUSPENSE

Colombia's revolution remains unachieved despite the ardour and desperate action of those hungry for reform. It is debatable whether the descent into terrorism has put significant reform into cold storage until government has security in steady hands. Writing in 1990 Pearce has no doubt about the delay and she quotes from one of Colombia's academic journals:

As Colombia's guerrilla movements began to build popular support, they found their spaces for political work starting to close. Defending the civilian population was difficult, but recruiting large numbers of civilians under threat into the guerrilla movements was logistically and politically impossible. They were too weak in the urban areas to claim that a revolution was imminent in the short or medium term.

The guerrillas had to respond to the political impasse, but the government had yet to recognise that it could not defeat them militarily. A massive army campaign during 1989 had failed to weaken the ELN and, within this context, the guerrillas had to decide how to use their armed strength. Should they, as the ELN wished, deepen the revolutionary process through a prolonged popular war? Or, as the EPL insisted, find political openings by uniting all forces against 'fascism'? Or, as the FARC and M-19 argued from their different perspectives, win reforms and the right to participate electorally? In 1989 arguments for peace or war, reform or revolution were once again being debated. William Ramírez Tobón (*Analísis Política*, no. 5, 1988) feels that the 'enemy in the peace negotiations is more than a military opponent or an opposition force. The guerrilla represents, whether we like it or not, a dream of a new society, a project different from the established order in existence today in Colombia. Behind the guns are voices that cry out for employment, education, health and the right to life'.[23]

Perhaps in an already confused community there were simply too many voices urging differing styles of reform:

Many progressive urban intellectuals rejected armed struggle and traditional left-wing politics and wanted to build a third force based on civic movements and broad social alliances. They formed a movement in early September 1989, called *Colombia Unida*. The UP hankered for a still elusive 'bourgeois democracy'. In some regions the guerrillas had simply replaced the state. In others they were emphasising grass-roots politicisation and popular power, from which they could build a revolutionary alternative in Colombia.

No political project (right, left or centre) had national legitimacy and, though with insufficient bipolar conflict to generate civil war, this contributed to a sense of social and political decomposition. There were wars in regions such as Urabá and the Magdalena Medio, where class conflict was particularly acute, but in the cities, where there were no clear political options other than cocaine and crime, violence bred violence.

Meanwhile the traditional élite was still searching for a political formula that would restore its hegemony more permanently with a minimum loss of power. The modernisers wanted to strengthen the state further, reform institutions and pursue a peace plan on their own terms. The majority of the élite were concerned at the loss of political legitimacy but their main interest was the preservation of their own privileges. In that sense, a weak state served them best.[24]

To what extent terror incapacitated government in Colombia is arguable. The programmes of counter-terrorism could be thought over-reactive and negative as Pearce intimates:

The Colombian journalist Antonio Caballero once called Colombia a 'political time-bomb'. Can an economy that has created only 500,000 jobs in manufacturing, which a leaked World Bank report (July 1989) describes as closed and meeting the needs of only a minority, provide the majority of its population with a humane existence and the means to a livelihood? The archaic political order that has kept that minority in power has proved incapable of taking on this responsibility. The bomb will carry on ticking until it does, or until the left proves itself able to unite the people around an alternative social and political project.[25]

POSTSCRIPT

By way of conclusion one question needs to be addressed as we enter a new century: what are the chances of a peace process which has already stumbled over ten years ending forty years of conflict? A brief outline of progress to date makes for sober reading.

- Between 1990 and 1994 the Colombian government begins to soften its refusal to negotiate with 'terrorists'. Guerrillas, sensing the easier position, press for membership of the Constitutional Assembly as well as immunity for their leaders. Both sides explore some international monitoring of demobilisation and withdrawal but FARC says 'No' to any United Nations mediation. Negotiations 'freeze' though delegates meet unobtrusively in Venezuela and Mexico.
- 1995, guerrillas now strong and confident enough to line up as National Guerrilla Coordinating Group (NGCG). Consequently, the Government, fearful of lost ground and initiative, reopens prospects of army withdrawal, and frames a programme for assisted reincorporation of former guerrillas into civilian life. Unhelpfully, these proposals collapse as major army offensives roll by and NGCG recoils from Bogotá's 'ultimatum'. The FARC, over-confident, attacks Colombia's anti-drug task force.
- 1996–98, momentum quickens. Government now realises its popularity is being rapidly eroded by large-scale peasant protest; coincidentally, NGCG see their own ranks denuded as former terrorists increasingly prefer peaceful protest to orchestrated violence. NGCG now willing to talk provided their arrested members are treated as Prisoners of War. Bogotá wonders how 'inhuman terrorists' could be accorded Geneva Convention rights.
- 1998, guerrilla schisms as ELN and National Peace Council (successor to NGCG) meet in a monastery in Mainz, Germany (a German Catholic initiative) and together work out a framework for a convention enabling Colombian non-governmental delegates to press Bogotá continuously for widespread political, economic and social reforms. Preliminary outlines for army evacuation, amnesties, guerrilla resettlement are drawn up.
- 1999 begins with ELN and FARC differing as to how to deal with the army's continued punitive sweeps. The government now acknowledges that the embryo revolution thirty years earlier had no alternative than to adopt terrorist methods. Did weak governments too readily resort to insensitive strategies and

over-reactive tactics? In May 1999 optimism and consensus are evident as in Bogotá disarmed terrorists and government ministers decide a Common Agenda for Change – to build a new Colombia with reforms of the bureaucracy, the army, the judiciary, new agrarian and environmental policies and codified citizens' basic rights.

- The objectives of Colombia's peace process are now discernible. In what black ways did the employment of terror on all sides force the pace of peaceful settlement? Will the fragile consensus of the summer of 1999 be an effective one? After decades of internal conflict and terrorism, Colombians are desperately anxious for sound and lasting reconciliation.

Chapter 13

Germany

THE SUBJECT OF THIS CASE-STUDY is the Red Army Faction (the Rote Armee Faktion or RAF), once known as the Baader-Meinhof Gang. During the 1960s and 1970s this notorious organisation terrorised what was then known as West Germany and operated as a number of hard-line cells carrying out a desperate terrorist strategy and recruiting a network of supporters. Its logistics of attrition and its propaganda were impressive until a determined German government and an alarmed public managed to reduce the conspiracy to its present-day secretive and much more heterogeneous remnant.

Essentially, political terrorism in Germany has illustrated an escalation from protest to violent demonstration and lethal action. It still raises many puzzling questions. How was it that the protest movement of young Germans developed into brutal and senseless terrorism? They were the first generation, after all, to enjoy life in a democratic community after the horrors of National Socialism. Many, too, were from affluent and privileged families. Were there distinctive socio-cultural or psychological factors to account for fanaticism in post-war Germany? Could some of the influences on their attitudes and behaviour have been imported from abroad while others were perhaps the product of a nation divided unhappily into West Germany and East Germany?

PROTEST TO TERRORISM: SOCIO-CULTURAL ORIGINS

As regards protest, already in the 1950s students in German universities were kicking their heels at conservatism and authoritarianism among the staff, regarding them as infuriatingly slow in responding to the changing circumstances of society and to the great increase in student numbers. This cry for reform was linked with some degree of resentment of control by an older generation (somewhat tainted by Nazi

memories). The growing student protest, chiefly led by the Socialist Student Association (SDS) was influenced by many external issues – America's war in Vietnam,
the liberation struggles of Third World peoples, the anti-nuclear war campaign, the
anti-apartheid movement, the vibrant mobilising appeals of Che Guevara, and the radical critiques of Herbert Marcuse and Jean-Paul Sartre. If reforms were not urgently
implemented constitutionally, then youth would have to take reform measures into
their own hands, for instance, through extra-parliamentary opposition,
Ausserparlamentarische Opposition (APO). Students increasingly despaired about the
prospect of significant improvements and about any reliable alliance with what was
for them a too conservative left wing front betraying student revolutionary fervour
and ideals. When large student gatherings in Berlin, Frankfurt, Hanover and Marburg
were addressed by such 'inflammatory' activists as Andreas Baader, Ulrike Meinhof,
or Rudi Dutschke the tenor of these assemblies was swiftly regarded by the state
security division as illegal and confrontational. Eventually, in 1967, police tear gas
and live bullets were used to disperse 'terrorist agitators'.

PROTEST TO TERRORISM: PSYCHOLOGICAL FACTORS

An attempt to throw light on the origins of German terrorism from a psychological
standpoint is provided in the analysis of Schura Cook (1982), a 'psychopolitics consul-
tant' in Southern California. Her hypothetical case (which may not convince
everyone) is that some young Germans 'over-identified' with imported cultural
elements, and political and social issues. American problems, so dynamic, counter-
cultural and anti-authoritarian, became the problems of Europe's youth. At the same
time, Cook argues, they 'under-identified' with the contemporary German system,
for they were uncomfortably aware of the dictatorial past and although they were
born and raised after 1945 there was for them the crucial need to resolve an identity:

The need of many young Germans to be totally different from their parents' generation resulted in identification problems. How could they identify with their parents'
generation which exterminated millions in concentration camps and fought brutal
and aggressive wars? Therefore, the German youth was characterized by a hypersensitivity towards all authoritarian structures in society. Anxiety and tension were
the result of this identification conflict. Collective guilt feelings for the horrible
deeds of the parents' generation predestined them for the anti-authoritarian role
of the youth movement. In Germany this resulted in a generation conflict manifested in a particular 'hypersensitive' atmosphere.

The unrelieved gap between the subconscious need to identify with the German
system and the conscious hate against this system created a large section of estranged
hypersensitive German youth. They felt they had become chronic injustice collectors, constantly aware of the insincerity, hypocrisy and greed of their environment,
which they had learned to hate with unmitigated passion. Providing a remedy for
injustices is the basic motivation for terrorism and the hypersensitive Germans saw
evidence of this injustice everywhere and reacted accordingly.[1]

Cook continues the argument with the supposition that many young people in Germany found it difficult to discern the difference between the former Fascist Germany and the new democratic ambience which surrounded them. For them this was a 'reality loss' which became a key factor in regression from what Cook terms psychological and social 'sensitivity' through 'hypersensitivity' (strong views about political and social injustice) to 'hyposensitivity' (the complete negation of sensitivity and lapse into terroristic brutality).

The young terrorist reaction, Cook concludes, moved through uncertainty about themselves to a search for group solidarity, to preference for anti-conformist attitudes and behaviour, to a longing for 'kicks' and the excitement of violent action, and, all together, to a gradual loss of inhibition about using violence as a means of political protest. In their growing hatred and rage and in response to what they saw as a biased press and their elders' lack of understanding, a wave of violent protest in some quarters became virtually unstoppable:

The transition from an anti-authoritarian youth protest movement to a political movement that eventually deteriorated into a hard core group of fanatically determined terrorists was brought about as much by the role of the press and police actions as by any intrinsic characteristics of the movement itself. In the course of political polarization and violent escalation, determined terrorists, criminals and crazies succeeded in infiltrating the anti-authoritarian youth movement and used its moral prestige for terroristic violence. At this point, indiscriminate activism for the sake of action was eventually transformed into strategic terror.[2]

They had become action addicts, interested only in living out their fantasies. In their self-imposed isolation in the underground these fantasies had become realities for them, the only realities they knew.[3]

ORIGINS OF GERMAN TERRORISM: THE HISTORICAL DIMENSIONS

A wider and more historical interpretation of German terrorism is to be found in the political analyses of Geoffrey Pridham (1981) and of Peter H. Merkl (1995). Their reference points are: first, the historical origins of terrorism; second, the question of ideological orientation among German protest groups; and third, sociological aspects. For them, historical factors in Germany's domestic politics are all-important in aiding understanding. Merkl, for instance, sees inevitability in the growing violence between West German police and students:

But the students' and other rebels' attitude towards the police, encouraged also by later clashes, remained impotent rage, frequently aggravated by the self-serving, hateful explanations of police conduct given by the press and by various Berlin establishment figures. It was very easy in this setting to feel that one had to defend oneself with lethal force against a lawless, violently repressive, and arbitrary authority that seemingly ignored its own legal and constitutional standards. It was also most plausible to perceive the established authorities as a crypto-fascist, or closet Nazi, force – in spite of democratic elections and majority support – which would inevitably reveal its true nature upon a little provocation. As Rudi Dutschke put it, 'If we were in Latin America, it's clear I would fight weapon in hand. [But here] we are fighting so none will ever need to take up arms'.

The use of police violence out of all proportion to a legitimate state interest removed much of the well-inculcated taboo against the oppositional use of similar violence in self-defense and lent legitimacy to the terrorist acts to come. Against the ugly pogrom mood among the West Berlin establishment, violence escalated quickly.

The genie of violence was out of the bottle, untrammelled by bourgeois inhibitions, ready for attack on the hostile media and authorities, and all this with an exhilarating sense of freedom after years of repression and frustration. Perhaps their very success and its reverberations brought about their undoing – on 1 May 1968 the SDS assembled a demonstration of 30,000 in Berlin; ten days later 50,000 demonstrated in Bonn against the acceptance of the Emergency Laws; and in Paris *les événements* broke out. Soon sober reflection set in, the 'manic phase' ended, and there was a renewed sense of impotence and frustration. The student movement began to disintegrate into many directions: Young Socialists, the newly founded Communists (DKP), Maoists, Trotskyists, trade-union activists, gay and feminist groups, child-care groups (*Kinderläden*), and rural communes.

As the mighty student movement died, following its most activist, even violent peak, it spun off small but intensely violent movements much as a dying hurricane might spawn tornadoes. The German literature on terrorism calls them the *Zerfallprodukt* (by-product of disintegration) of a brilliant social movement, and in a comparative context, I have called this the fire-sale theory of terrorism – after the revolutionary fire burnt out, its high-sounding, though fire-damaged, values became the easy rationalizations of trigger-happy zealots. Some critics of the German terrorism literature have warned against the tunnel vision of both the terrorists themselves and the conservative enemies of the student movement, who insist that the student movement directly and logically led to terrorist excesses, when in fact it had many and varied consequences, including political apathy and depression, a rueful return to the major parties, a 'long march through West German institutions', the citizen initiatives, the women's movement, and peace, ecological and alternative movements – all of them rather nonviolent. The same caveat, of course, applies to the logic of condemnation: it should be possible at the same time to condemn the later terrorist violence, to approve of most of the police measures to apprehend the guilty, to support the constitutional right of APO [Extra-Parliamentary Opposition] and the student movement to demonstrate, and to condemn the public hate campaign and police lawlessness unleashed on them by the Berlin Senate and the media.[4]

Pridham has reservations as to the extent that this early German terrorism was in any real way a unified movement:

Whatever the impact of German terrorists as a whole, especially with reference to their early years of involvement, they did not themselves represent a movement in any conventional sense. The New Left, or the Extra-Parliamentary Opposition

(APO) as it was formally known, faded rapidly before the 1969 change of power in Bonn, and its participants went in a variety of directions: a substantial number, so far as they remained in politics, were absorbed into the SPD [Social Democrats], a much smaller number into orthodox communism, some became anti-communist publicists and only a minuscule proportion became engaged in any way in terrorist activity. At the same time one should not underrate the symbolism of '1968', for whatever the APO's failure as a movement it was bound to have indirect political consequences of some kind. The student background of many individual terrorists and the involvement of some in the vogue habits of commune-living and the drug scene suggested a link with the mood of radical protest against conformist bourgeois society, but the specific relationship between APO and the later terrorists demands closer examination before any general points can be inferred.[5]

Looking at the domestic political context, Pridham adds student 'disillusionment' with the left's establishment as well as hostility towards what they regarded as rightist, authoritarian government:

While it is accepted there is no simple explanation for the appearance of terrorism, a number of different factors relating to its origins can be deciphered. One of these often neglected in the discussion of German terrorism and its causes is the domestic political context in which it arose. This is worth emphasising because, although the Vietnam question undoubtedly became a classic object for youthful indignation, the early terrorists spent more time in polemical attacks on the Federal Republic (albeit sometimes described as a 'colony' of the USA) rather than on 'American imperialism' as such. The desire to create a 'Vietnam feeling' did feature prominently in leaflets distributed by them in connection with the first actions in 1968–69. Some of them were later to claim that the motive for the Frankfurt department store fires of April 1968 had been 'to light a torch for Vietnam', just as Gudrun Ensslin, one of them, asserted: 'We did it out of protest against the indifference towards the war in Vietnam'.

All the same, the chief 'enemy' for the terrorists remained West Germany itself and its postwar system and this continued to be so once their actions became a trend from 1970. Various political developments inside the Federal Republic, as confirmed by some terrorist writings of the time, seemed to help ignite their determination to embark on their course of violent protest – above all, a general disillusionment with the constitutional left, as represented by the Social Democrats (SPD), which could be traced back to the break between the party and the Socialist Student Organisation (SDS) in the early 1960s but which came to a head with the Grand Coalition of the SPD with the Christian Democrats (CDU) and Christian Socialists (CSU) (especially over the issue of the emergency laws) and thereafter was fostered by the general failure of the much promised 'inner reforms' once the SPD became the principal governing party from 1969. Since the SPD's coalition with the CDU/CSU was clearly viewed by the radical student movement as a fundamental challenge, several later terrorist figures then involved in minority activist circles within the SDS (notably Horst Mahler and Ulrike Meinhof) were influenced by this viewpoint.[6]

ORIGINS OF GERMAN TERRORISM: THE IDEOLOGICAL DIMENSIONS

Most commentators on German terrorism have found some difficulty in making out the ideological content and orientation of the early terrorists. Pridham believes that divergence from conventional socialist principles in time widened the gap between terrorists and the broad left:

A first glance at German terrorism would certainly locate its ideological home on the left, or as more left than anything else in the sense that its main ideological targets and phobias were distinctly 'right wing', e.g. Nazism/fascism, American imperialism and Vietnam, bourgeois opposition to the 'class struggle', capitalist society. The historical link with the New Left, the political background of individual terrorists and the fact that their circles of 'sympathisers', both active and passive, all came from the political left suggested the same ideological location. West Germany did not undergo any phase equivalent to Italy's period of neo-fascist inspired violence in the early 1970s. Violent activities (for 'terrorism' is too strong a word here) deriving from the extreme right have occurred spasmodically in the Federal Republic through the 1970s, with some fluctuation and occasional growth in incidents, but they cannot *in toto* be considered and have not been perceived as presenting the same challenge as 'red' terrorism.

Yet, the problem of identifying specifically the ideological left-wingness of the German terrorists remains and is underlined by their complicated relationship, or really lack of it, with the constitutional left. A good illustration of this problem is Willy Brandt's commentary in his speech to the Bundestag during the debate on terrorist legislation in March 1975:

> It is customary to speak of the terrorists as of the 'left'. This is a use of speech which has been taken over only too thoughtlessly, also by me and therefore I criticise not only others but also myself. There is certainly a reason behind this in some cases – therefore two comments. Firstly, those who decree the terrorists the title of 'left' in the sense of the proper political spectrum of our country – I emphasise, political – are doing them an honour to which they have no right. This includes them in a schema – about which one can of course argue – that is taken from the parliamentary sphere. I say emphatically: the terrorists are everything other than 'left' in the sense of the political and parliamentary spectrum of parties. They have nothing to do with it. They are rather people who play into the hands of reaction. Secondly, those who nevertheless characterise them as 'left' in an ambiguous way are defining consciously or unconsciously the parliamentary left so as to place it, again consciously or unconsciously, close to the terrorists. In the name of the parliamentary left – and this is the role of Social Democracy, also when it is part of the new centre – I reject firmly these views.

So far as the terrorists themselves were concerned it could be said they represented unorthodox variations based on Marxism. This assertion is only possible because of the political divisions of the Marxist tradition in German history. The terrorists themselves laid claim to 'Marxist' or even 'communist' inspiration, firmly rejecting the 'anarchist' label, in which their ideological loyalty was to Mao-tse-tung or Che Guevara rather than Lenin – as in their criticism of the DKP for being 'embourgeoised' and not wanting to overthrow the state. Insofar as they had any German historical reference points, these were the 'purist' martyrs of Rosa Luxembourg and Karl Liebknecht. Yet it is also possible to add that insofar as they resembled features of German romanticism they were more akin to right-wing politics. All the same, by any usual standards it is still difficult to measure the ideological dimension of German terrorism. Various authorities or observers have commented that for the terrorists ideology has provided a 'camouflage' or that it is eclectic and taken at face value, that at best it is utopian (or 'criminal utopianism') and finally that it is theoretically weak as it offers no clearly defined alternative society, only the belief that the system should be 'different'. There is some element of truth in all these remarks but it still remains to identify more specifically the ideological content and orientation of the German terrorists.[7]

Three overarching leitmotivs may be said to have contained key concepts in terrorist thinking since they were regularly included in underground publications. Pridham considers these as central to motivation:

(a) *The concept of the 'armed struggle' and the model of Third World liberation movements.* This probably had the greatest individual influence on terrorist thinking, especially as it gave the groups a sense of international solidarity in the face of their lack of popular following in the Federal Republic. However, this leitmotiv had a definite history of its own deriving from the New Left (e.g. the hero-worshipping of Che Guevara), and it undoubtedly provided the salient 'theoretical' basis for terrorist activity. Numerous terrorist booklets, manuals or statements gave expression to it: 'The concept of the urban guerrilla' (1971, written by Ulrike Meinhof), 'Concerning the armed struggle in Western Europe' (allegedly authored by Horst Mahler), 'Serve the people – Red Army Faction: urban guerrilla and class struggle' (sent to *Der Spiegel* for publication in April 1972) and 'Lead the anti-imperialistic struggle – Create the Red Army – the action of Black September in Munich' (November 1972). It was repeated by other shorter statements from the RAF's two ideological leaders, Horst Mahler and Ulrike Meinhof, on various occasions. Briefly, while identifying with 'oppressed' people in the Third World in opposition to 'US imperialism', the theory involved following Carlos Marighela's application of guerrilla warfare to urban areas and drew succour from the theoretical blessing given by Frantz Fanon to violence as an intrinsic element of revolution. The terrorists' fervent adherence to these concepts had something of a simplistic ring when applied to German conditions. [. . .] This clearly involved a fundamental rejection of legal methods and parliamentarianism, but two further points are worth a mention. The absolutist and cathartic view of violence, in asserting that the destruction of the existing order was an essential precondition for a 'free' society, was nevertheless hedged with conceptual ambiguities in a German context. The other point concerned the terrorists' idea of their relationship with the masses. These theories contained an automatic belief that 'armed struggle' would inspire mass support, but here they were criticised from within the 'unconventional left' – Jean-Paul Sartre emphasised their failure to construct a mass basis, and eventually Mahler left the RAF on these grounds. In answer to such criticism they argued that it was not a question of 'supporters' or 'fellow-travellers' but of the 'effects' of their politics in 'changing people's attitude to the state' following the government's anti-terrorist measures.

(b) *The Nazi 'connection' and 'formal democracy' in the Federal Republic.* Although Nazism was defeated militarily in 1945, it was in the view of the terrorists still living 'spiritually' and politically. This basic association of the postwar democracy with the Third Reich – whereby the Federal Republic was only 'formally' a democracy (a term borrowed from the New Left) because it served only the interests of the 'bourgeoisie' – was, of course, in the intensity with which it was applied, a special feature of the German version of terrorism for obvious historical reasons. As an emotively charged concept it involved not so much a theory as a theoretical assumption and it covered a variety of other or related attitudes, e.g. problems of generational conflict, postwar Germany's 'neglect' of the 'spiritual' education of the young and above all the thesis of 'structural violence' on the part of the existing system (a concept elaborated theoretically by Galtung at this time) and the need to oppose it with counter-force. This socio-political anti-Nazism, expressed through the frequent use by the terrorists of the term 'resistance' to describe their own activities, was said to be influenced by their personal complexes about the past, but it also clearly drew on the revival of anti-authoritarianism in the late 1960s as a virtually sub-cultural attitude of the younger generation by no means confined to the New Left.

On a more directly political level, the terrorists' main claim was that anti-communism from the time of the Cold War had opened the way for 're-fascistisation' in the Federal Republic, especially as Germany had unlike many other European countries experienced no 'mass-scale armed anti-fascist resistance'. This particular thesis of the terrorists predictably aroused more controversy in West Germany than many of their other ideas, with perhaps the most pertinent argument coming from the political historian Bracher that the terrorists were making the mistake of confusing 'totalitarianism' and 'fascism', so that the discussion centred around the confrontation of fascism versus socialism while ignoring the difference between parliamentary and totalitarian rule. It is worth noting that on a psychological plane the views of the terrorists occasioned much debate focusing on the thesis of their being 'Hitler's children'. This thesis worked in two different directions: on the one hand, that they were reacting against the recent past and sought to compensate for it, and on the other that they were subconsciously identifying with it. The latter interpretation produced the idea that the terrorists were 'left-wing fascists', although as a concluding point it is worth distinguishing in political terms between their ideological anti-Nazism and the fact that their *methods*, violent as they were, resembled those employed by Nazis.

(c) *The rejection of consumer society.* This leitmotiv overlapped somewhat with the preceding two, both because of the terrorists' sympathies with the Third World 'proletariat' and because they were influenced by New Left theories about what Habermas called 'a form of modern, noiseless fascism', above all Marcuse's critique of capitalist society as having a 'fascist' potential sociologically speaking in its 'degradation' of humanity. This anti-capitalist leitmotiv again allowed an outlet for generational conflict because of the terrorists' attack on the materialistic preoccupations of the parental generations, and provided a further basis for over-throwing the established system. For this reason they have been called 'refugees from affluence' or 'the spoiled children of the economic miracle' (a reference to the prosperous middle-class background of many of them). Generally speaking, terrorist thinking on this matter hardly offered anything new or original.

This last point is certainly stressed by Pridham:

These ideological leitmotivs and the various concepts they included were largely negative, certainly utopian and very much second-hand. Because of these charac-teristics doubts have to be cast on how far terrorist thinking involved any integral or systematic assessment of the wrongs and deficiencies of West Germany. One particular problem is that terrorist language, while familiar in its use of jargonistic terminology, has been both confused and confusing as a means of communicating ideas.[8]

Pridham goes on to refer to the organisational underpinning of the terrorists' ideo-logical positions:

It is no secret, and obvious from the nature of their planned actions, that the terror-ists have usually been well organised. Their methods of preparation have been systematic with various common features such as the procurement of arms from abroad or by stealing from military depots, the renting of so-called 'conspirative flats' usually in anonymous blocks, a strong mobility with the use of fast cars and other details like the forging of passports and driving licences. One key factor has of course been finance, a vital precondition of all these expensive modes of oper-ation. Aside from the pattern of bank robberies (which produced DM 5.4 million during 1970–78 with another DM 6.2 million from other forms of robbery) as the main source, financial demands have been made on active sympathisers, there has been some blackmailing of those implicated in small ways with assisting the terror-ists who prefer this not to become known and apparently material support from international terrorist contacts, notably the Palestinians. These international links have been an important backdrop to German terrorism for other reasons since various leaders have at times received guerrilla training in the Middle East, some German terrorists have participated in actions abroad (e.g. the attack on the OPEC headquarters in 1975) while, more notably, Palestinian terrorists have sometimes played a central part in German activities (the Munich Olympics massacre in 1972, and the Lufthansa hijacking during the Schleyer affair in 1977).

In the later 1970s this efficiency seemed less evident, for a principal change had by then occurred in the structure of German terrorism. Whereas in the first phase of 1970–72 the terrorist scene had been dominated by the centralised and nationwide RAF, in the latter half of the decade several autonomous groups were operating, although all committed to a form of 'strategic' agreement. The mere dynamism of terrorism itself, together with the fact that the West German secu-rity authorities were now 'biting', made it in any case unlikely that its structural nature would remain stable. This more hydra-headed leadership situation made it in turn more difficult for security to be effective in tracking down the terrorists. Already by 1975 a lack of contact and coordination was apparent between the different groups: the so-called 'Central Info-Office' had been disbanded, terrorists were more cautious in avoiding contact with other groups and there developed a preference for a strict division of labour through smaller units, which could easily disperse when necessary. One could add to this a further qualitative difference and speak of a second generation of terrorists, for many of them were distinctly younger than the original Baader-Meinhof group – born in the late 1940s or early 1950s rather than 1930s or early 1940s – and therefore had no direct experience of participation in the student protest movement of the late 1960s. It is possible to suggest that they were differently influenced, if at all, by the ideological assumptions of the New Left. The 'belief system' of the terrorists was seemingly inherited by later groups, but what is clear is that they drew inspiration from the very act of terrorism itself with the Baader-Meinhof acting as trail-blazers.[9]

ORIGINS OF GERMAN TERRORISM: THE SOCIOLOGICAL DIMENSIONS

Pridham does not find it easy to distinguish the social context within which early German terrorism was operating since in many respects the cells were isolated on the left and were marked by shifting numbers of 'active' and 'passive' adherents to a cause. There are, however, some basic social elements:

First, the predominantly bourgeois background of the terrorists and the prominence among them of women accord with patterns in other West European countries. [. . .] Second, the relative political isolation of the terrorists naturally had its social side. As we have seen, it has been necessary to differentiate between the various tendencies in the West German political left – between the constitutional/anti-constitutional left in general and among the extreme left between orthodox and 'unconventional' communists – because these historical divisions derive from conflicting aims for German society and divergent means of achieving them. The country's long background of fratricidal antagonism between these divisions created added pressures for the deliberate isolation of the radically activist minority within the left. Moreover, the terrorists' reminder of the Nazi past in such brutal terms was hardly comfortable to those outside circles committed unswervingly to their beliefs. Consequently, recruitment into terrorism involved an act of finality that expressed itself in the absolutist demands of the various groups.

One final question in this context is the degree to which the German terrorists as a phenomenon may be said to have social roots, that is with which social groups they have had any relationship and which may provide a potential recruitment basin.

The most valid point to make at this stage is to distinguish between the 'active' and the 'passive' among the 'sympathisers'. The former would include those involved in some form of practical assistance for the terrorists, notably in providing temporary accommodation; while 'passive sympathisers' comprised the much larger audience receptive of the terrorists' theories (which after all had never been confined to the terrorists) but who had reservations about or disagreed with their violent methods. Even this distinction had its weaknesses as a sociological description, not only because of inevitable overlap but also on account of the variety and complexity of motives that led some people into active support (and maybe even terrorism) and others close to its border but never actually across it. Various official estimates have been given at different times of the numbers of 'sympathisers', sometimes confusingly totalling them all together, with ranges of up to several thousand 'active' supporters around a hard core of some 60–200 terrorists. They have been drawn from the intelligentsia or academic and professional classes (e.g. doctors, lawyers, some priests, but above all students), but clearly they have been a fluctuating and unquantifiable number.[10]

Merkl (1995) interprets extensive analytical and statistical material published by the West German Government in 1977–78:

Quite illuminating and comparable to the findings and surveys in other countries are the results of the study of the life histories and individual case records of some 227 left-wing terrorists charged or sentenced by the end of 1978, most of them RAF and June 2nd members. Unlike the terrorists of the German radical Right, the 227 had four times the number of parents in the higher occupational categories (independents, higher white-collar and executive and civil service status, and the professions) as the population average. Female left-wing terrorists were to an even higher degree the daughters of the German upper classes: five times the average. Workers and farmers were distinctly underrepresented among the 227, which may help to explain the terrorists' disdain for the working masses of their country. Their ages were typically concentrated in the second postwar generation (born between 1941 and 1955), which also supplied most of the '1968ers' of the student movement, especially the birth cohorts of 1941–47.

About one-third of the left-wing terrorists of the seventies were women. [. . .] Disproportionate numbers of the female terrorists had graduated from a *Gymnasium* and had attended a university. A much larger percentage of both sexes than the average population of comparable age were unemployed or employed only partly or intermittently. There are strong signs of downward social mobility between the fathers and their terrorist offspring, and disproportionate numbers left the university without completing their course of studies. From this basis the life-history research proceeds to the more revealing but also slippery areas of how the family and school background of the terrorists may be different from that of young people of comparable age.

No less than 69 per cent of the men and 52 per cent of the women reportedly had major clashes with parents, schools or employers – 33 per cent with their parents, 18 per cent with employers – of prior records of criminal or juvenile offenses, many of them repeated entries. Although there are no exact population averages or control groups with which to compare, the percentages are so large as to suggest in many cases a conflict-ridden youth aggravated by parental death, divorce, remarriage, and other misfortunes of modern societies. German social scientists sometimes refuse to accept such evidence, because it falls short of a theory of causation of terrorism, but the parallels to such information about other violent movements, for example, the Weimar storm troopers of 1928–33, are striking. Human behavior, of course, has never been subject to simple cause-and-effect relations. In spite of their socialization patterns, every German terrorist could just as well have turned away from terrorism, being a creature endowed with free will; and some did.

Why, then, did some terrorists desert the cause? Merkl adds a point to this:

Some of the researchers asked why some terrorists had turned away from their engagement and when. About one fourth did, most while in jail – a major reason for keeping them separated from each other – and most among those were specialized in a relevant skill rather than in exercising leadership. Although only a few indicated why they quit the group, usually because of the means employed or because of both means and goals, disproportionate numbers of defectors attempted suicide (11 per cent), and many appear to have been swayed by such factors as breaking off their education or job training, drastic mood swings, or the end of a significant personal relationship in their lives. They were generally less violent and somewhat less involved in the groups and had also exhibited better social integration in their personal backgrounds, suggesting, perhaps, the ego strength required for the turnaround.[11]

THE TALLY OF TERRORISM

Joanne Wright (1990) has enumerated the terrorist actions of the RAF and its affiliates over the period 1967–85. There were fierce demonstrations greeting the Shah of Iran's state visit in June 1967 and the shooting then of one student. (This was to give birth to the splinter group, the June 2nd Movement.) Ten months later part of Frankfurt's shopping area was burned to the ground. In May 1972 US army bases in Frankfurt and Hamburg were bombed, with four deaths. Judges, prosecuting counsel, prison governors and leading Christian Democrat politicians were ambushed and threatened between 1974 and 1977. These the RAF labelled as 'necessary actions' since any return of the police-state of the Nazi Third Reich must be aborted. Between 1970 and 1978 there had been 108 attempted murders (one in three succeeded) and 163 kidnappings.

It was in August 1975 that an RAF squad seized the West German embassy in Stockholm demanding the release of twenty-six prisoners, among them Andreas Baader and Ulrike Meinhof. The Bonn Government refused to concede, two embassy officials were shot, and explosives went off by accident.[12]

Jillian Becker (1989) takes the list of incidents further:

With the deaths by suicide of Andreas Baader, Gudrun Ensslin and Jan-Carl Raspe on the night of October 17th–18th, 1977, about a year and a half after the death of Ulrike Meinhof also by suicide, the 'Baader-Meinhof' terrorist group – as it was dubbed by the news media – may be said to have come to an end. The group had called itself the 'Red Army Faction' (Rote Armee Faktion), or 'RAF'. Some terrorists who had belonged to the group when Baader was alive continued to be active after his death, and new members joined it in subsequent years. They went on calling it the 'RAF'. Sometimes in news reports and commentaries the surviving group was still referred to as 'Baader-Meinhof', but the term seemed increasingly inappropriate. The character of the group changed with the changing circumstances of the late 1970s and early 1980s. The original impetus, that is to say the political atmosphere and particular issues which had stimulated the founder-members to mount their campaign of terrorism, was gone by then. The sort of young rebels who were attracted to the secret life dedicated to violent subversion changed too. Those who came to it later seemed less complicated, showed less need for self-justification, and carried out attacks ever more blatantly callous and brutal.

Yet it was not until 1984 that there was a resurgence of terrorist violence by the RAF. At the same time, newer groups struck with bombs and fire-bombs, and the number of explosive and arson attacks in cities and towns throughout the Federal Republic rose steeply over the next two years to well over 400 a year in 1986. Other acts of terrorist crime amounted to about 1,300 in that year.[13]

Wright and Becker agree that after 1981 the principal targets were connected with NATO and the United States. US air bases were bombed and officers, even civilian contractors, shot at. In justification, the RAF used familiar themes of imperialism and liberation. Now West Germany and other states of Western Europe needed to be liberated rather than Vietnam or Palestine.

Throughout the two decades of terror those terrorists who were imprisoned went on hunger strike. In Wright's words:

The hunger strike can be a particularly effective weapon, as the state can be presented as barbaric if it lets the prisoner die, and barbaric if it intervenes to force feed. The purpose of the RAF's hunger strikes was to force the state to change the conditions under which it held the prisoner, and to recognize the political component of the RAF's crimes. The RAF prisoners invariably described themselves as political and demanded treatment as such.[14]

Deaths and injuries as a consequence of terrorism in Germany were insignificant compared with the number of road accident casualties during the same period. The terrorists were comparatively few in number yet their activity was effective measured against the atmosphere of crisis and real fear that was widespread in the population at large. Again, their activity meant a massive deployment of counter-terrorism where there was a trebling of security forces and a five-fold increase in the budget of the Federal Criminal Police Department. Almost certainly, it was the vigorous and wide propaganda work of the terrorists that yielded them a profile never commensurate with their thin numbers.

THE PUBLIC'S RESPONSE TO TERRORISM

In general terms, as we have seen, the effect of German terrorism in its early days led to confusion, fear and even panic until it was seen that the counter-terrorism measures of the government were taking hold. More specifically at the outset, and taking into account the customary black-and-white, unanalytical style of press reporting, there was real perplexity as to the motivation and future intentions of bombers and incendiarists. Given the nature of unforeseen terrorist incidents with their destructive outcome it is hardly surprising that public response was over-whelmingly censorious as to effect and rarely enquiring as to cause. Pridham sees this as an understandable response:

Mass opinion was undoubtedly disturbed by the major terrorist crises. In this sense, the terrorists achieved one of their aims although with the opposite consequences they had predicted, for far from undermining the popular base of the Federal Republic the attacks on prominent figures produced a feeling of outrage in which one could perceive a certain attribution to the state of a sacrosanct quality.

The picture presented by the media, especially the press, was often one of unmitigated hysteria. [. . .] It was commonly stated during the debate over terrorism that attention concentrated exclusively on its effects rather than its causes. This was not strictly true, as is already evident, but it is more apt to say that in searching for the causes political debate was very much more *geistig-politisch* than *sozial-politisch* orientated – that is, it was characterised by a moralistic and often abstract cultural–historical approach to the problem rather than one that followed a 'social–scientific' mode of enquiry and would have allowed a more differentiating approach. Hence, the historically coloured insistence on defending the *Rechtsstaat* at all costs and the accusations levelled against the liberal press of trying to 'under-stand' the terrorists.[15]

Like terrorists in other countries the RAF and associated groups manufactured and transmitted a range of propaganda to clarify and expound their message. It is not at all sure that they were successful in putting their aims in terms easily grasped by the common man, especially where rhetoric was coated in violence. There is every indication that their own far-from-clear rationale not only failed to penetrate the target but also rebounded unproductively. Wright (1990) takes a close look at RAF propaganda enterprise. She conjectures that terrorist propaganda has specific targets and messages which are adjusted or emphasised according to the target selected or the particular tactic being adopted. Wright goes on to identify three target audiences – the 'uncommitted', the 'sympathetic', and the 'active', using these categories to aid definition:

Propaganda is not neutral; it aims to further the aims of the propagandist. One assumption of terrorist strategy is that violence will bring the terrorists mass support by provoking the state to adopt repressive counter-measures. Violence as propa-ganda 'by deed' is certainly instrumental in this, but accompanying it are themes designed to discredit the state and present the state as disadvantaging a particular section of society. These themes, and the channels through which they are promoted, are aimed essentially, although not exclusively, at an 'uncommitted' audience. Once the uncommitted actor begins to ask why an organization perpetrates such terrorist acts, propaganda shifts its emphasis and reclassifies the actor as at least potentially 'sympathetic'. Here propaganda concentrates on justifying the need for violence, and attempts to widen the sympathetic audience usually by focusing on issues much narrower than the overall objective. The objective as regards the 'sympathetic' audience can be said to be to provoke action, and once this happens propaganda again shifts its emphasis. Within the 'active' audience, propaganda aims to keep the individual bound to the cause, and stresses morale-boosting themes such as the inevitability of victory and the justness of the cause.[16]

This seems an interesting theory but the reader may have difficulties with it (as Wright seems to do). It is perhaps the 'uncommitted audience' that both Wright and the RAF see as elusive:

The Marxist terminology and communist utterances of the RAF were not credible reference points for a people who saw themselves as being in the forefront of the battle against communism. Therefore, it is not surprising that the RAF aroused hostility amongst most of the uncommitted audience, rather than encouraging any movement towards the sympathetic audience.

In the case of the so-called 'sympathetic audience' two major elements appear to have formed the foundations of RAF propaganda:

One is the expansion of the ideological appeal to an analysis of what is perceived to be wrong with the current situation, and a rejection of all nonviolent means of achieving it. The second is the use of specific issues to expand the base of support. Both components are very evident in the propaganda of the two groups involved in this study.

The RAF argued that the capitalist mode of production had brought new forms of repressive terror. The people most subject to this terror had become so tied to the processes of production that they could not see their oppressed situation. The violence perpetuated by the RAF would itself help the oppressed see their true situation, and demonstrate that an alternative was possible. The RAF's violence would force the state to reveal its real fascist nature, and thus the people would rally to the RAF as their defenders and saviours. The parliamentary and extra-parliamentary left had failed totally to respond to the situation, and therefore there was no option but to resort to violence, or in the RAF's terminology 'urban guerrilla warfare'.

However, as the RAF's most general ideological appeal was rejected by the uncommitted audience, so was its more detailed one by the sympathetic audience. Orthodox communists had already given up the notion of a violent revolution within the Western democracies by the time the RAF emerged. Others on the Left also rejected the RAF's analysis, and the students' main concern proved to be university reform, not a violent revolution. The RAF clearly identified a potentially sympathetic audience and directed a considerable propaganda effort towards it. But this sympathetic audience was not generally the disadvantaged group defined by the RAF's ideology. It was, like the RAF, essentially middle class and educated. Those defined as disadvantaged by the RAF did not see themselves as disadvantaged, and were subject primarily to messages of violence and threat.

None the less the RAF was at times able to discernibly increase its sympathy. This sympathy was limited to fairly specific objectives, and was more a result of government reaction than of actions by the RAF itself. As mentioned earlier, the climate of fear generated by the RAF led to increased police powers and to changes in the criminal code. The West German state also argued that even in prison the RAF presented such a danger to the state that special holding conditions were necessary. The actions of the police, legislative changes and the prison conditions were successful for the RAF because they were based on a credible derivation of fact acceptable to the target audience. The RAF's sympathetic audience was amenable to suggestions of increasing repression, which the state's treatment of the RAF seemed to show. But while many were critical of the police's behavior and of the legislative changes, and supported a considerable easing of the conditions under which RAF prisoners were held, the linkage with the RAF's overall objectives was inherently weak. In the early 1980s the RAF tried to strengthen this link by presenting West Germany as an American colony within NATO. Its 1984 strategy paper advocated attacks on NATO, but these attacks were to be accompanied by attacks on representatives of West German 'fascism', and a hunger strike by RAF prisoners.[17]

As for the 'active audience', in Wright's view, this is where terrorist propaganda must be directed 'inwards' to seek out adhesion to the group and to cement it:

The aim of propaganda as regards the active volunteer is to further bind the individual to the cause. Thus it is not surprising to find propaganda stressing the need for further action, and emphasizing morale-boosting themes such as the inevitability of victory. The organizational structure of the terrorist group also plays a part in isolating the individual from alternative propaganda sources. Ideology plays its part by providing further justifications for the need to commit acts of terrorism and reassurances that the 'cause' justifies such acts. Prisoners too seem to assume a role of some significance in propaganda directed inwards. Certainly prisoners and the state's treatment of them seem to provide the terrorists with the most tangible link to their sympathetic audience and ways to increase it, but how the terrorist group itself treats its imprisoned members has obvious internal implications. While successful operations freeing prisoners undoubtedly send messages to the uncommitted and sympathetic audiences, their primary effect is on internal morale especially if an 'experienced' volunteer is returned to active service.[18]

STATE RESPONSE TO TERRORISM

Three pervasive themes illumined the debate about democratic values and the challenge of terrorism from the start, according to Pridham. First, then and today,

terrorism is regarded in the eyes of the state and by all sides of the political spectrum as presenting a threat to West Germany's constitutional order or *Rechtsstaat*
(state of law). Second, there was and still is the expectation that a German citizen
has to be an 'active democrat' prepared to uphold and defend basic order. Third, a
balance must be maintained between the individual rights of citizens within a liberal
state and the need to implement security measures without infringing individual
rights. Between 1971 and 1978 the German parliament, the *Bundestag*, enacted
numerous restraining provisions. New laws were passed in respect of hijacking
and abduction, and there was a tightening up of the searching for and arrest of
suspected terrorists who would then be put into solitary confinement. In Bonn a
new government department was created, the Federal Office for the Protection
of the Constitution, with powers to obtain intelligence about the movements and
activities of designated persons and, if necessary, to use informers and police
agents provocateurs. Not all these devices were approved in liberal quarters. If trials
were to be 'expedited' under a new code, might this not limit the rights of the
accused? Was it legitimate to put defence lawyers in treason trials under higher
court 'supervision' because of the possibility of their being regarded as 'terrorist
lawyers'?

A counter-terrorism measure arousing contention was the *Berufsverbot* (job ban)
of 1972. This was a government edict to ban suspected terrorist sympathisers from
tenured employment in all state-sponsored occupations. In the first four years of the
ban nearly half a million people were officially screened not merely for supposed
terrorist activity but also for any behaviour which might put their political reliability
in doubt. By many this edict was alleged to be a tool of a repressive, fascist state.
Not all Federal Government response was seen as hazarding constitutional freedoms. It could be said, apart from panic here and there, that a good many Germans
were inclined to be reflective rather than obsessive about threats to their community, as Pridham indicates:

Yet, the debate over the effects of terrorism on the political scene has revealed an
evident and often passionate interest in the *quality* of the democratic system and
not merely its stability.

Two effects have been popularly attributed to the rise of terrorism in the
Federal Republic: promotion of a strong internal security system and encouragement of a trend to the right. The first is without doubt, but the second demands
some qualification. Other left-wing circles accused the Baader-Meinhof and later
groups of provoking a right-wing reaction, but in conventional political terms
this is difficult to establish. The Social and Free Democrats were in power in
Bonn throughout the course of terrorism in the 1970s, but despite some political
setbacks and security failures they have by and large managed to contain the issue
in the party-political sense, this being confirmed by their image of competence in
the area of law and order. Nevertheless, there is always the possibility of severe
political repercussions in the event of disaster in another major terrorist attack,
particularly in view of the widespread West German obsession with all matters of
security.[19]

Law statutes, he points out, were unlikely to get rid of the malevolence, persistence and ingenuity of those who intended to mete out revolutionary terror:

Terrorism simply could not be legislated out of existence, an assumption that owed something to a traditional belief that political conflicts could be solved with administrative means and that quite ignored the sociological roots of this new phenomenon.[20]

POSTSCRIPT

It would be beyond the bounds of this brief account of terrorism in Germany to go too deeply into analysing motives and methods. (It is said that the analysts studying terrorists have always far outnumbered the terrorists themselves.)

The enigmas remain. We now know a good deal about the origins and the shape of German terrorism as a result of autobiographies, interviewing, prison confessions, and seized documents. Nevertheless, there are numerous questions. How did a dedicated few suppose that their plea for a better deal for the downtrodden and their comradeship with the exploited in every land would ever have a magnetic appeal if it were accompanied by end-justifies-the-means violence? When terrorist propaganda shifted from warranting a genuine struggle to advocating deliberate attacks on persons and property was this not likely to be considered destructive self-indulgence and nihilistic? Were the would-be revolutionaries not in danger of being branded (even by the 'sympathetic') as irrational fanatics, prisoners of unreality?

In conclusion, this case-study seems to point up two common features of the terrorist – his defensiveness and his apocalyptic visions. Kellen (1998) has this to say about defensiveness:

In fact, probably all terrorists, whether of the religious, ethnic, nationalist, or political/social variety, believe that their targets, individually and collectively, are not only guilty because of what they do and represent, but because they oppress and mistreat the terrorists. It seems to be extremely difficult for Western observers to see and accept that terrorists, whom society regards as the ultimate aggressors, believe that they themselves act out of self-defense. How can that be in West Germany? Very simply, from the beginning, West German terrorists have regarded themselves as the innocent victims of an aggressive, intrusive, repressive West German state ready to use violence – structural violence, they call it – to keep itself in power and to repress them and other 'rightminded people'.

Most people and their leaders in the Western democracies refuse to accept this psychological phenomenon. In fact, it seems they are no more aware of it than they realize that the Soviet Union is honestly afraid of the West and generally acts from that impulse. Psychologically, however, by far the most important key to understanding terrorists is that they feel they are defending themselves against an aggressive, evil, intrusive and murderous world.[21]

Those in the Baader-Meinhof brigade and the RAF who confidently awaited the Moment of Truth, the rainbow's end to the Right Way Forward, were millenarians. Jillian Becker (1989) quotes the scholarly conclusion of Norman Cohn about the nature of this predilection:

It is characteristic of this kind of movement that its aims and premises are bound-less. A social struggle is seen not as a struggle for specific, limited objectives, but as an event of unique importance, different in kind from all other struggles known to history, a cataclysm from which the world is to emerge totally transformed and redeemed. This is the essence of the recurrent phenomenon or [. . .] persistent tradition – that we have called 'revolutionary millenarianism'.[22]

Given the earnestness and absoluteness of the German terrorist (similar to that met with elsewhere) there is no easy response to terrorist campaigning and outrage. As Kellen put it, terrorism is an intellectual challenge to us all:

In the end, as important as the penchants for ideology and rebellion are in provoking and shaping terrorist behavior, they are not all-important. At least as significant are the realities that infringe upon, and affect, the world that the terrorist experiences. And among the most affecting of these is the rhetoric that governments articulate in response to the terrorists' acts. Bombastic threats followed by abject cave-ins do more to sustain the terrorists than does any id or ego – or, for that matter, any ideology or rebellion.[23]

Chapter 14

Italy

THE CASE OF TERRORISM IN ITALY is interesting in several
respects. Social and economic deprivation are seen to breed violent agitation
and response. A small group of determined students came together in 1970 to fashion
an instrument to carry through political action-at-all-costs. This was to be known as
the Red Brigade, the Brigate Rosse or BR. Unavoidably, the outcome was to be a
violent one. Italian terrorism flourished between 1970 and 1989 on account of the
tardy unresolve of governments rent by factionalism and corruption to frame consistent strategies of counter-terrorism. How, then, have Italians learned to live with
thirty or so years of terrorism in their midst? Is it credible, as some believe, that
Italy as a country is distinctive in harbouring negative millenarian tendencies, a
culture of violence, which a well-organised group may exploit? 'Why did they do it,
those Red Brigadists?' asks Alison Jamieson (1989):

Most of the Red Brigadists were intelligent and young, some of them genuinely
dedicated to ideals of brotherhood and justice; they had acquired at university the
political skills of analysis, communication and persuasion, skills which should have
enabled them to contribute more than most to influencing peaceful progress in
society. Why did they throw these skills aside and turn instead to the gun, killing
people in cold blood, often preceding the killing with the prolonged and excruci-
ating mental torture of kidnap – perhaps the most loathsome and inhuman of all
man's inhumanities to man?

How did a few dozen such people, a hard core aided by a few hundred part-
timers, dominate the political life of Italy for ten years, killing and kidnapping
politicians, judges and industrialists, disrupting the process of law? And how, in
the end, did the fragile, chaotic and corrupt system of Italian democracy, already
bombarded by criminal gangs and constant economic crises, survive this onslaught
and emerge with its rule of law strengthened by the ordeal?[1]

THE ORIGINS OF TERRORISM

The BR, originating in Milan in 1970, was an outgrowth of the Europe-wide radical student movement of 1968–69. A small circle of leaders directed political struggle in the belief that against an authoritative state which often employed violence, a recourse to violence by subjects and victims was justified. Clandestine conspiracies and provocative action and what nineteenth-century anarchists termed 'the propaganda of deeds' were legitimate. As the leaders of the BR understood it and in numerous broadsheets proclaimed it, their actions were not those of a mindless class war. The BR would be the vanguard of proletarian resistance against its fundamental enemy, the Italian incarnation of a 'multinational imperialist state'. This was 'liberation' strategy in sour, uncompromising terms. 'Justificational violence' was to be the exercise of retribution for what the Marxist-Leninists among them considered to be injustices against the working class. Magistrates, industrial managers, political and social figures could be abducted as hostages in a move towards 'incipient Socialist revolution'. As means to an end, opponents would have to be marked down and 'terrorised'. Danila Salvioni and Anders Stephanson (1985) have studied the organisational permutations of the BR:

The most important elements stemmed from two groups of (former) northern Italian students: one (mainly sociologists) from Trento led by Renato Curcio, and the other from Reggio Emilia in which Alberto Franceschini was the most prominent. In 1969, they became part of the Metropolitan Political Collective in Milan, and it was from this experience that the Red Brigade was most directly to emerge. On the whole, these were students of middle-class or working-class background who had become part of the enormous expansion of the university system in the 1960s. There were notably few upper-class or upper-middle-class members. But whatever their social roots, they were clearly not 'marginal' people, social outcasts, as would often be the case with subsequent forms of left-wing terrorism. Nor, as is sometimes done, can their background simply be described as predominantly left-wing Catholic. The Trento group contained a fair number of old Catholics – some still practising – but the Emilia group was chiefly of Communist parentage. Neither fact is surprising. Catholicism and the Communist party have traditionally been the two outlets for personal activism in Italy, and the BR's founders had an extensive history of such efforts.[2]

Paul Furlong (1981) has looked at the social and economic preconditions of Italy's terrorism and at the national and political context within which they operate. Left-wing terrorism seems to depend upon international models, right-wing groups are close to earlier fascist traditions. Three strands in the political culture are: first, a classic state liberalism, second, tenacity derived from wartime resistance, third, a tradition of popular opposition to centralised government. Varied influences, often contradictory, help explain a minority feeling permanently excluded politically. Organised violence has been a predictable consequence of political confusion and economic malaise:

In Italy, recent history certainly from the Risorgimento is scattered with minority groups committed to political activism that finally issued into organised violence and sometimes into terrorism. Left-wing political terrorism in Italy in its contemporary form is in its ideological expressions and organisation very much dependent on international models, in some cases with explicit rejection of indigenous theories of political violence; right-wing political terrorism on the other hand is ideologically close to the fascist traditions of 1920–22, though in its operations it differs somewhat from that model. Despite these differences, the traditions of violence in Italy are important for an understanding of its modern political terrorism.

Italy presents us with conflicting and confused strands of political culture that result in a wide variety both of forms of political violence and of attitudes towards political violence on the part of political actors. There is the traditional authoritarianism of the Liberal state that developed after the unification of Italy, exaggerated and developed by the fascist state, which has residual survival in areas within the central administration, the judiciary and the armed forces. Second, the guerrilla warfare carried out with some success by the partisans against the occupying German forces is significant as a model for some modern terrorists, but not only for that. The idealism and tenacity of the resistance movement found only partial expression in the constitution of the Republic, but their tradition is claimed as a source of legitimacy by many contemporary political actors. Third, there is a specifically Italian tradition found in the violence, almost invariably unsuccessful, of those who opposed the Liberal state, whether in an organised form as anarcho-socialists or 'bourgeois patriots' or in a disorganised and spontaneous fashion as brigands and outlaws, particularly in the South. The modern Italian state is an amalgam of these strands. It has inherited both the tradition of centralised administration and the emphasis on the supremacy of the law that characterised the Liberal state, with its formalism, its authoritarianism and some of the practical failings, in particular its vulnerability to political pressure. The combination of this 'strong state' tradition with the relatively radical democratic and federalist state that appears in parts of the postwar constitution is uneasy, but it is these two together that influence in different directions both the development of organised political violence and the response to it by the state.

Against the 'redneck Marxism' of the left-wing terrorists and the grandiose operations of the neo-fascists, the Italian polity presents an ambiguous and polyvalent set of tactics, torn between its liberal–democratic constitution and origins and its authoritarian heavy-handed tradition. Political terrorism is implicitly an attack on the authority of the state, and may be closely connected with the development of a minority that believes itself to be permanently excluded from the political system; the questions that arise in the Italian case might therefore concern the authority of the Italian Republic and the economic, social and political conditions that have led to the emergence of a 'permanent minority'.

The social and political origins of Italian terrorism can be found in the contradictory influences that produced the Italian constitution and that resulted in the radical expectations engendered by the resistance movement; in the tempering of the populist democratic elements in the Constituent Assembly; and in the delays and lapses that accompanied the implementation of the constitution. The political system that has developed is characterised by the continuous occupation of power by one party, the Christian Democrats (DC), for over thirty years and the exclusion from ministerial posts since 1947 of the next largest party, the Italian Communist Party (PCI). The electorate, divided for much of this period into two hostile and exclusive blocs supporting one or other of these parties, is extremely stable in its voting patterns.

The continuous occupation of power by the DC has fostered the development of a system of government based on clientelism and petty compromise, known commonly as immobilism, in which unstable coalitions are cobbled together on the basis of distribution of ministerial posts with programmes nominally supported by the coalition parties rarely reaching the stage of implementation. The coalitions are beset by inter-party and intra-party wrangling, by personal feuds and ideological rigidities, by vacuous adherence to fine-sounding principles and by cynical opportunism.[3]

Thus, for Furlong political terrorism is a predictable consequence of so much malaise:

An economic crisis producing unemployment particularly among the younger age-groups, political parties that are unable to agree on appropriate measures, a social fabric severely threatened by the industrial mobilisation of the immediate postwar period, and not least a political culture that supports radical expectations and gives legitimacy to the unsatisfied hopes and programmes of the postwar political reconstruction.[4]

David Apter (1997) sees those who commit violent acts (like the BR) seeking broad public support through confrontational acts, a moral crusade in a sense, but a presumptuous one to outside observers:

Mobilizing oppositional forces for the forcible overthrow of the state, or terrorism, in which small bands use acts of violence to render the state impotent, turn citizens into bystanders, and force the state to engage in violent retaliation which undermines both its credibility and legitimacy. [. . .]

The Red Brigades in Italy [. . .] played a cat and mouse game with the Italian state which it tried to make stupid and incompetent by daring acts which left the authorities helpless. It also revealed the corruption at the core of the state, a critique which was not as wrong as the solution. The Red Brigades, as a movement, represent other similar ones, like Baader-Meinhof (Red Army Faction), and Action Directe. These came to regard themselves as the last pure crystalline structure, the radical residue of the 'generation of '68', the others having become compromised and corrupted. For the Red Brigades, the story-telling includes a classic tale of betrayal, the proletariat betrayed by the Italian Communist Party. The hegemonic enemy represents world capitalism. Loss is double, the product of the proletariat to a hegemonic bourgeoisie, and the domination of that bourgeoisie, and the state itself, by NATO, the chief instrument of the American military–industrial complex. Terrorism is necessary to up-end the state and reclaim the national patrimony, returning it by means of revolution to its rightful owners.[5]

THE NATURE OF ITALIAN TERRORISM

Furlong (1981) surveying the interwoven reaction and response to terrorism in Italy considers that the incidence of terrorism developed largely in two phases. The first phase, 1969–73, begins with neo-fascist public outrages, then more selective and symbolic targeting by the BR setting themselves up as legitimate strong-arm defenders of the proletariat. Despite terrorist 'success' there is a sense of isolation among many *brigatisti* doubting whether clandestine violence effectively promotes Socialist advance:

In the first years of terrorism post-1968, it was clearly the right-wing terrorists who dominated the scene with a series of spectacular gestures. On 12 December 1969 a bomb exploded in the Piazza della Fontana in Milan. There were fourteen deaths and eighty people injured. Three days later the police arrested Pietro Valpreda, a known anarchist, and the mass media loudly proclaimed his guilt. But it was nearly nine years before the case was to be closed with Valpreda acquitted on all charges, two neo-fascists convicted for the attack after having fled from house arrest, and damaging revelations made both in court and out concerning the involvement of security services in the manipulation of right-wing terrorism. In the five years from 1969 to the end of 1973 there also occurred a series of bomb attacks against political targets, an abortive *coup d'état* in December 1970, the long drawn out riots in Reggio Calabria fomented by the MSI, and the development of the so-called strategy of tension. This was the period of mass political terrorism operated by the neo-fascists in which the victims were indiscriminately selected from the target group – the general public – with the aim of producing panic prior to the armed takeover of power.

At the same time there was the steady growth of a more selective form of political terrorism, in which the target group was narrower and the victims therefore more limited: this was the terrorism of the Red Brigades, in this period overshadowed by the terrorism of the right, but later to come into its own. A major difference between the two forms of terrorism, which indicates their differing objectives, is the frequency with which the neo-fascist groups use bombs in crowded places, while the BR rarely use bombs and do not appear to have aimed any operations directly against the public at large. The activity of the BR began in August 1970 in Milan. They were a development of the Collettivo Politico Metropolitano (Metropolitan Political Collective), later termed Sinistra Proletaria (Proletarian Left), a group restricted to Milan some of whose leading members, in particular Renato Curcio and Margherita Cagol, had been together at the University of Trento and had their first known taste of political activity in left-wing Catholic groups there. Others who joined the BR at this stage or soon after, such as Alberto Franceschini and Roberto Ognibene, came from the PCI-dominated area of Reggio Emilia. Though the BR appear to have chosen clandestinity early in 1971, the terrorist attacks mounted by them were high in symbolic content and low on physical injury for a considerable period. Arson against cars belonging to managers of large firms or against known neo-fascists appears to have been their trademark, with occasional well-planned and well-publicised kidnappings that inevitably resulted in a 'proletarian trial' and the release of the prisoner. Throughout this period the BR showed a gradual increase both in expertise and in ambition. The arson attacks constituted bread-and-butter operations undertaken against representative targets with the aim both of inducing terror among the 'ruling class' and of stimulating the working class to take up arms. The BR also showed at this stage a great interest in and knowledge of factory conditions and organisation. Many of their 'proletarian trials' were little more than interrogations to extract information about suitable targets. Their purpose appeared to be to establish themselves as 'vigilantes of the workers', and their operations were usually explained in the inevitable leaflets as actions on behalf of particular groups of workers.

The experiences of those years, though not marked by any obvious success in achieving their overall objectives, may paradoxically have confirmed the BR and other left-wing groups in the validity of their strategy. Clandestinity and 'proletarian justice' may have begun as a reaction to the heady days of 1968 and the labour struggles of the 'hot autumn' of 1969 in the belief that the intensification of the class struggle was both desirable and necessary.

Furlong sees this first phase, despite its moments of terrorist 'success', as pointing up feelings of isolation (even a sense of futility) among many of the *brigatisti*. Clandestine activity was never to be altogether effective in promoting the advance of Socialism:

Because [it was] clandestine, it was the violence of an isolated group, unable to achieve any direct relationship with the masses it was supposed to be serving. Though to some extent BR has been able to overcome this isolation in recent years, the pattern of its activity is still characterised by reliance on clandestine violence as the single valid instrument of revolutionary activity. In this also it is to be distinguished from the revolutionary groups on the extreme left that have not chosen clandestinity, whose view of the BR is well summarised in the description of them as '*compagni che sbagliano*' – comrades who are in error.[6]

Furlong's second phase is given as 1974–79. The attacks of the BR on prominent political figures are seen as an armed struggle raising their horrific public image without any consequential increase in proletarian support. The BR's following may have been thin and erratic but the group is now mature enough to know how to strike at the government in Rome. (As we shall see later there is, among commentators, speculation as to how far the BR were prisoners of a myth about the centre when in reality Italian power was much diffused.) Generally, the discipline, expertise and confidence of the BR stand out in contrast to the shrill terrorist clamour of an indecisive left wing and a much weakened neo-fascist front. Even so, BR, in using both full-time and part-time terrorist members, does not coordinate activities easily. They cannot take for granted popular support for their violent methods. Yet, BR confidence had its ups and downs as Furlong relates:

The years 1974–79 were the boom years for BR with several major operations against their name and the clear assertion of their leadership over the pullulating left-wing terrorist groups. As well as the regular attacks on representative figures, the declared strategy of the BR was to strike at the heart of the state. This they attempted to do with the kidnap of Mario Sossi, a public prosecutor in Genova, on 18 April 1974, three weeks before the divorce referendum; the murder of Francesco Coco, chief magistrate in Genova, on 8 June 1976; and the kidnap of Aldo Moro, president of the DC, on 16 March 1978, who was murdered (presumably on 8 or 9 May) and whose body was found in the centre of Rome on 9 May. These grand manoeuvres appear to have been expressly designed to have the maximum political impact, since they invariably occurred either during election campaigns or at times of government crisis. Sossi was kidnapped during an extremely divisive referendum campaign, which pitched the DC against its governmental allies and the PCI and in which the issues raised spread wider than the single question of the divorce law to cover the fundamental political direction of the country. Coco, who had been responsible for the rejection of the terms previously agreed with the BR for Sossi's release, was murdered exactly a fortnight before the parliamentary elections of 20 June 1976 in which the PCI were expected to make large gains. Moro was kidnapped on the day that Prime Minister Andreotti, after a prolonged government crisis resolved with the considerable help of Moro's negotiating skills, was presenting his new government's programme to parliament, with the support of the PCI. But the dual strategy of the BR, comprising persistent attacks on middle-ranking officials, industrialists and police with the occasional grand attack, has so far failed to incite the working class to civil war or even to mobilise them against the state and the parties. [. . .]

The BR now [1974–79] have an articulated organisation with established groups – 'columns' – of full-time clandestine terrorists in at least four major cities and probably elsewhere. Each column consists of about six members, one of whom is in touch with the central control; the columns are kept strictly separate from one another. The BR are directed by a national executive known as the 'Strategic Control' (Direzione Strategica). Though the organisation is well able to preserve clandestinity, the isolation of the columns appears to have led to problems for the Strategic Control of keeping the operations of the individual columns under central direction. The BR are well equipped, well trained, thorough and determined. They are extremely careful in their recruiting and appear successfully to have resisted significant infiltration since 1975. They are not short of finance, which they obtain by robbing banks and from kidnappings. Unusually for groups of the extreme left they have survived for nine years under difficult circumstances apparently without major defections or divisions, and have not been deterred from their operations either by the overall failure of their strategy or by the increasing frequency of arrests of their members.

In an effort to avoid the isolation from which the BR suffer, their main rival group, Prima Linea, operate on part-time clandestinity. The members of PL are expected to hold ordinary full-time jobs and as far as possible live the lives of normal members of society, though any involvement in 'mainstream' politics is not feasible. PL operates therefore like a traditional 'secret society'. This 'part-time' clandestinity probably explains the restricted quantity of PL's operations; it does not appear to have increased their capacity to establish direct relationships with working-class organisations.

Despite the continued success of the anti-terrorist group led by General Dalla Chiesa, it is not a hazardous speculation that the operations of BR and PL will continue for some time to come and that they will be increasingly determined and ruthless. In January 1979 for the first time the BR murdered a member of the PCI who had notified the police of the presence of a BR informant in the factory where he worked. This operation could only be necessary if the BR had failed to win the argument with the PCI and other organised groups over the political direction of the Marxist left, and may be interpreted as indicating the reliance of the BR on terrorist tactics to achieve some control over the area they claim to be organising and leading.

At the same time, it must be acknowledged that left-wing terrorism attracts significant consent in certain sectors of society and sympathy in others. BR and PL both rely on the support and cover provided by 'irregulars', and both appear to have good contacts in some of the major industrial complexes in the North, as well as in the larger universities (in particular, Rome, Bologna, Turin and Milan). BR appear to recruit mainly from the universities, among the urban unemployed and in the prisons; PL, because of their different strategy, cannot be so reliant on the urban unemployed. These sources are likely to continue to supply the groups both with permanent activists and with irregulars. Administrative rearrangements have produced some change in the prisons, where the policy of establishing top-security prisons preferably on outlying islands, such as the Asinara, for long-term and dangerous prisoners appears to be having some success both in keeping captured terrorists behind bars and in preventing their proselytising activities in the ordinary prisons. The left-wing terrorists appear able at present to retain these links with limited sectors of society while the overwhelming majority of the population appear either to reject them completely or to prefer to ignore them. This is perhaps more a function of the failure of the political system adequately to cope with chronic social problems than a result of any great success of the BR in winning support for their strategy. The sympathy of the unemployed and the anarchic student groups is ambivalent and unstable. Political terrorism of both left and right is likely to lose sympathy and consent because of the increasing intensity of their methods; combined with the increased efficiency of the security services who now appear to be taking terrorism seriously, this means a bleak future for the terrorists, though the short-term prospects for the Italian citizen are not good either.[7]

Two distinctive features of Italian terrorism are emphasised by David Moss (1997). First, there is the reliance on working towards social-revolutionary objectives rather than ethnic nationalist ones:

A comparison with Northern Ireland suggests a further distinctive feature of the Italian case. In advanced industrial societies attempts to promote clandestine social-revolutionary violence have to contend with a difficulty not encountered in cases of ethnic-nationalist violence. The activists of ethno-nationalist violence at least share a clear set of religious or ethnic characteristics with the populations on whose behalf they are fighting, as well as some straightforward political goals, even if the identification of exactly which hostile group stands between the population and its goals may be a matter of controversy. But the social-revolutionary users of violence in liberal-democratic societies such as Italy have to make violence not only an instrumental technique for damaging opponents but also the symbolic basis of the community of activists. Solidarities have to be built around availability for violence in order to attract sympathizers, encourage affiliates and identify enemies. Whatever support for social-revolutionary violence may be claimed from class identification, the dispersed social classes of present-day capitalist societies can only on very rare occasions provide the kind of direct explicit solidarity that ethnicity or religion confers.[8]

A second characteristic of Italian terrorism is an element of 'exchange' of violence between the political left and right, ritualistic in that 'macro-violence' is displayed and exploited for different constituencies and contrasted political ends especially in the main cities:

Most violence had occurred more or less openly in the course of the student and worker mobilizations, characterized by direct confrontations between extremists of the Right and Left and clashes with police in the course of mass demonstrations. Given the importance of the practice and discourse of violence in recent Italian history and the scale of mass mobilization and confrontations across all major institutions between 1967 and 1969, what is surprising about the first phase of clandestine violence is less its appearance than the reluctance to exploit it [. . .] both exploited the symbolic capital of the Resistance in creating a model for their actions and appealing for the support of the wider communities in which they claimed membership. As a result the violence which ensued fell rapidly into a predictable sequence of exchanges which reflected the dominant empirical and discursive opposition between Left and Right in post-war Italian politics.

   The examples of macro-violence by the extreme Right and extreme Left revealed their different approaches to the distinction between politics and violence. The bomb massacres of the Right – four across Italy between 1969 and 1974 – were designed to create the sense that violence had become a pervasive element of everyday life. Making victims indiscriminately, the bombs demonstrated that violence was no longer a separate domain, remote from all but political extremists, but a potential threat to everyone. Trust in the governing parties to protect their electors and other citizens would be undermined. Similarly, by leaving their attacks unclaimed or trying to throw responsibility for them onto the Left, the extreme Right was also seeking to weaken the significance of the general distinction between Right and Left and the kinds of political strategy each was prepared to use. The disruption of these taken-for-granted distinctions was part of a general strategy to subvert the boundaries which had excluded the Right from full political legitimacy since the fall of Fascism.

   A quite different relation between the fields of violence and politics was represented in the macro-violence of the extreme Left – the five bloodless kidnappings carried out by the Red Brigades between 1972 and 1974. They provided a carefully structured occasion for demonstrating the separate existence but mutual accessibility of the fields of open and clandestine politics by moving the victim across the boundary between them during his capture. His confessions – confirming the role of extreme Right violence in repressing working-class mobilization on the shop floor – were designed to transform the accusations of his captors into established knowledge for dissemination to the widest possible audience. Kidnappings – lasting up to several weeks – thus served as an elaborate mechanism for the production of knowledge about politics. In contrast to the incorporation of violence into everyday life and politics by the extreme Right, they represented a highly structured exterior site from which the reality of politics could be revealed.

Within the contrasting frames created by macro-violence, both Right and Left practiced the micro-violence of attacks on opponents and their property. Right-wing militants attacked the activists of the extreme Left; members of the Left retaliated. [. . .] Their attacks were concentrated against neo-Fascist activists, accusing them of waging class war against the working class on the street and shopfloor, protected by the local representatives of an increasingly repressive state. To assess the results of their displays of 'counter-power', they sought direct reports from factory floor or sympathizers from the extreme Left.[9]

THE TALLY OF TERRORISM

The statistics of Italian terrorism are appalling. During the years 1969–87 there were 14,591 recorded terrorist attacks. One third of these incidents occurred in 1980. It was right-wing terrorism that ranged most widely and brutally in the first phase of terrorism – 9,000 attacks were attributed to them and one in four incidents featured the use of explosives. Left-wing terrorists belonged to 181 different groups. The BR captured most attention in Italy's press with the daring kidnapping of former Italian Prime Minister Aldo Moro in 1978 and of US Army Brigadier-General Dozier two years later. The BR also claimed responsibility for murdering Leamon Hunt, the US Chief of the United Nations Multinational Force and Observer Group, in Sinai in 1984. Nothing was left to chance by the BR, which may explain why their 'score' of vicious attacks between 1972 and 1986 was rather lower at eighteen abductions and sixty-nine murders. Even so, in one year, 1979–80, the BR admitted to 439 terror attacks. For David Moss (1997) the tally of Italian casualties and property destroyed needs to be seen in broader perspective and he gives the example of Northern Ireland:

The Italian case, involving radical terrorism, did not exact its casualties from among the proletariat – the class of preference in keeping with the Leninist tradition of the Red Brigades. Nevertheless there was plenty of political violence. It was inaugurated by a right-wing bomb massacre in 1969; it ended with the murder of a Christian Democrat intellectual by the residual members of the left-wing Red Brigades in 1988. The damage to people and property in those two decades – circa 400 murders, 5,000 injuries, and 12,500 attacks on property – was certainly substantial; yet it amounted to only half the number of deaths from political violence in Spain and barely one-sixth of the deaths in Northern Ireland over comparable periods (Hewitt, 1988). Wider comparisons, too, will help to put the Italian case in perspective. In half the time and among a population little more than one-third of Italy's, left-wing and state violence in Peru produced 25,000 deaths and 22,000 attacks on property; and in Sri Lanka, over an even shorter period, ethnic and political strife caused between 70,000 and 90,000 deaths and the physical displacement of more than 10 per cent of the population.

These crude contrasts can tell us little directly about the social and political perceptions of violence in the different cases. But they do suggest a rather different degree of saturation of everyday life by violence. The chances of dangerous encounters, and the urgency of the need to choose openly to support, tolerate or oppose violence, vary greatly. Even allowing for territorial and temporal variations in the concentration of attacks, 'living with violence' must have been different in Peru, where 25,000 insurgents were active among a population of 20 million, than it was in Italy, with no more than a few hundred people directly responsible for clandestine violence active at any one time and widely dispersed among 57 million people. These contrasts can be linked to two further differences. First, the greater or lesser density of violence is likely to have consequences for the force and stability of the meanings that violence carries. In Northern Ireland, for example, the concentration of violence on a miniaturized terrain supports the highly personalized theme of 'victimhood' in a way that the dispersed, mostly experience-distant, violence in Italy could not. The Northern Irish conflict has produced a much more stable and elaborate set of conventions governing the meaning of violence than could ever be established in Italy. A second difference concerns the relative importance of particular channels of communication. The discourse community of participants, sympathizers and audiences in Italy was linked by ties that were relatively weak, indirect and impersonal.[10]

Crucial to the early successes of BR was its organisation on military lines – there was a strategic directorate, an executive committee variously in charge of logistics and mass propaganda nationwide (occasioning some cynical comment from elsewhere that Italian terrorism was becoming too bureaucratic). Field activities were the work of seven 'columns' in different areas of Italy known as 'poles' each with a delegated leader and with some operational autonomy. Actual 'missions' were assigned to subordinate 'brigades' co-ordinated by the column commanders. Targets were selected from a 'hit list' of some 1,100 individuals and properties on account of symbolic value and vulnerability. Prior reconnaissance and evidence from a network of informers would decide the tactics to be used, whether it would be abduction, ambush, raid, fire bomb or assassination. Robberies would bring in funds. As counter-terrorist identification and arrest increased so the proportion of regulars grew less. The BR headquarters constantly put out communiqués and strategic resolutions. In its early stages the BR owed a good deal to carefully maintained international connections. Training camps for Italian activists were offered by Angola, Cuba and Czechoslovakia. Automatic weapons were sent from the Soviet Union. France, Libya and Bulgaria offered finance and liaison personnel.

THE MORO AFFAIR

Italy's terrorists made world headlines on 16 March 1977 when a BR hit squad snatched out of Rome's traffic Aldo Moro, former Prime Minister, Foreign Minister and prominent Christian Democrat. His five-man bodyguard were all gunned down. Moro was bundled away to be imprisoned and interrogated by his captors as Public Enemy No. 1. This abduction coincided with the arrest in Turin of Renato Curci, one of the BR leaders. Curci and others were to be put on trial, caged in a court guarded by no less than 8,000 armed police. 'We believed,' Curci shouted, 'it was necessary to kill today in order to live tomorrow'. Moro was kept in solitary confinement in Rome. He wrote numerous letters to family and friends seeking their mediation with the terrorists. The Pope and United Nations Secretary-General Kurt Waldheim did their best to intercede, but unavailingly. At length, after fifty-five days, Moro was tried by a BR's 'People's Court', executed, and his body dumped in a Rome side-street near the Christian Democrat headquarters.

This daring incident was, in fact, counter-productive in more than one respect. The Italian public were more cynical than sad, shaking their heads at so much political chicanery. The savage kidnapping alienated many members of the wider revolutionary movement. Moreover, there was now increasing disenchantment with these ruthless tactics among imprisoned terrorists – the 'soft' penitents who had earned some remission, the 'hard' dedicated prisoners on life-sentence, and those who were wavering in their loyalties.

David Moss is one of the commentators on the Moro affair who sees the whole tragic event as posing questions. Was the abduction planned to make a clear political point or was it the outcome of some who leaned more to symbolic violence? Were the connections between intention, action and consequence carefully thought out in advance? Was the government's response to the kidnapping anything like as well-informed and well-managed as Moro's importance deserved? The conclusions of Moss are speculative:

The controversy over the 'real authorship' of Moro's letters from his 'people's prison' exhaustively rehearsed the interpretive difficulties of reading documents emanating from clandestine sources. The intentions of the BR remained uncertain: the document explaining the meaning of the attack was only distributed one year after the kidnapping and had been authored, not by those directly responsible, but by the intelligentsia [the directors of BR]. Notoriously, the 'official' BR version of the attack failed to fix its meaning. [. . .] Those uncertainties were coupled with ambiguities about the primary intentions of the Red Brigades' opponents: to secure Moro's release or to use the ritual to display their own identities. These interpretive conflicts lasted throughout the 1980s, aired extensively during the sequence of trials and resurfacing unpredictably in wider party-political disputes. The prolonged interpretive sequel to the kidnapping has shown clearly their escape from determination by reference either to the intentions of the protagonists or the consequences of the events. Finally, whatever impact it may have had on its opponents, the kidnapping ritual revealed very clearly the divisions of various kinds within the community of armed struggle: between the *autonomi*, who refused the

BR invitation to show support by increasing their attacks; between the BR apparatchiks, leading to the first public scission from the group, followed shortly by its
definitive breakup into hostile factions; and between the BR apparatchiks and the
intelligentsia, who had been in clandestine conflict for one year already.

Awareness of these multiple confusions of intention, identity and time
prompted some activists to start calling publicly for an end to armed struggle in
1979.[11]

The Moro attack, indeed, the whole approach and subsequent handling of it by the
BR, has been the subject of much comment. There is some agreement that in 1977
the BR was already losing ground and doing it in a confused way.

THE STATE'S RESPONSE TO TERRORISM

There is more than a touch of irony in the way in which the Italian state responded
to terrorism during the years that Furlong has described as 'first phase'. What better
way could there be for a weak government hamstrung by discord and compromise
than to announce a concerted drive to remove a social and political cancer? However,
it was never to be the strident voice of an authoritative regime. Somehow, Rome
must assuage the cynicism and fatalism of the electorate at large. Furlong (1981)
has scrutinised the early response of government. A slow-to-act government coined
the term 'strategy of tensions' to assure the public that their security would be safe
in Rome's hands, provided a DC majority received firm support for its long-term
strategies if not its competence in crisis management:

It took the Italian political classes at least five years to alert themselves seriously
to the problem of terrorism, in the sense that their initial reactions to it were
immobilist, using the events for short-term political gains and leaving their sources
untouched. Initially, successive governments appeared disposed to use terrorism to
reinforce the position of the DC and to a lesser extent of the minor lay parties as
bulwarks of democracy. The term 'the strategy of tension' was coined to refer to
the apparent coincidence of increases in terrorist activity with critical political events
such as elections or the formation of new governments. The use of the phrase
particularly on the left was intended to imply that terrorism was in fact being
directed in a strategic manner to favour the short-term aims of the government
parties, as if somewhere a 'mastermind', probably an established politician, was in
control. Though a lot of evidence has come to light on the close relationship between
the security services and the right-wing terrorist groups, there is no evidence to
indicate that there is or was a 'mastermind' of terrorism, inside or outside the DC.
There were undoubtedly neo-fascist sympathisers occupying senior positions in the
security services, and some left-wing terrorist groups appear to have sympathisers
at a lower level in the police and civil service. The links with the security services
probably helped the right-wing groups sustain a certain level of activity, and the
secret intelligence services appear to have known in advance of some of their major
operations, in particular of the attempted occupation of the Ministry of the Interior

in 1970 and the similar operation in August 1974. But it is not necessary to find a 'mastermind' to explain the apparent strategy of tension, for the operations of terrorists must surely be most effective when political awareness is already heightened, and it would be surprising if terrorists did not attempt to plan their activity to take account of this. To say that successive governments used terrorism reflects not 'strategy of tension' conspiracy theories but the rather less contentious observation that governments did not react vigorously against terrorism in this period and that leading politicians (of the DC in particular) took the opportunity to attack communists and socialists and to affirm their own centrality to the political system.[12]
[. . .]

To talk of 'crisis management' in this period would be something of a misnomer, since the state was faced on the whole with a steady escalation of violence that required not short-term 'management' but long-term strategy. Crises of relatively lengthy duration occasioned by terrorist activity did not occur while the neo-fascist strategy predominated. In practice, as I have indicated, little was done to halt the increase in frequency and seriousness of terrorist incidents.[13]

During the 1970s and into the 1980s the failure of the Italian state to respond adequately to terrorism had a double-edged significance: it strengthened the image of a force dedicated to reform-through-violence and it eroded public confidence in the competence of a democratic government. Furlong, writing in 1981, as terrorists battled, evaluates the formidable 'professionalism' of the BR, its sharp-edged profile in media and political circles and the desperate ineffectualness of government response. He sees modern Italy both as fostering terrorism and as learning to live with it. Furlong detects *ad hoc* government manipulation of organised political violence (both left and right wing) by politicians intent on drawing together their own divisive tendencies, needing to strike recognisably strong attitudes to dispel public cynicism. Thus, terrorism menaces not only public security but also élitist political groups:

The responses of the state to political terrorism in Italy provide an instructive example of how the modern industrialised state may both foster terrorism and learn to survive with it. The inefficiency of the administration, of the police and of the judicial system make it unlikely that in the immediate future political terrorism can be significantly weakened by a strategy dependent on administrative efficiency in the carrying out of policy directives from elected politicians. At the same time, though some agreement has been reached over short-term measures, it is not clear that elected politicians are united either over the appropriate strategy to be followed against terrorism or over the administrative reforms that would be a necessary precondition of any long-term approach to the problem.

I have argued that the major failings in the response to terrorism have been the deliberate manipulation of organised political violence to satisfy short-term goals – goals that have been predominantly electoral but that have also been concerned with the formation of alliances within and between the parties – and, more broadly, the continued underestimation by politicians and senior civil servants of the capacity of clandestine groups to strike politically significant targets and of their intention to do so. This applies both to left-wing and to right-wing terrorism. These failings are intricately connected. The Italian state has been attempting to 'ride the tiger'. The continued support given to General Dalla Chiesa by all the major parliamentary parties is perhaps an acknowledgement of their own incapacity to produce consistent policy direction, but it is also very much a traditional solution for this political system to give a non-elected figure large amounts of free rein and to pay little attention to the less satisfactory aspects of his approach.

I have attempted in this short case study to understand political terrorism within a fragmented yet highly developed political system. If the response of the state has been less than adequate, it may be argued that the inadequacy results from the disparity between a dynamic and open political culture, based on a radical constitution and populist traditions, and the stultifying immobilism of the governmental system. The dangers for the political system are not, as may be elsewhere, that civil liberties will be snuffed out at the behest of an oppressive and authoritarian political culture but that in the face of the inefficiency and indecisiveness of the formal institutions individual actors may operate outside formal controls. The continued tendency of sectors of state administration to seek and indeed to achieve autonomy from political control is to some extent a function of the survival within the state of residues from the fascist dictatorship and from the Liberal state that preceded it. The personnel and institutions that carry these residues constitute a would-be alternative élite to the unchanging political élite of the postwar republic, just as do the terrorist groups on the left. The growth of terrorism and the responses of the state may thus both be related to the unbalanced economic development and incomplete political development of the postwar period.[14]

David Moss (1997) argues that the BR and other terrorist groups view intended actions through the 'frames' of politics and violence. Actions are legitimated when frames converge, separating frames points to violence as an end in itself without achieving credible political gains. Thus, terrorist zeal might diminish, not necessarily because of the state's counter-terrorism but almost in spite of it. Terrorists were offered the chance to recant. Restrained counter-terrorism indicated the belief that a less strident response might prevent opponents proclaiming a unified, highly symbolic identity. The description of 'terrorist' was to be deflated in significance, the term 'terrorism' less explicitly condemned. The Moss argument is in these terms:

The increasing scale and scope of the rites of violence forced opponents and participants to clarify their commitments publicly. Opposition to violence on the Left grew, making it much more difficult for the users of violence to combine armed struggle with grassroots politics. They could no longer claim that their attacks were simply supplements to existing conflicts and spontaneous violence: the frames for violence and politics grew further apart.[15]

On particular occasions the political parties were called on to display a more focused rejection of the rites of violence. In kidnapping cases, for example, the government was invited to recognize the kidnappers as direct political antagonists and, by negotiating for the release of the victim, accept the reality of the passage between the two frames. Negotiations also carried the clear message that activities in the two frames of politics and violence were symbolically and instrumentally linked.

In sum, the obstacles which the nature of the Italian political system and the substantive disagreements of its major parties placed in the way of an agreed macro-level interpretation of violence helped to prevent the translation of highly varied local meanings into a plausible narrative of a unified assault on the Italian state. It frustrated any opportunity for the users of violence to seize on a clear set of meanings to reinforce their own understandings of what they were doing and might achieve. Moreover, the low-key, particularized defense of the state also served to undermine the Red Brigades' identification of the monolithic state as the primary antagonist for armed struggle – an identification required for assailants to be able to claim 'disarticulating' results for their actions.[16]

CONCLUSIONS

Italy's terrorists, rather like those in Algeria and Lebanon, in time became locked within a spiral of violence, a vortex of their own making. However rational terrorist pronouncements appeared at the beginning of their campaigning, a descent through hit-and-miss targeting to indiscriminate attacks was viewed in general as 'mindless' and 'non-negotiable' activity, obsessed with unattractive symbolism, and destructive in the main. Almost inevitably, the BR began to lose its effectiveness and credibility with the advent of the 1980s, culminating at about 1986 with a process of systematic failure which would not have surprised Furlong writing in 1981:

The terrorists chose clandestinity and 'hit and run' tactics in Italy as an instrument of political activity, and developed around their choice a considerable volume of strategic theorising aimed at justifying *a posteriori* a choice made for quite other reasons. The world they appear to move in is inhabited by symbols, not by people. Within the terrorist groups there is, as in other exclusive homogeneous institutions, a large element of cognitive dissonance. As their violence is unsuccessful, they are drawn not to a reconsideration of their initial choice but to an exacerbation of the violence. In this sense, the system 'forces' them; granted their initial choice against other more conventional forms of political activity, the failure of their strategy leads them further into violence, and further into exclusivity and isolation.

One of the reasons for their lack of success and for the inevitable spiral of violence in which they find themselves is that the instruments they have chosen are simply not sufficient for the task. I would not argue complacently that terrorism is necessarily unsuccessful because 'pathological' or 'irrational'; but it does seem to me that where it is successful it is because whatever the long-term strategic aims of the terrorists, between them and their goal there is a series of negotiable demands or intermediate goals which may under certain circumstances be met by the opponent with less harm than is threatened directly by terrorist action. In some cases one of the intermediate goals most useful to terrorists and most readily obtainable is the publicity given to them and their action. But to take on the authority of the state with hit and run terrorism or with bomb attacks against civilians is to over-estimate the effectiveness of the symbol, and in such cases publicity is of little value. There is little the Italian state can give the terrorists other than its own dissolu-tion; the liberation of prisoners demanded by the BR during the Sossi and Moro kidnappings was invested with such symbolic significance that to have granted it would have been to give the BR the legitimacy of the title of 'guerrilla fighters' that they are seeking. They have succeeded in criminalising dissent, in rendering large sectors of the left, including some members of the PCI, vulnerable to the suspicion of being 'pro-terrorist'. Their actions have certainly made the task of government by consensus more difficult, and they have amply demonstrated the vulnerability of politically significant individuals to terrorist attack. But the frag-mentation of the Italian state and the dispersion of authority within it make symbolic attacks against it by clandestine terrorists a particularly inefficient form of warfare.[17]

Donatella della Porta (1995) has studied at length the emergence of left-wing terrorism in Italy:

Clandestine organizations were founded by individuals who were tied to one another by a common militance in protest organizations. These organizations were not distinctive as far as interests, ideologies, or tactics were concerned. Their shared characteristic was, instead, the presence of semi-legal structures. [. . .] In the case of armed formations solidarity networks were mainly composed of individuals who had previously used violent forms of political action.

Groups using illegal strategies arose when interests were not effectively medi-ated by the institutional system, when the political culture predisposed them to violence, and when social movements used violent tactics. By experimenting with different strategies, some organizations found that the adoption of more and more violent tactics attracted recruits. To counter state repression, clandestinity offered the advantage of minimizing some costs, such as the risk of arrest, even at the price of minimizing the benefits available in the short run.

Furthermore, with regard to the evolution of the Italian terrorist groups, the same condition of clandestinity brought about a series of vicious circles in which each attempt to face problems at a certain level produced new difficulties at the next. The centralization and structuration of the organizational model met the task of protecting the militants and involving them deeper and deeper inside the orga-nization. Its consequence was, nevertheless, their further isolation from the outside world and, with it, the loss of channels for information and recruitment. Also, an increasingly compartmentalized structure was aimed at protecting the group and strengthening personal involvement. One of its effects was, however, to fuel personal rivalries, producing new splits.

Under pressure from the police, contacts with the external world were reduced to demands for logistical support. The tactics terrorist organizations adopted for getting financial resources were those typical of common criminality, exposed them to increased risks of armed fights with police, and damaged the image of the orga-nizations before the public. The urgency of finding money and arms for the survival of the growing number of militants forced into clandestinity brought about a dangerous dependence on secret services and organized crime. To deny the defeats, the clandestine groups developed cryptic ideologies of highly symbolic value for insiders but with no meaning for the external world.

Underground organizations are also highly isolated from external reality, making it extremely difficult for their militants to perceive defeat. By reducing the possibilities of communicating with the external world, the terrorist organization becomes, in fact, the only source of information. This facilitates the internalization by the militants of the organization's ideology. Justification for the use of violence is therefore found in a highly abstract and simplified image of the world, where the victims are presented as small wheels of a mechanism, a small elite of 'freedom fighters'. [. . .]

In Italy, this kind of dynamic delayed the process of quitting the underground organizations but could not, however, prevent it. After frequently lengthy processes of individual and collective reflections, almost all the militants of the left-wing terrorist groups decided to abandon their commitment to violent political action. The abandonment of this commitment, as well as the reintegration of those who had quit, was facilitated by particular laws that allowed former members to maintain a collective identity and solidarity bonds among one another outside the terrorist organization. These widespread 'exits' from the terrorist groups indicate that the cycle of political violence in Italy is over. The remaining small nuclei, only sporadically active underground, represent a different, far less dangerous phenomenon.[18]

What della Porta has to say about Italian terrorism in particular would surely also apply to facets of terrorism elsewhere.

Chapter 15

South Africa

THIS CASE-STUDY DIFFERS from the others, chiefly in two respects. First, it swings a spotlight onto a question frequently debated by those in South Africa urging vigorous protest against apartheid, namely, since there seems to be no alternative must there be a resort to violence? Second, it describes an ambitious social experiment, as terrorism against oppression subsides, when a government attempts to unify a nation torn by conflict. The truth about terrorism is to be disclosed publicly as a prelude to reflection, amnesty, reparation, and rehabilitation.

THE NATURE OF APARTHEID

The backdrop to the dramatic debate about the employment of violence was the racialist regime imposed by successive South African governments. It was in South Africa that racial segregation was translated into an ideological creed known since the 1940s as apartheid, separateness.

The origins of apartheid and its later development have been described, among others, by Whittaker (1999), who surveys the early principles and the divide-and-rule practice and concludes citing fresh views on the nature and extent of apartheid:

The forced separation of black and white in South Africa originated mainly as a protective response among Dutch settlers at the Cape in the 1650s who faced and feared the surrounding Bantu natives. British soldiers and farmers 150 years later displaced the Dutch (then termed 'Boers') who trekked northwards to found independent republics. The growth of industrialisation and the tapping of vast mineral resources after 1900 made South Africa dependent upon large numbers of black male workers migrating to white cities from 'reserves' where their families were left to sparse subsistence farming. Segregation of white and black was seen as defending and preserving white culture, residence and the social order, as well as operating a 'colour bar' to protect 'lower-class' whites from competition in the job market. Nelson Mandela has spoken of apartheid as 'a new term but an old idea [. . .] a monolithic system that was diabolical in its detail, inescapable in its reach and overwhelming in its power'. A creed it was, too, in that the Dutch Reformed Church regularly provided the ideologues with theological justification for white supremacy.

Apartheid was organised by parcelling out the country into white areas and African reserves. Six million white *Herrenvolk* went on to occupy 87 per cent of the land, enjoying high living standards and every amenity yet, as a 'vulture culture', growing ever more apprehensive about their future. Around the white settlements loomed a disconsolate mass of 30 million black Bantu. Originators of apartheid had an ingenious solution to the problem of finding cheap labour for factories and gold-mines. Workers were bussed in from shacks in teeming 'townships' located downwind from the big cities. After 1962, country people were relegated to eight 'Bantustans' – up-country 'homeland reserves' – to develop in their own way, or so the theory went. The notion of separate development was, of course, apartheid at a remove and it was a spurious idea, for without fertile land, investment and infrastructure, no appreciable development is possible. These facilities were never made available. There were also 4 million Indians or mixed-race 'Coloured' people assigned to particular living places and occupations.

The divide-and-rule strategy of apartheid was deliberately employed to reduce black solidarity. In the reserves, government policies took advantage of long-standing tribal parochialism and feuding among Xhosa and Zulu clans. Elsewhere, the urban migrant was soon introduced to divisive perceptions of status common to white society: namely, persons who were skilled, semi-skilled, unskilled or servants. In the struggle for survival, as the Black Freedom Movement was to find, it was everyone for himself and for nobody else under the yoke. It was to take many years and much feverish political management before a black response to white overlordship shaped itself into united civil disobedience campaigns. In the 1950s the apartheid regime at last found itself engaged in conflict, as latent discontent sparked off a general strike against the Treason Trials of 1956. A fractured community was faced with draconian white laws. All Africans over the age of 16 were compelled to carry a Native Pass issued by the government for showing to any employer, policeman or civil official. Failure to produce this pass meant a fine, even detention for up to ninety days. No travel was possible without a permit. The signs 'WHITES ONLY' or 'AFRICANS ONLY' emblazoned on park benches, or at the entrance to a hotel, swimming pool, hospital, dance hall or beach, betokened the strict exclusion of the inferior race under the 1953 Separate Amenities Act. The Group Areas Act of 1950 confined Africans and Indians to specific residential areas in towns. Any trespass into white urban areas would lead to forced relocation or even imprisonment. Overall, in the white perception there was the fear of *svart gevaar*, a black danger which would always infiltrate both the white material culture and the confidence of *baasskap*, that inalienable supremacy. Exclusion through 200 legal statutes had the dual function of guaranteeing the security of white mastery and the preordained servitude of the rest. An ironical consequence of this position was the emergence of a group of middle-class Bantu professionals and intellectuals. They were lawyers, teachers, doctors, journalists and clergy – people able to recruit supporters not only for the African National Congress (ANC) but for a 'resistance front' of other political and cultural groups. They were joined by a growing band of sympathetic whites and Indians in the universities and the media. Meanwhile, the mass of the population, certainly by the 1970s, began to stir from lethargy into liberationist zeal.

Apartheid as a set of principles was never quite watertight. There were compelling reasons why apartheid could never be 'total' in spite of shrill racialist clamour and repressive legislation. White Afrikaner farmers and businessmen needed ample supplies of black labour, provided they were rigorously controlled in residence and movement. Many liberals felt they had a Christian mission to promote the 'differential development' and self-determination of blacks who had been herded away in tribal chiefdoms. As the South African economy grew ever more powerful, so apartheid policies had to address the problems of urbanisation magnetising an inflow of many thousands of black job-seekers and the consequent economic and social malaise of the reserves. 'Black power' in numbers and force-fulness was to force apartheid, that protective system for white interests, on to the defensive, revealing it as an expression of weakness rather than strength. From weakness sprang a dilemma: without a privileged position whites could not survive; without safeguarding racial separation privilege was not maintainable. For white leaders such as Hertzog, Malan and Verwoerd, apartheid was a survival mechanism, a life-raft supporting power, unity and the growth of group identity. Theirs was a backs-to-the-wall position, a fruitless posture given the dependence of the minority on the servile complacency of the majority.

Recent South African scholarship has published fresh views on the nature of apartheid:

- Ideological disunity was always more obvious than solidarity. 'Hardliners' and 'softliners' seldom agreed about the complexities of defusing potential class conflict, maintaining white supremacy, and steering between the counter-productive areas of all-out dominance and assimilation (through racial mixture or 'miscegenation').

- Apartheid was probably never a long-term Master Plan. Its principles were often hastily devised in an *ad hoc* manner to meet economic and social changes. Party leaders, industrial magnates, farmers, financiers frequently resorted to provisional and often contradictory styles of situation management.

- Already by 1930 conservative as well as liberal elements in South Africa were aware of the impossibility of ordering separate development of white and black 'to a large extent on lines of their own'. Calls for ethnic mobilisation might express nationalistic urges in rival white and black camps but the eventual emergence of a multi-racial South Africa was hardly in doubt. Equally certain was the prospect of conflict.

- Racist intolerance often had less to do with skin colour prejudice and more to do with feelings of vulnerability, fear and loss of group identity, particularly among a peripheralised white working class.[1]

APARTHEID INTERNATIONALLY CONDEMNED

At his presidential inauguration on 10 May 1994, Nelson Mandela declared that never again would his country 'suffer the indignity of being the skunk of the world'. The era of world contempt and forced isolation was now at an end. Whittaker (1999) takes up the story:

National governments, the UN, and a host of non-governmental organisations voiced a swelling protest from generalised, disapproving rhetoric just after the end of the Second World War to more specific and earnest campaigning in the 1960s. In 1952, India and states newly enfranchised from imperialism, such as Ethiopia, Iraq and Liberia, had asked the UN's General Assembly to consider urgently the question of 'Race conflict in South Africa resulting from the policies of apartheid'. Discrimination on so great a scale was a negation of the UN and its Charter and could easily lead to international conflict. South Africa resisted the allegation stating that the policies complained of were a domestic matter. This contemptuous response failed to deflect UN members from pressing home increasingly strong condemnation over the next twenty years. Attempts at persuasion and negotiation by UN Secretary-Generals and their representatives got nowhere. To help advance freedom in South Africa, many African and Arab states were prepared to supply whatever they could afford in the way of material and military aid.

By 1976 a majority in the General Assembly was explicitly supporting 'armed struggle' in South Africa as a way of defeating apartheid. Moral pressure was spearheaded by the Anti-Apartheid Movement in Britain, which recruited almost 40,000 vigorous campaigners at one point during its time of activity, 1959–94. There were similar action groups in the USA, in Scandinavia and in Holland. From time to time the US Congress expressed outrage and went on to pass legislation restricting South African trade. Indirect pressure eventually took the form of consumers and dock worker unions in Europe and the USA boycotting South African goods, and in 1977 led to mandatory embargoes on the shipment of arms, ammunition and military vehicles to Cape Town. During the following fifteen years the UN pressed, never too effectively, for the application of mandatory sanctions against South Africa and for disinvestment by trading partners, although there were certain governments, such as those of the USA, UK and France, who preferred to retain their links under the guise of 'constructive engagement', in the belief that penalising a delinquent state would lead to a siege mentality and render it impervious to dialogue and negotiation.

In 1974 the UN called for the total exclusion of South Africa from all international organisations and conferences held under the auspices of the UN, so long as apartheid was practised and in 1978 the UN established an International Anti-Apartheid Year. There was now in many lands quite uncompromising support for the 'liberation' struggles of the South Africans. The Security Council, for instance, in October 1977, had demanded the cessation of violent repression and torture, the release of detainees, the abrogation of bans on freedom groups and news media, the ending of the inferior and marginalising Bantustan system and, conclusively, a recourse to democratic elections and the establishment of black majority rule.

The apartheid scenario was now one of explicit conflict. Month by month and year by year the UN and an array of 400 liberal non-governmental organisations issued condemnation of apartheid and calls for action. Sadly and quite predictably, tightening the screw from outside only led to fiercer repression and opposition. Even so, no other fight for basic freedoms has ever gained such wide political support and concrete assistance from other nations, perhaps 130 of them.[2]

THE GROWTH OF AFRICAN PROTEST

Uncertainty within South Africa and international pressure from without shook the country's confidence and brought tension to an unendurable pitch as Whittaker (1995 and 1999) relates, stressing the excesses of government action, the prominence of youth protest, and the dilemmas facing an international community over the extent to which their condemnation should move towards support for an armed struggle within South Africa:

Inevitably, the government sought to screw down dissent and opposition by recourse to a state of emergency in 36 areas, to the use of the armed police posse, detention and censorship. The original ANC claim that a struggle for liberation could be peaceful was no longer credible. South Africa's military budget, increased twelve times between 1960 and 1980, indicated mobilisation for civil war. Three great protests had severed the nation and angered the world: Sharpeville in 1960, Soweto in 1976, and the national strikes of 1984. It was obvious that the flailing efforts to silence the oppressed only made the voices of protest more audible.

A highly visible aspect of the liberation struggle against apartheid was the participation of young people in South Africa. One in two detainees was 18 or younger. The so-called 'children' were the most deprived and the most assertive (as they are in reports from the Palestinian conflict). There was great poignancy in 1985 when the UN proclaimed the year International Youth Year and from South Africa came the cry, 'Nothing demonstrates the utter bankruptcy of apartheid as the revolt of our youth. Never on our knees! Victory is certain!' This was a poignant message from Nelson Mandela, smuggled out of Robben Island Prison in 1980.

After forty years of a consistent stand the UN found itself faced with the issue of supporting violence as a legitimate vehicle of protest against apartheid. If the opposition persistently resorted to violent tactics as the contest burst out in virulence, what moral position should the outside world adopt? What, for instance, were the ultimate implications of the Rev. Allan Boesak's statement before the UN Special Committee on Apartheid in January 1988 when this South African freedom campaigner declared: 'Apartheid is so wrong, so indefensible, so intrinsically evil that it cannot be modernised, streamlined or reformed; it can only be irrevocably eradicated'? The UN's lawyers had found that a legally permissible right to use violence arises only in extreme situations as the final response to systematic violation. Furthermore, means used to resist violation of rights of individuals or of peoples should be 'proportionate' to the gravity of that violation. But is the right to violent combat legitimate only if it is accorded to a responsible group? Is it disproportionate to allow any individual guerrilla the option of violent tactics, perhaps irresponsibly?

With some impatience another question was being asked in South Africa: if our active resistance becomes violent can the international community really sit on its hands and take refuge in the non-violent liberalism of the Charter while our persecuted community and its oppressors are exploding? The General Assembly, after all, had challenged Pretoria in establishing the 'inalienable right' of the anti-apartheid wing to use all available means 'including armed struggle'. The ANC lost no time in blessing the militaristic efforts of its armed guerrilla force, *Umkhonto we Sizwe*, the Spear of the Nation – and it felt justified on hearing such last-ditch statements as that of President P. W. Botha in 1986, 'If we respect minority rights, we won't have black majority rule'.[3]

Black opposition to white apartheid in South Africa has moved through a number of stages. The first decade after the Second World War was one of 'soft' conflict and resentful alienation. Slowly the ANC began to build structured means of resistance through action committees, an illicit press and legal representation for detainees and the evicted. Student Power and Youth Power sharpened the intensity of conflict. They filled the prisons too. Three out of four detainees were aged between 18 and 25.

It was in March 1960 that police brutality in Sharpeville, when sixty-nine unarmed protestors were gunned down inescapably, brought 'hard' conflict in its train. There was now a polarisation of forces – a white solidarity, preventive with law and rifle, and a black solidarity movement making a stand for Black Consciousness.

> Mandela and others were taken off to years of penal servitude, their associates in the courtroom clenching fists invoking 'the anvil of united mass action and the hammer of armed struggle'. The accused used their trials as platforms for declaring beliefs rather than as any test of the law. They defended themselves in a moral sense, instead of resorting to fine forensic points. Growing protest gave way reluctantly to military training and the deployment of armed 'freedom fighters'. From its inception in 1912 the ANC had regarded non-violence as an indisputable core principle. It was best for the oppressed to pursue the unavoidable conflict in ways that saved lives, not threw them away. Guerrilla warriors, termed the Spear of the Nation, would seek to achieve liberation as far as possible without bloodshed and civil war.[4]

Black protest at the excesses of apartheid has been studied by Gibson (1972) who traces the transition from early reliance on non-violent protest by the African National Congress (founded in 1912), through a period of faith in the 1940s and 1950s in the pacific principles of Mahatma Gandhi, allied to more interest in framing an activist strategy, and then to an ultimate phase after 1962 when resistance turns violent and initiates armed struggle:

The lengthy history of the ANC can conveniently be divided into four major periods. First, its founding as an élitist social movement of limited membership, enjoying mixed fortunes. Second, after a brief decline and near eclipse by the All-African Convention, the revival of the organisation by its Youth League, which was committed to a more nationalistic, activist programme and its transformation into a mass movement. Third, the failure of the passive resistance campaign and the split of the ANC, with the most active nationalists leaving to form the Pan Africanist Congress. Fourth, its banning by the white minority regime, followed by the transfer of its leadership abroad and the belated adoption of the principle of armed struggle as the sole effective means of creating a democratic, multiracial state in South Africa.[5]

Gandhian tactics were equally out of place in South Africa, whose history is one continuous record of white brutality against black. The Afrikaner Nationalists might indeed be bigoted, racist fanatics, but, unlike their African adversaries, they had a remarkably clear vision of the goals they sought and had no scruples about the means they would use to reach them. Multiracialism as a concept, offering guarantees to the minority against arbitrary and discriminatory rule by an African majority, could only have been justified if there had been – as there was not – a substantial number of Europeans and Indians who were prepared to close ranks with the oppressed majority. As it was, the paltry numbers of European, Coloured, and Indian allies that came forward under the Congress Alliance blunted the driving force of African nationalism, the only ideology likely – as the subsequent history of the PAC [Pan-African Congress] demonstrates – to appeal to the broad masses of the black proletariat. In addition, while non-violence might have been acceptable in the short term as a tactic, nothing in the record of African struggle against European encroachment indicated that it could have any deep, long-term appeal to the African people, who passed their daily lives in conditions of often extreme social violence and brutality, harassed by white bosses and anti-social black thugs, as well as the ever-vigilant and violent South African police. Only a political programme of counter-violence on a massive scale, decided upon years earlier by an African organisation, might have mobilised the masses and permitted them to force an early clash with the regime before its repressive apparatus had been installed.[6]

The end of 1962 marked the beginning of violence, a sort of preparation for the major uprising. Groups of Africans, in the past generally docile and non-violent, even when not law-abiding, in their dealings with Europeans, mercilessly struck down individual whites in a number of localities [. . .] oppressed masses finding catharsis in the killing of their enemies. [. . .] It seemed that the South African powder keg was at last exploding.[7]

The transition from non-violent protest to violent confrontation took place as part of the liberation movement that began tentatively throughout colonial Africa and then surged as a wave all through the post-colonial Africa that emerged after the Second World War. This is a process noted by Braganca and Wallerstein (1982) who go on to see the advent of the 1960s as the time when massing for peace was to give way to mobilising for war. They cite the dramatic way in which the peaceful preferences of Gandhi's approach now succumbed – because all else failed – to an anxious dependence on violent assertiveness. They quote both Gandhi and Nelson Mandela as recognising the limits of non-violence:

All the national liberation movements in Portuguese and southern Africa started off by seeking to achieve change peacefully, by the pure route of dialogue and persuasion. All without exception found after a while that this route was foreclosed to them by those who held power.

The violence of conquest was repeated in the violence of suppression of protest. Each movement paid its price, found its adherents massacred in the course of a public demonstration or a strike. [. . .] Each concluded that the only road to national liberation open to them was the road of armed struggle.

It was not that they rejected dialogue. Rather they found regretfully that it was only via armed struggle that one day a real dialogue of coloniser and colonised would be possible, a dialogue rendered possible by the equalising impact of military combat.

While each movement ended at the same point, each came to it via a different logic and thus each felt it necessary to explain publicly the particular route it has taken.

The decision was particularly hard for the three countries that had a contact with the British parliamentary tradition – South Africa, Namibia and Zimbabwe. It was not that Africans were ever allowed to play a meaningful role in the local parliaments. It was rather that the values and the style of parliamentary struggle were persuasive in the society. Thus the ANC in South Africa had to overcome a long commitment to non-violence. How and why they did so is clear from the successive statements of Chief Luthuli in 1952 and 1964, Nelson Mandela in 1962, and Oliver Tambo in 1968. Furthermore they had to reconcile their views with the ideas and influence of Mahatma Gandhi who developed his theme of *satyagraha* not in India but in South Africa.[8]

Where the choice is set [wrote Gandhi in 1938] between cowardice and violence I would advise violence. I praise and extol the serene courage of dying without killing. Yet I desire that those who have not this courage should rather cultivate the art of killing and being killed, than basely avoid the danger. This is because he who runs away commits mental violence; he has not the courage of facing death by killing. I would a thousand times prefer violence than the emasculation of a whole race. I prefer to use arms in defence of honour rather than remain the vile witness of dishonour. (Mahatma Gandhi, Declaration on question of the use of violence in defence of rights, *Guardian*, 16 December 1938).[9]

THE DEBATE OVER THE USE OF VIOLENCE

This debate, mainly among members of the ANC, was to be long, strident and comprehensive in its range of issues. Its course has been charted by one of its leading participants, Nelson Mandela, in his autobiography (1997). Mandela outlines the shift from a passive mode in the 1940s featuring civil disobedience with a Programme of Action dangerously on the edge of the law to a much more active mode. Debate focuses on the uselessness, indeed, impossibility, of non-cooperation, non-violence and mass-defiance; however well-planned and executed, it would earn the relent-less crackdown of the Establishment. Even the doyen of the non-violent movement, Chief Luthuli (a Nobel Peace Prize winner), is seen eventually to come round to Mandela's way of thinking that black liberation must espouse violent methods. Mandela then goes on to show how, in the debate, the more conservative and the more radical present their arguments with candour and with fear that they will soon be branded as irresponsible terrorists. A consensus is reached that a new path must now be planned – that of 'organised violence'. Mandela describes how he, though never a solider, is given the task of forming a resistance army, as an alternative to guerrilla warfare. Leaflets describing the role of the new army were to be widely distributed and Mandela and his fellow-liberators are now convinced that their policy is right:

The Programme of Action approved at the annual conference [ANC, 1949] called for the pursuit of political rights through the use of boycotts, strikes, civil disobe-dience and non-cooperation. In addition, it called for a national day of work stoppage in protest against the racist and reactionary policies of the government. This was a departure from the days of decorous protest, and many of the old stalwarts of the ANC were to fade away in this new era of greater militancy. Youth League members had now graduated to the senior organization. We had now guided the ANC to a more radical and revolutionary path.[10]

Mass action was perilous in South Africa, where it was a criminal offence for an African to strike, and where the rights of free speech and movement were unmercifully curtailed. By striking, an African worker stood to lose not only his job but his entire livelihood and his right to stay in the area in which he was living.[11]

We also discussed whether the campaign should follow the Gandhian princi-ples of non-violence or what the Mahatma called *satyagraha*, a non-violence that seeks to conquer through conversion. Some argued for non-violence on purely ethical grounds, saying it was morally superior to any other method.

Others said that we should approach this issue not from the point of view of principles but of tactics, and that we should employ the method demanded by the conditions. If a particular method or tactic enabled us to defeat the enemy, then it should be used. In this case, the state was far more powerful than we, and any attempts at violence by us would be devastatingly crushed. This made non-violence a practical necessity rather than an option. This was my view, and I saw non-violence on the Gandhian model not as an inviolable principle but as a tactic to be used as the situation demanded.

The joint planning council agreed upon an open-ended programme of non-cooperation and non-violence. Two stages of defiance were proposed. In the first stage, a small number of well-trained volunteers would break selected laws in a handful of urban areas. They would enter proscribed areas without permits, use Whites Only facilities such as toilets, Whites Only railway compartments, waiting rooms and post office entrances. They would deliberately remain in town after curfew. Each batch of defiers would have a leader who would inform the police in advance of the act of disobedience so that the arrests could take place with a minimum of disturbance. The second stage was envisioned as mass defiance, accompanied by strikes and industrial actions across the country.[12]

I said the government was now scared of the might of the African people. As I condemned the government for its ruthlessness and lawlessness, I overstepped the line: I said that the time for passive resistance had ended, that non-violence was a useless strategy and could never overturn a white minority regime bent on retaining its power at any cost. At the end of the day, I said, violence was the only weapon that would destroy apartheid and we must be prepared, in the near future, to use that weapon.

I had begun to analyse the struggle in different terms. The ambition of the ANC was to wage a mass struggle, to engage the workers and peasants of South Africa in a campaign so large and powerful that it might overcome the *status quo* of white oppression. But the Nationalist government was making any legal expression of dissent or protest impossible. I saw that it would ruthlessly suppress any legitimate protest on the part of the African majority. A police state did not seem far off.[13]

In discussing the ANC's policy of non-violence, he [Chief Luthuli] emphasized that there was a difference between non-violence and pacifism. Pacifists refused to defend themselves even when violently attacked, but that was not necessarily the case with those who espoused non-violence. Sometimes men and nations, even when non-violent, had to defend themselves when they were attacked.[14]

The debate on the use of violence had been going on among us since early 1960. I had first discussed the armed struggle as far back as 1952 with Walter Sisulu. Now, I again conferred with him and we agreed that the organization had to set out on a new course. The Communist Party had secretly reconstituted itself underground and was now considering forming its own military wing. We decided that I should raise the issue of the armed struggle within the Working Committee [ANC], and I did so in a meeting in June of 1961.

I had barely commenced my proposal when Moses Kotane, the secretary of the Communist Party and one of the most powerful figures in the ANC Executive, staged a counter-assault, accusing me of not having thought out the proposal carefully enough. He said that I had been outmanoeuvred and paralysed by the government's actions, and now in desperation I was resorting to revolutionary language. 'There is still room', he stressed, 'for the old methods if we are imaginative and determined enough. If we embark on the course Mandela is suggesting, we will be exposing innocent people to massacres by the enemy'.

I was candid and explained why I believed we had no choice but to turn to violence. I used an old African expression: '*Sebatana ha se bokwe ka diatla*' ('The attacks of the wild beast cannot be averted with only bare hands'). Moses was a long-time communist, and I told him that his opposition was like the Communist Party in Cuba under Batista. The party had insisted that the appropriate conditions had not yet arrived, and waited because they were simply following the textbook definitions of Lenin and Stalin. Castro did not wait, he acted – and he triumphed. If you wait for textbook conditions, they will never occur. I told Moses point blank that his mind was stuck in the old mould of the ANC being a legal organization. People were already forming military units on their own, and the only organization that had the muscle to lead them was the ANC. We had always maintained that the people were ahead of us, and now they were.[15]

The Executive meeting in Durban, like all ANC meetings at the time, was held in secret and at night in order to avoid the police. I suspected I would encounter difficulties because Chief Luthuli was to be in attendance and I knew of his moral commitment to non-violence. I was also wary because of the timing: I was raising the issue of violence so soon after the Treason Trial, where we had contended that for the ANC non-violence was an inviolate principle, not a tactic to be changed as conditions warranted. I myself believed precisely the opposite; that non-violence was a tactic that should be abandoned when it no longer worked.

At the meeting I argued that the state had given us no alternative to violence. I said it was wrong and immoral to subject our people to armed attacks by the state without offering them some kind of alternative. I mentioned again that people on their own had taken up arms. Violence would begin whether we initiated it or not. Would it not be better to guide this violence ourselves, according to principles where we saved lives by attacking symbols of oppression, and not people? If we did not take the lead now, I said, we would soon be latecomers and followers to a movement we did not control.

The chief initially resisted my arguments. For him, non-violence was not simply a tactic. But we worked on him the whole night; and I think that in his heart he realised we were right. He ultimately agreed that a military campaign was inevitable. The National Executive formally endorsed the preliminary decision of the Working Committee.

The chief and others suggested that we should treat this new resolution as if the ANC had not discussed it. He did not want to jeopardize the legality of our unbanned allies. His idea [Luthuli's] was that a military movement should be a separate and independent organ, linked to the ANC and under the overall control of the ANC, but fundamentally autonomous. There would be two separate streams of the struggle. We readily accepted the chief's suggestion. The chief and others warned against this new phase becoming an excuse for neglecting the essential tasks of organization and the traditional methods of struggle. That, too, would be self-defeating because the armed struggle, at least in the beginning, would not be the centrepiece of the movement.

The following night a meeting of the joint Executive was scheduled in Durban. This would include the Indian Congress, the Coloured People's Congress, the South African Congress of Trade Unions and the Congress of Democrats. Although these other groups customarily accepted ANC decisions, I knew that some of my Indian colleagues would strenuously oppose the move towards violence.

The meeting had an inauspicious beginning. Chief Luthuli, who was presiding, announced that even though the ANC had endorsed a decision on violence, 'it is a matter of such gravity, I would like my colleagues here tonight to consider the issue afresh'. It was apparent that the chief was not fully reconciled to our new course.

We began our session at 8 p.m., and it was tumultuous. I made the identical arguments that I had been making all along, but many people expressed reservations.

We argued the entire night, and in the early hours of the morning I began to feel we were making progress. Many of the Indian leaders were now speaking in a sorrowful tone about the end of non-violence. The entire debate went back to square one. But towards dawn, there was a resolution. The Congresses authorized me to go ahead and form a new military organization, separate from the ANC. The policy of the ANC would still be that of non-violence. I was authorized to join with whomever I wanted or needed to create this organization and would not be subject to the direct control of the mother organization.

This was a fateful step. For fifty years, the ANC had treated non-violence as a core principle, beyond question or debate. Henceforth, the ANC would be a different kind of organization. We were embarking on a new and more dangerous path, a path of organized violence, the results of which we did not and could not know.[16]

I, who had never been a soldier, who had never fought in battle, who had never fired a gun at an enemy, had been given the task of starting an army. It would be a daunting task for a veteran general, much less a military novice. The name of this new organization was Umkhonto we Sizwe (The Spear of the Nation) – or MK for short. The symbol of the spear was chosen because with this simple weapon Africans had resisted the incursions of whites for centuries.

Our mandate was to wage acts of violence against the state – precisely what form those acts would take was yet to be decided. Our intention was to begin with what was least violent to individuals but most damaging to the state.

I began in the only way I knew how, by reading and talking to experts. What I wanted to find out were the fundamental principles for starting a revolution. I discovered that there was a great deal of writing on this very subject, and I made my way through the available literature on armed warfare and in particular guerrilla warfare. I wanted to know what circumstances were appropriate for a guerrilla war; how one created, trained and maintained a guerrilla force; how it should be armed; where it gets its supplies – all basic and fundamental questions.

Any and every source was of interest to me. I read the report of Blas Roca, the general secretary of the Communist Party of Cuba, about their years as an illegal organization during the Batista regime. In *Commando* by Deneys Reitz, I read of the unconventional guerrilla tactics of the Boer generals during the Anglo–Boer War. I read works by and about Che Guevara, Mao Tse-tung, Fidel Castro. In Edgar Snow's brilliant *Red Star Over China* I saw that it was Mao's determination and non-traditional thinking that had led him to victory. I read *The Revolt* by Menachem Begin and was encouraged by the fact that the Israeli leader had led a guerrilla force in a country with neither mountains nor forests, a situation similar to our own. I was eager to know more about the armed struggle of the people of Ethiopia against Mussolini, and of the guerrilla armies of Kenya, Algeria and the Cameroons.

I went into the South African past. I studied our history both before and after the white man. I probed the wars of African against African, of African against white, of white against white. I made a survey of the country's chief industrial areas, the nation's transportation system, its communication network. I accumulated detailed maps and systematically analysed the terrain of different regions of the country.[17]

In planning the direction and form that MK would take, we considered four types of violent activities: sabotage, guerrilla warfare, terrorism and open revolution. For a small and fledgling army, open revolution was inconceivable. Terrorism inevitably reflected poorly on those who used it, undermining any public support it might otherwise garner. Guerrilla warfare was a possibility, but since the ANC had been reluctant to embrace violence at all, it made sense to start with the form of violence that inflicted the least harm against individuals: sabotage.

Because it did not involve loss of life, it offered the best hope for reconciliation among the races afterwards. We did not want to start a blood-feud between white and black. Animosity between Afrikaner and Englishman was still sharp fifty years after the Anglo–Boer war; what would race relations be like between white and black if we provoked a civil war? Sabotage had the added virtue of requiring the least manpower.

Our strategy was to make selective forays against military installations, power plants, telephone lines and transportation links; targets that would not only hamper the military effectiveness of the state, but frighten National Party supporters, scare away foreign capital, and weaken the economy. This we hoped would bring the government to the bargaining table. Strict instructions were given to members of MK that we would countenance no loss of life. But if sabotage did not produce the results we wanted, we were prepared to move on to the next stage: guerrilla warfare and terrorism [. . .] thousands of leaflets with the new MK Manifesto were [to be] circulated all over the country announcing the birth of Umkhonto we Sizwe.[18]

Experience convinced us that rebellion would offer the government limitless opportunities for the indiscriminate slaughter of our people. But it was precisely because the soil of South Africa is already drenched with the blood of innocent Africans that we felt it our duty to make preparations as a long-term undertaking to use force in order to defend ourselves against force. If war were inevitable, we wanted the fight to be conducted on terms most favourable to our people. The fight which held out prospects best for us and the least risk of life to both sides was guerrilla warfare. We decided, therefore, in our preparations for the future, to make provision for the possibility of guerrilla warfare.

All whites undergo compulsory military training, but no such training was given to Africans. It was in our view essential to build up a nucleus of trained men who would be able to provide the leadership which would be required if guerrilla warfare started. We had to prepare for such a situation before it became too late to make proper preparations.[19]

THE DEFEAT OF APARTHEID

The crumbling of apartheid happened with unexpected rapidity as Whittaker (1999) relates and its demise brought elections and a new Government of National Unity:

In the late 1980s there were secret talks between the Pretoria government and the ANC, which explored the middle ground between white fears (and a sense of retreat) and black hopes. In February 1990 President F. W. de Klerk sounded an auspicious note, declaring in Parliament, 'Now is the time to speak out loud and clear about the dreams that unite us, because these dreams are the foundation of our new South African nation'. Thus was the urgency of reconciling conflict proclaimed, and officially so. The ANC was now loosed from its ban. Mandela was released to take his 'long walk to freedom' after thirty-seven years in jail. By degrees the demeaning restrictions of apartheid were lifted. Segregation in public places was ended. Steadily, the noxious laws that had inflamed protest were repealed. As the white National Party gradually lost ground, they could dream only of a fragile retention of some of their commercial and investment privileges. Exploited black masses shared visions handicapped by 50 per cent illiteracy and 25 per cent unemployment. Right-wing factions reviled de Klerk as a traitor as he engaged in working-party discussions for a new constitution that would smoothly but irrevocably transfer power to the majority. A time of transition would be a time of compromise when a black government had to provide structural guarantees for the white minority. At the same time, 22 million black people had to be coaxed into careful acceptance of compromise. They must be ready to be enfranchised for democratic voting. For much of the time the prospects of an end to conflict and of any lasting reconciliation were bedevilled by savage fighting between the more fanatical activists of the ANC and Zulu nationalists.

Only one way of reconciling South Africa's conflict seemed practicable and fair. Power and reconciliation were to be shared. A Government of National Unity would put an end to the isolation and rejection of both black and white. ANC leaders made much of the significance of their logo of the spear and the wheel. Freedom for the deprived had required an advancing thrust; freedom for all South Africans would need a common revolution. There would be no time for recrimination: enemies must become partners. A new united government was elected, with the ANC getting 60 per cent of total votes and the National Party 20 per cent, and it took office in Pretoria in April 1994. Nelson Mandela became the first black President with F. W. de Klerk, the former President, as a Vice-President. In a Cabinet of twenty-seven there were ten white members, six of them from the National Party. South Africa was now a nation on a new footing; no longer were most South Africans co-existing in an occupied territory.[20]

TERRORISM IN THE LIGHT OF TRUTH

The newly elected Government of National Unity decided in May 1994 to set up a Truth and Reconciliation Commission (TRC) with a charge to investigate human rights abuses under the former apartheid regime which had been sanctioned by the state or were the result of action by liberation groups. Under scrutiny would be the period 1960–94. South Africa would now have its violent past acknowledged rather than covered over. Coming to terms with terror in the past must advance means of reconciliation in the present and in the future. This mammoth exercise was scheduled to take some four years of public disclosure, a process which Whittaker (1999) has summarised:

The TRC would investigate abuses by publicly hearing testimony from victims and statements from the accused. Further steps would involve report, recommendation, arrangements for reparation and rehabilitation. The truth laid bare would be beamed to all South Africans regardless of colour. [. . .] Eighteen commissioners, impartial and broadly representative of the nation, were to be chosen by President Nelson Mandela. Their unenviable task was to prise apart thirty-three years of repression and counter-violence and to do it within four years. The Final Report of the TRC had to go to the State President by 31 July 1998.

The objectives of South Africa's TRC seem clear enough. Organisational arrangements provide for public disclosure before a tribunal of commissioners who are mainly figures from professional and public fields, not lawyers. Their chairman is Archbishop Desmond Tutu. The public sessions are held in Cape Town and at various locales in the countryside. The unremitting efforts to secure reliable and at times dramatic evidence are followed closely by the media. Very little is heard in camera – this would defeat the purpose of the exercise.

Three committees were formed: Human Rights Violation; Amnesty; Reparation and Rehabilitation. Agendas were carefully thought out but aroused great debate. The first committee was restricted to considering ill-treatment, torture, abduction and murder.[21]

The final report of the TRC is now available in four comprehensive volumes. In this case-study it is, of course, not possible to examine the findings in detail but even a short résumé casts light on the web of terrorism in South Africa. The TRC began its work by asking questions of the main participants in South Africa's apartheid conflict, that is, the ANC and the National Party (who had a majority in the former de Klerk Government). Answers to these questions, in written form and in countless statements by witnesses, occupy 400 pages in volume 1 of the report.

A brief inspection of the actual questions throws into relief a number of the crucial issues raised by terrorism, in this case, a terrorism that was widely shared by members of the South African community. First, there are the questions directed to the ANC; second, those that went to the National Party:

Questions to the ANC

In its submission the ANC uses a definition of gross human rights violations different from that in the legislation governing the TRC: 'Actions carried out in the course of the just war of national liberation do not constitute gross violations of human rights' [. . .] What does the ANC mean by this, especially with regard to amnesty application?

[. . .] does the ANC encourage all those who committed gross human rights violations as defined by the TRC to apply for amnesty?

[. . .] The ANC quotes a pamphlet identifying justified targets (page 52) as 'the racist army, police, death squads, agents and stooges in our midst'. Can this definition possibly be used to legitimise the killing of policemen, alleged informers, community councillors, and co-opted parliamentarians? [. . .] Can the ANC elaborate what is meant by 'stooges in our midst'?

Can the ANC elaborate and substantiate efforts made to avoid such attacks on civilian targets? What steps were taken, after the incidents, to investigate them? Were ANC cadres disciplined for their involvement in such activities?

Can the ANC supply any evidence substantiating the involvement of South African security forces in the death or disappearance of MK cadres and ANC members?

Questions to the National Party

The submission [by the National Party] states that 'we defended South Africa against those who planned to seize power by violent and unconstitutional means'. How does one achieve power constitutionally if one is disenfranchised and denied many of one's most basic constitutional rights? [. . .] Can one legitimately equate the struggle against apartheid with the struggle to defend it?

In the submission of the NP it is stated: 'We never hesitated to submit reasonably substantiated allegations [concerning serious violations of human rights] to vigorous investigation'.

Is this true of all periods during which the NP was in office? [. . .] Anti-apartheid perpetrators were pursued with vigour and tenacity. Did the government make an equal commitment to investigating human rights abuse by the security forces?

How does one explain the alleged ignorance of the former State President and his predecessors of gross human rights violations committed by the security forces and others? Why were the accusations of the state's critics, the media and former agents of the state not adequately investigated?

The submission indicates that no one in a position of authority can 'know everything which takes place in the realm of his or her managerial responsibilities'. This raises the question of accountability. Who should ultimately be held responsible for gross human rights violations?

Did any resolution of the SSC [State Security Council] authorise the security forces to use the same methods as revolutionaries to counter the revolutionary threat? If so, what was contemplated hereby? If this is so, to what extent is it legitimate to blame 'revolutionary strategies adopted by the government's opponent' for blurring the traditional distinctions between combatants and non-combatants, legitimate and illegitimate targets and between acceptable and unacceptable methods of police and military action?[22]

Each of those questioned was asked to furnish the TRC with a two- to three-page statement in regard to the party's underlying ideology, values, motives, and reasons for involvement in violations. 'It is important,' stated the TRC, 'for these views to be boldly, and yet sensitively, articulated in order to facilitate the reconciliation process'. The mind of the terrorist in South Africa was to be scrutinised.

Apart from the main issues highlighted by TRC questioning there is in the textual accompaniment explicit reference to a whole range of terrorist methods employed by both sides – death squads, demolition and burning of property, forced eviction, torture, water and food poisoning, garotting, summary execution, 'smear' and disinformation campaigns, 'disappearances' without trace, car bombs, assassination, land-mine planting.[23]

The traumatic experience of terrorism in South Africa is unlikely to bring about either swift or easy reconciliation as Whittaker (1999) points out:

If reconciliation is to be the desirable outcome, then objective understanding of the situation is furthered by regarding both parties as victims of apartheid. There is some thought among TRC officials that the term 'victim' is better replaced by 'survivor', implying a degree of control and perhaps recovery which the other term does not connote.[24]

Rather more carefully than the authorities in the other scenarios we have studied, the South Africans are very carefully attempting to take their 'survivors' into a unified and multi-racial, post-terrorist, 'rainbow' society. It is a breathtaking experiment.

Chapter 16

Twelve terrorism case-studies: conclusion

SOMETHING OF THE EXTENT and variety of terrorism during the last half-century has been illustrated in the twelve case-studies presented in Part Two. This concluding section will be brief. There are two reasons for this. In the first place, each case-study should stand by itself as a distinctive example of how terrorism, as we understand it, can arise and develop. In a number of these case-studies there are already conclusions in the form of a postscript and there would be no need of duplication. One or two points about each will suffice. Hizbullah in the Lebanon demonstrates the force of political action becoming violent as an alliance of religious fundamentalists and secular radicals set out to mobilise an Islamic constituency in addition to ousting Israeli and Western influence from the Middle East. Their doctrinaire stance leads them to venerate the martyr and by way of a mission, the jihad, to use bombs, guns and hostages to advance their cause. They remain an enigma to Western countries whose response has been uncertain and inconsistent. Another enigma is that of Libya's state-sponsoring of terrorist activities. Transformed from the desert fringe to an oil-rich, Socialist community and with a charismatic leader, Libya's provocative behaviour and networking of terrorist enterprise in other countries has seen it consigned as a pariah state. Lately, in the summer of 1999, the terrorists of Libya have entered the market-place, scenting the possibility of dependable trade contacts. Sanctions against them have been lifted. Their arch-terrorist Leader, Colonel Quaddafi, has made conciliatory approaches towards his former 'imperialist' enemies. The British Government is renewing diplomatic relations. The transition from terrorist exporter to internationally acknowledged respectability is an intriguing one. Sri Lanka's problem with the fanaticism of the Tamil Tigers remains unsolved. A desperate vortex of internal ruthless violence is fuelled by the external support of many Tamils who fund armed resistance to a government they see as unwilling to grant the Tamil minority self-determination as a separate entity. Northern Ireland, for so long imprisoned by myth and sectarian memories feeding decades of fratricide, is now, it seems, entering an era of 'seismic change' and an end to terrorist outrage. Unhappily, in the cases of Argentina, Basque Spain, Algeria, Peru and Colombia we have situations of whole societies caught up in many years of frenzy. The first impulses of nationalistic fervour, liberationist zeal, proletarian discontent in towns, the grinding poverty of peasantry have variously set elements of society against one another and brought upon those resorting to impassioned and frustrated violence the repressive force of government counter-action in the shape of 'dirty war'. Only in the instances of Spain and Colombia has there been the prospect of edging towards settlement and perhaps a chance of reconciliation. Germany and Italy reveal, in differing ways, the over-optimism of radical youth, a transition from protest demonstration to sporadic then planned violence and in these two countries a draining away of public support for activity regarded as mindless and nihilistic. Interestingly, in Germany, the terrorist aim of attacking what they saw as a bourgeois (neo-Nazi) dictatorship counter-productively engendered in most Germans a feeling that they had a duty to defend a young post-Nazi and liberal New Germany. Lastly, in the case of South Africa, terrorism comes under intense scrutiny. If the 'victims' of monolithic apartheid are to emerge as 'survivors' then massing for peace might have to become mobilisation for war. Organised violence might then be the only feasible option. Terror would have its place. Ultimately, sabotage, and other means of 'guided violence', helped bring about the dissolution of apartheid and the emergence of a peaceful and nominally united 'rainbow nation'. After the welter of division, the new South Africa hoisted into place a process of Truth and Reconciliation to look squarely at the historic incidence of discrimination and terrorist violence and to seek to make amends for it.

There is a second reason for the brevity of this conclusion. It was pointed out earlier that these twelve case-studies ought to stand separately from one another. They tell us a good deal about terrorism and its practitioners and they do so in contrasted fashion, although, of course, there are some common characteristics. It is not difficult to theorise about cause and effect across a range of examples of violent political action. This is frequently done. The result is often simplistic and leads to invalid and unreliable judgements. In Part One attempts to define terrorism and to analyse motivation were discussed and seen as problematic.

M. R. L. Smith in Alan O'Day (1995) has identified a number of rather distorted (if not fallacious) interpretations of terrorism which are common in print. Among them are a stress on non-state political actors and superficial comparison of diverse terrorist scenarios. Smith argues that such procedures are weak explanatory tools. The Editor of this reader agrees with these views and in conclusion quotes some of the points Smith makes:

It is possible to identify a number of problem areas with the contemporary study of terrorism. In the first instance, there has been a tendency to focus attention on non-state political actors while ignoring other agencies of terror like governments and quasi-government organisations. This has led to the assumption that most, if not all, terrorism is practised exclusively by those without direct political power and thereby equating all forms of insurgency with terrorism. This assumption is quite common in public discourse and over the years has helped foster the notion of terrorism as a pejorative term denoting criminality, psychopathology and an ethical void where the ability to distinguish between right and wrong has been lost. Such thinking can result in commentators merely making moral condemnations of those political groups with whom they happen to disagree. [. . .]

The distorted focus on non-state actors has reduced a lot of terrorist studies to a series of typologies and historical catalogues which try to identify the alleged incidence of terrorism around the world. Not only does this make the subject fairly dull, above all, it decontextualises low level conflicts by trying to connect an assortment of diverse political groups merely on the basis of their *modus operandi*. If one thinks about it for a moment, the proposition seems intellectually quite dubious. No serious historian would contend that World War Two and the Arab–Israel Six Day War in 1967 are analogous [. . .] merely because the combatants at various stages happened to use tanks. At best this would be a rather crass observation. At worst, a thoroughly misleading and bogus linkage. Yet linking the unlinkable is exactly what terrorist studies has sometimes tried to do. There is no reason why the violence of the Red Army Faction in West Germany during the 1970s, ostensibly the product of 1960s student radicalism and a frustrated post-war generation, should be associated with Irish nationalist violence the roots of which go back centuries. Even so, one will find all sorts of studies which try to link these and other disparate groups with each other as if they were in some way comparable. Instead of treating agents of political violence and the conflicts of which they are a part as singularly distinctive, each deserving separate treatment, the study of terrorism often draws together these varied low-level wars by trying to make theoretical generalisations primarily on the basis of tactical modality. Individual wars are thus disconnected from their historical and cultural backgrounds. Clearly this is an unsatisfactory way to analyse what are usually complex and highly divergent conflicts. The damage caused to the decent study of low intensity wars by the decontextualisation of conflicts as a result of terrorist studies methodology, seen in the superficiality of some works in the area, has been vast. So who are the experts on terrorism? Answer: there are no experts, just people who know a little about a lot of small conflicts.

For the strategic analyst who sees terrorism purely as an instrument of policy to be selected by any political actor from a range of options be they peaceful or violent, speculating on 'what gives rise to terrorism?' is like saying 'what gives rise to conventional war?' The question holds no meaning. All of the difficulties over causality, the over-concentration on tactical minutiae, counter-measures and so on, merely illustrates how the public debate on terrorism is flawed at the point of departure, namely at the definitional level. Nowhere is this best captured than in the expression which continues to take up an inordinate amount of space in terrorist studies literature: 'One man's terrorist is another man's freedom fighter'. This 'weary cliché', as Peter Sederburg says, 'suggests that all attempts to formulate the concept [of terrorism] will be hopelessly compromised by essentially arbitrary personal biases. Consequently, any analysis based upon such conceptual foundations will be inevitably distorted and vacuous'. Vacuous is certainly a word which can probably describe many of the tortured dissertations which have tried to resolve this alleged conundrum. Whatever significance the aphorism may have had once has now been mangled out of existence by those who have attached far more intellectual weight to the phrase than it really deserved.

Without wishing to rehearse the debate in detail, the notion of one man's terrorist is another man's freedom fighter is, to a strategic theorist at any rate, a false dichotomy. You can be both. For example, few would dispute that in its fight for independence from France between the mid-1950s and the early 1960s the Algerian *Front de Liberation Nationale* (FLN) could be justifiably described as freedom fighters. At the same time, the FLN carried out operations, most notably in the capital Algiers, which were clearly intended to terrorise the French settler population. The point is that one part of the terrorist–freedom fighter equation is a description of policy (terrorist/terrorism) while the other is a moral judgement on the nature of a belligerent (freedom fighter). They are two entirely separate intellectual issues. Why try to link them? It is illogical [. . .]

[. . .] The persistence of the old saw 'one man's terrorist is another man's freedom fighter', and the time wasted trying to force this false linkage, illustrates both the weakness of terrorist studies as an explanatory tool and the tyranny of simplistic slogans when they become a substitute for thought.[1]

PART THREE

Prevention and control of terrorism

THE SUBJECT OF PART THREE of this book is the prevention and control of terrorism, generally referred to as counter-terrorism. In all countries prevention and control of terrorism is an ever-shifting field of purpose, enquiry and *ad hoc* management of events. Governments strive to cope with a diversity of motive and organisation which frequently leads to some individuals and groups being hounded as suspects and even outlawed. Thus, the practice of counter-terrorism is indisputably affected by considerations of principle and legality and it is these matters which will be considered in Chapter 17.

Chapter 17 discusses ethical considerations such as whether terrorism should be treated as a crime or under the conventions of warfare, and in what respects counter-terrorism measures are commonly justified. Legal aspects are then outlined with the conclusion that counter-terrorism does not yet have a legal underpinning that is internationally rigorous and viable.

Chapter 18 surveys a number of counter-terrorism programmes and discusses the principles on which they are based. State-sponsored terrorism is also looked at, again, with an outline of programmed approaches to control. There is a note about what international institutions such as the United Nations and the European Union are able to do in this field. In conclusion, the threat of terrorists using mass-destruction devices is mentioned together with a rejoinder that since terrorism has its own hideous dynamic then counter-terrorism must try to match its pace.

Counter-terrorism: ethical and legal considerations

ETHICAL CONSIDERATIONS

THERE ARE MAINLY THREE basic questions that cause contemporary governments much anxiety. First, what are the factors that steer public and legitimate protest into destructive and illegitimate violence and to what extent can this transition to violence be handled peacefully without leading to injustice? Second, given the variety of protest goals, those that are political, economic, social, even ecological, what degree of call-for-change may be permitted so long as it does not threaten institutional collapse? Third, and a growing problem, in which ways can a government effectively deter and prevent any export of terrorism, personnel, methods and funds, from activist cells domiciled within its frontiers? Each of these questions raises further qualification if it is granted that there must be a world of difference between an individual's right to protest and individual and collective incitement to violence.

Questions such as those above are being fiercely debated in Europe and in the Americas. In Britain, for example, the government brought a new terrorism bill to the House of Commons at the end of 1999 which was carefully designed to meet the multivariate challenges of contemporary political violence. Predictably, the drafted terms of this bill have occasioned much public discussion of ethical and legal issues. From the British government's point of view there had to be in place a comprehensive approach to the protection of democracy and the securing of society's ordered and peaceful existence. Opponents of the proposed measures are viewing a number of them as infringement of human and civil rights. In some liberal quarters there is dismay that statements of intent and proclamations which do not strike everyone as extreme and destabilising can be vilified as conspiratorial by a process of mere say-so and without legal evidence sustainable in a court.

Ethical and legal arguments are complex. An example of the way in which they are being shaped is to be found in the *Guardian* of 14 December 1999. There,

the United Kingdom Home Secretary, Jack Straw MP, defends the protective purpose of the new bill as widening and clarifying present legislation and at the same
time as providing a 'robust' response to challenged democratic values without dimin-
ishing an individual's right to protest. The legislation is to fit in with measures
coordinated within the European Union to fight international crime. Over against
this, on the same newspaper page, is a strong riposte from John Wadham, the
director of the civil rights group, Liberty.

Straw addresses the newspaper's readers directly:

Given recent coverage, *Guardian* readers could be forgiven for believing that the
new terrorism bill marks the end of liberal democracy as we know it. As ever,
however, the reality is very different.

Legislating in this area is difficult. By its nature, terrorism is designed to strike
at the heart of our democratic values. That is all the more reason why we must
ensure that we get right the balance between defending the public from acts of
organised terror and ensuring that human rights are protected.

The main disagreement between the government and those like John Wadham
is our long-held belief that we need specific legislation to counter the on-going
terrorist threat.

It has, however, long been recognised that we need special laws to prevent
and deal with particular threats – just witness the success of the legislation covering
serious fraud and drug trafficking. Yet these have not resulted in complaints about
the injustices of a 'twin-track system'.

With the new terrorism bill, we are proposing to move away from the rather
piecemeal and temporary approach that characterises current anti-terrorism legislation.

For a quarter of a century, the prevention of terrorism act [PTA] – introduced
by one of my more liberal predecessors, Roy Jenkins – has provided the police
with extra powers to counter the terrorist threat.

In opposition, the Labour party objected to three parts of that act. The terrorism
bill deals with each of them.

First, the PTA allowed ministers to exclude British citizens entering the mainland from Northern Ireland, and vice versa – a form of internal exile which was
ineffective, wrong and opposed by nationalists and unionists alike. I lapsed exclusion powers in early 1998 and, under this bill, they are to be scrapped altogether.

Second, the PTA allowed ministers – not judges – to decide whether a terrorist
suspect should be detained by the police for longer than 48 hours. With this bill,
extensions to detention will require approval by a stipendiary magistrate (or equivalent) – and at last allow the UK to overturn its derogation from a key part of the
European Convention on Human Rights.

Third, the PTA was a temporary measure to deal mainly with Irish terrorism,
and took no account of the changing nature of the terrorist threat. This legislation
puts that right too.

The powers available under the terrorism bill will be subject to a series of
checks and balances to ensure that they are used proportionately. As well as the
judicial oversight of extensions of detentions, proscribed organisations will have a

right of appeal to an independent body and all future authorisations of the use of stop and search powers under the bill will have to be confirmed by me or another minister.

Opponents of the bill have cited the proposed new definition of terrorism as an affront to the individual's peaceful right to protest. It is no such thing. The bill (which defines terrorism as 'the use or threat, for the purpose of advancing a political, religious or ideological cause of action which involves serious violence against any person or property, endangers the life of any person or creates a serious risk to the health or safety of the public or a section of the public'), in fact distinguishes more clearly than ever before the situations in which anti-terrorist legislation should apply.

It increases the level of the threshold before which certain powers within the bill can be activated, by making it clear that it refers to activities which constitute 'serious violence'. Moreover, the definition itself does not create any new criminal offence. Rather it is primarily the trigger for the use of the powers in the bill. Terrorists committing serious acts of violence will continue to be charged with the usual such offences, from murder to causing explosions.

The legislation is not intended to deal with alleged offences properly dealt with under the existing criminal law. Neither will it in any way curb individuals' democratic rights to protest peacefully. The difference between 'serious violence' and 'violence' will not be meaningless in a court of law, as some have suggested. Our courts are well used and perfectly able to apply the word 'serious' in the context of specific circumstances, and do so, for instance, when considering aggravating features in criminal cases. So this will make a difference.

At the same time the new bill widens the scope of the legislation, extending it to include the threats posed by terrorists both domestically and internationally. It must be right for the law to deal on the same basis with all groups or individuals intent on causing death and injury here in Britain to further a cause. This is particularly necessary as the nature of the terrorist threat changes.

Finally, some have claimed that the new legislation will prevent individuals and organisations opposing oppressive regimes overseas – the 'Mandela' effect. Protest from here, as they see it, will brand them terrorists.

But there is a world of difference between an individual's rights to freedom of expression and protest and the plotting of serious violence. What the bill will do is also to outlaw the incitement of murder and other extremely serious terroristrelated crimes of violence. Any prosecution would also require the consent of the director of public prosecutions if it is to proceed. This part of the bill fills a gap in the law.

Existing legislation which has implemented various international conventions means that it is already an offence here to incite anyone abroad to hijack an aircraft, or someone in Turkey or India to commit murder. Why should similar incitement of terrorist murder in Japan or Australia not also be an offence?

This bill strengthens the powers to meet an ever-changing, ever-present threat, yet is properly regulated by a series of safeguards. Every terrorist attack represents a violation of our democratic values, and as such our response must be sufficiently robust to challenge and defeat these vile activities at all times. I think we have got the balance right.[1]

Wadham is in no doubt that if the new bill becomes law then all who protest are liable to be branded as 'criminals':

Where can you be sentenced to 10 years in prison for speaking at a meeting? The answer, I am afraid, is this country and the proposal is contained in clause 11 (3) (b) of the terrorism bill which has its second reading in the House of Commons today. The bill gives the government the power to 'proscribe' organisations. Membership of a proscribed organisation would not be the only offence created. To speak at a meeting where a member of that organisation was speaking would also be a crime – even if your speech opposed terrorism, the use of violence, or of any criminal action.

While the only organisations currently proscribed are those associated with Northern Ireland, the bill gives the secretary of state the power to add to these. If direct action organisations are being targeted as potential 'terrorists', then proscription is the next logical step.

The prevention of terrorism act is currently restricted to those suspected of involvement in international terrorism or terrorism connected with Northern Ireland. The government wants some of these special provisions to apply to any kind of 'terrorism'. People suspected of such 'terrorist' offences would also have fewer rights than other criminals. Surely it is wrong in principle to have a twin-track criminal justice system.

There is a diversity of views about the morality of damaging property to prevent a new road scheme or making threats of violence to try to halt experimentation on animals. But there is no logic to a system that assumes that those suspected of such offences should have fewer rights than a person who assaults another for revenge or for greed.

The anti-terrorism laws have led to some of the worst human rights abuses in this country over the past 25 years, contributed to miscarriages of justice and have led to the unnecessary detention of thousands of innocent people, most of them Irish. Only a tiny percentage of those detained have ever been charged and almost without exception they could have been detained under ordinary criminal laws.

This bill will create a duty to report people to the police in certain circumstances. If, during the course of your work, you find information about, or become suspicious of, someone who you suspect may be using money or property to contribute to the causes of terrorism, you must report them. Failure to do so will make you liable to a five-year prison sentence. This could have a serious effect on journalistic investigations.

Furthermore, under this bill exiled supporters of Nelson Mandela who publicly supported the armed struggle in South Africa would be classified as terrorists. The offence of 'incitement' may be committed by mere words and there will be clashes with the right to freedom of expression. Investigation of such offences will often be brought about by political forces such as overseas governments complaining about the tactics of pressure groups and government opponents based in this country.

When these same offences were introduced in 1994, Lord Williams of Mostyn QC, the Labour home affairs spokesman in the House of Lords and now the attorney general, described the offences as 'alarming'; said that the offences were 'far too harsh and draconian' and would bring the law into disrepute; and that they would 'bring us into serious conflict with the European convention on human rights'.

The lord chief justice in the divisional court on March 30 this year decided that these same provisions in a 'blatant and obvious way undermined the presumption of innocence'.

The home secretary believes that this bill complies with the European convention on human rights. We would have to disagree. It risks infringing the rights to a fair trial, to freedom from unlawful detention, to freedom of speech and freedom of association. Yet the powers in the police and criminal evidence act are more than sufficient to deal with the criminal activities described under the bill.

Draconian anti-terrorist laws should be abolished and not extended: such laws have a far greater impact on human rights than they ever will on crime.[2]

TERRORISM AS CRIME; TERRORISM AS WARFARE

As we have seen earlier, there are few definitions of terrorism adequate to provide clear grounds for fair and square counteraction. Is an arrested terrorist to be indicted according to civilian criminal codes? If collaborators are found, are they to be treated in the same way? Are terrorists to be regarded as participants in armed conflict and so subject to the conventional rules of war? Distinctions such as these have been considered by Brian Jenkins (1986). They go some way to explain the terrorism control policies of many governments and they also point to lack of agreement especially in the case of Third World States where there were campaigns of liberation and 'freedom fighting'. Jenkins has this to say:

Civilized nations have through law identified modes of conduct that are criminal. Homicide, kidnapping, threats to life, and the willful destruction of property appear in the criminal codes of every country. True, some of the prohibitions may legally be violated in times of war – the law against killing, for example, may be violated by those we call 'lawful combatants'. Terrorists claim to be soldiers at war, who are therefore privileged to break ordinary laws. But even in war there are rules outlawing the use of certain weapons and tactics.

The rules of war grant civilian combatants who are not associated with 'valid' targets at least theoretical immunity from deliberate attack. They prohibit taking hostages. They prohibit violence against those held captive. They define belligerents. They define neutral territory. These rules are sometimes violated – and those responsible for the violations become war criminals. But violations in no way diminish the validity of the rules.

Some international lawyers see the laws of war as possible solution to the dilemma of definition. They suggest that rather than trying to negotiate new treaties on terrorism that are not likely to be ratified or enforced, nations should apply the laws of war, to which almost all have agreed. Terrorists, they say, should be dealt with as soldiers who commit atrocities. Nearly all countries have agreed to try or extradite soldiers who commit atrocities in international armed conflicts. Why should persons not explicitly granted soldiers' status be given greater leeway to commit violence? Under the laws-of-war approach, terrorism would comprise all acts committed in peacetime that, if committed during war, would constitute war crimes.

Terrorism thus can be objectively defined by the quality of the act, but not by the identity of the perpetrators or the nature of their cause. All terrorist acts are crimes, many of which would also be war crimes or 'grave breaches' of the rules of war if we accepted the terrorists' assertion that they are waging war. All terrorist acts involve violence or the threat of violence, sometimes coupled with explicit demands. The violence is usually directed against noncombatants. The purposes are political. The actions are often carried out in a way that will achieve maximum publicity. The perpetrators are usually members of an organized group. Their organizations are by necessity clandestine, but unlike other criminals, terrorists often claim credit for their acts. And finally – the hallmark of terrorism – the acts are intended to produce psychological effects beyond the immediate physical damage.

While these criteria do not eliminate all ambiguity, they enable us to draw some limits and answer some questions. Terrorism differs from ordinary crime in its political purpose and in its primary objective. Neither the ordinary bank robber nor the man who shot President Ronald Reagan is a terrorist. Likewise, not all politically motivated violence is terrorism. The Minuteman of the American Revolution and the rebel in Central America both have political motives, but they are not automatically terrorists. Terrorism is not synonymous with guerrilla war or any other kind of war, and it is not reserved exclusively for those trying to overthrow governments.

International terrorism can be defined as incidents that have clear international consequences: incidents in which terrorists go abroad to strike their targets, stay at home but select victims because of their connections to a foreign state (for example, diplomats or the executives of foreign corporations), or attack international lines of commerce (airliners). It excludes the considerable amount of terrorist violence carried out by terrorists operating within their own country against their own nationals and in many countries by governments against their own citizens.

This definition of international terrorism admittedly reflects the particular concern of the United States and the handful of other governments frequently targeted by terrorists abroad. The issue is not the general problem of political violence or terrorism or its causes – these are domestic matters. The unit of measure is the spillover of this violence into the international domain. The terrorists would argue that the established rules of diplomacy and war were contrived by a small group of primarily western nations for their own advantage and that they deprive groups without recognized governments, territory, or armies from exercising their 'right' to resort to violence. The above definition of international terrorism is also criticized as being an artificial distinction that encompasses only a narrow slice of the total volume of political violence.

Lack of agreement on definition is further complicated by differing concepts of conflict. Many Third World governments, particularly those in Africa and Asia, may not cooperate with American and European efforts to identify and combat international terrorism, not because these governments approve of terrorist tactics, but because they see the antiterrorist efforts as part of a broader campaign aimed at outlawing the irregular methods of warfare that were developed in the Third

World during the civil war in China and the anticolonial struggles in Asia and Africa. Not a few of the Third World's insurgent chiefs — today's leaders — were once called terrorists themselves. Their governments, particularly the ones that lack the tools of modern conventional war, therefore deliberately exclude from their definition of terrorism 'wars of liberation', guerrilla warfare, other means of struggle that they themselves once employed or which are now being employed on behalf of causes they support.

The position taken by the Third World governments on international terrorism is consistent with the position they took at the Geneva negotiations to revise the laws of war. They sought to extend the rights and protections of the original Geneva Conventions to irregular forces as well as regular soldiers in international wars. They noted that the Geneva Conventions and other treaties regulating war were drafted by Europeans to regulate warfare among Europeans, but that they omitted from 'international warfare' military force used by the Europeans in gaining and maintaining colonies. In other words, when Europeans shot at Europeans, it was a closely regulated affair, but when Europeans shot at Africans or Asians, they could do what they wanted. The Third World governments feared that the Americans and Europeans now wanted to brand the irregular methods used by the natives to fight back as 'terrorism' and thereby outlaw them.[3]

At another point in his argument, Jenkins refers to the common readiness of many governments to press for an immediate military response to terrorism even though it might be dubious legally:

In a speech made in February 1985, Secretary of State George Shultz said, 'International terrorism has rapidly become one of the gravest challenges to American interests around the world. In the Middle East, in Latin America, and in Western Europe, we have suffered heavy casualties, and the threat has not diminished!' In an earlier speech, he warned that in response to further state-sponsored terrorist attacks, the United States might be compelled to resort to military force, possibly 'before each and every fact is known or on evidence that would not stand up in an American court'.[4]

The control policy that Secretary of State Shultz was outlining was to be an active one that was understandable as a military one:

In a major policy address on the changing nature of power and diplomacy in the 1980s and the particular threat posed by state-sponsored terrorism, Secretary of State Shultz in April 1984 spoke of the 'grey area' that falls 'between major war and millennial peace' and the contemporary weapons of state-sponsored terrorism, which he described as a new form of warfare. He said it was 'increasingly doubtful that a purely passive strategy can even begin to cope with the problem'. The United States needed an *active defense* — and that meant the use of military force.

By the time he delivered the speech, Shultz had in effect already won his battle with those in government who opposed a formal military response to terrorism. On that same day, the President signed a National Security Directive dealing with terrorism, which ordered the appropriate government departments to develop military options. Shultz's speech was thus a call to arms, an exhortation to use force if that is necessary to combat terrorism. The speech, together with the National Security Directive, constituted a declaration of war against an unspecified terrorist [sic], to be fought at an unknown place and time with weapons yet to be chosen.[5]

Jenkins's conclusion is that Americans see international terrorism, so often directed at their own nationals, as menacing to their common defence. In this perception there is perhaps an ethical component as well as a political one:

State-sponsored terrorism is increasingly seen, at least in the United States, as a threat to national security, a form of war that must be countered like any other form of war. Accordingly, military force is seen as an appropriate response, not every time, but clearly an option for which the armed forces must be prepared.[6]

MORAL JUSTIFICATION OF COUNTER-TERRORIST MEASURES

Albert Bandura, an eminent United States social psychologist, argues that effective counter-terrorism must regard terrorism itself as a form of 'cognitive reconstrual' (reconstruction) and 'moral disengagement' transforming normally socialised individuals into dedicated and skilled combatants. Terrorists are social 'challengers' who morally justify their activities. Government authority justifies the need of a militant counter-response. Regimes that are markedly authoritarian have less trouble devising tough tactics of control than democratic societies. (The case-studies in Part Two indicate that this was largely true of Argentina, Peru, Spain and Colombia.) Dilemmas face those states where too harsh or too hasty control imperils the life of hostages or, indeed, is held to violate fundamental principles in a civilised society. (Germany, Italy, Northern Ireland, Sri Lanka have been seen wrestling with the possibilities and limits of stern control policies.) Bandura outlines his thinking about moral justification in these terms:

People do not ordinarily engage in reprehensible conduct until they have justified to themselves the morality of their actions. What is culpable can be made honorable through cognitive reconstrual. In this process, destructive conduct is made personally and socially acceptable by portraying it in the service of moral purposes. People then act on a moral imperative. Radical shifts in destructive behaviour through moral justification are most strikingly revealed in military conduct.

People who have been socialized to deplore killing as morally condemnable can be transformed rapidly into skilled combatants, who may feel little compunction and even a sense of pride in taking human life. Moral reconstrual of killing is dramatically illustrated by the case of Sergeant York, one of the phenomenal fighters in the history of modern warfare. Because of his deep religious convictions, Sergeant York registered as a conscientious objector, but his numerous appeals were denied. At camp, his battalion commander quoted chapter and verse from the Bible to persuade him that under appropriate conditions it was Christian to fight and kill. A marathon mountainside prayer finally convinced him that he could serve both God and country by becoming a dedicated fighter.

The conversion of socialized people into dedicated combatants is not achieved by altering their personality structures, aggressive drives, or moral standards. Rather, it is accomplished by cognitively restructuring the moral value of killing, so that the killing can be done free from self-censuring restraints. Through moral sanction of violent means, people see themselves as fighting ruthless oppressors who have an unquenchable appetite for conquest, protecting their cherished values and way of life, preserving world peace, saving humanity from subjugation to an evil ideology, and honoring their country's international commitments. The task of making violence morally defensible is facilitated when nonviolent options are judged to have been ineffective and utilitarian justifications portray the suffering caused by violent counterattacks as greatly outweighed by the human suffering inflicted by the foe.

Over the years, much reprehensible and destructive conduct has been perpetrated by ordinary, decent people in the name of religious principles, righteous ideologies, and nationalistic imperatives. Throughout history, countless people have suffered at the hands of self-righteous crusaders bent on stamping out what they consider evil. Elsewhere, Rapoport and Alexander have documented the lengthy blood-stained history of holy terror wrought by religious justifications. Acting on moral or ideological imperatives reflects a conscious offense mechanism, not an unconscious defense mechanism.

Although moral cognitive restructuring can easily be used to support self-serving and destructive purposes, it can also serve militant action aimed at changing inhumane social conditions. By appealing to morality, social reformers are able to use coercive, and even violent, tactics to force social change. Vigorous disputes arise over the morality of aggressive action directed against institutional practices. Power holders often resist, by forcible means if necessary, making needed social changes that jeopardize their own self-interest. Such tactics provoke social activism. Challengers consider their militant actions to be morally justifiable because they serve to eradicate harmful social practices. Power holders condemn violent means as unjustified and unnecessary because nonviolent means exist to effect social change. They tend to view resorts to violence as efforts to coerce changes that lack popular support. Finally, they may argue that terrorist acts are condemnable because they violate civilized standards of conduct. Anarchy would flourish in a climate in which individuals considered violent tactics acceptable whenever they disliked particular social practices or policies.

Challengers refute such moral arguments by appealing to what they regard as a higher level of morality, derived from communal concerns. They see their constituencies as comprising all people, both at home and abroad, who are victimized either directly or indirectly by injurious social practices. Challengers argue that, when many people benefit from a system that is deleterious to disfavored segments of the society, the harmful social practices secure widespread public support. From the challengers' perspective, they are acting under a moral imperative to stop the maltreatment of people who have no way of modifying injurious social policies, either because they are outside the system that victimizes them, or because they lack the social power to effect changes from within by peaceable means. They regard militant action as the only recourse available to them.

Clearly, adversaries can easily marshal moral reasons for the use of aggressive actions for social control or for social change. Different people view violent acts in different ways. In conflicts of power, one person's violence is another person's selfless benevolence. It is often proclaimed that one group's criminal terroristic activity is another group's liberation movement fought by heroic freedom fighters. This is why moral appeals against violence usually fall on deaf ears. Adversaries sanctify their own militant actions but condemn those of their antagonists as barbarity masquerading behind a mask of outrageous moral reasoning.[7]

For Bandura, justifications spiral away as outrage calls for punitive response and as institutional repression hardens the resolve of the violent. Utilitarian principles come to the fore on all sides, narrowing the scope for options and reducing the room for compromise:

So far, the discussion has centred on how terrorists invoke moral principles to justify human atrocities. Moral justification is also brought into play in selecting counter-terrorist measures. This poses more troublesome problems for democratic societies than for totalitarian ones. Totalitarian regimes have fewer constraints against using institutional power to control media coverage of terrorist events, to restrict individual rights, to sacrifice individuals for the benefit of the state rather than to make concessions to terrorists, and to combat threats with lethal means. Terrorists can wield greater power over nations that place high value on human life and are thereby constrained in the ways they can act.

Hostage taking has become a common terrorist strategy for wielding control over governments. If nations make the release of hostages a dominant national concern, they place themselves in a highly manipulable position. Tightly concealed captivity thwarts rescue action. Heightened national attention, along with an inability to free hostages independently, conveys a sense of weakness and invests terrorists with considerable importance and coercive power to extract concessions. Overreactions in which nations render themselves hostage to a small band of terrorists inspire and invite further terrorist acts. In contrast, hostage taking is stripped of functional value if it is treated as a criminal act that gains terrorists neither any coercive concessionary power nor much media attention.

Democratic societies face the dilemma of how to morally justify counter-measures that will stop terrorists' atrocities without violating the societies' own fundamental principles and standards of civilized conduct. A set of critical conditions under which violent counterattacks are morally justified can be spelled out. It is generally considered legitimate to resort to violent defense in response to grave threats that inflict extensive human suffering or endanger the very survival of the society. But the criterion of 'grave threat', while fine in principle, is slippery in specific application. Like most human judgments, gauging the gravity of threats involves some subjectivity. Moreover, violence is often used as a weapon against threats of lesser magnitude on the grounds that, if left unchecked, they will escalate in severity to the point at which they will eventually exact a high toll in loss of liberties and in suffering. Gauging potential gravity involves even greater subjectivity and fallibility of judgment than does assessment of present danger. Construal of gravity prescribes choice of options, but choice of violent options also often shapes construal of gravity. Thus, projected grave dangers to the society are commonly involved to morally justify violent means that are used to squelch limited present threats.

It is hard to find any inherent moral rightness in violent acts that are designed to kill assailants or to deter them from future assaults but that inevitably risk the lives of some innocent people as well. Because of many uncertain factors, the toll that counter-terrorist assaults take on innocent life is neither easily controllable nor accurately calculable in advance. To sacrifice innocent lives in the process of punishing terrorists raises fundamental moral problems. Democratic societies that happen to kill some innocent people in the process of counter-terrorist actions find themselves in the vexing predicament of violating the values of their society in defense of those values. Therefore, the use of violent counter-measures is typically justified on utilitarian grounds – that is, in terms of the benefits to humanity and the social order that curbing terrorist attacks will bring. On the assumption that fighting terror with terror will achieve a deterrent effect, it is argued that retaliatory assaults will reduce the total amount of human suffering. As Carmichael notes, utilitarian justifications place few constraints on violent countermeasures because, in the utilitarian calculus, sacrificing the lives of some innocent persons can be greatly outweighed by the halt to repeated massacres and the perpetual terrorizing of entire populations.[8]

All states face the double necessity of trying to make sense of terrorist motives and methods and of allaying public fear through feasible counter-policies. A moral requirement would be that such policies exclude the retaliatory cycle of violence fuelling more violence. Extreme counter-measures, Bandura concludes, can play into terrorist hands:

In coping with problems of terrorism, societies face a dual task: how to reduce terrorist acts and how to combat the fear of terrorism. Because the number of terrorist acts is small, the widespread public fear and the intrusive and costly security counter-measures pose the more serious problems. Utilitarian justifications can readily win the support of a frightened public for violent counter-terrorist measures. A frightened and angered populace does not spend much time agonizing over the morality of lethal modes of self-defense. Should any concern arise over the taking of innocent lives, it can be assuaged by stripping the victims of their innocence by blaming them for not controlling the terrorists in their midst. The perturbing appearance of national impotence in the face of terrorist acts creates additional social pressures on targeted nations to strike back powerfully.

Extreme counter-terrorist reactions may produce effects that are worse than the terrorist acts themselves. Widespread retaliatory death and destruction may advance the political cause of terrorists by arousing a backlash of sympathy for innocent victims and moral condemnation of the brutal nature of the counter-reactions. To fight terror with terror often spawns new terrorists and provides new justifications for violence that are more likely to escalate terrorism than to diminish it. Indeed, some terrorist activities are designed precisely to provoke curtailment of personal liberties and other domestic repressive measures that might breed public disaffection with the system. Extreme counter-measures can, thus, play into the hands of terrorists.[9]

LEGAL CONSIDERATIONS

Ethical debate raises many complicated issues for those who would seek to prevent terrorism. The same is true of legal approaches and this has led to a wealth of international controversy. This chapter can only attempt a summary of a number of legal issues. Rosalyn Higgins, for instance, eminent in the field of international law, argued in 1997 that terrorism is not a discrete element of international law with its own recognised norms, procedures and codes. It is rather, she says, 'a pernicious contemporary phenomenon' which presents complicated legal problems. Foremost among these problems is the question of adequate definition as an indispensable prelude to control – something that has not been resolved at all satisfactorily when the United Nations has given it intensive discussion:

Underlining all the initial efforts of the United Nations to address the problem of terrorism has been a debate about whether the concept of terrorism should, and could, be defined. On the one side were those who contended that normative responses to prohibited conduct could not be devised without agreement as to what conduct was indeed prohibited. In particular, what uses of force, by whom and in what circumstances, were to be considered as 'terrorism', thus triggering certain legal consequences? On the other side were those who responded that agreement upon definition was doomed to failure, and that it was better to proceed pragmatically with building up agreed norms that were relevant to different aspects of the overall problem. Intellectually, the former view is clearly right. There will always be room for controversy as to whether normative community responses are or are not to be invoked on a given occasion, if it is unclear whether the triggering conduct is or is not terrorism. At the same time, the pragmatic response was the only possible one, because there simply was not the consensus to identify what acts did or did not constitute terrorism. That was certainly true in the 1970s, when the United Nations began to address this problem, and when the Cold War was at its height. Even in today's vastly improved climate at the United Nations, the definition of terrorism would still present enormous problems.

In 1972 the General Assembly established an Ad Hoc Committee on Terrorism. Early discussions on agreeing a definition revealed that some regarded certain types of action as characterising terrorism; others emphasised the relevance to any definition of a prohibited target; others pointed to the purposes of the action undertaken; while yet others thought that the characteristics of the perpetrator were a key factor in any definition. Thus 'hostage taking, aircraft piracy, sabotage, assassination, threats, hoaxes, indiscriminate bombings or shootings' have been viewed by some as acts of terrorism. But at the same time it is apparent that not every assassination, threat, or shooting, by whomsoever, is to be characterised as terrorism; the killing of one soldier on the field of battle by another is not 'terrorism'; the threat by one State that it will assist another if that other is attacked is not 'terrorism'; the shooting of a person in a store during a robbery raid is not 'terrorism'. It is apparent that while these acts *can* constitute terrorism, the definitional answer depends on other factors too. Terrorism cannot be defined by reference alone to the acts committed.

Nor can it be defined by reference alone to the targets. We have all come to share a perception that acts against aircraft, or against kidnapped hostages, constitute 'terrorism'. Civil aircraft and individuals should be able to go about their business without the fear of detention or other violence. But what does the status of the target add to our understanding? Aircraft and individuals have no special 'protected' status – it is simply self-evident that it is intolerable for them to be the target of attacks. Diplomats, and non-combatants in warfare, do have a special status, conferred on them by international treaties. They too are not to be harmed. But even then is every harm to them 'terrorism'?

If a State uses rockets to coerce another State, that may be lawful or unlawful, depending on all the circumstances. But we do not usually describe it as 'terrorism'. If rockets are launched by an individual, we are apt to speak of 'terrorism'. Is terrorism something that is perpetrated only by private persons or can States engage in 'terrorism'? If a government kills those demonstrating against it, is this unlawful killing, or is it 'terrorism'? Again, does an individual have to be acting from ideology to be a terrorist? Or are mercenaries to be described as terrorists?

The answer to all of these questions leads to yet other difficulties and problems, and to profoundly divergent views. The view of most Western and many Third World States was that attempts to define terrorism were doomed to failure and were therefore to be strongly resisted. When it reported to the General Assembly in 1979, the Ad Hoc Committee on International Terrorism avoided any attempt at a definition.

If the West was nervous that a definition of terrorism could be used to include 'state terrorism', the Third World was nervous that any definition which emphasised non-State actors would fail to differentiate between terrorism properly so called, and the struggle for national liberation. The Secretary General was asked to report to the General Assembly on the possibility of convening an international conference 'to define terrorism and to differentiate it from the struggle of peoples for national liberation'. It is clear from his Report, submitted in 1989, that the problems about definition had not disappeared with the improved East–West situation, and that differences remained about the usefulness of a definition. Thus Mexico used the occasion to point out that although it had participated positively in all the international measures to contain terrorism, it none the less believed that:

> the basic problem which has arisen in tackling the question of terrorism
> is the lack of a single criterion determining the fundamental component
> elements of the definition of the term. Only the adoption of such a
> criterion would make it possible to establish mechanisms to help elim-
> inate the practice of terrorism.[10]

The United Nations General Assembly, in practice, has looked to a subsidiary body, the International Law Commission, for authoritative advice about the legal implications of international terrorist control. Higgins (1997) concludes her sketch of controversial legal issues with a note about the efforts of the Commission in this difficult area: Higgins admits that this rudimentary definition is so loose that it offers little scope for universal jurisdiction. Her reference to activities which are 'widely disapproved of' and to 'community condemnation' indicates that the lawyers and the rest of us are falling back on ethical considerations rather than rigorous legislation:

The impression of the term 'terrorism' being a term of convenience is emphasised by the work of the International Law Commission. In the Draft Code on the Peace and Security of Mankind, initially under study by the ILC in 1954, 'terrorist acts' formed part of the definition of the concept of aggression. Aggression was defined, *inter alia*, as 'the undertaking or encouragement by the authorities of a state of terrorist activities in another state'. After a prolonged period of inattention, the Draft Code came under renewed consideration from 1985–91. The text was almost completed in 1990 by which stage terrorism was the subject of a separate article in the Draft Code. But then the Draft Code itself is widely regarded by many writers (including this one) as a compendium of elements of existing international law, and not as a 'real' topic itself.

The concept of aggression, as ultimately defined in General Assembly resolution 3314 of 1974, does not contain any reference to terrorism as such. But some of the component elements that we have come to associate with state terrorism (including the sending of armed bands to the territory of another, or allowing one's territory to be used as a base for violence against another state) are to be found within the definition.

We may conclude thus:

The term 'terrorism' has no specific legal meaning. It covers compendiously the following:

1   Offences by States against diplomats.
2   Offences by States against other protected persons (e.g. civilians in times of war).
3   Offences by States, or those in the service of States, against aircraft or vessels.
4   The offence of State hostage-taking.
5   The offence by States of allowing their territory to be used by non-State groups for military action against other States, if that action clearly includes prohibited targeting (i.e. against civilians), or prohibited means of force.
6   Action by non-State actors entailing either prohibited targets or prohibited means.
7   Connivance in, or a failure to control, such non-State action. This engages the indirect responsibility of the State, and is subsumed under 'State terrorism'.

Item (6) above does not at first sight come within the scope of international law, which is largely concerned with the norms that govern the behaviour of States. But it has become a matter for international legal concern because of the concept of 'international crimes' and the possibility, under international law, of international jurisdiction over them. That being said, although all acts by private persons using prohibited means, or directed against prohibited targets, may loosely be termed 'terrorism', not all such acts give rise to universal jurisdiction. Certain major offences against persons protected by the 1949 Geneva Conventions do give rise to such jurisdiction. In *that* context we could say 'terrorism is a crime which allows of universal jurisdiction'. But as we have seen above, the aircraft offences, deemed 'criminal' as a term of approbation, still do not give rise to universal jurisdiction. Put differently, although individuals may be said to bear criminal responsibility for a range of activities coming within the general scope of the term 'terrorism', only a very few of them (war crimes, crimes against humanity) give rise to universal jurisdiction. But most of them do allow of the possibility of trial within various national jurisdictions, because of broadly based (even if not universal) jurisdiction permitted under international law.

'Terrorism' is a term without legal significance. It is merely a convenient way of alluding to activities, whether of States or of individuals, widely disapproved of and in which either the methods used are unlawful, or the targets protected, or both. International law generally, and the mechanisms of the United Nations specifically, have sought painstakingly over the years to specify exactly what is prohibited, and to provide wide possibilities for jurisdiction over such events and persons. None of that activity has in fact required an umbrella concept of 'terrorism', over and above the specific topics of hostages, aircraft, protected persons etc. The term is at once a shorthand to allude to a variety of problems with some common elements, and a method of indicating community condemnation for the conduct concerned.[11]

Chapter 18

Counter-terrorism: programmes and strategies

FOR M. R. L. SMITH (1995) there is an important question of standpoint: does too much dwelling on control and prevention of political violence cloud a necessary attempt to analyse and understand the causes of terrorism?

The consequence of the rather narrow concentration on the supposed tactics of terrorism, gives rise to a second area of concern which is the extent to which research has dwelt on the control and prevention of political violence. To a degree this is understandable. For many people who live in environments afflicted by terrorism, howsoever defined, their sole experience of the problem is likely to be of its disruptive effects on everyday life. The immediate inclination is likely to want to be rid of the problem – not to engage in some contorted hypothetical discourse on the subject. Nevertheless, at an academic level, too much concentration on counter-responses to sub-state terrorism can make research narrowly policy prescriptive. The violent symptoms of political conflict certainly do have to be controlled by the responsible authorities charged with upholding the public good. While not denying the right of scholars or anyone else to have their say on how to tackle such matters, academics do have to tread carefully if they start to advocate detailed policy and if they are to remain true to their vocation. Part of the problem has been that much of the literature on terrorism published over the years has betrayed an over-emphasis on, and sometimes even an obsessive concern for, tactical counter-measures which leaves the analyst poorly placed to undertake the more considered long-term diagnosis of the crisis. Undue stress on counter-terrorist techniques can also lead to an equally obsessive search for a general theory of the causes of terrorism and political violence: the thinking being that if one discovers the 'causes of terrorism' then one will be that much more able to devise policies to eliminate the problem. Since all conflicts have very diverse origins, one is not going to obtain a very meaningful theory, only ones which are so nebulous, like 'human nature is the cause of violence' that they explain everything yet nothing at the same time.[1]

Notwithstanding caution such as this the non-academic community of governments, police forces and armed services devise policies and operate programmes to pinpoint any originators of violence, to deter them from committing outrages, and to deal as best they can with a traumatised public.

COUNTER-TERRORISM PROGRAMMES

An example of clearly laid out practice in counter-terrorism is to be found in a broadsheet published in 1998 by the Terrorism Research Center in the United States in association with the Department of Defense. It is a statement of principles and an outline of practice couched in a style soberly reminiscent of an army manual. It discusses objective, unified effort, control legitimacy, the need for perseverance and restraint, security, and ends with notes about United States counter-terrorism policy:

Objective

The general objective of combatting terrorism programs is neutralizing terrorist groups. As in most stability and support operations, neutralization in this context means rendering the source of threat benign, not necessarily killing the terrorists. In antiterrorism, the objective can be further refined as preventing attacks and minimizing the effects if one should occur. It includes any action to weaken the terrorist organization and its political power and to make potential targets more difficult to attack. Counterterrorism includes spoiling action, deterrence, and response.

Unity of effort

As in all stability and support operations, interagency action is required to combat terrorism. Unity of effort requires ways to integrate the actions of various responsible agencies of the US and foreign governments. Intelligence is particularly important and sensitive. [. . .]

Unfortunately, it is easier to prescribe unity of effort than to achieve it. In circumstances where multiple police and intelligence agencies have vague and overlapping charters and jurisdictions, friction is bound to occur. As in other aspects of stability and support operations, the solution lies in negotiation and consensus-building. Fortunately, experience has proved that cooperation at the local unit or installation level is relatively easy to obtain.

Legitimacy

Legitimacy is not usually a problem in combatting terrorism since the right of self-defense is universally recognized and, as indicated above, terrorist acts are crimes in peace, conflict, or war. Security forces might bring their legitimacy into question by failing to distinguish between those perpetrating, aiding, or abetting terrorism and others who might sympathize with their cause but do not engage in violent acts. [. . .] An overreaction that results in the avoidable deaths of hostages while security forces are attempting to neutralize terrorists, for example, raises questions of judgement as well as the legitimacy of the undertaking.

Patience and perseverance

Patience and perseverance are the hallmarks of successful programs to combat terrorism. In any country or region, there are few terrorists relative to the population. Identifying and capturing them is difficult and entails tedious police and intelligence work. It is filled with frustration. [. . .] Perhaps the most irritating aspect of defence against terrorism is that success is hard to identify. For example, if there is no incident, it may be because the defensive measures are effective. On the other hand, it is equally likely that the terrorists never intended to attack in the first place. Rarely will success be measurable, but defensive efforts must continue.

Restraint

Restraint is necessary to both objective and legitimacy in the context of combatting terrorism. Premature action against individuals, for example, can be counterproductive if it interferes with developing intelligence in depth that might neutralize an entire terrorist group. Similarly, overreaction, such as imposing severe populace and resource control measures, can undermine legitimacy and unnecessarily irritate the civilian populace.

Security

Security is the most obvious requirement in combatting terrorism. Terrorists rely on surprise and the victim's confusion at the time of an incident. Antiterrorism involves physical security, operational security [. . .] and the practice of personal protective measures by all personnel. [. . .]

In combatting terrorism, intelligence is extraordinarily important. The essential elements of information [. . .] differ somewhat from those normally found in traditional combat situations. In addition to the terrorists' strength, skills, equipment, logistic capabilities, leader profiles, source of supply, and tactics, more specific information is needed. This includes the groups' goals, affiliations, indication of their willingness to kill or die for their cause, and significant events in their history, such as the death of martyrs or some symbolic event. [. . .] Unless terrorists' specific interests are known, predicting the likely target is pure chance.

US policy for combatting terrorism

Until the 1980s, the US government, like most other Western governments, considered terrorism to be primarily a police matter. The seizure of the US embassy in Teheran and subsequent car and truck bomb attacks on our facilities in Lebanon forced us to reevaluate that position. Current US policy regarding terrorism encompasses acts against Americans at home and abroad.

The United States considers all terrorist acts criminal and intolerable and condemns them without regard for their motivation. The United States will support all lawful measures to prevent terrorism and bring perpetrators to justice. We will not make any concessions to terrorist blackmail because to do so will merely invite more terrorist actions. (No concessions does not mean no negotiations.)

The Department of Defense has identified five threat levels to standardize reporting. They are based on terrorists' existence, capability, intentions, history, targeting, and the security environment. The five levels are described below:

- Critical, which means that a terrorist group has entered the country or is able to do so. It has the capability to attack and is engaged in target selection. Its history and intentions may or may not be known.
- High indicates that a terrorist group exists which has the capability, history, and intention to attack.
- Medium describes the same conditions as high except that intentions are unknown.
- Low is a situation in which terrorist groups exist and have a capability to attack. Their history may or may not be known.
- Negligible describes a situation in which the existence or capability of terrorist groups may or may not be present.[2]

Another rather earlier example of a counter-terrorism programme is that suggested by a research criminologist, Grant Wardlaw (1982):

The following options might be suggested as parts of an anti-terrorist campaign.

1. Attempt to find long-term solutions to the underlying causes of terrorism. This approach involves a decision to acknowledge that there are remediable inequities in society which may provide objective causes of terrorism. Such an approach probably is the most significant because of the widespread policy changes with extensive effects on other aspects of the social milieu which might be occasioned by it.
2. Increase the size and powers of the security forces (for example, increase manpower, search and entry powers, power to detain without trial, etc.). This would involve major policy decisions about the nature of policing our society, civil rights, etc.
3. Introduce capital punishment for terrorist activities. Such a move involves policy decisions about the role of capital punishment, whether terrorists are to be treated as a separate class of offenders (as opposed to reintroducing

capital punishment generally), which types of terrorist acts are to be made capital offences.

4. Enact legislation limiting rights of assembly and increasing controls over the members of society by way of identification cards, registration of residence and extensive use of computerised files. This has implications for the type of society we have, police powers, civil rights, etc.

5. Establish a 'third force' or special military units to cope with terrorist attacks. The decision to employ new types of force involves policy decisions about how early to commit military forces, the role of police in anti-terrorist operations, and civil–military relations.

6. Announce a policy of 'no negotiations' with terrorists. Such a policy implies a wide range of decisions about such issues as the value of individual life, the authority and prestige of the state, and how far in reality such a policy would be pursued (for example, would the government refuse to negotiate in the face of a credible nuclear threat?).

7. Increase physical and procedural security. Such an increase revolves around related issues of the economics of such measures, powers given to security officers (particularly those employed by private security organisations), and civil rights.

8. Introduce internment without trial or special legal procedures designed to limit intimidation of witnesses (such as the so-called Diplock courts in Northern Ireland). The introduction of measures outside of the normal legal process requires major policy decisions about the legal system, civil rights, and the political consequences of such changes.

9. Place legal limits on the ability of the media to report terrorist acts. This may involve suggestions as to the timing, duration, or content of news reports. Such restrictions involve some of the most controversial policy decisions about freedom of the press, free speech, and the nature of government.

10. Introduce special anti-terrorist legislation which may mandate a combination of the above or other measures. Such legislation implies that a decision has been taken that terrorists cannot be dealt with by normal legal processes and leads to consequential policy changes in the law, police powers, civil rights, and governmental intrusion into everyday life.

11. Make it illegal for individuals or private organisations to pay ransom to terrorists or to take out ransom insurance and place a legal duty on people to report hostage takings to the police. Such measures involve decisions about the rights of individuals to take whatever action they consider necessary to safeguard the lives of those for whom they are responsible when a conflict exists with what the authorities see as undesirable consequences for society in general.

12. Promote and become a signatory to international treaties providing for extradition or trial of captured terrorists, suspension of air services to countries providing safe havens for hijackers, etc. This involves decisions about the effectiveness of international measures, the definition of terrorism and whether or not to allow 'political exception' clauses.

13. Research and develop alternatives to hostage negotiations. This implies a recognition that hostage taking is likely to decrease in frequency or take on new forms as negotiation techniques appear more successful. Consequently

important policy decisions would have to be made about research directions and issues such as attitudes towards more aggressive incident resolution techniques.

14. Suggest that terrorist groups be encouraged to adhere to the norms articulated by the customary laws of war, the Geneva Conventions, and the Nuremberg Principles (a suggestion which has been characterised as 'patently valueless, representing the *reductio ad absurdum* of legalistic naïveté'). To support such a suggestion would require a policy decision to recognise terrorist groups as political entities and to accord them special prisoner-of-war status if captured.

15. Develop and deploy highly intrusive technologies as pre-emptive moves (for example, technologies for monitoring and surveillance). Such deployment requires major policy decisions about civil rights, police powers, and the nature of society.

The foregoing list illustrates the complexity of the decisions facing authorities in the field of counter-terrorist policy. Again it is emphasised that the list is not exhaustive. Many other equally important issues face the policy makers. What is evident though is that the major decisions focus around a relatively small number of major issues, namely the general nature of the society in which we live and, specifically, police powers, civil rights, and the rule of law. Many of the specific issues enumerated above will be examined in detail in the following chapters. However, specific policies need to be formulated in the context of a general understanding of how a society views itself and its legitimate responses to violence and subversion. The question which first needs answering is: What are the major principles around which we should build our counter-terrorist strategy?[3]

PROGRAMMES AND PRINCIPLES

Democratic societies generally find definitive action against political violence problematic. This is understandable on account of the public's customary high regard for private opinion and action and their prompt censure of anything they believe is authoritarian intervention. Security services find it hard to initiate what is seen as 'irregular' police work, to carry out surveillance, and to resort to planted 'informers'. Walter Laqueur (1999) sees much modern counter-terrorism as hampered by bureaucracy and inconsistent collaboration among states:

Counter-terrorism naturally goes hand in hand with terrorism, but over the ages it has become less successful for a variety of reasons. Modern technology in this area has made enormous progress; for example, it can trace the movements of even small units and single tanks over a wide area day and night. But it cannot keep track of the movements of single individuals in a town carrying miniaturised bombs. The only effective weapon against terrorism in the modern era has been the infiltration of their ranks and the use of informers. Police in the last century had a much freer hand against terrorism than today's police: they placed their agents in all major and most minor terrorist movements, and paid them from special funds to which only they had access. It is probably no exaggeration to state that most of the terrorist journals at the time were paid for by secret police funds. If a police informer in the course of his duty had to carry out a terrorist act, no questions would be asked, nor would he be put to trial or lose his pension rights.

Present-day police forces in democratic societies have little freedom of manoeuvre. Too many people are involved in decisions and operations, and bureaucratic formalities have to be observed. Payments to informers have to be signed and countersigned; the interception of communications between terrorist suspects has to be approved by the judiciary; and a skilful lawyer has a good chance to get his client, the terrorist, off the hook even if he was apprehended *in flagranti*. Because of these factors the successful infiltration of terrorist groups is almost impossible.

Counter-terrorism's success in democratic societies is mainly the result of advanced computer technology and the cooperation of a population that provides important leads. On the other hand, cooperation in the international arena has been less than perfect. Governments have been afraid of extraditing terrorists for fear of retaliation and for other reasons, or they have released convicted foreign terrorists from prison after a token stay. Also, governments have invoked 'higher interests of state' – France and Greece are examples – as reasons for not dealing with terrorists harshly. In a few cases, terrorists who have lost their usefulness or lacked influential protectors have been extradited. But by and large, counter-efforts against terrorists by democratic states have been only partly effective in recent times.[4]

The difficulty of sustaining an adequate counter-terrorism strategy in a democratic state is also discussed by Martha Crenshaw (1995). The practice of a state resorting to exemplary violence both to punish violent dissidence and to discourage its further spread is for Crenshaw also terrorism, 'reactive terrorism' even though it is less intimidating than that practised by authoritarian states. Although this point would not be acceptable to everybody, there would be more agreement with Crenshaw's belief that counter-terrorism policies often use political labelling which may be modified should a state's interests require it. Moreover, there is little doubt that government repression may result in unforeseen consequences for public attitudes. Crenshaw goes on to speculate why reform as an element in counter-terrorism has not always brought an end to terrorism. This and other problems highlight the question: how can governments best control terrorism while maintaining democratic freedoms? Specifically, how may the terrorists' individual motivations best be changed?

The term [terrorism] has to be limited to the systematic resort to exemplary violence or the threat of violence against a small number of victims in order to change the attitudes of much larger popular audiences. Thus, only specific government practices can qualify as terrorism. In this sense, the use of torture or the resort to the guillotine, a particularly dreadful form of execution, may be considered terrorism when they are intended to create fear in the population and to discourage potential resistance, rather than simply to acquire information or to punish. Similarly, if terrorism is defined as violence that society regards as unacceptable, whether

according to the rules of war or the standards of peace, then violence that is unusually cruel or arbitrary in the view of the targeted audience, and that the perpetrator
knows to be such, can reasonably be considered terrorism.

The usage of the term *counterterrorism* is even more perplexing. It is used to
describe both a government's use of terrorism to oppose terrorism from a chal-
lenger and any official response, legal or otherwise, to terrorism. I use it here to
refer to reactive terrorism by those in power. This approach draws a distinction
between a policy of counterterrorism and what Eugene V. Walter has termed a
regime of terror, which implies that the foundations of government are built on
creating a state of emotional terror in its citizens. Democracies, for example, might
practice counterterrorism in specific instances, although their authority is not
comprehensively based on stifling potential resistance from society through intimidation. These instances seem often to occur in foreign or 'occupied' territory,
where the military is in charge and procedures for democratic accountability are
weak.[5] [. . .]

In contemporary politics, calling adversaries 'terrorists' is a way of depicting
them as fanatic and irrational so as to foreclose the possibility of compromise, draw
attention to the real or imagined threat to security, and promote solidarity among
the threatened. Using the term terrorism can imply not only that an adversary
employs a particular strategy or style of violence but also that the 'true nature' of
the opponent is thereby revealed. By defining the PLO as a terrorist organization,
for example, Israeli policy makers precluded recognition or negotiations. Furthermore, the government was bound by its own label; dealing with the PLO appeared
as a major concession. This example also reminds us of the international dimensions of political labeling. The United States and Israel tend to share common
conceptions of terrorism, but when talking to the PLO became a matter of American
political interest, these conceptions diverged. In 1988 the United States accepted
the PLO's formal renunciation of 'terrorism' (although the two sides did not agree
on a precise definition), but to Israel the group remained a 'terrorist organization'.

Thus, conceptions of terrorism affect the ways in which governments define
their interests, and interests also determine reliance on labels or their abandonment when politically convenient. The label can, however, blind governments to
the distinction between violent and nonviolent dissent. It can also influence the
selection of targets for state repression. For example, because the Argentine military conceived of terrorism as the symptom of a disease to be eradicated, the whole
of society was seen as contaminated, and thus society itself became the target of
terrorism from above. The government determined not only to destroy organized
opposition but to cleanse society of the tendencies that had motivated resistance.
In Italy, the term 'terrorism' was not used until midway through the Red Brigade's
campaign of violence, although their activities remained essentially the same. In
Northern Ireland, the official criminalization of the IRA was part of an effort to
deny special status; such criminalization led to prison hunger strikes. West Germany
pursued a similar policy. Labeling minorities as terrorist may intensify communal
conflict, as it has in India. Labeling revolutionary movements terrorist risks minimizing their importance. The Peruvian government may have delayed responding
to Sendero Luminoso, because it was initially dismissed as a mere 'terrorist organization', implying the absence of popular support or military power. Possibly

reintegration of 'repentant' terrorists was easier in Italy because left-wing militants were considered misguided youth, not professional revolutionaries.[6] [. . .]

But government repression may frighten would-be supporters of terrorists' goals into passivity; the costs of resistance may become too high. The oppositional groups who use terrorism extensively can rarely protect the populations they put at risk from government persecution or communal vengeance. Indiscriminate repression or vengeance equalizes risk, but it is not clear whether a coercive reaction to terrorism increases support for the government or for the opposition. Public attitudes with regard to these issues are difficult to discover; whether people act out of loyalty or fear, or a combination of the two, is hard to know. In Peru, for example, rural populations in Ayacucho province are exposed to pressure from both government and Sendero Luminoso.

The political changes in Northern Ireland might suggest, perhaps paradoxically, that terrorism can work as protest, leading to reform of underlying conditions (greater equality or regional autonomy, for example). In India, Spain, and Northern Ireland, governments have responded to nationalist terrorism by increasing coercive powers in attempts to destroy the infrastructure of the terrorist organizations but also by pursuing reforms intended to remedy the grievances that underlie public support for or tolerance of violent extremism. Are governments responding to terrorism or to collective action that seems to be a more spontaneous expression of popular opinion? We should also ask how reforms have affected the internal stability and cohesiveness of violent oppositions. Have reforms, for example, benefited moderates or extremists? Why have reforms in Spain, India, and Ireland, even the transition to democracy in Spain, not yet ended terrorism? The context seems to have been transformed, but terrorism has not.

In other circumstances democracies as well as authoritarian regimes respond to terrorism with repression rather than reforms. An early example was the response to anarchist terrorism in the nineteenth century. Such a choice might be a deliberate policy of counterterrorism or the result of constraints on the ability to implement reforms. The agricultural reforms that might alleviate rural discontent are expensive. For example, both because of the cost (for a country already in dire economic straits) and because of the state of insecurity in areas dominated by Sendero Luminoso, the economic reforms that might make a political difference are problematic for the Peruvian government. In divided societies, opposition from the majority may pose obstacles to making concessions to minority demands.

The western European democracies confronting terrorism saw a growth in power of state security institutions. West German and Italian governments also upgraded intelligence-gathering and surveillance functions, bringing the government into a more intrusive role vis-à-vis society. In West Germany, Spain, Italy, and the United Kingdom, anti-terrorist legislation restricted civil liberties. The normative context for political action might also have changed as radical ideologies that appeared to support terrorism were discredited in the eyes of the public.

An important question for many of these case-studies [in Crenshaw, 1995] is how governments can control terrorism while maintaining democratic freedoms. There appears to be no single easy answer. Democracies struggle with terrorism from the Left and from the Right, as well as from nationalist or separatist interests.

They must balance a perceived need to control the direct consequences of terrorism, by maintaining order and security, with the realization that any coercive response to terrorism reduces democratic freedoms. Is it possible to deal successfully with terrorism without resorting to coercion? Are reforms alone ever sufficient to prevent or to halt terrorism? Can repression and reform be combined?

Ending terrorism may require a change in the motivations of the individuals involved. How do conditions change so as to decrease incentives for terrorism? What might cause individuals to abandon the initial commitment that bound them to a terrorist role? When do people who use terrorism cease to believe in their own justifications? Under what circumstances can the individuals who have participated in terrorism be reintegrated into society? Environments may be more or less hospitable to exit and reentry. The reabsorption potential of a society may depend on public attitudes (for example, sympathy for the cause, if not the method) or public policies (such as the Italian policy of rewarding 'repentance'). In divided societies, where terrorism is likely to be continuous with nonviolent collective action, reintegration may be simpler. Yet in Spain, offers of negotiations and of amnesty appear only to have provoked factional violence. In Italy, the Catholic church played an important role as an institutional mediator for reintegration. Successful adaptation may thus depend on many factors: a social environment that does not provide justifications for terrorism but permits reintegration, appropriate government policies that reward exit, and institutions that facilitate the process.[7]

COUNTERING STATE-SPONSORED TERRORISM

There is a long history of terrorists finding support in a patron state which has an interest in furthering dramatic political change elsewhere. Today, Iran, Iraq, Libya, Cuba, North Korea, Syria and Sudan are all considered 'rogue states' in facilitating and harbouring terrorist elements. Since the second half of the twentieth century there has been a considerable increase in this sponsorship. Other states have attempted some form of counter-action using, for example, diplomatic pressures, negotiation, third-party mediation, even economic sanctions and blockades. They have done this either unilaterally or in association, say, with those who have ratified the conventions and declarations of the United Nations or the European Union. Fighting state-sponsored terrorism is a problematic and frustrating concern and discussion of it deserves prominence in this section of Part Three.

Boaz Ganor (1998) has comprehensively surveyed the issues that arise in dealing with state-sponsored terrorism. He begins by pointing to the contemporary wide incidence of this type of involvement, outlining the main characteristics, namely, ideological support, financial support, military support, operational support, direction of terrorist attacks, and direct state involvement in terrorist attacks. Ganor goes on to consider strategies of counter-terrorism which endeavour to treat sponsoring states as capable of rational decision. Such states are likely to respond constructively to a range of deterrent options employed against them by contemplating the ratio of cost to benefit. Ganor takes the familiar point of national conflict of interest where security and politico-economic interests seem incompatible. There is a brief discussion of the utilitarian approaches of 'critical dialogue' and 'buying silence'. Finally, given that offending states are apt to look around for loopholes in any unified counteraction, Ganor makes a case for some sort of international institution to fight terrorism although the United Nations is not highly mentioned in this regard. His conclusion defines an agenda for internationally co-ordinated counter-terrorism:

Instead of the 'weapon of the weak' – minority groups, liberation movements, and revolutionary organizations – terrorism has become a tool of states and even of superpowers. In some cases, states established 'puppet' terrorist organizations, whose purpose was to act on behalf of the sponsoring state, to further the interests of the state, and to represent its positions in domestic or regional fronts. In other cases, states sponsored or supported existing organizations, thereby creating mutually profitable connections.

The patron state provided its beneficiary terrorist organization with political support, financial assistance, and the sponsorship necessary to maintain and expand the struggle until the attainment of its objectives had been achieved. The patron used the beneficiary to perpetrate acts of terrorism as a means of spreading the former's ideology throughout the world, or in other cases, the patron ultimately expected that the beneficiary would assume control over the state in which it resided or impart its ideology to broad sections of the general public. [. . .]

The high costs of modern warfare, the Cold War, and concern about non-conventional escalation, as well as the danger of defeat and the unwillingness to appear as the aggressor, have turned terrorism into an efficient, convenient, and generally discrete weapon for attaining state interests in the international realm.

Ideological support

The basic level of state support for terrorism is 'ideological support'. Terrorist organizations, as noted, are a convenient instrument for spreading ideological doctrines, particularly revolutionary ones. States such as the Soviet Union and Iran, which set themselves the operative-strategic aim of spreading their revolutionary ideology (Communism in the former case and Islamic fundamentalism in the latter) found suitable allies in terrorist organizations.

In some cases, however, terrorist organizations were founded by extreme radical activists, who were inspired to found their group by a state which supported terrorism or who had accepted the ideological sponsorship of a state sponsor in an effort to attain material assistance, after having already founded their organization. In such cases, the terrorist organization is provided with political, ideological or religious indoctrination via agents of the supporting state or is trained by institutions of the sponsoring state. (In this context one should mention communist terrorist organizations, such as the 'Popular Front for the Liberation of Palestine', which enjoyed support from the Soviet Union, and organizations with an Islamic fundamentalist outlook, such as Hizballah, with close ideological and religious ties to Iran.)

Financial support

A higher level of state support for a terrorist organization is 'financial support'. In order to continue operations and develop further, a terrorist organization requires large sums of money, which are sometimes unavailable through its own independent resources. In such cases, terrorist organizations rely on the generous support of sponsoring states. Today Iran is one of the main contributors to terrorist organizations. [. . .]

Military support

A higher level of aid involves 'military support'. Within this framework, the state supplies the terrorist organization with a broad range of weapons, provides military training, organizes courses for activists, and so on. Iran also falls in this category. [. . .]

Operational support

The next level of aid is 'operational support'. It entails the direct provision of state assistance in the perpetration of specific attacks. Operational support takes various forms: false documents, special weapons, safe havens, etc. Iranian embassies throughout the world, for instance, play a crucial role in this context. [. . .]

Initiating terrorist attacks

The next level of state involvement in terrorism is 'initiating and directing terrorist attacks'. In this category, the state no longer limits itself to providing aid indirectly to terrorist organizations. Instead, it gives specific instructions concerning attacks, it initiates terrorist activities, and it sets their aims. [. . .]

Direct involvement in terrorist attacks

The highest level of state involvement in terrorism is 'perpetrating direct attacks by government agencies'. In these cases, the state carries out terrorist attacks in order to further its interests, using agencies from its own intelligence services and security forces, or through people directly responsible to them. [. . .]

Rationality of states involvement in terrorism

Having established the various features of state sponsorship of international terrorism, we are faced with determining the possibility of preventing states interested in assisting terrorist organizations or in perpetrating terrorist acts on their own. Before turning to this issue, however, we must determine the extent to which one can view the decision to engage in terrorist activities as a rational act.

The most widely accepted strategy for coping with terrorism in general, and with states involved in terrorism in particular, is deterrence. However, if the state's decision to sponsor terrorism does not follow from rational considerations, deterrent activities against it will be meaningless. Indeed, a policy of retribution against irrational states might be ineffective, and could even lead to further escalation. [. . .]

Most states engaged in terrorism choose to do so. They take into account the price they will be required to pay for their activity, in exchange for the benefits gained by the attainment of their policy goals. Usually, these states adhere to rational cost-benefit analyses. Indeed, most countries which sponsor terrorism are not democratic, and their decision-making processes are limited to the consideration of a single ruler. The variables entering the cost and benefits equation in such cases might seem irrational to Western sensibilities, as they seemingly assign exaggerated and disproportionate weight to ideology, religion, and emotions. But even the lone decision maker tests the extent to which his activity will ultimately promote his goals, as he himself has defined them, and whether countermeasures adopted against his country, if and when its involvement in terrorism is disclosed, will endanger his and his country's basic interests.

For every country, there is a limit to the amount it is willing to pay for its continued involvement in terrorism. The price scale varies from country to country, as does each one's 'breaking point'. Hence, in order for deterrence to be successful, countries contending with terrorism must raise the costs of terrorism involvement to the point where the costs outweigh the benefits, and they must do so according to the specific characteristics of the individual state sponsors.

What is the range of activities available in the deterrence of states sponsoring terrorist activities? What is the 'price scale' that the international community can endorse in an attempt to alter the costs and benefits analysis of those states which are involved in terrorism?

The 'price scale'

[There is a] rising scale of prices of international [deterrent] efforts, each one conveying a more stringent sanction than the previous one, beginning with a warning to cease terrorism sponsorship, to international condemnation and cultural boycott (including banning the sponsor from international events, removing it from international cultural or educational programmes, and the expulsion of its citizens who live, work, or study in other countries). The next stage is a diplomatic boycott, including the removal of terrorism sponsors from international institutions, the suspension of its membership in UN institutions, removal from the UN General Assembly and even a cessation of bilateral relations (no country has ever been expelled from the UN). At the next stage (or parallel to the previous one) is an economic boycott. Such a measure could include restricting the state's ability to purchase military or dual-use equipment (in a military conflict or in its involvement in terrorism), preventing exports to it and purchases from it, freezing and confiscating its assets throughout the world, and the construction of a blockade, by air, land and sea. In addition, a secondary boycott could be imposed on countries and companies which insist on maintaining commercial ties with the sponsor. The next phase is the legal stage. Here, the sponsoring state's political and military leaders are defined as 'war criminals' or charged with 'crimes against humanity', with international show trials set to punish them (even if not in their presence). The highest stage of punishment and deterrence against a state sponsoring terrorism is the offensive stage – international coordinated military actions against the terrorist organization's facilities in the sponsoring country and the sponsor's military installations.

Conflicts of interests

The struggle against states involved in terrorism reflects many conflicts of interests in the international arena – between states and superpowers, alliances and leagues of states, groups, and organizations. At times, however, the counter terrorism effort creates conflicts of interests within a state, between its security and economic interests. Thus far, economic interests have had the upper hand, whereas security interests, expressed in the will for a more effective struggle against states engaging in terrorism, have been relegated second-class status.

An analysis of the international measures adopted against countries involved in terrorism reveals that most states are unwilling to sacrifice their economic interests for the cessation of terrorism. The most prominent example of such a tendency can be found in the attitude of European states (headed by Germany, France and Italy) towards Iran, the world's leading terrorism sponsor. Contrary to the American approach, which is intended to restrict Iranian activities and to force it to abandon terrorism by further damaging Iran's precarious economy with additional sanctions, the countries of Europe have relied on a varied set of practical arguments to justify their extensive economic and commercial ties with Iran.

The 'critical dialogue' – a utilitarian argument

Countries maintaining extensive economic links with states involved in terrorism choose to justify their policy in utilitarian-international terms rather than in economic ones. Their claim is that imposing sanctions on such states will not lead them to restrict their sponsorship of terrorism. Indeed they claim that the opposite will result, and such policies will corner them into even more extreme, violent tactics and a further escalation of international terrorism. According to such an outlook, the preferred policy is one of 'critical dialogue' – keeping channels open with states sponsoring terrorism by maintaining economic and cultural links with them. Such 'open channels' can be used as a means to voice criticism of terrorism policies and to influence terrorism sponsors against the continuation of their sponsorship.

At the Paris summit of the industrialized countries (G-7), in August 1996, which dealt with international terrorism, the Europeans blocked an American attempt to impose sanctions on four terrorism sponsoring states – Iran, Libya, Iraq and Sudan. The European participants claimed that isolating countries such as Iran has no moderating influence whatsoever on terrorism, but rather the opposite. In support of their 'critical dialogue' approach, they claimed they can make ingenious use of the 'carrot and stick' approach, thereby preserving the effectiveness of their own actions against terrorism sponsors.

Buying silence – the security argument

As previously mentioned, critics of the use of sanctions often claim that imposing sanctions on states engaged in terrorism closes channels of communication and may lead to escalation. This claim is compatible with another conciliatory strategy towards terrorists, mainly that which supports a 'dialogue' with terrorist organizations in an attempt to influence their policies. Such a policy is in effect 'buying silence'. In such cases, a terrorist organization (or sponsor) agrees to refrain from carrying out attacks within the borders of a certain country, in exchange for a commitment by that country to turn a blind eye to terrorist activities of the organization or the ideological influence or support of the sponsor. In so doing, the country conceals the responsibility of the organization or its sponsor, and can even prevent the extradition of terrorists caught in that country or lead to the release of terrorists without, or shortly after a trial.

Such a strategy is opportunist at best. It promotes particularistic interests while jeopardizing the safety of the entire international community and of other sovereign states. It also hampers all chances of effective international cooperation in the struggle against terrorism; it defeats the international effort to coerce terrorism sponsors to refrain from further involvement in the use of terror. [. . .]

Breakdown of international unity

International struggle against states which are involved in terrorism should not be limited to the imposition of economic sanctions. Rather, it should cover a full range of diplomatic, legal, economic, and offensive actions. Ultimately, such measures will raise the costs of involvement in terrorism, and therefore reduce the terrorism-related activities of sponsoring states.

States sponsoring terrorism will resort to any means to find loopholes in international boycotts and will seek out countries ready to maintain cultural, diplomatic, and economic ties, either openly or surreptitiously. In return, they will be ready to pay a high price and grant economic and other benefits to anyone prepared to cooperate with them. Alternatively, these states may threaten to harm foreign investments or assets within their territories or execute massive acts of terrorism or even an all-out war. [. . .]

The late Prime Minister of Israel, Yitzhak Rabin, also addressed this issue:

> The response to international terrorism must also be international.
> Nations must find ways of cooperating against the terrorist network

[. . .] I propose that this type of cooperation be institutionalized and made concrete. Countries that choose to coordinate their activities against international terrorism should create a special international organization for this purpose. Obviously, this organization cannot be created within the framework of the United Nations. It can come into being only if the United States, the most powerful country in the free world, will take the initiative and call for its establishment. [. . .] This organization should coordinate four main functions: first, intelligence gathering and counterintelligence; second, protection of facilities and transportation routes [. . .] third, military operations in cases of emergency [. . .] fourth, and most difficult, political action against states that initiate and promote terror. Countries that initiate terrorism must be made to understand that they will face an organized, united front of states, a union ready to take measures that an attacked country would not be able to undertake alone. The existence of such an agency might help serve as a deterrent, and possibly an effective means of sanctions and punishment.

An international agenda for the struggle against states involved in terrorism

In conclusion, developing an effective international strategy against states which are engaged in terrorism requires the international community to adopt the following steps:

- To reach an international agreement regarding an exhaustive definition of terrorism.
- To endorse a means of classifying countries according to the features and the level of their sponsorship of terrorism.
- To publish an updated list of countries' involvement in terrorism according to their level of involvement.
- To acknowledge the necessity and the duty to punish countries because of their involvement in terrorism.
- To define a clear 'price scale' to be paid by countries engaged in terrorism.
- To adjust the 'price scale' to the various types of state sponsorship of terrorism, aiming to change their balance of interests.
- To impose a secondary boycott on states and companies that continue to maintain economic and other ties, whether open or covert, with states on which a boycott was imposed because of their involvement in terrorism.
- To establish a permanent international mechanism to combat terrorism, one of whose aims will be to ensure that punitive steps are taken against states engaged in terrorism and to warn against any infringement of these measures.

Only the careful fulfillment of all these steps can ensure effective action against terrorism sponsors. Otherwise, it will be impossible to alter the cost-benefit calculus, to reduce their involvement, or limit the scope of their attacks or their damaging effects.[8]

COUNTER-TERRORISM AND INTERNATIONAL INSTITUTIONS

Ganor's point as to the desirability of international institutions taking on a role in counter-terrorism can be taken further with a note about what the United Nations is doing globally and what the European Union is doing regionally. The United Nations has neither the constitutional authority nor the resources to discharge an executive function. Primarily, this is up to governments alone or in association. What the United Nations can do and does do is to mobilise resolve among its 185 member states to combat terrorism by framing resolutions, conventions and declarations and then to persuade states to ratify these enabling instruments. Much is being done, too, to promote research into the causes of terrorism, to convene workshops in co-ordinating intelligence exchange, in setting up an advisory service, and in devising training opportunities for field workers. It is the last-named who have been brought into mediation work in the Middle East and in South-east Asia especially in crises over hostage release and the hijacking of aircraft. In Colombia, Panama, Thailand, and Cambodia, teams of experts and relief workers have been drafted into areas where a growing terrorist enterprise – drug-related narco-terrorism – has devastated entire communities.

Only very slowly are the legal components of international counter-terrorism assuming shape in thirteen global or regional treaties. Progress is hampered, first, by the reluctance of many states jealous about their sovereignty to give overall priority to humane considerations rather than political ones, and, second, by the fact that international law provisions, however definite, still require translation into domestic laws before offenders in those countries can be prosecuted. A statement from the United Nations in 1996 lists a number of aspects of international terrorism where co-ordinated counteraction has yet to be realised:

Most of the international legal instruments pertaining to international terrorism were introduced after significant international incidents had already taken place. International terrorism is in many instances associated with drug trafficking, the arms trade, smuggling or money laundering, and acts by groups with extremist persuasions. A number of subjects are not covered by existing international treaties. These include terrorist bombings, terrorist fundraising, traffic in arms, money laundering, exchange of information concerning persons or organizations suspected of terrorist-linked activities, the disruption of global communications networks, the use of weapons of mass destruction, falsification of travel documents, and technical cooperation in training for counter-terrorism. Preventing the use of weapons of mass destruction by terrorists and the use of modern information technology for terrorist purposes, such as disrupting a communications network by altering data or disseminating on a wide scale extremist ideologies inciting persons to commit terrorist acts, also requires to be addressed.[9]

European states have also worked together to draft the beginnings of a legislative approach to controlling terrorism. In 1982 Grant Wardlaw listed many provisions in a European convention which appeared to offer firm grounds for states to act together: but would there be sufficient common will?

The second existing major anti-terrorist Convention is the Council of Europe's 1977 European Convention on the Suppression of Terrorism. This may on paper be seen as an advance on previous Conventions in that it strips many offences of the protection afforded by the classic 'political exception clause' (that is a clause which exempts from the criminal category those acts which are politically motivated). Article 1 of the Convention declares the following offences to be outside the purview of a political exception clause:

1.   Offences within the scope of the 1970 Hague Convention for the Unlawful Seizure of Aircraft.
2.   Offences within the scope of the 1971 Montreal Convention for the Suppression of Unlawful Acts Against the Safety of Civil Aviation.
3.   Serious offences involving an attack against the life, physical integrity, or liberty of internationally protected persons, including diplomatic agents.
4.   Offences involving kidnapping, hostage taking or serious unlawful detention.
5.   Offences involving the use of bombs, grenades, rockets, automatic weapons, or letter or parcel bombs where people's lives are endangered.
6.   Attempts to commit any of the above offences, or being an accomplice to such offences or attempts to commit them.

Article 2 stipulates that other particularly serious acts involving innocent persons may also be regarded as non-political. Much of the Convention deals with provisions for extradition and Article 7 states that refusal to extradite under the terms of the Convention requires the detaining State to initiate prosecution of the offender. On the face of it, the European Convention seems a worthwhile contribution to international attempts (or, in this case, regional) to combat terrorism. However, as with other cases, it is flawed by the fact that not all members of the Council of Europe have ratified it and that it contains no enforcement provisions for breaches by signatories. Thus, there is no guarantee that it will be adhered to in the cruel test of a crisis. [. . .] In general, it can be expected that many, if not all, nations will put national self-interest before international treaty obligations in a crisis. This is the fatal flaw in international regulatory attempts.[10]

More recently, Antonio Vercher (1992) has compiled an international comparative legal analysis of counter-terrorism moves in Europe. A good deal of progress has been made – on paper. Summit meetings, workshops, conferences, reports, inter-governmental liaison have all given the topics on cross-border terrorism many hours of earnest discussion. Numerous agendas and documents from the European Parliament in Brussels and from the European Court in Strasbourg have envisaged the facilities and rulings of a 'homogeneous judicial area'. European states, members of the European Union, have preferred a much less unified approach, that of political co-operation and police liaison. (Interpol is constrained by its narrow founding terms of reference and by a dearth of resources by mounting and sustaining any monitoring of terrorist intent.) Vercher does not doubt that much more is possible to realise a unified counter-terrorism strategy in Europe: provided that examination of feasibility does not confine itself to what he terms 'legal–technical' points. There is need of wider horizons:

It is not sufficient only to examine the legal–technical feasibility of a unified anti-terrorist system in Europe. Various other questions must be addressed simultaneously. These are concerned with the investigation of the root causes of terrorism and the protection of the fundamental rights of individuals within the EEC. Such questions are partially outside the purely legal scope of this thesis, but their importance cannot be underestimated since they are as much a guarantee of a long-standing and definite solution to the terrorist problem as the legal–technical measures themselves.

The legal measures which are part of an anti-terrorist system are intended to deal directly with the violence and social disruption provoked by terrorism. This does not mean that in themselves they will solve the causes of that violence and disruption. In fact, an investigation of the root causes of terrorism in any particular part of Europe may suggest the adoption of different measures, more social and political than legal.[11]

COUNTER-TERRORISM AND MASS-DESTRUCTION DEVICES

The face of terrorism and the demands on counter-action are changing fast in many ways. The potential for nuclear terrorism has been widely discussed in recent years along with the possible use of chemical, biological and computerised devices ('cyber-terrorism'). A good deal of the theory and practice of counter-terrorism becomes out of date month by month as Bruce Hoffman (1999) believes:

Meanwhile, the face of terrorism is changing in other ways. New adversaries, new motivations and new rationales have emerged in recent years to challenge at least some of the conventional wisdom on both terrorists and terrorism. More critically, perhaps, many of our old preconceptions – as well as government policies – date from the emergence of terrorism as a global security problem more than a quarter of a century ago. They originated, and took hold, during the Cold War, when radical left-wing terrorist groups then active throughout the world were widely regarded as posing the most serious threat to Western security. Even such modifications or 'fine-tuning' as have been undertaken since that time are arguably no less dated by now, having been implemented a decade ago in response to the series of suicide bombings against American diplomatic and military targets in the Middle East that at the time had underscored the rising threat of state-sponsored terrorism.

In no area, perhaps, is the potential irrelevance of much of this thinking clearer, or the critical lacuna more apparent, than with regard to the potential use by terrorists of weapons of mass destruction (WMD): that is, nuclear, chemical or biological weapons. Most of the handful of publications that have authoritatively addressed this issue are themselves now seriously dated, having been conceived and written in some instances nearly two decades ago when very different situations, circumstances and international dynamics existed. Indeed, much of the research on potential uses of WMD during the Cold War understandably concentrated on nuclear confrontation involving almost exclusively the two superpowers and their allies. Potential terrorist use of such devices was either addressed within the Cold War/superpowers framework or else dismissed, given the prevailing patterns of substate violence and the aims and objectives of violent non-state groups active at the time.

Today, the threat of a general war – nuclear and/or conventional – between the superpowers of the Cold War era and their respective alliances has faded. But it has been replaced by new security challenges of a potentially far more amorphous, less quantifiable and perhaps even more ominous character, that may also be far more difficult to meet. [. . .] the increasing salience of religious motives for terrorist activity has already contributed to the increasing lethality of international terrorism. Moreover, many of the constraints (both self-imposed and technical) which previously inhibited terrorist use of WMD are eroding. The particular characteristics, justifications and mindsets of religious and quasi-religious – as compared with secular – terrorists suggest that religious terrorists will be among the most likely of the potential categories of non-state perpetrators to use WMD.[12]

Is it possible that a terrorist group could produce a nuclear device? A democratic state needing to counteract such an eventuality would face agonising choices in the view of Laqueur (1999):

Democracies that have faced a terrorist challenge have tended toward underreaction, because the identity of the perpetrator may not have been clear, or because restraint and a response commensurate with the damage caused and the number of victims suffered was called for. But the reaction to the use of a weapon of mass destruction might be the opposite, one of overreaction. in such a case there is bound to be overwhelming pressure to retaliate on a bigger scale, both as an act of revenge and to forestall future attacks.

Despite the reasons one can marshal against the use of nuclear bombs by terrorists acting as substitutes for foreign countries, one can still think of a variety of scenarios in which this could happen, whether because a country with a nuclear capacity has descended into chaos, or a government has temporarily lost control, or any other circumstance in which those in power have ceased to act rationally.

What if a domestic terrorist group should produce one or more nuclear devices without any foreign help at at all? It is difficult to think at the present time of an effective defence to prevent an attack in this case. Given the amount of fissionable material that is available, the voluminous literature on nuclear weaponry, and military and state budgets in which hundreds of millions of dollars is a paltry sum, the chance that a terrorist group will come into possession of a nuclear device is significant.[13]

Laqueur at the same time has speculatively surveyed what he terms the 'terrorism of the future' in which sophisticated lethal devices pose problems both for the would-be terrorist and for those called to counteract.

There are many questions regarding the effective use of chemical and biological weapons. Chemical substances and biological organisms have to be more than highly toxic; they also need the right atmospheric conditions. Success depends on a variety of factors, including the direction and strength of the wind, the temperature, and other climatic factors. A massive dispersal may have a very limited effect, or it may create enormous damage.

Recent research in biotechnology has made the construction of fusion toxins possible, and bacteria and viruses can now be made more dangerous and resistant to antibiotics through genetic modification. But at the same time, biotechnology makes it possible to manufacture antisera and vaccines to protect a civilian population.[14]

THE DYNAMIC OF TERRORISM AND THE NEED OF RESPONSE

However sophisticated the means employed, the essence of political violence is that it is dynamic and constantly evolving. Counter-terrorism to have any success at all must keep in pace. Again, it is Bruce Hoffman (1999) sensing the urgency of mounting intelligible and intelligent strategies to contain something that can drain life out of ordered living:

At the same time, perhaps the most sobering realisation that arises from addressing the phenomenon of terrorism is that the threat and the problems that fuel it can never be eradicated completely. Their complexity, diversity and often idiosyncratic characteristics mean that there is no magic bullet, no single solution to be found and applied *pari passu*. This conclusion, however, reinforces the need for creative solutions if not to solve, then at least to ameliorate both the underlying causes and the violent manifestations. Only in this way will the international community be able prudently, effectively and productively to marshal its resources where and against whom they will have the greatest positive effect.

In sum, the emergence of this new breed of terrorist adversary means that nothing less than a sea-change in our thinking about terrorism and the policies required to counter it will be required. Too often in the past we have lulled ourselves into believing that terrorism was among the least serious or complex of security issues. We cannot afford to go on making this mistake.[15]

Notes

1 Definition of terrorism

1. Terrorism Research Center, United States. Website: www.terrorism.com/terrorism/basics.html. Print out pp. 11–12 (listing definitions).
2. Hoffman, Bruce (1998), *Inside Terrorism*, London: Indigo, pp. 13–15.
3. Hoffman, pp. 25–7.
4. Hoffman, pp. 28–31.
5. Hoffman, pp. 33–4, 35–6.
6. Hoffman, pp. 41–2, 43–4.
7. Crenshaw, Martha (1995), *Terrorism in Context*, Pennsylvania State University Press, pp. 7–10.
8. Crenshaw, pp. 11–12.

2 Motivation for terrorism

1. Crenshaw, Martha (1981), The causes of terrorism, *Comparative Politics*, July, pp. 381–5.
2. Reprinted from US Army's Command and General Staff College, Fort Leavenworth, Kansas, by Terrorism Research Center (cf. Note 1, Chapter 1), Extracts from print out of 31 December 1998, pp. 1–5.
3. Post, Jerrold, M. (1998), Terrorist psycho-logic: terrorist behavior as a product of psychological forces, in Reich, Walter, *Origins of Terrorism*, Baltimore: John Hopkins University Press, pp. 25–8.
4. Post, pp. 31–2.
5. Post, p. 33.
6. Post, pp. 35–6.
7. Post, p. 38.

3   Terrorism's worldwide occurrence

1.   Laqueur, Walter (1999), *The New Terrorism*, Oxford: Oxford University Press, pp. 22–30.
2.   Laqueur, pp. 31–6.
3.   See Note 1, Chapter 1. Print out p. 6.
4.   Shultz, Richard (1978), Conceptualizing political terrorism, *Journal of International Affairs*, vol. 32, no. 1, Spring/Summer. Extracted from discussion, pp. 7–15.
5.   International Policy Institute for Counter-Terrorism, Herzliya, Israel. Website: www.ict.org.il/interter/org.cfm. Print out 9 December 1999, pp. 1–2.
6.   As for Note 5. Print out p. 1.

4   Lebanon

1.   Picard, Elizabeth (1997), The Lebanese Shi'a and political violence in Lebanon, in Apter, David (ed.), *The Legitimization of Violence*, New York: New York University Press, p. 190.
2.   Picard, p. 191.
3.   Picard, pp. 193–4.
4.   Picard, p. 197.
5.   Picard, p. 199.
6.   Picard, pp. 206–8.
7.   Khalil, A. A. (1991), Ideology and practice of Hizballah in Lebanon. Islamization of Leninist organization and principles, *Middle Eastern Studies*, vol. 27, no. 3, pp. 390–1.
8.   Khalil, pp. 392–3.
9.   Khalil, p. 394.
10.   Khalil, p. 395.
11.   Khalil, p. 395.
12.   Khalil, p. 396.
13.   Khalil, p. 398.
14.   Khalil, pp. 398–9.
15.   Kramer, Martin (1998), The moral logic of Hizballah, in Reich, Walter (ed.), *Origins of Terrorism*, Baltimore: John Hopkins University Press, p. 132.
16.   Kramer, p. 136.
17.   Kramer, p. 137.
18.   Ranstorp, Magnus (1997), *Hizb'allah in Lebanon: the Politics of the Western Hostage Crisis*, London: Macmillan, pp. 60–1.
19.   Ranstorp, pp. 108–9.
20.   Ranstorp, pp. 134–5.
21.   Ranstorp, pp. 135–6.
22.   Ranstorp, pp. 192–4.
23.   Kramer, pp. 156–7.
24.   Kramer, p. 132.

5   Libya

1.   Laqueur, Walter (1999), *The New Terrorism*, Oxford: Oxford University Press, pp. 168–72.
2.   Habib, H. P. (1975), *Politics and Government of Revolutionary Libya*, Ottawa: Le Cercle du Livre de France, pp. 13–15.
3.   Blundy, David, and Lycett, Andrew (1987), *Quaddafi and the Libyan Revolution*, Boston: Little, Brown and Co., p. 44.
4.   Blundy and Lycett, p. 64.
5.   Blundy and Lycett, p. 68.
6.   Habib, p. 121.
7.   Habib, p. 122.
8.   Habib, p. 124.
9.   Habib, p. 127.
10.   Habib, p. 151.
11.   Ibrahaim, Ahmed (1983), *Revolutionary Organization, Revolutionary Committees: The Instruments of Popular Revolution*, Tripoli: Socialist Peoples Libyan Arab Jamahiriya (General Publications), p. 89 ff.
12.   Ibrahaim, p. 121.
13.   Haley, P. E. (1984), *Qaddafi and the United States since 1969*, New York: Praeger Special Studies, p. 35.
14.   Haley, pp. 37–8.
15.   Haley, p. 39.
16.   Haley, pp. 49–50.
17.   Haley, pp. 51–2.
18.   Haley, p. 54.
19.   Haley, pp. 231–2.
20.   Haley, p. 224.
21.   Blundy and Lycett, pp. 74–5.
22.   Blundy and Lycett, p. 212.
23.   Falk, Richard (1986), Rethinking counterterrorism, in Thompson, E. P. and Kaldor, Mary (eds), *Mad Dogs, The US Raids on Libya*, London: Pluto, p. 139.
24.   Hoffman, Bruce (1998), *Inside Terrorism*, London: Indigo, pp. 191–2.
25.   Quoted in the *Guardian*, 27 September 1999.

6   Sri Lanka

1.   Tamil website: www.tamilnation.org/overview.htm. Print out pp. 1–2.
2.   Laqueur, Walter (1999), *The New Terrorism*, Oxford: Oxford University Press, pp. 191–6.
3.   Tamil website: www.tamilnation.org/diaspora.htm. Print out pp. 2–7.
4.   *Asiaweek*, 26 July 1996, p. 30.
5.   *Mackenzie Briefing Notes* (1995), Mackenzie Institute, Toronto, pp. 9–10.
6.   *The Times*, 23 October 1997.
7.   Kapferer, Bruce (1997), Remythologizing discourses: state and insurrectionary violence in Sri Lanka, in Apter, David (ed.), *The Legitimization of Violence*, New York: New York University Press, p. 174.

8. Kapferer, pp. 178–9.
9. Kapferer, p. 175.
10. Joshi, Manoj (1996), On the razor's edge: the Liberation Tigers of Tamil Elam, *Studies in Conflict and Terrorism*, vol. 19, 19–42, p. 21.
11. Kapferer, p. 163.
12. Kapferer, p. 183.
13. Kapferer, pp. 181–2.
14. Joshi, p. 27.
15. Laqueur, pp. 230–1.
16. Laqueur, pp. 100–1.
17. Joshi, pp. 25–6.
18. Sri Lanka Outlook, Summer 1997, reprint of article in the *Indian Express*, 27 May 1997.

7   Northern Ireland

1. Whittaker, David J. (1999), *Conflict and Reconciliation*, London: Routledge, pp. 80–3.
2. Whittaker, pp. 83–4.
3. Whittaker, pp. 84–7.
4. Arthur, Paul (1997), 'Reading' Violence, in Apter, David (ed.), *The Legitimization of Violence*, New York: New York University Press, p. 234.
5. Arthur, pp. 238–9.
6. Arthur, pp. 240–1.
7. Arthur, p. 241.
8. Arthur, pp. 242–3.
9. Arthur, pp. 254–5.
10. Arthur, pp. 255–6.
11. Kearney, Richard (1997), *Postnationalist Ireland*, London: Routledge, p. 109.
12. Townshend, Charles (1995), The culture of paramilitarism in Ireland, in Crenshaw, Martha (ed.), *Terrorism in Context*, Pennsylvania State University Press, pp. 330–1.
13. Townshend, p. 324.
14. Townshend, p. 317.
15. Townshend, p. 317.
16. Townshend, pp. 336–7.
17. Arthur, pp. 270–2.
18. Kearney, pp. 110–12.
19. Kearney, p. 121.
20. Arthur, p. 235.
21. Townshend, pp. 339–40.
22. Whittaker, pp. 89–90.
23. Ref. Northern Ireland website: www.nio.gov.uk/agreement.htm.
24. Quoted in Mitchell Report to British and Irish Governments, January 1996. For text ref. the above website.

8   Argentina

1. Gillespie, Richard (1982), *Soldiers of Peron: Argentina's Montoneros,* Oxford: Oxford University Press, pp. 217–19.
2. Crassweller, R. D. (1987), *Peron and the Enigmas of Argentina,* New York: W. W. Norton, p. 337.
3. Gillespie, pp. 47–8.
4. Gillespie, pp. 70–1.
5. Gillespie, Preface.
6. Gillespie, Richard (1995), Political violence in Argentina, terrorists and carapintadas, in Crenshaw, Martha (ed.), *Terrorism in Context,* Pennsylvania State University Press, p. 213.
7. Gillespie (1995), p. 214.
8. Gillespie (1982), pp. 76–7.
9. Gillespie (1995), pp. 215–16.
10. Gillespie (1995), pp. 224–5.
11. Gillespie (1982), pp. 79–80.
12. Gillespie (1982), pp. 79–80, footnote.
13. Gillespie (1982), pp. 81–2.
14. Gillespie (1995), pp. 226–8.
15. Gillespie (1982), pp. 84–5.
16. Gillespie (1995), pp. 232–3.
17. Gillespie (1982), p. 102.
18. Hodges, D. C. (1976), *Argentina 1943–76. The National Revolution and Resistance,* Albuquerque: University of New Mexico Press.
19. Gillespie (1995), pp. 240–1.
20. Gillespie (1982), p. 268.
21. Gillespie (1982), p. 247.
22. Gillespie (1995), p. 243.
23. Gillespie (1995), pp. 246–7.

9   Spain

1. Shabad, Goldie and Ramo, F. J. L. (1995), Political violence in a democratic state: Basque terrorism in Spain, in Crenshaw, Martha (ed.), *Terrorism in Context,* Pennsylvania State University Press, pp. 411–13.
2. Shabad and Ramo, pp. 415–17.
3. Shabad and Ramo, pp. 418–19.
4. Shabad and Ramo, p. 422.
5. Shabad and Ramo, p. 423.
6. Shabad and Ramo, pp. 427–8.
7. Shabad and Ramo, p. 436.
8. Wieviorka, Michel (1997), ETA and Basque political violence, in Apter, David (ed.), *The Legitimization of Violence,* New York: New York University Press, p. 300.
9. Wieviorka, p. 294.
10. Shabad and Ramo, pp. 444–5.
11. Zirakzadeh, Cyrus E. (1991), *A Rebellious People. Basques, Protests and Politics,* University of Nevada Press, p. 204.

12.   Shabad and Ramo, pp. 441–3.
13.   Trevino, Jose A. (1982), Spain's internal security: the Basque autonomous police force, in Alexander, Y. and Myers, K. A., *Terrorism in Europe*, London: Croom Helm, p. 142.
14.   Shabad and Ramo, p. 465.
15.   Shabad and Ramo, pp. 466–9.

10   Algeria

1.   United Nations General Assembly (July–August 1998) Report of the Panel Appointed by the Secretary-General to Gather Information on the Situation in Algeria [. . .] (Report of Eminent Panel). Extracts from website print out (published April 1999), pp. 1–7.Website is www.un.org/NewLinks/dpi2007/contents.htm.
2.   Stone, Martin (1997), *The Establishment of Algeria*, London: Hurst & Co, pp. 1–3.
3.   Stone, p. 37, p. 42.
4.   Stone, pp. 177–8.
5.   Stone, pp. 180–1.
6.   Stone, pp. 185–6.
7.   Stone, pp. 189–96.
8.   United Nations: Report of Eminent Persons Panel print out (see Note 1).
9.   United Nations: Report of Eminent Persons Panel print out, p. 20.

11   Peru

1.   Scott Palmer, David (1995), The revolutionary terrorism of Peru's Shining Path, in Crenshaw, Martha, *Terrorism in Context*, Pennsylvania State University Press.
2.   Scott Palmer, pp. 251–3.
3.   Scott Palmer, pp. 254–5.
4.   Scott Palmer, p. 257.
5.   Scott Palmer, pp. 260–1.
6.   Scott Palmer, pp. 262–3.
7.   Scott Palmer, pp. 265–6.
8.   Scott Palmer, pp. 267–8.
9.   McClintock, Cynthia (1984), Why peasants rebel: the case of Peru's Sendero Luminoso, *World Politics*, October, pp. 81–2.
10.   Scott Palmer, p. 270.
11.   Scott Palmer, pp. 270–8.
12.   Scott Palmer, p. 285.
13.   Scott Palmer, p. 280.
14.   Izaguirre, C. R. (1996), *Shining Path in the Twenty-First Century. Actors in search of a new script*, NACLA Report on the Americas, vol. XXX, no. 1, July/August, pp. 37–8.
15.   Izaguirre, p. 38.
16.   Scott Palmer, pp. 301–2.
17.   Izaguirre, p. 38.
18.   Scott Palmer, p. 305.

12   Colombia

1. Pearce, Jenny (1990), *Colombia, Inside the Labyrinth*, London: Latin American Bureau, pp. 4–5.
2. Pearce, pp. 64–5.
3. Pearce, p. 69.
4. Pearce, pp. 76–9.
5. Oquist, Paul (1980), *Violence, Conflict and Politics in Colombia*, London: New York Academic Press, pp. 1–6.
6. Oquist, p. 153.
7. Oquist, p. 133.
8. Oquist, pp. 134–5, quoting Antonio Garcia (1971).
9. Oquist, p. 135.
10. Oquist, p. 138.
11. Oquist, p. 139.
12. Oquist, pp. 143–4, 145–6, 147.
13. Oquist, p. 150.
14. Pearce, pp. 52–4, 55–6, 56–7.
15. Pearce, pp. 61–2.
16. Pearce, pp. 165–6.
17. Pearce, pp. 167–8. The quotation is from *L'Humanité*, 3 June 1966.
18. Pearce, pp. 168–9. See the useful references to the relationship between the guerrillas and the drug cartels in Laqueur, Walter (1999), *The New Terrorism*, Oxford: Oxford University Press, pp. 27, 188–91, 212–4.
19. Pearce, pp. 171–2, 173.
20. Pearce, p. 207.
21. Pearce, p. 231.
22. Pearce, pp. 278–9.
23. Pearce, p. 284, quoting from Tobón, W. R. (1988), *Análisis Política*, no. 5.
24. Pearce, pp. 286–7.
25. Pearce, p. 287.

13   Germany

1. Cook, Schura (1982), Germany, from protest to terrorism, in Alexander, Y. and Myers, K. A., *Terrorism in Europe*, London: Croom Helm, p. 165.
2. Cook, p. 161.
3. Cook, p. 170.
4. Merkl, P. H. (1995), West German Left-wing Terrorism, in Crenshaw, Martha (ed.), *Terrorism in Context*, Pennsylvania State University Press, pp. 176–8.
5. Pridham, Geoffrey (1981), Terrorism and the state in West Germany during the 1970s: a threat to stability or a case of political over-reaction?, in Lodge, Juliet (ed.), *Terrorism: a Challenge to the State*, Oxford: Martin Robertson, p. 18.
6. Pridham, pp. 16–17.
7. Pridham, pp. 20–2.
8. Pridham, pp. 22–5.
9. Pridham, pp. 27–8.

10.   Pridham, pp. 28–9.
11.   Merkl, pp. 202–5.
12.   Wright, Joanne (1990), *Terrorist Propaganda: the Red Army Faction and the Provisional IRA 1968–86*, New York: St Martins Press.
13.   Becker, Jillian (1989), *Hitler's Children*, London: Pickwick, pp. ix–x.
14.   Wright, p. 116.
15.   Pridham, p. 41, p. 44.
16.   Wright, p. xiii.
17.   Wright, pp. 226–9.
18.   Wright, p. 168.
19.   Pridham, p. 52.
20.   Pridham, p. 52.
21.   Kellen, Konrad (1998), Ideology and rebellion: terrorism in West Germany, in Reich, Walter (ed.), *Origins of Terrorism*, Baltimore: Johns Hopkins University Press, pp. 54–5.
22.   Becker, p. 250, quoting Cohn, Norman (1970), *The Pursuit of the Millennium*, London: Paladin.
23.   Kellen, p. 58.

14   Italy

1.   Jamieson, Alison (1989), *The Heart Attacked*, London: Marion Boyars, p. 9.
2.   Salvioni, Danila, and Stephanson, Anders (1985), Reflections on the Red Brigades, in *Orbis*, Forum, Fall, p. 491.
3.   Furlong, Paul (1981), Political terrorism in Italy: responses, reaction and immobilism, in Lodge, Juliet (ed.), *Terrorism, a Challenge to the State*, Oxford: Martin Robertson, pp. 61–2.
4.   Furlong, p. 63.
5.   Apter, D. E. (1997), Political violence in analytical perspective, in Apter, D. E., *The Legitimization of Violence*, New York: New York University Press, p. 19.
6.   Furlong, pp. 69–71.
7.   Furlong, pp. 74–8.
8.   Moss, David (1997), Politics, violence, writing: the rituals of 'armed struggle' in Italy, in Apter, D. E., *The Legitimization of Violence*, New York: New York University Press, p. 85.
9.   Moss, pp. 92–3.
10.   Moss, p. 83.
11.   Moss, pp. 105–6.
12.   Furlong, p. 77.
13.   Furlong, p. 80.
14.   Furlong, pp. 85–6.
15.   Moss, pp. 103–4.
16.   Moss, pp. 114–15.
17.   Furlong, pp. 88–9.
18.   Della Porta, Donatella (1995), Left-wing terrorism in Italy, in Crenshaw, Martha (ed.), *Terrorism in Context*, New York: New York University Press, pp. 156–9.

15   South Africa

1.   Whittaker, David J. (1999), *Conflict and Reconciliation*, London: Routledge, pp. 21–4.
2.   Whittaker, pp. 24–5.
3.   Whittaker, David J. (1995), *United Nations in Action*, London: UCL Press, p. 168.
4.   Whittaker (1999), pp. 25–6.
5.   Gibson, Richard (1972), *African Liberation Movements: Contemporary Struggle against White Minority Rule*, London: Oxford University Press for Race Relations Institute, p. 38.
6.   Gibson, p. 64.
7.   Gibson, p. 92.
8.   Braganca, A. de, and Wallerstein, I. M. (1982), *The African Liberation Reader*, vol. 2, London: Zed Press, p. 33.
9.   Braganca, and Wallerstein, p. 43.
10. Mandela, Nelson (1997), *Long Walk to Freedom*, London: Abacus, p. 132.
11. Mandela, p. 135.
12. Mandela, pp. 146–7.
13. Mandela, pp. 181–2.
14. Mandela, p. 277.
15. Mandela, pp. 320–1.
16. Mandela, pp. 321–4.
17. Mandela, pp. 325–6.
18. Mandela, pp. 336–8.
19. Mandela, p. 434.
20. Whittaker (1999), pp. 27–8.
21. Whittaker (1999), p. 30.
22. Detail as to questioning process obtained from South Africa's Truth and Reconciliation (TRC) website, October 1999:
     www.truth.org.za/submit/q-anc.htm and
     www.truth.org.za/submit/q-np.htm
     and from print out extracts pp. 1–9.
23. Further TRC detail may be obtained by searching the website noted above.
24. Whittaker (1999), p. 33.

16   Twelve terrorism case-studies: conclusion

1.   Smith, M. R. L. (1995), Holding fire, in O'Day, Alan (ed.), *Terrorism's Laboratory: the Case of Northern Ireland*, Aldershot: Dartmouth.

17   Counter-terrorism: ethical and legal considerations

1.   The *Guardian*, 14 December 1999, Jack Straw MP, p. 18.
2.   The *Guardian*, 14 December 1999, John Wadham, p. 18.
3.   Jenkins, Brian (1986), Defense against terrorism, *Political Science Quarterly*, 101, 5, pp. 779–81.

4. Jenkins, p. 774.
5. Jenkins, p. 783.
6. Jenkins, p. 786.
7. Bandura, Albert (1998), Mechanisms of moral disengagement, in Reich, Walter (ed.), *Origins of Terrorism*, Baltimore: Johns Hopkins University Press, pp. 163–5.
8. Bandura, pp. 165–7.
9. Bandura, p. 169.
10. Higgins, R. O. and Flory, M. (1997), *Terrorism and International Law*, London: Routledge, pp. 14, 15, 16. (For specific detail on international law and terrorism, consult the United Nations Website: www.un.org/law/terrorism.htm)
11. Higgins, R. O. and Flory, M., pp. 27–8.

18 Counter-terrorism: programmes and strategies

1. Smith, M. R. L., (1995), Holding fire, in O'Day, Alan (ed.), *Terrorism's Laboratory: the Case of Northern Ireland*, Aldershot: Dartmouth, p. 23.
2. Terrorism Research Center, United States Website: www.terrorism.com/terrorism/basics.html. Print out of 31 December 1998, pp. 7–9.
3. Wardlaw, Grant (1982), *Political Theory, Tactics and Counter-measures*, Cambridge: Cambridge University Press.
4. Laqueur, Walter (1999), *The New Terrorism*, Oxford: Oxford University Press, pp. 45–6.
5. Crenshaw, Martha (1995), *Terrorism in Context*, Pennsylvania State University Press, pp. 481–2.
6. Crenshaw, pp. 9–10.
7. Crenshaw, pp. 21, 22, 23, 24.
8. Ganor, Boaz (1998), Countering state-sponsored terrorism. Full text article dated 25 April 1998, in print out 12 January 1999, from International Policy Institute for Counter-terrorism, Herzliya, Israel. Website: www.ict.org.il/interter/org.cfm. pp. 1–19.
9. United Nations, *UN Chronicle*, no. 3, 1996, p. 31.
10. Wardlaw, p. 114.
11. Vercher, Antonio (1992), *Terrorism in Europe. An International Comparative Legal Analysis*, Oxford: Clarendon Press, p. 369.
12. Hoffman, Bruce (1998), *Inside Terrorism*, London: Indigo, pp. 196–7.
13. Laqueur, pp. 256–7.
14. Laqueur, pp. 259–60.
15. Hoffman, pp. 211–12.

Guide to further reading

There are two reasons why this guide lists fewer books than might be expected. First, most people who consult this reader on terrorism will be able to search for relevant literature and, to some extent, select it, via computer terminals and internet facilities in today's libraries and through the on-line catalogue AMAZON (www.amazon.co.uk).

Second, in the twelve case-studies in Part Two of this book there are ample references which need no repetition in this guide. A number of additional references are listed. It is worth looking at the extensive, up-to-date bibliography in Laqueur, Walter (1999), *The New Terrorism*.

Most of the other references are fairly general recent texts useful for readers of Part One (chiefly about definition and motivation) and of Part Three (counter-terrorism). The author has found these sources invaluable.

PART ONE

Bjorgo, T. (1995), *Terror from the Extreme Right*, London: Cassell.

Bremer, L. P. (1989), *Terrorism, its Evolving Nature*, Washington DC: Bureau of Public Affairs.

Clutterbuck, Richard (1973), *Protest and the Urban Guerrilla*, London: Cassell.

Clutterbuck, Richard (1994), *Terrorism in an Unstable World*, New York: Routledge.

Crederberg, P. C. (1989), *Terrorism, Myths, Illusions, Rhetoric and Reality*, Oxford: Prentice Hall.

Gaines, Ann (1998), *Terrorism*, Philadelphia: Chelsea House.

Hobsbawn, Eric (1995), *Age of Extremes*, London: Michael Joseph. See particularly Chapter 15.

Kushner, H. H. (1998), *Terrorism in America: a Structured Approach to Understanding the Terrorist Threat*, Springfield, Illinois: C. C. Thomas.

Kushner, H. H. (1998), *The Future of Terrorism: Violence in the New Millennium*, Thousand Oaks, CA: Sage Publications.

Laqueur, Walter (1986), Reflections on terrorism, *Foreign Affairs*, Fall, pp. 86–100.

Laqueur, Walter (1996), Postmodern Terrorism, *Foreign Affairs*, Sept/Oct.

Long, D. E. (1990), *The Anatomy of Terrorism*, New York: Free Press.

Moxon-Browne, E., Alexander, Y. and O'Day, A. (1994), *European Terrorism* (International Library of Terrorism No. 3).

Nash, J. R. (1998), *Terrorists in the Twentieth Century: a Narrative Encyclopaedia*, New York: M. Evans & Co.

O'Kane, R. H. T. (1991), *The Revolutionary Reign of Terror: the Role of Violence in Political Change*, Aldershot: Elgar.

Rapoport, D. C. (1998), *Inside Terrorist Organizations*, New York: Columbia University Press.

Schmid, A. (1983), *Political Terrorism*, New Brunswick: Transaction Books.

Shubik, Martin (1998), *Terrorism, Technology and the Socio-economics of Death*, New Haven, CT: Cowles Foundation, Yale.

Stohl, M. (ed.) (1979), *The Politics of Terrorism: a Reader in Theory and Practice*, New York: Marcel Dekker.

Wilkinson, Paul (1974), *Political Terrorism*, London: Macmillan.

Wilkinson, Paul (1977), *Terrorism and the Liberal State*, London: Macmillan.

PART TWO

Alexander, Y. and Myers, K. A. (1982), *Terrorism in Europe*, London: Croom Helm.

4   Lebanon

Jaber, Hala (1977), *Hezbollah: Born with a Vengeance*, New York: Columbia University Press.

5   Libya

Harris, L. C. (1986), *Libya: Qaddafi's Revolution and the Modern State*, London: Westview.

6   Sri Lanka

Schwartz, Walter (1998), *The Tamils of Sri Lanka*, London: Minority Rights Group.

Spencer, J. (ed.) (1990), *History in Sri Lanka: the Roots of Conflict*, London: Routledge.

7   Northern Ireland

Bruce, Steve (1992), *The Red Hand. Protestant Paramilitaries in Northern Ireland*, Oxford: Oxford University Press.

Coogan, T. Pat (1995), *The Troubles*, London: Hutchinson.

O'Brien, Brenda (1999), *The Long War: the IRA and Sinn Féin*, Dublin: The O'Brien Press.
O'Day, A. and Alexander, Y. (1994), *Dimensions of Irish Terrorism*, Aldershot: Dartmouth.
Smith, M. I. R. (1994), *Fighting for Ireland? The Military Structure of the Irish Republican Movement*, London: Routledge.

9   Spain

Medhurst, Ken (1982), Basques and Basque nationalists, in Williams, C. H. (ed.), *National Separatism*, Cardiff: University of Wales Press.
Sullivan, John (1988), *ETA and Basque Nationalism, the Fight for Euskadi 1890–1986*, London: Routledge.

10   Algeria

Abucar, M. A. (1996), *The Post-colonial Society. The Algerian Struggle for Economic, Social and Political Change 1965–90*, New York: Peter Long Publishing Co.
Jackson, H. F. (1977), *The FLN in Algeria: Party Development in a Revolutionary Society*, London: Greenwood Press.
Stone, Martin (1997), *The Agony of Algeria*, London: Hurst & Co.

13   Germany

Aust, Stefan (1987), *The Baader-Meinhof Group*, London: Bodley Head.

14   Italy

Cantanzaro, R. (1991), *The Red Brigade and Left-wing Terrorism in Italy*, London: Pinter.
Pisano, V. S. (1981), *The Dynamics of Subversion and Violence in Contemporary Italy*, Stanford, California: Hoover Press.

15   South Africa

Beinart, William, and Dubow, Saul (eds) (1995), *Segregation and Apartheid in Twentieth Century South Africa*, London: Routledge.

PART THREE

Bassiouni, M. C. (ed.) (1988), *Legal Response to International Terrorism*, The Hague: M. Nijhoff.
Blakesley, C. L. (1992), *Terrorism, Drugs, International Law and the Protection of Human Liberty: a Comparative Study*, Ardsley-on-Hudson: Transnational Books.
Evans, A. E. and Murphy, J. F. (1978), *Legal Aspects of International Terrorism*, Lexington Press, D. C. Heath.

Hyunwook, H. H. (1993), *Terrorism and Political Violence: Limits and Possibilities of Legal Control*, New York: Oceana Publications.

Jenkins. B. M. (1997), *The Potential for Nuclear Terrorism*, Santa Maria, CA: Rand.

Schmid, A. P. and Crelinstein, R. D. (eds) (1993), *Western Responses to Terrorism*, London: Cassell.

United Nations General Assembly (1973), Report of the Ad Hoc Committee on International Terrorism, XXVIII, A/9028, Supplement 28, 1973.

OTHER SOURCES OF FURTHER INFORMATION

From time to time articles of relevant interest appear:

Foreign Affairs, International Affairs, International Relations, International Studies, Millennium Review of International Studies (not just the year 2000!), *Political Science Quarterly, Studies in Conflict and Terrorism, Terrorism and Political Violence, The World Today, Third World Quarterly.*

USEFUL ADDRESSES

United Nations Department of Public Information, Public Enquiries Unit, UN Plaza, New York NV 10017, United States.

United Nations Information Centre, Millbank Tower (21st floor), 21–24 Millbank, London SW1P 4QH.

Apart from printed material readily obtainable from the above, these international websites will yield a great deal of information:

United Nations
www.un.org

Terrorism Research Center (USA)
www.terrorism.com

International Policy Institute for Counter-terrorism (Israel)
www.ict.org.il/interter/main.httm

British Library (UK), OPAC 97 Service
http//opac97.bl.uk

Index